Decision Making
& the Will of God

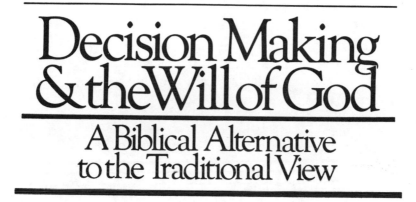

Decision Making & the Will of God

A Biblical Alternative to the Traditional View

GARRY FRIESEN
WITH J. ROBIN MAXSON

MULTNOMAH PRESS
Portland, Oregon 97266

Unless otherwise indicated, all Scripture quotations are from the *New American Standard Bible*, © 1960, 1962, 1963, 1968, 1971, 1972, 1973, 1975, 1977 by The Lockman Foundation, La Habra, California. Used by permission.

Cover design and illustration by Britt Taylor Collins

DECISION MAKING AND THE WILL OF GOD
© 1980 by Multnomah Press
Portland, Oregon 97266

Printed in the United States of America

Library of Congress Cataloging in Publication Data

Friesen, Garry, 1947-
    Decision making and the will of God.

    Includes indexes.
    1. God—Will.   2. Decision-making (Ethics)   3. Christian life—1960-
I. Maxson, J. Robin, 1947- joint author. II. Title.
BV4501.2.F767   248.4   80-24592
ISBN 0-930014-47-2 (hdbk.)
ISBN 0-88070-024-6 (pbk.)

86 87 88 89 90 91 – 14 13 12 11 10 9 8

Dedication

To Muzz and Dad who provided us
children with a home where the moral will
of God was encouraged and practical
wisdom was demonstrated.

To the students of Multnomah School of
the Bible and the believers at Klamath
Evangelical Free Church who matured this
book through their practical help and
penetrating questions.

Table of Contents

Illustrations

11

12   Illustrations

Foreword

Sacred cows make the best hamburger, but the meat can be hard to swallow.

Christians cherish a mythology that—along with their theology— shapes and directs their lives. Perhaps no myth more strongly influences us than our understanding of how to know the will of God. We want to make right decisions, for we realize that the decisions we make turn around and make us. As we choose one end of the road we choose the other. When we select a life's work, a life's partner, or a college, we desire God's direction in those choices.

Yet when we ask, "How can I know the will of God?" we may be raising a pagan question. In the ancient world kings and generals consulted the oracles to gain guidance from the gods for their plans. The oracles provided such direction by vague and illusive counsel and worshipers could read into the enigmatic responses what their hunches told them to do. Convinced that their plans had the stamp of the gods, generals could lead their troops into battle with unfounded courage. By 300 B.C., however, the oracles had gone out of business. Too often they had led their devotees to staggering defeat.

If we ask, "How can I know the will of God?" we may be asking the wrong question. The Scriptures do not command us to find God's will for most of life's choices nor do we have any passage instructing us on how it can be determined. Equally significant, the Christian community has never agreed on how God provides us with such special revelation. Yet we persist in searching for God's will because decisions require thought and sap energy. We seek relief from the responsibility of decision making and we feel less threatened by being passive rather than active when making important choices.

In this book, Dr. Garry Friesen insists that we must change the question. Instead of wondering, "How do I find the will of God?" a better question to pursue is, "How do I make good decisions?" Answering that question stands as the central purpose of this book. While the author challenges the traditional Christian approach to

13

decision making as both unbiblical and unworkable, he does not stop there. He moves on to give us specific practical principles that we can apply when making everyday decisions that range from minor choices to vital problems. Through a study of these pages we are delivered from two crippling extremes—unwarranted delay and vacillation on the one hand and impulsive, emotionally-loaded judgments on the other. As a result, we achieve freedom to live spiritually productive lives.

The Bible does not provide a map for life—only a compass. But through this book you will discover how the compass can guide you over the bewildering terrain.

Haddon W. Robinson
President
Conservative Baptist Theological
Seminary

Introduction

Is It Worth Another Look?

This book needs an introduction — or at least an explanation. For Solomon's lament that "the writing of many books is endless" (Ecclesiastes 12:12) seems especially applicable to volumes on the subject of knowing God's will. What could possibly justify another book on a subject that has received such exhaustive treatment?

Then again, the fact that you are investigating a book that claims to be "a biblical alternative" to decision making and the will of God may be an indication of a further need for understanding in this area. In fact, I rather expect that most of the people who pick up this book will have already been exposed to some teaching (or even a lot of teaching) on how to know God's will. Yet many, if not most Christians, find knowledge of God's will difficult to come by. It's not that they don't know what to do. It's just that after they have followed all the steps, the clear picture that is supposed to materialize, doesn't. I have met many believers who were frustrated because they were convinced that God loved them and had a wonderful plan for their lives, but for some reason He was not telling them what it was. Are Christians like so many laboratory rats, consigned to explore every dead end in the maze of life, while the One who knows the way through just watches?

No. God *does guide* His people. It's important to know that. The question is: *How* does He guide?

15

That question, above all others, occupied my waking thoughts some fifteen years ago as I faced the most important decision in my Christian life: I had to choose where I would go to college. The seriousness of that decision is immediately apparent to anyone who has ever prepared to make a similar investment of four determinative years.

A full year before the decision had to be made, I had narrowed the options to two schools. In the course of that year, I carefully sought to discover God's will for that decision. I obtained relevant data on the two colleges, weighed circumstances, sought mature counsel, read books on God's will, and sincerely prayed. Both schools appeared to offer excellent opportunities to study God's Word; circumstances seemed to be favorable for both; my available information gave me no indication of obvious superiority of one school over the other; and counselors I respected recommended them both. The inner impressions in my heart were not decisive. In fact, I wavered back and forth a lot—one day I leaned toward this school, the next day the other looked better.

The decision had to be made by the first of September. In the absence of any certain leading, the pace at which the deadline approached seemed to accelerate with each passing day. The year of prayer and evaluation seemed to dissolve into apparent irrelevance. I prayed more fervently and specifically: "Lord, You know that I am willing to go to any school You want. I will go to either of these colleges, or any other that You have chosen. But Lord, I must know what to do, for the deadline for my decision is at hand."

And yet there was no definite leading. Finally, not knowing what else to do, I established a circumstantial "fleece," and followed where it pointed. As things turned out, it proved to be an excellent choice. For those four years of college training were very constructive in my overall development as a person and as a Christian.

Still, my experience in the making of that decision left me perplexed. Why had it been so hard for me to find God's will when I so sincerely sought for it? And why, after I had made the decision, did I lack the certainty that the decision I had made was the correct one? I knew enough from good Bible teaching to realize that I could not base doctrine on experience. On the other hand, should not my experience conform to and confirm doctrine? It was at that point that I began my pilgrimage to seek the reason for my difficulty in finding God's will for that particular decision.

As I reflected on my experience, it became apparent that there could be three possible causes for my lack of success in discovering God's will:

1. Perhaps God was unable to reveal His will. In such a case, the problem would lie with Him.

2. Perhaps there was sinfulness or insincerity on my part. Then, obviously, I would be the cause for my own failure.

3. Perhaps my understanding of the nature of God's will was biblically deficient. If that were true, then the problem would be ignorance.

As I considered these possibilities, I immediately ruled out the first one. For God is perfect in His character, and infinite in His ability. Sinfulness or insincerity on my part was a much more likely cause. Yet, as I searched my own heart in all honesty before God, I felt I had been as open and sincere as I knew how to be.

Could it be that my understanding of biblical guidance was incorrect at some point? There were a couple of things that excited me as I thought about this third possibility. The first was that one's understanding of biblical truth can be objectively evaluated. In fact, it ought to be so scrutinized. The Word of God is our final authority on every issue. As a believer, I am encouraged to test everything I am taught by that single standard—the Bible itself.

The other thing that excited me about the prospect of restudying the biblical material on this subject was that all such effort was bound to have positive results. What Paul wrote is true: "All Scripture is inspired by God and *profitable* for teaching, for reproof, for correction, for training in righteousness; that the man of God may be adequate, equipped for every good work" (2 Timothy 3:16-17). It encouraged me to realize that the result of further investigation would either be valuable training or needed correction. On the one hand, I might become more fully convinced and articulate concerning the accuracy of what I had been taught. On the other hand, whatever deficiencies in understanding I might have would be subject to correction or revision. Either way, God's Word would be honored as my final authority, and my mind would be renewed by exposure to its transforming character.

So I pursued that third possibility—that there might be some part of my understanding of God's will that was in need of scriptural adjustment. And I found that such was indeed the case. But it took a while. By the time I graduated from seminary eight years later, the pieces of a biblical picture of guidance were falling into place. Five additional years of more concentrated research provided more than enough data for my doctoral dissertation on the subject. Seminars conducted for my students and a few churches provided the opportunity and motivation to put the material into teachable form. Penetrating questions from thoughtful Bible students prompted further refinement of controversial points.

As I pursued this project, I became aware of three significant facts that have motivated me to put what I have learned into a book:

Fact One, to which I have already alluded, is that my experience of frustration in decision making was by no means unique. Over the years, it has become evident to me that for many Christians, that same sense of anxiety emerges from the closet every time an important decision must be made. As a result, some believers that I have talked to have openly admitted that they dislike, or even dread, the process of making important decisions in life.

Fact Two is that interest in the subject of guidance is consistently high. Pastors and Bible teachers in Christian schools report that questions related to knowing God's will rank among the most frequently asked. The demand for magazine articles and books on the subject continues unabated. People continue to seek guidance on guidance.

Fact Three is that the instruction on this subject has remained relatively uniform over the past several decades. Whenever anyone in evangelical circles talks about "discovering God's will," everyone else has pretty much the same idea about what that means and what is involved. A few important modifications have been made in recent years as writers have recognized difficulties with the basic position. But no book, to my knowledge, has given a detailed challenge of the presuppositions of the consensus viewpoint.

This book shares the overall goal of its predecessors: to help Christians understand what the Bible says about God's will as it pertains to decision making. Where it differs is in some of its conclusions. That's why I call it an "alternative" view. For my study of God's Word has led me to the conviction that the consensus position—what I call the "traditional view"—is flawed at several critical points. As a result, this book must do two things: It must reveal the errors in the traditional view that have resulted in applicational frustration; and it must reconstruct a correct theology of guidance.

The book is divided into four parts. Part 1 is a survey of the traditional view of guidance. In Part 2, that view is critiqued and, where necessary, refuted. Part 3 contains the constructive development of a biblical approach to guidance. In Part 4, the principles established in Part 3 are applied to specific important decisions that are commonly encountered.

In speaking of "a biblical approach" to guidance, I do not mean to imply that the traditional view is unbiblical or antibiblical. Every evangelical book I have read on knowing God's will has sought to faithfully reflect the teaching of Scripture with integrity. Neither do I intend to convey the notion that all the other books are just plain wrong. I have gained much valuable insight from many of the books I have read.

It is my conviction, however, that the view of guidance developed in this book is a more accurate explanation of biblical revelation. So my responsibility is to present my conclusions as clearly as I can. Your responsibility is to judge whether those conclusions do, in fact, comprise a truly biblical approach to decision making. Since the Word of God is our authority, we do well to emulate the example of the Bereans who "received the word with great eagerness, examining the Scriptures daily, to see whether these things were so" (Acts 17:11).

To return to our tour, Part 1 is intended to give an accurate overview of the teaching most often presented in our churches, schools, and literature—the traditional view. The reader will sit in on a fictional seminar in which the salient points of that view are developed. That presentation will also provide specific content for evaluation later on in the book.

The vehicle of fiction was chosen in an effort to depersonalize the traditional position. For while I disagree with some aspects of the traditional view, I do not wish to disparage any specific individuals who have sincerely taught it. And so the documentation that is appropriate to a formal dissertation has been omitted from this volume.[1] Of course the opposite danger of erecting a "straw man" for the purpose of simple dissection is very real. But I believe that when you leave the fictional seminar, you will say, "Yes, that is essentially what I have heard taught about God's will."

Part 2 concentrates on those aspects of the traditional view that call for correction. The specific supporting arguments presented in Part 1 are systematically critiqued. The heart of Part 2 is Chapter 6 which contains careful exposition of the Scripture passages most often cited by the consensus teaching.

Part 3 presents the "biblical alternative" promised in the title. It is in this section that I offer my answer to the question: "How does God guide believers in the process of decision making?"

In Part 4, the biblical principles of guidance are applied to specific important decisions: singleness and marriage, choosing a vocation, giving to the Lord's work, and disagreeing with other Christians without blowing the church apart!

Now that you have some understanding of where this book has come from and where it is going, I am confident that you can profit from *Decision Making and The Will of God.* My hope is that when you have finished reading this volume, you will agree: "Yes, it was worth another look."

May God be glorified through this effort according to the wisdom of His sovereign will.

Notes

1. For specific documentation of the traditional view, see Garry Lee Friesen, "God's Will As It Relates To Decision Making" (Th.D. diss., Dallas Theological Seminary, 1978), pp. 7-148.

PART 1

You Have Heard It Said

The Traditional View Presented

Chapter 1

On Marriage and Missions

*E*ven a second, insistent buzzing of the intercom failed to fully penetrate Bill Thompson's concentration. Blindly, his left hand probed the paper strewn surface of his desk in search of the button that would silence the interruption. It was only when three paperbacks and a pile of notes toppled into the metal trash can below that he actually stopped writing. Uncovering the partially buried intercom, he pushed the button.

"Yes, Mary. What is it?" His tone scarcely masked his irritation.

"I'm sorry to disturb you, Pastor Bill," the voice apologized, "but Ted Bradford just came in and asked if he could talk with you. I thought you'd want to see him."

A smile quickly erased the frown from Bill's face. Again he pushed the button. "You're right, Mary. Send him in."

Bill retrieved the errant books and notes and was attempting to arrange them in a less vulnerable position when Ted entered the study. Bill got up and extended his hand. "Hi, Ted. Good to see you."

"It's good to be home," Ted replied, shaking Bill's hand. "I've been looking forward to semester break for a long time, or so it seems."

Bill motioned to the chair facing his desk. "Have a seat. You don't look too much the worse for wear. I like your mustache."

Ted grinned and self-consciously brushed his lip with his fingers. "I've gotten used to it. I almost forget it's there. My folks haven't decided what they think about it yet."

Bill laughed. "Don't worry about them. They'll adjust. They always do."

"Yeah, I guess so," said Ted as he sat down.

Bill walked back around to his swivel chair, sat down, and leaned back. "So, how does it feel to be one semester away from graduation?"

"I'm pretty excited about it for the most part," replied Ted.

"For the most part?"

"Well, that's what I wanted to talk to you about, pastor. I'm going to have to make some pretty big decisions in the next few months and I'd like to get your advice on some of the things I've been thinking about."

Bill leaned forward in his chair. "Before we go any further," he said in mock seriousness, "I want you to know that my advice is free—and worth every cent of it."

Ted grimaced appropriately and continued. "I'll bear that in mind." He hesitated. "I'm not sure where to start. It's all gotten kind of complicated."

"Complicated, huh?" Bill leaned back and arched his eyebrow. "What's her name?"

Ted was momentarily startled. "How did you know?" Then he laughed. "Her name is Annette—Annette Miller. And she's a remarkable girl."

"She'd have to be to get your attention," Bill chided. "Does she like mustaches?"

Ted colored slightly as he grinned. "She doesn't let them get in her way. Not this one at least."

"I bet with a little arm twisting you could be persuaded to produce a picture of this young lady."

"Thought you'd never ask," said Ted, reaching for his wallet. He extracted a photograph from the plastic holder and passed it across the desk to the pastor. "It's a little worn around the edges, but I think it bears a close resemblance to the real thing."

Bill studied the picture for a moment. "Annette Miller is one very attractive young lady, Ted. I can see why you would notice her."

"She really is a remarkable girl, pastor."

"You said that already," replied Bill as he handed the picture back. "Tell me something objective about her, if that's possible."

"Well, she enrolled in the one-year Bible program at the beginning of this school year. Before that she graduated with a B.A. from the state university with a major in African history and a minor in anthropology. I met her during the first week in a Bible class. She was so easy to talk to, pastor, I didn't even have to work up courage to ask her out for the first time. I took her to a reception for new students and we really had a great time. The relationship just kind of took off from there."

"She sounds really sharp," said Bill. "Where does she live?"

Ted hesitated. "I'm never really sure how to answer that one, pastor. You see, her folks are missionaries in Kenya. That's where Annette grew up. When they come back to the states on furlough, their home base is Chicago. Of course, Annette is pretty much on her own now, so I guess her home is wherever she happens to be going to school."

"Well, that accounts for the major in African history," observed Bill. "It sounds like she's preparing to return to Kenya as a missionary herself."

"She's not positive that she should go to Kenya specifically," explained Ted, "but she does feel that the Lord has called her to a ministry in Africa. Of course she's most familiar with Kenya, but the tribe her parents have been working in extends across national boundaries. For that matter, she's not even sure yet that she should return to that same tribe. She's just preparing as much as she can so that when she does receive a more specific call, she'll be ready to go anywhere."

"It sounds like she's very committed to the Lord."

"Yes, she is, pastor. That's what I appreciate most about her." Ted paused and looked down at the floor. It was quiet in the study for a few moments. Then Bill spoke.

"Do you love her, Ted?"

Ted raised his head and looked Bill in the eye. "Yes, I do—very much."

"Do you want to marry her?"

"Yes."

"Does she know that?"

"We've talked about it quite a bit."

"How does she feel about the idea?"

"She would like to marry me, too."

"So what's the problem?"

Ted's gaze returned to the floor and he sighed. "There seem to be several problems, pastor, and they're not going away. The more I think about them, the harder they seem to get, and the more confused I become."

"Why don't you just list them one at a time," suggested Bill. "Sometimes a forest seems more manageable when you tackle one tree at a time."

"All right," replied Ted. He paused to think a moment. "One thing that concerns me is that I don't know whether it's the Lord's will for us to get married. When we first started dating, I never stopped to think about whether Annette might be the girl God had chosen for me to marry. I know that the Lord has a plan for my life, and I know that plan includes the one person I should marry. I also know that the same thing is true for Annette and her future husband. We're just not sure we were meant for each other, you know, as far as God's plan is concerned."

"Are you willing *not* to marry Annette if it's not the Lord's will?" probed Bill.

"I've agonized over that question a lot, pastor. And I think I can honestly say that I'm willing to give her up if that's His will. Both of us realize that if the Lord doesn't mean for us to marry it would be a big mistake for us to go ahead on our own. We want the Lord's best for our lives — for both of our lives." Ted hesitated for a moment. Then he continued, "In fact, we've kind of broken things off until we get a clear answer on this matter from the Lord."

"I imagine it's been kind of rough on you."

Ted nodded.

Bill continued, "I really have a lot of admiration for you two. It takes considerable inner strength to do what you've done. I think you are demonstrating real maturity and sincerity in this matter. The Lord will reward that, I'm sure."

Ted took a deep breath and cleared his throat. "Annette and I have had a wonderful relationship. I'm glad that I don't have to be ashamed of any part of it. And there are several things that seem to indicate that we'd make good marriage partners. We seem to complement each other in personality and abilities and things like that. The only major indicator that might point in a different direction is this African business."

"You don't want to go to Africa?" asked Bill.

"Oh, I'd be willing to go," answered Ted. "It's just that Annette has had such a strong feeling that that's where she should serve the Lord, and I haven't received any kind of a call. Until I met Annette, I never thought about Africa at all."

"What do you plan to do after graduation?"

Ted shrugged his shoulders. "I haven't had any strong leading in any specific direction. I've been thinking about going to seminary. In fact, I've applied to a couple of different schools. But even that was frustrating."

"Why?" asked Bill. "I think you'd do real well in seminary. I'm glad to hear you're thinking about it."

"I'm excited about the idea," replied Ted. "It's just that on the application forms they wanted me to describe my 'Call to the Ministry of the Gospel.' I had to tell them that I don't yet know exactly what the Lord wants me to do. But I feel that I need more training in the Word for whatever it is."

"I see," said Bill.

"The thing is," continued Ted, "I don't see how Annette and I can be married unless we both feel called to the same ministry. Or at least our calls should be compatible. Another thing that bothers me is that since we began discussing marriage, Annette has been wondering about her commitment to Africa. What if she didn't go there because she married me instead? That's the question that's been haunting me."

"Perhaps the Lord wants Annette to spend a term in Africa while you go to seminary," suggested Bill.

"That's a possibility, pastor," replied Ted. "And I think we're both willing to do that, as hard as it would be. I guess the thing I really want to know is, how can we know for sure what the Lord wants us to do? We have to make some decisions pretty soon, and we need to know clearly what God's will is for us."

"That's very interesting," mused Bill as he stared off into space.

"I thought you'd think so," laughed Ted. "Are you going to give me any of that free advice you promised?"

"As a matter of fact, yes," replied the pastor. "But not right now."

Ted looked puzzled. "Not now?"

It was Bill's turn to laugh. He waved at the materials on and around his desk. "You see all that chaos?"

Ted nodded.

"It just so happens that this weekend we're holding our annual youth conference for all the young people in our district. I was asked to lead a seminar on 'Knowing God's Will for Your Life.' I've been working on it for several weeks. In fact, that's what I was doing when you came in."

Ted's eyes registered his amazement as he surveyed the materials on the desk and the volumes in the cardboard box next to the pastor's chair. "Are all those books on the will of God? You must have twenty-five paperbacks alone!"

"Well, I've been collecting them for a couple of years, but new titles seem to come off the press faster than I can read them. The subject is very popular—always has been."

Ted nodded. "I guess that means I'm not the Lone Ranger when it comes to questions about God's will for my life."

"Exactly," replied Bill. "I've probably been asked more questions on that subject than any other—especially by young people. That's why I've been working so hard on this seminar presentation."

Bill stood up. "I'll tell you what let's do, Ted. You come to the seminar this Saturday morning and take in the entire presentation. Mary can give you the details on your way out. Then, if you wish, we can get together next week and see how the principles apply to your situation."

"That sounds good, Pastor Bill," said Ted as he rose from his chair. The two men shook hands. "I'll be in the front row Saturday morning," Ted promised. He started toward the door, then stopped, turned back to Bill, and added, "Lord willing, of course."

Chapter 2

Hitting the Bull's-eye

*B*ill Thompson surveyed the church auditorium from his seat on the platform. He would have preferred the more intimate setting of a classroom, but the number of registrants precluded that. As anticipated, the seminar on "How to Know God's Will For Your Life" had generated the greatest interest among the young people. And the front half of the auditorium was filled with an almost even mix of high school upperclassmen and college students.

As he looked out over his audience, Bill also noted, with some amusement but little surprise, the presence of several pastors and youth leaders. "I guess this is where I would be too," he mused to himself, "if I wasn't the speaker."

The conference director, having already led in prayer, was completing his introduction of Bill. Everything was in readiness. To the right of the pulpit stood the overhead projector. On the left side was a small table on which Bill had carefully stacked his collection of books on the will of God. "It's nice to be an authority on something," he kidded himself.

"So now, without any further delays, we'll turn the rest of this session over to our speaker, Pastor Bill Thompson." There was a smattering of polite applause as the director nodded to Bill, then left the platform to find a seat among the young people. Bill stepped to the pulpit, placed his notes before him, and began.

"God wants to reveal His will to you more than you want to know it. God's ability to communicate His will is perfect. He never stutters. On the basis of God's desire to communicate and His ability to communicate, I can say to you that you can know God's will for your life with complete certainty."

Bill Thompson felt his introduction had gone well. It reflected a genuine confidence that could only be reassuring to the young people in the audience.

"That's good to know, isn't it?" he continued. "For in every life, there are hundreds, perhaps thousands of decisions to be made—some major, some minor. The non-Christian individual must make those decisions alone, asking each time, 'What is my best course of action? What will bring me greatest happiness?' But the Christian, knowing that he has a wise and loving Heavenly Father who has a special plan for his life, asks a different question: 'What is God's will for me in this situation?' Few experiences can compare with the peace that comes with knowing that a decision has been made in accordance with the perfect will of God. Whether one is selecting a vocation or choosing a mate, the key to spiritual success in decisions lies not in our own feeble insights, but in knowing God's will and doing it. As it says in Proverbs 3:5-6: 'Trust in the Lord with all your heart, and do not lean on your own understanding. In all your ways acknowledge Him, and He will make your paths straight.' Or as the King James Version says it, 'He shall *direct* thy paths.'"

Bill was impressed by the attentiveness of the young people as they listened to him. Noticeably absent were the telltale signs of restlessness that so often characterized these sessions. Many were taking notes. Among them was a college student sitting by himself on the front row. Ted Bradford had kept his promise.

"Knowing God's will is hardly an academic subject. Today there are many husbands and wives who are frustrated in their marriages because they did not choose the one person God wanted them to marry. There are students who are discouraged because they went to the wrong school. Some Christian men experience dissatisfaction in their jobs because they did not seek and follow God's vocational calling for them. Christian women are unhappy in their office positions because they ran ahead of God in accepting an offer that was less than His best. The shortage of workers on the mission field and in local churches gives further evidence that many people have missed or ignored God's call. And those who have missed that call are missing the unparalleled joy of living in the center of God's will.

"Perhaps you are attending this seminar this morning because you are uncertain as to what the Lord's will is for you in a particular decision. Maybe you feel like the airline pilot who announced to his passengers: 'Folks, I have some good news and some bad news. First the bad news—our flight instruments are broken and we are completely lost. Now the good news—we are making excellent time!' Our problems in finding God's will do not lie with God; they lie with us and our failure to read God's 'instruments' and obey them.

"As we consider this subject this morning, I think it will be helpful for us to ask and answer four basic questions. I have put them on this overhead transparency so you can see where we are going [Figure 1]. First, we want to know: What do we mean by the term 'God's will'? Then we will ask: How do we know that God has a specific plan for each individual? Third, we will consider: What is the correct process for discovering God's will? And finally: How

Questions About God's Will

1. Definition: What does "God's will" mean?

2. Proof: Does God have a plan for *my* life?

3. Process: How can I discover God's will?

4. Certainty: How can I know God's will for sure in a specific situation?

Figure 1

can a believer be 100 percent certain of God's will in a particular matter?

"Before we consider the first question, I want to explain something about the material I will be presenting in this session. In my research on this subject, I found that a great deal has been written on God's will by a host of respected Christian teachers and leaders. For the most part these writers are in basic agreement on the correct understanding of God's will. I have drawn heavily from these excellent resources in the preparation of this seminar. My goal this morning is to give you an easy-to-follow presentation that summarizes the basic content of these books. On those issues where Christian teachers differ, I will mention the varying viewpoints before explaining the one I consider to be most in harmony with the teaching of Scripture.

DEFINING GOD'S WILL

"Now our first question is, *what does the term 'God's will' mean?* Most people are not aware that in normal conversation we use the term 'God's will' in three different, yet correct, ways. For instance, in talking to a grieving friend who has lost a close relative in a tragic accident, you might say, 'The Bible says that everything that happens is part of *God's will,* and though we may not understand why these things occur, we can receive comfort from the knowledge that a wise and loving God is in control.' In another situation you could be speaking to a Christian friend who is considering marriage to an unbeliever, and you would warn, 'If you marry her you will be violating *God's will.*' Finally, you might be in conversation with a friend who is contemplating a college education, and you ask, 'Have you discovered *God's will* about which school He wants you to attend?' In each of these statements, the term 'God's will' is used in a different sense. For the sake of clarity in this presentation I will refer to these three different aspects as God's *sovereign* will, God's *moral* will, and God's *individual* will.

"The first of these, God's *sovereign* will, can be defined as God's predetermined plan for everything that happens in the universe.

"When we say that God is sovereign, we are saying that He is the Almighty Ruler of the universe. In eternity past, God for-

Three Meanings of "God's Will"

Sovereign	Moral	Individual
"God's secret plan that determines everything that happens in the universe."		

Daniel 4:35
Proverbs 21:1
Revelation 4:11
Ephesians 1:11
Proverbs 16:33
Romans 9:19
Acts 2:23
Acts 4:27-28
Romans 11:33-36

mulated a perfect plan for all of history. He determines how nations will act and how their kings will rule. The world was created by His will and our salvation is the result of God working all things after the counsel of His sovereign will. He even determines each toss of the dice in a Monopoly game. No one or no thing can resist or frustrate His sovereign will. It will inevitably come to pass.

"And yet, though God determines all things, He does so without being the author of sin, without violating the will of man, and without destroying the reality of decision making. Each one of us is held responsible for every decision we make. This is a great mystery, but it is true. If we are not able to grasp it, we may rest assured that it all fits together perfectly in the mind of God.

"This explanation of God's sovereign will has been brief of necessity. Let me encourage you to write down and look up the references included on the chart. These are just a few of the passages in Scripture which tell us about God's sovereign will.

"Next we have God's *moral* will. This may be defined as God's moral commands that are revealed in the Bible teaching men how they ought to believe and live.

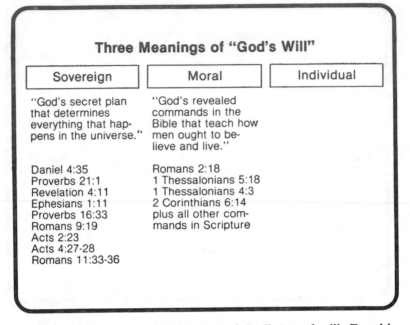

Three Meanings of "God's Will"

Sovereign	Moral	Individual
"God's secret plan that determines everything that happens in the universe."	"God's revealed commands in the Bible that teach how men ought to believe and live."	
Daniel 4:35 Proverbs 21:1 Revelation 4:11 Ephesians 1:11 Proverbs 16:33 Romans 9:19 Acts 2:23 Acts 4:27-28 Romans 11:33-36	Romans 2:18 1 Thessalonians 5:18 1 Thessalonians 4:3 2 Corinthians 6:14 plus all other commands in Scripture	

"The Bible reveals 100 percent of God's moral will. For this reason, the apostle Paul stated in Romans 2 that even the unbelieving Jews knew God's will because they had the Scriptures. That is, they knew how they ought to live. They knew right from wrong because they knew God's moral will.

"In some instances, a specific command is said to be 'God's will.' For example, giving thanks in everything and living a sanctified life are both said to be part of God's moral will.

"You see, the Bible gives general instructions which affect all of life, but do not determine each decision we make. For instance, a Christian is prohibited from marrying an unbeliever by the moral will of God; but Scripture cannot specify which particular person to marry, or even if a specific believer ought to get married at all. That is why God's moral will is sometimes referred to as His 'general' will.

"When it comes to making decisions, the important thing to note about this moral will is that all of our decisions must be in harmony with what God has said in the Bible. If you are considering cheating just a little bit on your income tax so that you can give money to missionaries, you don't need to ask for the Lord's direction—He's already given it. God will never lead you to do something that He has forbidden by His moral will in the Bible.

"The fact remains, however, that there are many things that the moral will of God does not declare—specific situations in which you must make choices. You will eventually have to decide where you will live, what school to attend, which church to join, which person to marry, and a host of smaller decisions every day. These specific decisions are not determined by God's moral will, but are to be guided by God's individual will.

Three Meanings of "God's Will"

Sovereign	Moral	Individual
"God's secret plan that determines everything that happens in the universe."	"God's revealed commands in the Bible that teach how men ought to believe and live."	"God's ideal, detailed life-plan uniquely designed for each person."
Daniel 4:35	Romans 2:18	Colossians 1:9
Proverbs 21:1	1 Thessalonians 5:18	Colossians 4:12
Revelation 4:11	1 Thessalonians 4:3	Romans 12:2
Ephesians 1:11	2 Corinthians 6:14	Ephesians 5:17
Proverbs 16:33	plus all other commands in Scripture	Ephesians 6:6
Romans 9:19		Proverbs 3:5-6
Acts 2:23		Psalm 32:8
Acts 4:27-28		Proverbs 16:9
Romans 11:33-36		Genesis 24

Figure 2

"God's *individual* will is that ideal, detailed life-plan which God has uniquely designed for each believer [Figure 2]. This life-plan encompasses every decision we make and is the basis of God's daily guidance. This guidance is given through the indwelling Holy Spirit who progressively reveals God's life-plan to the heart of the individual believer. The Spirit uses many means to reveal this life-plan as we shall see, but He always gives confirmation at the point of each decision.

"This individualized aspect of God's will is given different titles by different writers. It is called God's 'perfect' will because it is not only in harmony with the Bible, but it is the perfect life-plan to bring happiness and spiritual success to the individual. It is called God's 'specific' will because it reveals each specific decision that should be made. It is called God's 'ideal' will because, of all the possible alternatives, it shows the ideal life-plan for each situation. I have called it God's 'individual' will because it represents the life-plan for each particular individual. Perhaps the most descriptive phrase is 'the very center of God's will.' If you visualize an archer's target, the outer circle would represent the moral will of God, and the bull's-eye would be the very center of His will—or His individual will [Figure 3]. It is important to live and make one's decisions within the larger circle of God's moral will. But finding the 'dot' in the center, God's specific individual will, is essential in making correct decisions in daily life.

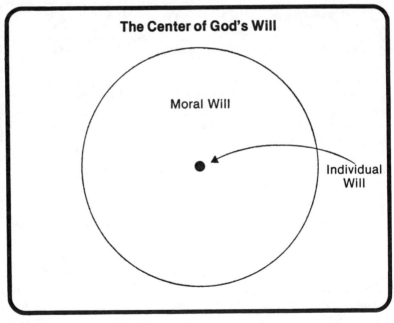

Figure 3

"Sometimes this is easier to see in concrete situations, so let's take marriage as an example. As we have noted repeatedly, it would be wrong for a Christian to marry an unbeliever. Such a decision would fall outside of the larger circle, for God's Word declares: 'Do not be bound together with unbelievers' (2 Corinthians 6:14). If the Christian married a believer who was nevertheless not the one God had selected, he would be acting within the larger sphere of God's moral will, but not precisely 'on target.' Some teachers call this 'God's second best.' Others refer to it as God's 'permissive' will. He permits it since it is not outside of the larger circle of His moral will, but it still falls short of God's best. He does allow the decision, but it will result in leanness of soul. The center dot represents God's individual will. In marriage, it is the one right mate, among all the believers permitted, that should be chosen. Our choice should mirror God's choice.

"Of course it is the choice of a marriage partner where finding or missing the 'dot'—God's individual will—is especially serious. For the choice one makes is permanent. Divorce, for the committed Christian, is not a live option. So the believer who has married the wrong person must live on within God's permissive will, settling for God's second best. You can change cars, houses, schools, or churches if you discover you have missed God's will, but the choice you make concerning your spouse is irreversible.

"What we have seen, then, is that there are three aspects to the will of God. We call them God's sovereign will, God's moral will, and God's individual will. As you can readily see, most questions about guidance concern God's individual will. Whenever someone asks, 'How can I know God's will for my life?', he is usually seeking God's guidance in some specific decision of his life.

"Since this is so, it is very important to avoid confusion between God's individual will and the other two aspects. Since these distinctions may be new to some of you, I've prepared a couple of additional charts that I think will clarify the similarities and differences between the individual will on the one hand and the sovereign and moral senses on the other.

"The first overhead chart compares and contrasts some of the defining characteristics of the individual will of God and the sovereign will of God [Figure 4].

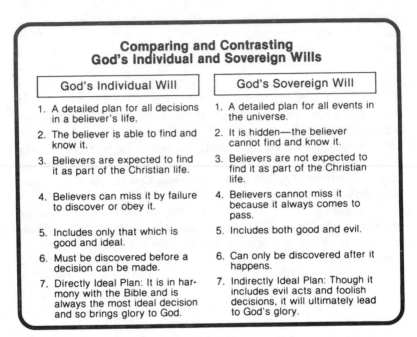

**Comparing and Contrasting
God's Individual and Sovereign Wills**

God's Individual Will	God's Sovereign Will
1. A detailed plan for all decisions in a believer's life.	1. A detailed plan for all events in the universe.
2. The believer is able to find and know it.	2. It is hidden—the believer cannot find and know it.
3. Believers are expected to find it as part of the Christian life.	3. Believers are not expected to find it as part of the Christian life.
4. Believers can miss it by failure to discover or obey it.	4. Believers cannot miss it because it always comes to pass.
5. Includes only that which is good and ideal.	5. Includes both good and evil.
6. Must be discovered before a decision can be made.	6. Can only be discovered after it happens.
7. Directly Ideal Plan: It is in harmony with the Bible and is always the most ideal decision and so brings glory to God.	7. Indirectly Ideal Plan: Though it includes evil acts and foolish decisions, it will ultimately lead to God's glory.

Figure 4

"Now, while most Bible teachers recognize these distinctions between the individual will and sovereign will of God, many treat the moral will and the individual will under the same heading. I believe that this can cause confusion. There are, to be sure, some points of similarity. But there are also some definite differences. I think you will clearly recognize both the differences and the similarities on this next chart [Figure 5].

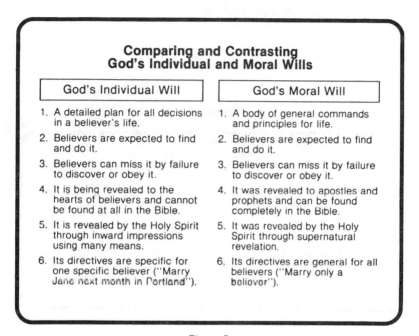

Figure 5

"Again, to sharpen these comparisons with a specific example, when someone asks you, 'Have you discovered God's will concerning which school He wants you to attend?', the question is about God's individual will. God's sovereign will cannot be known in advance. And God's moral will is not specific enough to direct you to any particular school. It is only God's individual will that can guide you to the right school."

Bill paused in his presentation for a few moments to give the note-takers a chance to finish copying down the last chart. He found the glass of water a thoughtful organizer had placed beside the lectern and took a couple of swallows.

PROVING GOD'S INDIVIDUAL WILL

"Now let's move on to our second question: *How do we know that God has an individual will for each believer?*

Questions About God's Will

1. Definition: What does "God's will" mean?

2. Proof: Does God have a plan for *my* life?

"Up to this point, we have assumed God's individual will for the sake of definition. It would not surprise me if many of you are wondering why further comment is necessary. The reasons for believing in an individual will are so compelling that the question is seldom raised and many books on God's will just assume that the reader knows and believes this truth. Still, it is important to be fully convinced in our minds so that we may help others and assure ourselves before God.

"The proof for the existence of God's individual will comes from four sources: reason, experience, biblical example, and biblical teaching [Figure 6].

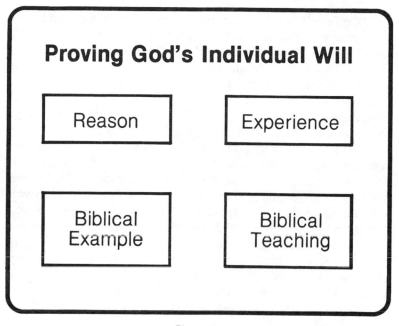

Figure 6

"The concept of an individual will of God is reasonable. It is reasonable because of the kind of God we have. God is a God of order and plans (1 Corinthians 14:40). He knows the future perfectly and He knows the outcome of any decision we might make (Matthew 11:21-22). It is only reasonable to conclude that God would use His ability to formulate an ideal life-plan for each of His children. If God has a beautiful plan and design for the planets and the tiniest snowflake, do you not think He would do the same for us? As Jesus said, we are of far more value to God than any of these created things (Matthew 6:26).

"The images used in the Bible to portray God and His relationship to believers argue strongly for the reasonableness of the individual will of God. God is our King, our Shepherd, and our Father. What great king has no plan for his people? What wise shepherd has no plan by which to guide his sheep? What loving father has no design for his son? It is unreasonable to say that our God does not have an individual plan for each of His precious children.

"God's individual will is proved not only by reason, but by the experience of dedicated believers. History abounds with men like Martin Luther, John Wesley, William Carey, David Livingstone, Hudson Taylor, and Adoniram Judson. In these lives God has demonstrated that He has a specific job for each believer to do. These men could say that they knew God's individual will and accomplished it. Their success in spiritual achievement strongly suggests that God has an individual plan for us as well.

"You can probably add your own testimony to theirs. Have you ever sensed in a particular situation that God was telling you to do a specific thing? In your heart it was as clear as if God was speaking to you audibly. You found no peace of heart until you were willing to do that particular thing. And when you followed through on it, you were filled with the peace and blessing of the Lord. Such is the common experience of all saints, but especially those who walk very close to their Lord. The unbeliever might try to write off such experiences as merely coincidental or psychological, but saints in every age testify that the Holy Spirit is our personal, indwelling Guide. Experience confirms that God has an individual plan for each believer.

"The evidences from reason and experience are impressive. But the most important and decisive proof comes from the Bible itself. The evidence from Scripture takes two forms: first, we have *examples* of men who show that God had an individual will for them; second, we have *direct teaching* about God's will.

"First, then, let's look at some examples from the Bible. Of course the greatest example is Jesus Christ. For He knew God's will perfectly and fulfilled it completely (Hebrews 10:7-9; John 4:34; 6:38; Luke 22:42). Christ did not come to earth on His own initiative, but was sent by the Father (John 8:42). As Jesus Himself was careful to point out, His teaching was from God (John 7:17; 8:26), and the works that He did were assigned to Him by the Father (John 5:36). If the Son of God placed such stress upon accomplishing God's specific will for Him, surely we can do no less.

"The apostle Paul is an outstanding example of someone who knew and obeyed God's individual will for his life. He continually reminded his readers that God had called him to be an apostle (1 Corinthians 1:1). His apostolic vocation was not 'from men, nor through the agency of man, but through Jesus Christ, and God the Father' (Galatians 1:1). He was obligated to preach (Romans 1:14).

Not only was his vocation selected for him, but God guided him specifically. He was directed to leave on his first missionary journey (Acts 13:1-2). Furthermore, he was directed to specific fields, as in the Macedonian vision (Acts 16:10), and away from other potential fields (Acts 16:6-7).

"Philip was directed to a specific road to speak to a particular needy man (Acts 8:26-29). If we would allow God to direct us that way today, our witnessing would surely show greater results. In other instances, the Lord led Ananias to Paul (Acts 9:10-11) and Peter to Cornelius (Acts 10:20). The Holy Spirit showed the Jerusalem Council what they should decide on a doctrinal issue (Acts 15:28).

"In the Old Testament, God had an individual plan for Joseph's life. Though hated and betrayed by his brothers, God exalted him to be a ruler over Egypt, thereby enabling him to rescue his family from the effects of a severe famine (Genesis 50:20).

"These individuals are not unique, for God's individual will is evident in the lives of Moses, Joshua, David, Elijah, Josiah, Ruth, Isaiah, Jeremiah, Ezekiel, Daniel, John the Baptist, and Mary, the mother of Jesus. Each of these godly believers knew enough to ask God, 'What do You want me to do?' just as Paul did (Acts 22:10). If we fail to ask the same question, the joy of following God's life-plan will be missed. God does not play favorites. He has an individual life-plan for us just as He did for the saints in the Bible.

"In addition to proof from scriptural examples, the Bible teaches directly that God has an individual will for each believer. In many passages, believers are instructed to know and do God's will. For example, Colossians 1:9-10 records this prayer: 'We have not ceased to pray for you and to ask that you may be filled with the *knowledge of His will* in all spiritual wisdom and understanding, so that you may walk in a manner worthy of the Lord, to please Him in all respects.' The only way to please God in all respects is to know and obey His individual will.

"In Romans 12:1-2, Paul urges believers to give themselves as a living sacrifice to God, to be transformed, and to resist conformity to the world so that they might be able to prove exactly what God's will is for them. As we noted in Proverbs 3:5-6, God promises that He will make His specific will known if we trust in Him rather than our own understanding. That is a promise of specific guidance into the exact paths of life that God wants us to take—a promise that still holds true.

"A parallel promise is found in Isaiah 30:21 which portrays the Holy Spirit working in us and directing us into the right path each time we begin to turn away from it. It says: 'And your ears will hear a word behind you, "This is the way, walk in it," whenever you turn to the right or to the left.' Again, God gives detailed guidance at each decision to keep us on that path which is God's individual will for us.

"Psalm 32:8 says, 'I will instruct you and teach you in the way which you should go; I will counsel you with My eye upon you.' This promise corresponds with the other promises for direction down the right path.

"We know that if a believer lives a righteous life, he will do good works. In Ephesians 2:10, however, Paul goes beyond that to say that God has specific good works which He wants us to do. These good works are mapped out by His individual will. It says: 'For we are His workmanship, created in Christ Jesus for good works, which God prepared beforehand, that we should walk in them.' This is God's way.

"The story of Genesis 24 provides further evidence that God has an individual plan for each person and will reveal it to the obedient believer. Abraham sent his servant to find a wife for Isaac. The servant prayed for God's specific guidance and was led to the exact woman that God had selected to be Isaac's wife (Genesis 24:14). In this case, God used a providential sign to confirm His individual will.

"It is no wonder, then, that saints throughout the ages have had a firm belief in God's individual will. To my mind the evidence from reason, experience, and Scripture is conclusive.

"Before we go on to the third question, I think it would be good if we took about a ten-minute break. I realize that you are probably most interested in the answers to the last two questions. Hopefully, this brief recess will help us to remain mentally alert as we tackle these most important issues related to God's will."

Chapter 3

Reading the Road Signs

"*I* was reminded by conversations with some of you during the break that I should announce that we will follow my presentation with an opportunity for questions and answers. You might want to jot down your questions as we go along." The stragglers hurried to find their seats as Bill Thompson prepared to continue his seminar.

"There is great joy in knowing that as believers we do not have to fumble through life trying to find our own way. We have seen that God has a blueprint for each of our lives, an ideal life-plan for each individual. Outside of knowing God as our Savior and knowing God as our Sanctifier, knowing God as our *Guide* is the most important knowledge in life.

DISCOVERING GOD'S INDIVIDUAL WILL

"The third question we are now ready to answer is: *What is the correct process for discovering the individual will of God?*

"God's individual will has been likened to a blueprint or a road map for a believer's life. Before such a blueprint or map can be useful it must be clearly understood. I recall an incident from my college days when a carload of us students were trying vainly to locate the home assigned for our evening lodging when someone

Questions About God's Will

1. Definition: What does "God's will" mean?

2. Proof: Does God have a plan for *my* life?

3. Process: How can I discover God's will?

figured out that our homemade map was upside down. We hadn't appreciated how lost we were until we realized that all of our lefts should have been rights, and all our rights should have been lefts!

"Similarly, Christians have misconceptions about God's individual road map for their lives. Some of these misconceptions are very common [Figure 7], and I think it would be helpful to correct them before we construct a proper approach to seeking God's guidance.

"Misconception number one is what I call the *Syllabus Search.* In college classes each teacher hands out a syllabus which outlines all of the required work for the whole semester. God's will, however, is not usually revealed like a complete syllabus. It is more like a scroll that is unrolled little by little. Normally, God will reveal your life-plan slowly and progressively. Just as God, by the pillar of cloud, led the children of Israel step by step and day by day, so He will lead you one step at a time. So don't pray for a syllabus, but rather ask God to unroll your scroll enough for you to see the next step that He wants you to take.

"The second misconception perceives God as a *Celestial Killjoy.* Some believers are not wholehearted in their search for God's will because they are afraid of what they might find! They unconsciously think of God as a Cosmic Scrooge who delights in sending people as missionaries to obscure African jungles where the heat is unbearable, the language unspeakable, the food indigestible, and the snakes inhospitable.

"That is a gross caricature of God. He is a loving Heavenly Father who delights in bringing joy to His children. There is no place in the world where you can find as much happiness, security, and fulfillment as in the very center of God's will.

"Misconception number three concerns the *Bionic Missionary*. The idea is that missionaries are a unique breed of superhuman Christians. People speak only of 'the call to the missionary,' or 'the call to the minister' as though these are the only believers that God calls.

"Now God does call missionaries and pastors. But He also calls printers, nurses, mechanics, carpenters, and housewives to their life-work as well. One's vocation is just one part of God's overall blueprint. Such an important aspect of your life could scarcely be omitted by the Master Designer. God's vocational call is for saints only—not for missionaries and pastors only.

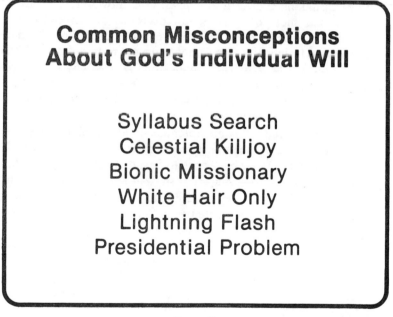

Figure 7

"The fourth misconception concerns the requirement for *White Hair Only*. Maturity will certainly help in discerning God's will, but the newest Christian who is properly taught can discover

God's will. Indeed, new believers must make decisions just like older believers. An open, willing heart is needed to know God's will—not white hair. God guided young Joseph, young Daniel, and young Jesus before they had a single grey hair.

"Misconception number five is that of the *Lightning Flash*. Now lightning did flash and a voice was heard when Saul of Tarsus received guidance on that Damascus road. But such a manifestation is neither normal nor necessary. The Holy Spirit dwells personally in your heart. It is more normal for God to speak through a still small voice, as He did with Elijah, rather than through fire, lightning, or earthquakes (1 Kings 19:12). If lightning flashes, you will not miss it. But do not think you have missed God's individual will because you saw no lightning.

"The final misunderstanding that we will correct this morning is one I have entitled the *Presidential Problem*. Some believers have inadvertently assumed that God's individual will is only concerned with earthshaking choices in our lives. God, however, is aware of the fact that most of our biggest decisions are preceded and brought into being by many smaller events and decisions. The date that seems so insignificant now could turn out to be a date with the woman you will later marry. That is one reason why God cares about the small things in your life and why His individual will for you is detailed. It is detailed so we can cast every decision upon Him—even the non-presidential ones.

"Having cleared out some potential stumbling blocks, we may now move on to consider that process by which we may properly discern God's will. As we have noted, the individual will of God has been compared to a road map that shows the one road we should take through life. God does not show us our whole journey all at once. It might be more accurate to say that we are given our directions by means of road signs along the way.

"Now literal road signs guide us in different ways. A huge sign over an expressway may guide us miles in advance: 'Highway 67/Exit 4 miles.' A small street sign on a corner pole may guide us moments before we must turn onto a side street: 'Lexington Ave'. God gives us ample road signs pointing to His individual will for us. In fact, there are seven such signs that He graciously provides to assure that we arrive safely [Figure 8].

"The first road sign is the *Word of God*. We noted earlier that the Bible does not reveal God's individual will, but only His moral

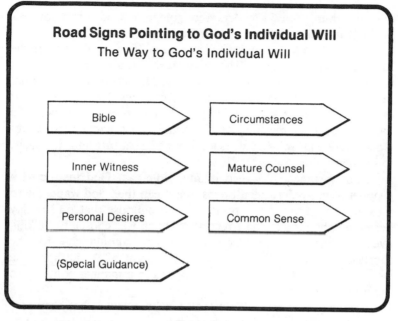

Road Signs Pointing to God's Individual Will
The Way to God's Individual Will

Bible

Circumstances

Inner Witness

Mature Counsel

Personal Desires

Common Sense

(Special Guidance)

Figure 8

will. However, since God's individual will (the "dot") is always within His moral will (the circle), the Bible is indispensable as a road sign. The individual will is always in the general direction to which the Bible points. It is like a sign that says: 'Divided Highway/Keep Right.' Anything to the left contradicts the Bible's commands, and God's will is never to be found in that direction.

"In choosing a mate, once again, God declares that all unbelievers are to the left—prohibited. The correct mate is always found among believers, so stay to the right. Further signs will have to be followed in addition to God's Word to find the specific person, but the road sign of the Bible is absolutely essential. If you miss this sign, you will not even remain on the right road to see the others.

"The Bible is filled with guidance that touches upon countless decisions. The committed Christian will read it, study it, and meditate upon it in order to find direct commands or principles that relate to specific decisions. Don't forget that the Old Testament is filled with hundreds of accounts of men and women of God making decisions. The book of Acts in the New Testament shows how the early church and its leaders were guided by God. Treat your Bible as if it were overflowing with God's guidance—for it is.

"I should add one word of caution concerning the use of the Bible in seeking guidance. The Bible must be understood according to the original intent of the author when he wrote to the original readers. In other words, it must be interpreted historically and grammatically as it was originally intended to be understood. To twist the original meaning of the text in an attempt to discover God's individual will for me is a misuse of Scripture and will prove to be misleading.

"For instance, if I read in my Bible that God instructed a prophet to go to Jerusalem, does that mean that God wants me to sign up for a Holy Land tour? No. Or suppose that on the day before a national election I read that David was chosen to be king over his taller brothers. Does that mean I should vote for the shortest candidate? No. That is not the point of the author. The words of the Bible should not be applied in a manner contrary to the original intent.

"Having said that, I must also acknowledge that there are godly men who disagree with me on this issue. They testify in principle and in practice that God does sometimes give specific guidance through the Bible. An effective modern-day missionary to China testifies that God used words directed to Moses to confirm his own leading to China. He had been concerned that he would not be able to learn the language of the people. But God said, 'Now then go, and I, even I, will be with your mouth, and teach you what you are to say.' He took the words personally and wrote 'China' over Exodus 4:12. Still, I do not suggest that you use the Bible in this way. Even these men, who do not agree with me, would tell you that such guidance from the Bible is uncommon and should be sought only with great caution.

"The second road sign is *circumstances*. The believer knows that no circumstance develops by chance. God is the sovereign Ruler over all things including the circumstances which surround the decisions you must make. You read your Bible because God wrote it. You should also read providence because God controls it. Through His control of circumstances God can reveal His individual will to you.

"Open and closed doors are two of the most obvious ways that God uses to reveal His will for you. If you apply to several medical schools, and they all turn you down, you should probably conclude that God is closing doors and saying, 'No'. This is not God's will for you, but He has something better behind another door. God also leads by opening doors that you never expected. This is often God's way of indicating, 'Yes, this is My will for you.' Paul was directed to stay in Ephesus by an open door (1 Corinthians 16:8-9), and he regularly prayed that God would open other doors for him (Colossians 4:3).

"At times God will bring unexpected, unlikely circumstances together with precise timing to reveal His will. The skeptic may claim that such remarkable combinations are merely coincidental, but the believer sees more and knows better. The believer also has the assurance that just as the Holy Spirit enlightens us to understand Scripture, so also He helps us to understand the meaning of providence. For He is the believer's Guide (John 16:13; Romans 8:14).

"We must, however, use caution with this road sign. Experienced saints know that sometimes a door may *look* closed, but in reality God is using that circumstance to test and strengthen that person's faith. You may find that God is saying, 'Wait, and I will open this door later.' Furthermore, one should not impulsively jump at every door that is not locked. A door could be open, but other road signs from God may tell you to pass it up.

"The most common question that is asked about circumstances is whether it is valid to 'put out a fleece.' This is the practice of asking God to speak directly through a providential sign agreed upon beforehand. For example, someone might pray, 'Lord, if You want us to sell our home, please have someone inquire about it next week without our advertising its availability.' An inquiry during the next week would be a 'yes' answer from God, and lack of such inquiry would amount to a negative reply.

"The term 'put out a fleece' comes from the story of Gideon in Judges 6:36-40. Gideon asked God to answer 'yes' or 'no' concerning his battle against the Midianites through the use of a fleece of wool. In the morning, if the fleece was wet with dew, but the threshing floor was dry, then God would be answering 'yes.' God granted Gideon his request for such guidance. Only the fleece was wet and Gideon did gain victory over the Midianites.

"Is such an approach valid today? Some Bible teachers do not think so. They reason, first, that this practice was used only in an age when the Holy Spirit did not indwell all believers. Furthermore, they point out that Gideon's request was not born of faith, but of his doubts and fears (Judges 6:15-18, 36-37). Finally they warn that such a practice could be easily misused.

"While these objections have merit and deserve our careful consideration, I believe that there are persuasive reasons from Scripture for using this method. The indwelling Holy Spirit does give us additional guidance today. But that does not change the fact that God also controls circumstances and can reveal His will through them. If God was gracious enough to reveal His will through this method to a doubter like Gideon, would He not be even more willing to respond in like manner to the request of faith? Indeed, that is exactly what He did with Abraham's servant in Genesis 24.

"Abraham sent his trusted servant to Haran to find a wife for his son Isaac. The servant obeyed Abraham and trusted God to guide him on the journey. He asked God to use a circumstantial sign to reveal the right bride for Isaac (Genesis 24:14). Even before he finished praying, Rebekah appeared and immediately fulfilled the 'yes' sign by providing water not only for the servant, but for his caravan of camels as well (Genesis 24:15-20).

"The experience of Abraham's servant has been shared by other saints through the ages, confirming that God is responsive to the sincere requests for guidance from His children even today.

"To guard against improper use of this method for finding God's individual will, I would suggest four guidelines which I see illustrated in the biblical examples: (1) put out a 'fleece' infrequently and only as a last resort — not as the first step in making a decision; (2) during a time of sincere prayer, agree with God on the circumstantial sign to be used; (3) select a sign that is a clear, definite, and somewhat uncommon occurrence; and (4) use this approach for more important decisions — not for trivial daily matters.

"The third road sign is the *inner witness of the Holy Spirit*. Since the Day of Pentecost, the Holy Spirit has come to dwell within each one who puts his trust in Jesus Christ. The Spirit has many wonderful ministries, but one of the most exciting is His leading and guiding of believers (John 16:13; Romans 8:14; Galatians 5:18).

"It is a somewhat delicate task to describe exactly *how* the Spirit speaks within the heart of the believer. This inward guidance is like God's peace which is clearly experienced, but beyond our full ability to put into words (Philippians 4:7). God is a Person and He speaks to us personally. Just as it is impossible to prove a salvation experience to an unbeliever, so it is impossible to prove the experience of the Spirit's inward guidance to the unbeliever.

"Bible teachers have attempted to find some words and expressions that help describe this guidance. Such guidance is called 'the voice of the Spirit' since it is the Holy Spirit speaking to us. It is called the 'inner voice' because it comes from within our heart and not from outside our body. It is described as 'the still small voice' in contrast to physically audible sounds such as the wind, earthquake, and fire perceived by Elijah (1 Kings 19:12).

"'Inner impression' is another expression that is used to distinguish such leading from direct supernatural revelation such as that given to the prophet Ezekiel (Ezekiel 1:1-3) or the Apostle Paul (2 Corinthians 12:1-4). It is called 'inner pressure' or 'inward urging' because it is so insistent that it cannot be ignored. The strength of such an impression is emphasized by calling it the 'inward burden' or 'inward compelling' of the Holy Spirit. Some refer to it as the 'guiding impulse' because the Spirit's direction often is unexpected and comes quickly when such immediate guidance is needed. It is also called the 'inner witness' because it is a testimony from the Spirit concerning the individual will of God (Romans 8:16).

"A most common designation for the Spirit's work in guidance is the expression 'peace of God.' We experience His peace when we are fully obedient and in the center of God's will. On the other hand, when we begin moving in the wrong direction, we experience restlessness and inward anxiety—in other words, lack of peace.

"Colossians 3:15 is an important verse on this subject. It says, 'Let the peace of Christ rule in your hearts.' The verb *rule* means 'to act as an arbitrator, or umpire.' In Paul's day, the word described the activity of officials ruling over the Greek games, making judgments and decisions at each event. Paul is saying that when we face decisions, we should allow the peace of God to call the decision like an umpire. Through this inner peace God says, 'Yes, this is My individual will for you.'

"From these descriptions, we can formulate a definition of the inward witness of the Holy Spirit. *It is that ministry of the Spirit in which He guides the believer through personal impressions and inner peace within the heart to reveal God's individual will.*

"The fourth road sign is *mature counsel* from other believers. A counselor who knows his Bible can help you to discover what the Word of God says about the decision you face. In addition to this, he may be able to share valuable insights from his own Christian experience which God can use to direct you into His individual will (Proverbs 24:6).

"As helpful as counselors are, this source of guidance does have definite limitations which makes it less reliable than some of the other signs already described. For instance, different counselors may give conflicting advice. Unfortunately, all fellow Christians are fallible, since they are human. One must remember that the Holy Spirit is our final Counselor in all leading, though He often uses human counselors along the way.

"The fifth road sign is *personal desires*. There are two extremes to avoid in evaluating your own desires in your search for guidance. The first extreme is what I call the 'filthy rags' complex. The Bible says that our righteousness before God is like filthy rags. It also says that the heart is 'deceitfully wicked' and not to be trusted. Some people assume from such statements that even after salvation all their personal desires are probably selfish. If such a person really wants to do something, he immediately suspects that it *cannot* be God's will! He forgets that God's salvation gives us a new heart and begins renewing our desires. As long as we live in these bodies in this world, our natural desires often will conflict with those of God. However, the more we grow in grace, the more our desires will begin to line up with God's desires. So don't automatically reject those options that you really want to do, for God is washing those rags a little more every-day as we grow.

"The second extreme is what I call the 'identical twins' theory, and is the exact opposite of the 'filthy rags' complex. Based on a possible interpretation of Psalm 37:4 and Philippians 2:13, the idea is that if I am really dedicated to the Lord, my desires will always be identical with the Lord's. This view looks inviting because it is always easier to determine one's own desires than it is to discover the Lord's will. The problem is that the 'twins' are not always identical. Even Jesus had to pray, 'Not My will, but Thine be done.' Paul experienced great inner conflict (Romans 7) and taught that Christians will always experience internal warfare as the flesh lusts against the Spirit (Galatians 5). Unfortunately, we will never be sinless in our desires until we are with Christ in heaven.

"The right approach is a balance between the two extremes. God is not a 'Celestial Killjoy,' as we have already said. God's individual will for each of us will bring happiness and joy. When we are in the center of His will, we can expect that our real desires will correspond perfectly to His. So we may expect that often our desires may be an indicator pointing to the very thing God wants us to do. As a Christian, you should not think of your desires as being 'filthy rags' or 'identical twins,' but they will serve as a valuable road sign to God's will.

"The sixth marker is *common sense.* Here is a road sign that is easy to see, but is often ignored by immature travelers in the faith. For some reason, there are many believers who think that God's individual will must always be something uncommon, unexpected, or even a bit bizarre. One has only to look at creation, however, to see that God is a God of order. He created man with common sense and He is not disappointed if we use it! In fact, the book of Proverbs repeatedly urges us to seek wisdom and shun the folly of the naive. The first deacons were expected to be full of wisdom (Acts 6:3) and it is required of church elders that they be prudent (1 Timothy 3.2) and sensible (Titus 1:8).

"Yet, we must always recognize that our common sense does not always see things the way God's divine wisdom does. Our thoughts are not always God's thoughts when we lean completely on our own understanding. God's will must never be boxed in by our common sense. For common sense would never have prompted Noah to build an ark in a land where rain had never fallen. Common sense would never have motivated Abraham to sacrifice his son Isaac. Common sense would not have compelled Philip to leave a successful revival to speak to one lone foreigner in the desert. The strategy for the battle of Jericho could hardly be the product of common sense.

"In my own ministry I was once impressed by the Spirit to abandon a sensible work schedule to go to the hospital for no apparent reason. Upon arrival, I found opportunity to speak with a dying man who had no pastor and had asked the nurse for a chaplain. I am sure that many of you have been prompted to pray for a certain individual you had not seen for some time. Later, you learned that on the very day you prayed, your friend was undergoing severe testing.

"I would suggest that guidance which appears to go against common sense should be followed only if the Lord gives you very clear and definite leading. In most cases, common sense will point in the direction of God's individual will. But never forget that we have a very uncommon God.

"The seventh road sign is that of *special supernatural guidance* through an audible voice, an angel, a vision, a trance, a dream, a prophecy, or a miracle. Has this road sign disappeared? Most saints travel the whole road of life and never receive a single supernatural message. As a matter of fact, that is true of the great majority of believers in the Bible. The book of Acts records only a handful of such experiences (Acts 8:26; 9:3-6; 10:3,10; 13:2; 16:9-10). Scripture and experience agree that such supernatural guidance is not to be normally expected. With the completed Word of God and the indwelling Holy Spirit, a strong case can be made that such further direct communication is no longer needed.

"Should we say, then, that such guidance *cannot* happen today? It is always risky, perhaps even presumptuous to tell God what He can or cannot do. So we must leave open the possibility that He could use such means. Do not, however, pray for such guidance, or feel that you must have it before you can make a decision. When God spoke through supernatural means in the Bible, He usually did it unexpectedly. Such revelation was usually the product of His initiative—not the long prayers of men. Thus we conclude that special supernatural guidance is neither normal nor necessary to find God's individual will for you . . . but if an angel should tap you on the shoulder, listen real good.

"To sum up, God has graciously mapped out a specific plan for your life which we call His individual will. Because He wants you to know that will, He has provided seven road signs which point the way. These signs are the Word of God, circumstances, the inner witness of the Holy Spirit, mature counsel, personal desires, common sense, and possibly special supernatural guidance. These road signs are fully sufficient to guide you directly into the center of His will."

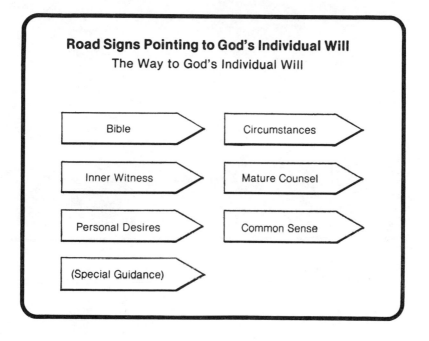

Road Signs Pointing to God's Individual Will

The Way to God's Individual Will

Bible

Circumstances

Inner Witness

Mature Counsel

Personal Desires

Common Sense

(Special Guidance)

Chapter 4

Letting the Umpire Rule

B ill Thompson paused in his presentation long enough to take another sip from the glass of water. The clock on the back wall and the attentiveness of the audience encouraged him to press on; so he continued.

"The age old question, 'How do you know when you are in love?' has through the ages been given the same answer: 'When you are in love, you won't have to ask.' That exchange is called to mind whenever I hear the fourth of our questions on God's will, for there is a similarity both in the question and its answer.

CONFIRMING GOD'S INDIVIDUAL WILL

"The fourth and final question is: *How can I know God's individual will with 100 percent certainty as it relates to a particular decision?* Such certainty is confirmed through essentially four means.

"The first means of finding 100 percent certainty concerning God's will is through *agreement of the road signs.* God has given us more than one road sign for a simple reason: He knows that one sign all by itself could be inadequate or misleading. But several of them together can give precise direction. In particular, when the three main signs of the Bible, the Holy Spirit, and circumstances all agree, you may rest assured that you have found God's will.

Questions About God's Will

1. Definition: What does "God's will" mean?

2. Proof: Does God have a plan for *my* life?

3. Process: How can I discover God's will?

4. Certainty: How can I know God's will for sure in a specific situation?

"An old familiar story illustrates this graphically. On an overcast night, a ship was fighting rough seas as it approached the narrow entrance to a harbor. To the inexperienced passenger, the chances of finding and navigating the path to safety seemed remote at best. The slightest miscalculation could spell disaster. Yet the captain appeared calm and relaxed. A nervous passenger, perhaps seeking reassurance to settle his own fears, asked the captain, 'Sir, how do you know when to guide the ship into the harbor entrance?' The captain pointed to the dark shore punctuated with random dots of light. 'Do you see those three brightest lights there on the land?' The passenger searched for a moment, then nodded. 'I have learned,' continued the captain, 'to steer my ship parallel to the shore until those three lights all line up as one. When the three lights agree, then I know that I can guide my ship safely into the narrow entrance of the harbor.'

"So it is with God's will. When you have agreement among the three lights of God's Word, circumstances, and the inward witness of the Holy Spirit, you can proceed with confidence. The other road signs may add support, but those three are essential. If one of those signs does not agree with the others, you should assume that something is wrong. If, for instance, you feel that the Spirit is prompting you, and that circumstances are positive, but your course of action violates God's Word, you can be certain that it is not God's will. Obeying this principle will save you great heartache and bring confidence into your decision making. It is exciting to watch God's Word, circumstances, and the inward witness slowly move into perfect alignment. With such agreement there is certainty that you have found the narrow entrance into God's perfect individual will.

"The second means of finding 100 percent certainty in God's will is through *results*. Finding God's will brings peace and blessing to the Christian. So the right results in a decision can give you certainty by confirming that your choice was correct. You may have felt confident that you were on the right road all along, but when you arrive at your destination there is additional certainty with this obvious confirmation. Results are like the sign at the park which says, 'Reunion Picnic—You Made It!' You were pretty sure you had accurately followed the arrows painted on the paper plates tacked to the telephone poles, but that final sign clinched it. In the matter of seeking God's will, you may find that the results of your correct decision are blessed beyond your expectation—though this is not necessarily so. The thing to note, however, is that your faith will always be tested. So do not be discouraged or intimidated by difficulties you may initially encounter. They do not necessarily mean that you have missed God's plan.

"Sometimes God, in His grace, uses results to give us an undeserved second chance. At times we run ahead of God in a decision and bypass the will of God in our haste. Results have a way of bringing us up short, informing us abruptly that we have lost our way. They are like the rude awakening experienced by the driver who suddenly discovers that the unfinished expressway has ended. Immediately he realizes how foolish he has been to drive around that warning sign encountered earlier. This can be a manifestation of God's grace, for in many cases, we can return to the point where the wrong decision was made and begin again. We still lose time, but God mercifully allows us to return to the right road of His will.

"God may also show His grace by closing a door in our face which otherwise would have led to disaster. On such occasions, though we are frustrated, we should give thanks. However, it would be presumptuous to expect God to continually run around slamming doors to protect us from our own foolishness or disobedience. God knows that often a burn on the hand or a good spanking teaches a mischievous child far more effectively than a thousand artificial roadblocks. Of course, such roadblocks will not be needed if we are sincere and obedient before God.

"The third means of finding 100 percent certainty in God's individual will is through *prayer*. Let me ask you a question at this point. How many hours did you spend in prayer during this past week? Would you be embarrassed to say it out loud?

"I often ask that very question of individuals who tell me they cannot find God's will. The answers I regularly hear have convinced me that 90 percent of those who cannot find God's will are not spending enough time in prayer. If you do not ask God, you will not receive (James 4:2). By the way, how many hours *did* you pray this past week? If believers spent as much time praying for God's will as they did frantically looking for it, most of our problems would be eliminated. Next time you are tempted to take an hour to go purchase another book on God's will, stay home instead and spend the time on your knees.

"Prayer is like a clean windshield when you are seeking God's will. It allows you to see the road and the signs clearly without distortion or distraction. Prayer is like a rush of cool air from a rolled down window. It brings the drowsy 'driver' back to full alertness.

"Godly saints will always tell you that the inward witness of the Spirit is most clearly heard when you are quiet before Him in prayer. It is then that His still, small voice can be most clearly heard. It is not then drowned out by the noisiness and busyness of our lives.

"Many Christians, if they are honest, will admit that it is hard for them to get started in prayer. And even once they have begun, the slightest distraction seems to cut it short. It may be hard to continue and wait in prayer, but it is even harder to live life after missing God's individual will from lack of prayer. If the answer does not come immediately, wait before God until it does. It may be that He is using this decision to get your undivided attention. If you will wait before Him in prayer, the answer will come, and it will not be too late.

"Let me say again that I am convinced that 90 percent of those who cannot find God's will are not spending enough time in prayer. Let prayer stimulate your alertness to the signs, cultivate your ability to hear the still, small voice, and develop your attentiveness to God. You may discover that prayer was the missing step in your search for certainty in knowing God's will.

"The fourth means of finding 100 percent certainty in God's individual will is through *personal communion* with God. It is frustrating to attempt to read a sign that is just a bit too far away, or to try to understand the words of someone who is slightly out of hearing range. The problem is distance. Distance complicates communication.

"In personal relationships distance also affects communion. When we say a husband and wife are distant from each other, we mean they are not enjoying marriage communion with each other. If this is the case, the lack of marriage *communion* will inevitably lead to a lack of marriage *communication*. On the other hand, it is a delight to watch a husband and wife who have grown in their love and communion through the years. They communicate on a level unknown by couples who merely live at the same address. Often one spouse can sense how his partner feels about a matter without even having to ask. Such people are able to communicate with each other with the slightest squeeze of the hand, the smallest facial expression, or even a certain glance of the eye.

"Such is the level of communion desired by the Lord, our personal Guide. He desires that our communion be so close that even the slightest glance of His eye will communicate His will to us. In Psalm 32:8 God says, 'I will instruct you and teach you in the way which you should go; I will counsel you with My eye upon you.' This guidance demands close communion that has no need of the bit and bridle required of horses and mules (Psalm 32:9). Such guidance is possible only when we are close to the Lord. When our fellowship is intimate so that we are walking by His side, then we will be aware of the slightest communication from the Holy Spirit.

"Nothing replaces closeness to the Lord: not formulas, not books on God's will, not seminars like this one, not college or Bible school degrees, not even perfect church attendance. The closer you are to Him, the closer you will be to finding certainty in the knowledge of His will. If you cannot quite hear God's leading, draw a little closer to Him. And be assured, that as you make that move, He will draw closer to you as well (James 4:8).

"What we have seen, then, is that there are four means by which a believer can find certainty of knowledge of God's individual will in a specific situation: agreement of the signs, results from a decision, prayer, and communion with the Lord [Figure 9].

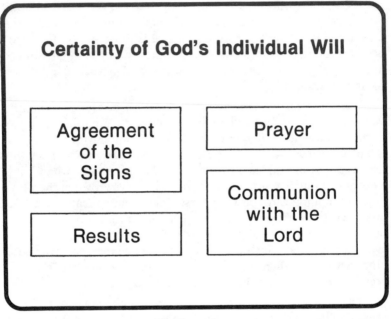

Certainty of God's Individual Will

Agreement
of the
Signs

Prayer

Results

Communion
with the
Lord

Figure 9

"Now I think it might prove helpful to look briefly at what we've covered this morning to this point before moving on to the question and answer period. So let's look to the overhead projector again to assist us in visualizing our review.

"At the beginning, we agreed that we would concentrate on answering four questions.

Questions About God's Will

1. Definition: What does "God's will" mean?

2. Proof: Does God have a plan for *my* life?

3. Process: How can I discover God's will?

4. Certainty: How can I know God's will for sure in a specific situation?

"As we considered the first question, we found that most references to God's will in daily conversation have to do with God's individual plan for a person's life. To give a more complete biblical perspective, we compared and contrasted God's individual will with His sovereign will on the one hand, and His moral will on the other. We used these brief definitions to clarify the distinctiveness of each of these aspects of God's will.

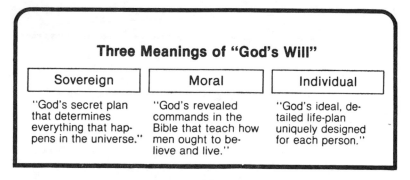

Three Meanings of "God's Will"

Sovereign	Moral	Individual
"God's secret plan that determines everything that happens in the universe."	"God's revealed commands in the Bible that teach how men ought to believe and live."	"God's ideal, detailed life-plan uniquely designed for each person."

"In seeking to answer the second question, we argued that the reality of God's individual will is clearly established by four lines of proof.

Proving God's Individual Will

Reason	Experience
Biblical Example	Biblical Teaching

"We began our consideration of the question of process by clearing up some common misconceptions that many Christians have about discovering God's will.

Common Misconceptions About God's Individual Will

Syllabus Search
Celestial Killjoy
Bionic Missionary
White Hair Only
Lightning Flash
Presidential Problem

"How, then, may we learn what God's will is? We likened God's plan for our lives to a road that we must follow. There are many possible roads to take, but only one correct one for each of us. To keep us from getting lost along the way, we learned that God has provided seven different kinds of road signs to point the way.

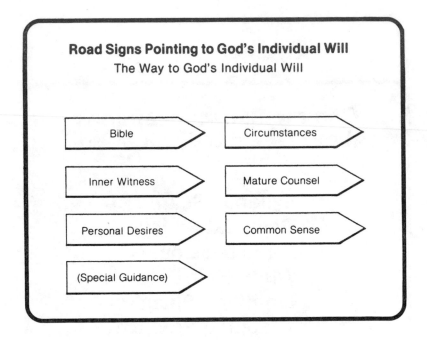

"Then, finally, we saw that there are four means by which the believer can find certainty of knowledge of God's individual will in a specific situation.

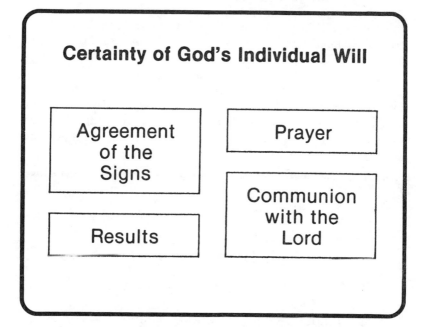

Certainty of God's Individual Will

Agreement of the Signs

Prayer

Results

Communion with the Lord

"I see by the clock on the back wall that even with the review I have not quite succeeded in using up all of the allotted time, so I'm afraid I will actually have to attempt to answer some of your questions." Bill's injection of levity into the proceedings was appreciated by the young people, some of whom actually laughed at the comment. A number began thumbing back through their notes to locate the memos they had made to themselves. Bill added, "Just bear in mind that I don't understand everything I know, and we'll get along just fine." More laughter.

A high school boy wearing glasses stood up in the third row. "Pastor Thompson," he signalled. Bill nodded to him. "Before coming to this seminar, I thought it might be a good idea to read this book my mother gave me on the will of God. The author only mentioned two ways of understanding the expression 'God's will.' Do most writers agree with him or you?"

"What you have to remember," began Bill, "is that writers on this subject are all working with essentially the same material. The differences are going to mostly be matters of organization, style, illustrations and varying viewpoints on minor points. I would like to think that if all such authors could hear the presentation I made this morning, they would agree that there are three aspects to God's will. They might not present it that way themselves, but I believe they would find my analysis to be acceptable.

"Those writers who develop only two categories either do not discuss God's sovereign will at all, or they present the moral and individual aspects together under the same heading. This is not surprising since, as we noted earlier, God's moral and individual wills have some important elements in common. Let me put these similarities on the overhead for you" [Figure 10].

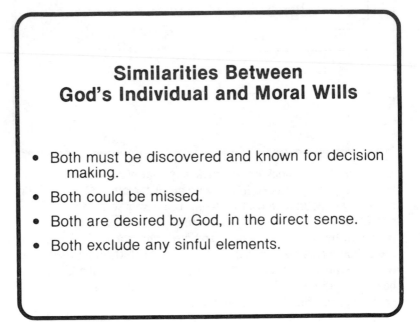

Similarities Between God's Individual and Moral Wills

- Both must be discovered and known for decision making.
- Both could be missed.
- Both are desired by God, in the direct sense.
- Both exclude any sinful elements.

Figure 10

"None of those characteristics are true of God's sovereign will, but all are true of both His moral will and His individual will. So, it is convenient to group the two under a single heading—such as, 'What God Wants Us to Do,' or 'God's Wishes,' or 'God's Desires.' But if this approach is taken, it is still important that the distinctions between the two aspects be clarified in some way. For they *are* different in some key respects, as you can readily see on this chart [Figure 11].

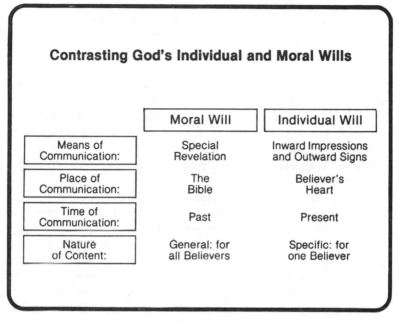

Contrasting God's Individual and Moral Wills

	Moral Will	Individual Will
Means of Communication:	Special Revelation	Inward Impressions and Outward Signs
Place of Communication:	The Bible	Believer's Heart
Time of Communication:	Past	Present
Nature of Content:	General: for all Believers	Specific: for one Believer

Figure 11

"I think that our designations of 'sovereign,' 'moral,' and 'individual' really help to prevent confusion in discussion of God's will. That's why I use them."

A dark haired girl stood up near the middle of the room. "Pastor Thompson, I'm a freshman in college, and when semester break is over, I'll be registering for my second-semester classes. My problem is that I don't know what vocation the Lord would have me follow. If I don't know that, how can I know His will for the courses I should take?"

"That's a good question, young lady," replied Bill. "There is much truth in the statement that anything you learn now will be of value to you in the future. So in a way, it's hard to go wrong. On the other hand, God does know what He wants you to do in the future, so it follows that He knows which courses would best prepare you for that future. Obviously, if He had revealed His vocational choice to you by now, that knowledge would be helpful in course selection. But the fact that He hasn't simply means that you must follow whatever other road signs He may choose to use. I would advise you to consider each course on its own merit, and make your choices on the basis of God's individual will as He makes it known to you—just like any other decision. Since He knows where He wants you to go and what He wants you to do in the future, the courses that He leads you to take will prepare you for that."

One of the youth sponsors from another church, a young woman in her late twenties, caught Bill's attention. "Pastor, I really appreciated what you said about the place of personal desires in finding God's will. The note I made to myself during that part of your presentation was this: How can I accurately distinguish between my own inward desires and those coming from the Holy Spirit?"

"In some cases it is obvious," replied Bill. "If I desire to do something that I know is contrary to the Word of God, then that desire cannot be from the Holy Spirit. The source of such a desire could only be my flesh. At other times, what I want and what the Spirit wants will be identical. On such occasions, it is not necessary to make a technical distinction since both are leading me in the same direction. What I have found is that much of the time, those desires that are prompted by the Holy Spirit have His distinctive stamp upon them. His desires are often holy beyond our own holiness, creative beyond our own creativity, wise beyond our natural wisdom, and discerning beyond our present level of maturity. That divine stamp will be evident, sooner or later, making it possible to clearly tell the difference."

"Well, what about hunches?" blurted a redheaded high school girl near the front. Embarrassed that in her eagerness she had neglected to raise her hand or stand, she blushed at the titters in the audience. Bill was grinning, too.

"What do you mean?" he returned.

The girl was slowly regaining her composure as she explained. "Sometimes I get these hunches that I should do something. Maybe I have a highly developed sense of women's intuition, I don't know. Anyway, could those feelings I seem to get for no reason at all be messages from the Holy Spirit?"

Bill appeared thoughtful as he spoke. "You really have to be careful about that sort of thing. Hunches and premonitions are experienced by Christians and non-Christians alike. We tend to remember the one that proved to be right, but as often as not, they don't pan out. I think that the thing to do when you get a hunch like that is to prayerfully evaluate it and test it by other road signs. If it is only a hunch, it will fade away under such scrutiny. My experience is that the impressions of the Spirit are much clearer than mere hunches, and they grow stronger, not weaker, with the passing of time."

Pastor Williams from a sister church in the next town stood to his feet. "Bill, have you thought about whether God has an individual will for churches as well as specific people?"

"I've thought about that some, Tom," Bill replied, "and I've come to the conclusion that He does. One biblical indication of that concept is the incident in Acts 13 where the Lord directed the church at Antioch to send out Barnabas and Paul as missionaries. That was, I believe, His individual will for that church as a whole.

"The idea of an individual will for each church not only fits with the doctrine of the church as one body, but actually fosters the unity demanded by it. If each individual member within a church sought God's will for that church on a specific decision, the resulting harmony ought to be much greater than that produced by the wisdom of men. Since God has an individual will for the church as a church, the practical conclusion is that, on important decisions, the church is not merely looking for a majority vote of its members, but unanimous recognition of God's will. Such an approach would, I believe, go a long way toward bringing the unity that our churches so desperately need today."

A young man that Bill recognized as a senior in his own high school group asked the next question. "Pastor Bill, my question concerns the road signs of circumstances and counsel. You said that at times, especially with very important decisions, it would be a good idea to set out a fleece. I was wondering whether I could use spiritual counsel as a fleece. Do you understand what I mean?"

"Yes, I do," replied Bill, "and no, I don't think that is a proper approach. If I do understand you correctly, you are talking about agreeing with God beforehand that you will consider whatever advice you are given by a counselor as indicating God's will. Is that right?"

The boy nodded.

"We have already established that spiritual counsel is one of the valid road signs which God has given us. But for it to have value, it must be used as it was intended. To turn it into a fleece is to require God to reveal His will through just one of the signs. Such an approach is not only presumptuous, it ignores one of the known areas of weakness characteristic of that sign—namely, that human counselors are fallible. Furthermore, the practice is unfair to the counselor. For, in reality, you are asking him for more than advice. You are asking him for leading. Such an approach ends up being a misuse of a counselor rather than a proper use of a fleece."

The girl sitting next to that boy raised her hand. "We learned the story of George Mueller in our Sunday school class. Our teacher said that before seeking God's will in a matter, he would try to completely empty himself of his own will and desires. Is that something I should do?"

"George Mueller was greatly used of God because of his child-like faith and zeal to serve the Lord," agreed Bill. "I think he took that approach because it helped him to better read the road signs that we have talked about. But I don't think that such 'self-emptying' is necessary for others. For, as we have already observed, often our own desires correspond perfectly with God's desires. We should take them into account and evaluate them so that God can use them to reveal His will to us. What we can appreciate about George Mueller is his concern that his own desires not block him from clearly seeing God's will."

A co-ed about a third of the way back was the next to take the floor. "Pastor Thompson, this past semester we studied spiritual gifts in our doctrine class in Bible school. How does my spiritual gift relate to God's guidance?"

"An excellent question," replied Bill. "We know from 1 Peter 4:10 that it is God's moral will for you to exercise your spiritual gift. Now in the specific matter of determining God's individual will for your vocation, knowledge of your spiritual gift will help to narrow your options. Not every occupation or profession will require your gift. For instance, to use a negative example, if you do not have the gift of teaching, you will not need to pursue a career as a seminary professor. If you have the gift of helps, a whole range of possibilities opens up while other fields are probably eliminated. Of course, the decision of how and where to use your spiritual gift is determined by God's individual will for you. Such specific choices should be made like every other decision governed by God's plan."

"Along that line, pastor," began a voice from the opposite end of the same row. It turned out to be another college-age fellow.

"What if God calls you to do something that you don't know how to do?"

"Perhaps some of you have seen that plaque that reads, 'The will of God will not lead you where the power of God cannot enable you and the grace of God cannot keep you.' I think that says it well. Usually, God places His soldiers at that point in the spiritual warfare for which He has prepared them—in terms of gifts, abilities, experience, personality, and so on. But there are times when He calls on someone, not because of his ability, but because of his availability.

"Biblical illustrations abound. Amos, in the Old Testament, was not a prophet by profession. He was a farmer who raised sheep and goats, and tended fig trees. But God called him to leave his farm and go north to declare God's message to Israel. As he obeyed, God enabled. Then there was that little boy with the five loaves and two fish in Galilee. A great miracle took place that day, not because of that boy's great talent, but because he gave what he had. If God clearly calls you to a difficult task, count on Him for the ability to do it. Remember what the Lord said to the Apostle Paul in 2 Corinthians 12:9: 'My grace is sufficient for you, for power is perfected in weakness.' Turn your weakness over to the Lord, and have at it."

"Pastor Bill." It was the familiar voice of Ted Bradford coming from the front row.

"Yes, Ted," acknowledged Bill.

"What should a person do when he is not certain of God's will, and yet he faces a deadline where a decision must be made?"

Bill nodded. "That's an all too common experience, isn't it?" Others in the audience indicated their agreement. "The first thing we must do in such a situation is admit that our lack of direction is due to some failure on our part, not God's. The Lord always does His part in revealing His individual will, but unfortunately we sometimes fail in our responsibility. Such an experience should be a warning to us that we need to be more sincere in seeking His will and meeting His requirements for leading. Failure to recognize this will only lead to repetition of the same problem further on down the road.

"Still, when a deadline comes, we must do something. In such a case, this is what I have done: I have humbly admitted my failure to God, prayed for last minute guidance, and then made the choice that seemed best to me at the time. If you ever have to do that, you should carefully watch the results to determine as quickly as possible whether the wrong decision was made. If you goofed, and it is possible to do so, you should backtrack to the point of decision and follow the other alternative. There have been times in my life when God has 'covered for me,' so to speak. But we must not presume upon His grace and count on Him to bail us out all the time. For there have also been times when, in His love, He has chosen to allow me to learn from my mistakes the hard way—lessons that were painful, but effective.

"Without a doubt, it's far better to follow God's direction and the road signs He has given from the very beginning. The words of the hymn are to the point: 'O what needless pain we bear.' Hopefully, we can learn from past mistakes, and apply what we know all the way."

Bill looked at the clock again and exclaimed, "We should wrap it up pretty soon—at least before I run out of answers."

"One more question, please, Pastor Thompson." It was the high school senior again.

"All right," allowed Bill, "one last question."

"Thank you, sir. It *is* important. What should you do when you face a decision and two options seem to be equal?"

"Are you sure you won't take my answer as a fleece?" chided Bill, grinning. Everyone laughed.

"No sir, or rather, yes sir," he stammered, to the great delight of the other kids. "What I mean is, it's not a fleece." A couple of people clapped and the laughter crescendoed. When the noise died down, the flustered boy explained. "The reason I asked the question in the first place is that I am in the process of applying for entrance to college. And frankly, from what I've been able to gather so far, I can't see any great differences between two or three of the schools I'm considering. I'm not sure I can get into any of them, but on the other hand, if they all accept me, I'm going to have a real problem."

"I can sympathize with that," replied Bill, "and it is an important question you are asking in spite of the hard time we've been giving you. From our human standpoint, two or more alternatives often do seem equal. This is because we are not able to see how each alternative will turn out in the future. God, however, in His omniscience, does know what would happen with each of the potential choices. That knowledge is part of His basis for selecting only one of those alternatives as part of His individual will for you. So, while the options may all be positive in terms of God's Word and circumstances, they are not equal in the mind of God. In such decisions, the inward witness of the Spirit is especially important and determinative.

"In your case, if you're accepted by two schools that seem equal to you, I would suggest that you do a more thorough study of them. Take their catalogs and compare them at every possible point. Make lists on paper showing the respective strengths and weaknesses of each school. Do this research prayerfully, and in all probability, God will make His choice clear in the process.

"If such further investigation does not lead to a definite conclusion, then submit the entire matter to the 'umpire' of God's peace. Go some place where you can be alone with God. Then close your eyes and, in your imagination, go to one of the schools. Visualize yourself packing your clothes, getting on the plane, arriving on campus. Go through this process with each of the schools under consideration. With one of them, you will experience the settled assurance of God's peace. This is the school you should attend.

"I really appreciate your attention and your thoughtful questions. I think it would be good for us to close this seminar with a word of prayer.

"Dear Lord, thank You for being our Guide. Help us to comprehend the meaning of 'God's will.' Direct our hearts in such a way that we will recognize Your individual plan for our lives. Give us the spiritual awareness to see and understand the road signs You give us to point the way to the center of Your will. Grant to these young people that blessed assurance of knowing for certain what Your will is in each decision that they make. And may they have the grace and courage to obey Your will as You reveal it. But most of all, teach us to pray and draw close to You. In Jesus' name we pray, Amen.

"You're dismissed."

PART 2

The Case of the Missing "Dot"

The Traditional View Critiqued

Chapter 5

Does God Have Three Wills?

*A*nd they lived happily ever after.

The high school senior was accepted by three fine colleges, and he had little difficulty determining the one he should attend. Ted and Annette got married that summer. After four years at seminary, and a one-year internship with Bill Thompson, the Bradfords began their first term as missionaries in Kenya. And Bill Thompson had a good set of cassette tapes of his seminar that saved dozens of counseling hours in the years ahead.

That is how one might expect the story to end. And it could end that way since the entire account is fictional. Real life, however, is seldom so cut-and-dried.

I know. That high school senior could have been me. And, as I explained in the introduction, my grasp of the principles explained by Bill Thompson proved to be more frustrating than helpful. As good as it sounds, the traditional view has serious weaknesses. And as long as those problems remain unexposed and uncorrected, the high school seniors and Ted Bradfords of this world will continue to have difficulty determining God's will for their decisions.

Accordingly, the pages that follow will provide a critique of the traditional view, revealing the underlying causes of decision-making frustrations. For purposes of outline, we will begin where Bill Thompson began with the first question: What does the expression "God's will" mean?

Two Out of Three

Bill Thompson explained that God's will may be understood in three senses. Using his terminology, there is God's *sovereign* will, His *moral* will, and His *individual* will. What we need to determine is whether each of these categories is, in fact, a biblical concept.

Does God have a sovereign will? The traditional view says yes, and we agree. The Bible clearly teaches that God has a sovereign will — "a predetermined plan for everything that happens in the universe" — as it was defined in Part 1. (Most, but not all, traditional view proponents accept this doctrine. And even for those who do not believe in the sovereign will, their view makes very little difference to their overall position on God's individual will.) We have concluded that God's sovereign will has a direct bearing on the decision-making process that Christians are to follow. So this aspect of God's will will be further developed and explored in chapters 12 and 13.

Does God have a moral will? Again, on this question virtually all evangelicals agree. The Scriptures, which are the Christian's final authority for faith and life, clearly reveal all of the moral will of God.

While there is agreement about the reality of God's moral will, there are differences about the extent to which that moral will provides guidance in the process of making specific decisions. The traditional view holds that the Bible (God's moral will) gives *most* of the guidance needed to make a decision; but, additionally, knowing God's individual will is essential for complete leading to the correct choice. The alternative view put forth in this book is that the Bible is *fully sufficient* to provide all the guidance needed for a believer to know and do God's will. That concept will be developed in chapter 9, "Thy Word Is Truth."

Does God have an individual will? With this question we come to the crux of the matter. For the traditional view, the concept of an ideal plan uniquely designed for each believer lies at the very heart of the whole system. To quote Bill Thompson, "It is important to live and make one's decisions within the larger circle of God's moral will. But finding the dot in the center, God's specific individual will, is essential in making correct decisions in daily life." (See Figure 3, page 36).

It is our contention, by contrast, that the idea of an *individual will* of God for every detail of a person's life is *not found in Scrip-*

ture. If we are right, the most startling ramification is that many believers are investing a great deal of time and energy searching for something that is nonexistent. By definition, the search for the proverbial needle in a haystack holds a greater promise of success than the quest for the vanishing dot.

Depending on one's mind-set, such an idea will either be liberating or unsettling. But in either case, the believer has a mandate to evaluate the biblical data. It simply will not do to *assume* that God has a unique plan for each life that must be discovered as the basis for making decisions. And yet that presupposition has been widely adopted as the starting point for most discussions on knowing God's will. The question as to whether such an assumption is biblically valid needs to be reconsidered.

Such reconsideration is called for in response to Bill Thompson's second question: "Does God have a plan for my life?" In the seminar presentation, the proofs for an individual will of God were argued on the basis of reason, experience, biblical example, and biblical teaching. We shall now examine each of these lines of evidence in order, dealing with the first three in this chapter (reason, experience, and biblical example), and reviewing the biblical teaching in the next (chapter 6, "Does Scripture Teach the 'Dot'?").

THE ARGUMENTS FROM REASON

The traditional view maintains that reason suggests several arguments for the reality of an individual will of God. The first line of evidence is based upon the combination of two of God's attributes: orderliness and omniscience. God's insistence upon order (1 Corinthians 14:40) and His advance knowledge of the outcome of every possible decision (Matthew 11:21-22) suggest that it is only reasonable that He would construct an ideal life-plan for each person. For all of creation, from the macrocosmic configuration of the galaxies to the microcosmic intricacies of molecular structure, testifies to the orderliness of the Master Designer.

Given God's nature as a Designer and His attribute of omniscience, it is certainly reasonable that He *could* develop an individual will for each person. But are we obligated to take the next step and contend that such observed orderliness in God's nature *demands* an individual will for people? We think not. The possibility of such an individual plan is not contrary to reason, but the necessity of such an individual plan is not required by reason.

Consider this illustration. It is reasonable to think that a man might drive his car down Main Street on his way to work because that is the shortest route to his place of business. But he does not *have* to go that way. He may, in fact, take a longer route which, because of a lower volume of traffic and fewer signal lights, allows him to get there more quickly. Reason permits either alternative.

Twinkle, Twinkle, Little Star

Everyone agrees that the Creator is a God of order. But while the galaxies and molecules reflect God's design, they do not demonstrate the individual will of God as described by the traditional view. The order of the galaxies is not the product of God's individual will, but rather of His *sovereign* will.[1] The universe is made up of inanimate objects that function in an orderly fashion by virtue of their sovereign conformity to God's laws of nature. The galaxies do not discover God's plan for them and then will to obey it. In that respect, there is a major difference between particles and people—people, and only people, make moral decisions. Apart from angels, people are the only creatures which have any concern about God's will.

And so, while the concept of an individual will of God is acceptable to reason, it is hardly required by it. Furthermore, reason can account for the orderly guidance of God in other ways. For instance, the theology of guidance presented later in this book also portrays God leading in an orderly fashion. In that model, an individual will of God is not necessary to such orderliness. Rather, God establishes His order through His moral and sovereign wills. His moral will regulates all behavior giving guidance into orderly living. And through His sovereign superintendence of our lives, God makes certain that all things work together for good. The end product is orderly guidance—without any need for the traditional "individual" will of God.

Father Knows Best

Another aspect of the traditional view's argument from reason is that the imagery of God as our Father, Shepherd, and King indicates the reasonableness of an individual will. The idea is that a good father, king, or shepherd would have a detailed plan for his charges.

But is that really the case? Does the wise father guide his child by formulating a plan that covers every detail of the child's life and then revealing that plan step-by-step as each decision must be made? Of course not. The father who is truly wise teaches his child the basic principles of life. He teaches what is right and wrong, what is wise over against what is foolish. He then seeks to train the child to make his own decisions making proper use of those correct guidelines. Such a father is overjoyed when he knows that the child has matured to the point where he is able to function independently as an adult, making wise decisions on the basis of principles learned in his youth. The grown-up son or daughter is thereby prepared to live in the real world and make responsible choices with respect to mate, vocation, and the other decisions of life.

The other images indicate a similar pattern. The good shepherd sets boundaries for his sheep, but allows freedom of movement within those boundaries. He establishes limits for the safety of the sheep, but does not use his staff to point out which specific tuft of grass ought to be eaten by which animal.

Likewise, the effective king does not seek to legislate every activity of his people. He establishes basic laws to promote righteousness and determines penalties as additional motivation for compliance. He does not desire a nation of slaves or robots, but a kingdom of people who respect their leader for his wisdom, and appreciate his protection. When such a relationship exists, those who are governed will act responsibly within the limits of the law.

If our development of these images is accurate, what we are seeing is that God is indeed a Guide. But His means of guidance may be different from that suggested by the traditional view. It may be more general than specific. It may give increasing freedom and responsibility to believers in their decision making.

Guidance and Child Rearing

Further support for such understanding comes from the scriptural analogy of God as a Father and believers as sons. The picture is developed by the Apostle Paul in Galatians 4:1-11. Throughout history, God has dealt with His people the way a wise father would rear his children. As children grow, they are given increased responsibility. With increased responsibility comes greater freedom and less restrictive rules.

In the progress of His revelation, God moved from a highly structured system of regulations governing a wide range of specific behaviors to a system where behavior is to be determined by principles and governed by personal relationship. There was progress from law to Christ; from the bondage of close, restrictive supervision appropriate to immature and willful children to the freedom of responsible adulthood.

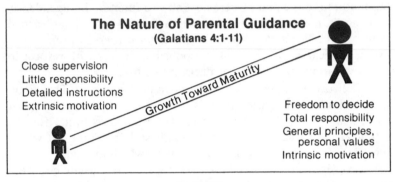

The Nature of Parental Guidance
(Galatians 4:1-11)

Close supervision
Little responsibility
Detailed instructions
Extrinsic motivation

Growth Toward Maturity

Freedom to decide
Total responsibility
General principles,
    personal values
Intrinsic motivation

Figure 12

One profound consequence of the coming of Christ is the believer's liberation from the Mosaic Law. By way of example, the effect of this freedom can be seen in the area of eating practices. Under the Mosaic Law, there were very precise restrictions and regulations governing what could be eaten and how it had to be prepared (Leviticus 11; Deuteronomy 14). With the death of Christ, such rigid requirements were removed (Acts 10-11), and there is now freedom in the choice of what one may eat with a clear conscience (1 Corinthians 10:25; 1 Timothy 4:1-4).

The point is this: God does guide His people like a father, shepherd, and king. These figures do not, however, argue for the existence of an individual will of God. In fact, it is reasonable to suggest that if these figures argue for anything, they support the idea that God guides through the basic principles of life He has given in the Bible (His moral will), thereby teaching His children to wisely use their freedom in the application of those principles to the decisions of life.

The Argument From Experience

The second line of proof advanced by the traditional view for the individual will of God is based on *experience*. All responsible Bible teachers agree that experience alone cannot determine truth. It can, however, confirm truth. And so, if it can be shown that experience conforms to the teaching that God has an ideal plan for each believer, such evidence would provide substantial support for that viewpoint.

Accounting for Hudson Taylor

To bring this question into focus, let's use a common illustration. Few believers would disagree that Hudson Taylor was highly successful in his missionary endeavors in China. The question is, how can we account for such success? The teaching of the traditional view is that Hudson Taylor's success can be attributed to his obedience to the call of God to take the gospel message to China. He followed God's individual will for his life, and God blessed him for that obedience. If God does have an individul plan for each believer, such an explanation for Taylor's success is indeed possible.

But is it the correct explanation? Are there any other factors which might account for such success? We believe there are. It seems equally possible that Hudson Taylor's accomplishments in evangelism stem from his obedience to God's *moral* will. Such spiritual success is *promised* to the one who will obey what God has revealed in His Word (Psalm 1:2-3; 1 Kings 2:3; 1 Chronicles 22:13).

> "Only be strong and very courageous; be careful to *do according to all the law* which Moses My servant commanded you; do not turn from it to the right or to the left, *so that you may have success wherever you go.* This book of the law shall not depart from your mouth, but you shall meditate on it day and night, so that you may be *careful to do according to all that is written in it; for then you will make your way prosperous, and then you will have success.*" (Joshua 1:7-8)

Blessing comes as the result of knowing and obeying the revealed moral will of God (John 13:17; 2 Timothy 3:16-17). How successful would Hudson Taylor have been if he had gone to Africa rather than China? We have no concrete way of knowing because he never went to Africa. But if his spiritual success was attributable, as we are suggesting, to his obedience to the Great Commission of Christ (Matthew 28:19-20), there is good reason to believe that he would have been an effective witness for Christ wherever he took the gospel, whether to China or Chinatown.

We cannot, of course, prove such universal spiritual success in endeavors not undertaken by Hudson Taylor. But in raising that possibility, we are insisting that the only thing experience proves is that Hudson Taylor did have success in China. It gives no undeniable explanation for the *reasons* for that success. And if we evaluate his ministry by the statements of Scripture, they seem to indicate that spiritual success comes because the sovereign God is working through believers who are dependently obedient to His moral will wherever they are. This would appear to be an acceptable explanation for Hudson Taylor's success judged by biblical standards.

A Still, Small Nudge?

But what is one to make of those strong inward impressions that seem to be pointing to a specific course of action? Examples of such promptings are abundant and appear to offer solid substantiation of an individual will from personal experience. Those who have followed such impulses have often seen genuine spiritual results produced upon obedience to the inner leading. Such experiences are usually perceived as very convincing demonstrations of the reality of God's precise guidance into an individual will.

This is an important question, and will be discussed at length in Chapter 8 "Impressions Are Impressions". For now, two observations will suffice. First, it is often forgotten that many, if not most, such inward impressions lead nowhere. Promptings are followed to dead ends as often as to avenues of service. For inward promptings to have value as proofs for the existence of an individual will, they would have to be uniformly productive of spiritual effects, at least with some degree of consistency. Second, spiritual accomplishments that result from following some inner leading can be accounted for in the same way as the success experienced by Hudson Taylor. That is, the believer in question seized upon the opportunity presented to minister in accordance with God's moral will (Ephesians 5:16-17). Such obedience brings blessing whether accompanied by an impression or not.

To sum up, the most that can be said about the applicability of experience to the question of God's individual will is that it neither proves nor disproves its existence. There are other adequate explanations for spiritual success that have specific biblical warrant.[2]

The Argument From Biblical Example

Having considered the arguments for the individual will from reason and experience, we may now turn to *biblical examples* that some construe to indicate an ideal plan for all believers.

Examples in Scripture must always be handled with care. For many of the events recorded in the Bible are included primarily because they were unique occurrences, or at least highly unusual. What must be determined in each case is whether the example referred to was intended to illustrate *normative* Christian behavior or experience. Should believers today practice the holy kiss (1 Corinthians 16:20)? Should one expect a light and a voice from heaven to accompany a call to the ministry (Acts 9:3-4)? God spoke to Balaam through a donkey (Numbers 22:28-30). Should each believer keep one in his back yard just in case? These suggestions may be extreme, but they remind us that while scriptural examples have real value, they must be interpreted with great care.

The scriptural examples adduced by the traditional view in support of an individual will invariably cite instances where God gave guidance, supernaturally revealed, that was much more specific and detailed than the moral will of God. The Old Testament is replete with accounts of men and women who received direct guidance leading them to take on a certain vocation (leader, prophet, king, etc.), or do a certain thing (e.g., Jonah 1:2). Paul received numerous divine directions which are recorded in the book of Acts. He was called, literally, to be an apostle by vocation (Galatians 1:1; 1 Corinthians 1:1; Acts 9). He was sent out as a missionary (Acts 13:1-2). During his missionary work he was directed to specific places of ministry and away from others (Acts 16:6-10; 18:9-10; 22:17-21; 23:11). Peter was told to go to the house of Cornelius (Acts 10:17-20) after Cornelius was directed to find Peter (Acts 10:5). Later Peter was led out of Herod's prison (Acts 12:7-8). Philip was directed to a desert road (Acts 8:26) to join a particular chariot (Acts 8:29), from which he was dispatched to the town of Azotus (Acts 8:39-40). Ananias was ordered to find Saul of Tarsus after the Damascus Road experience (Acts 9:10-16). There can be no doubt that these occurrences consisted of guidance that was more detailed and specific than the general moral commands of Scripture. The question is whether such examples prove that God has an individual will for *every* believer.

Consistently Sporadic

The traditional view has some weaknesses at this point. The first weakness is that the *number of recorded cases is not sufficient* to constitute normative experience. In the first thirty years of the church's history covered by the book of Acts, there were at most fifteen to twenty instances of direct, personal guidance. Many of these directions were given to the Apostle Paul. Yet within the framework of his total ministry, relatively few of his decisions were determined on the basis of such leading. Most of the time he had to weigh the apparent merits of various options before settling on a course of action.[3] In other words, when he had a decision to make, *he* had to decide (cf. Acts. 15:36; Acts 20:16; Romans 1:10-13; 1 Corinthians 16:4-9; 2 Corinthians 1:15-2:4). The cases of direct guidance are clearly the exception to the rule, even in Paul's case.

The second weakness of arguing for an individual will from such examples is that *most of the recipients of specific guidance occupied a special place in the outworking of God's program.* They were ordinary people selected by God to play an extraordinary role in His plan.

Most of the examples in the book of Acts occur in the ministries of Peter and Paul—*apostles* who received special revelation because of their unique office in the church. The nonapostolic recipients of direct guidance—Philip, Ananias, Cornelius, and the church at Antioch—found themselves at strategic historical crossroads in the spread of the gospel beyond the house of Israel. By virtue of their reception of divine revelation and their obedience to it, they became key figures in the worldwide propagation of the gospel.

Old Testament examples are usually prophets, judges, kings, or other leaders rather than the general populace. This is partially explained by the fact that the greatest part of biblical history focuses on "special" believers. Still from the standpoint of logic, to argue from such special cases that God has an individual will for all believers is unwarranted in the absence of further substantiation from the epistles.

The third weakness of the traditional view on this question is that the *examples are not sufficiently comprehensive*. That is, guidance was only provided for a handful of decisions. God's individual will for the believer's life is supposed to cover every decision that is made. But the examples do not touch upon the ordinary decisions in life. In fact, most of the instances in Acts had some direct bearing on the spread of the gospel. In other words, specific leading was given by God to insure expanding evangelistic outreach during the formative years of the church. Such a purpose is clearly seen in the guidance given to Peter, Cornelius, Philip, Ananias, Barnabas, the church at Antioch, and Paul. In the book of Acts, there is no indication of any specific word from God on the more ordinary decisions of life.[4]

What we have seen so far is that the examples of detailed divine guidance in Scripture are infrequent in appearance, limited in scope, and directed to persons who play a special role in the outworking of God's program on earth. Such selectivity on the part of God seems to weaken rather than strengthen the support for the concept of an individual will for all Christians.

There is one more factor worthy of consideration – namely, the *means of communication*. The examples indicate too much in this case. For, on the one hand, the traditional view holds that supernatural revelation is not normative experience for all believers. On the other hand, all of the examples which are selected to support individual guidance are clearly instances of *supernatural revelation*. In the book of Acts, such guidance came through visions (Acts 9:10-16; 10:3-8; 10:17; 16:9-10; 18:9; 22:17-21), angelic messenger (Acts 8:26; 12:7-8; 27:23), physical miracle (Acts 8:39), an audible voice from God (8:29; 9:3-6; 10:19-20; 23:11) or a prophet who had received direct revelation (Acts 21:10-11). Are there other recorded examples where detailed guidance was given through some means other than supernatural revelation? No. From the examples that are given, one could argue that God *may* give a believer guidance that is more specific than that found in the Bible. But if He does, it will be through supernatural means.

The absence of any indisputable examples of the traditional view's approach to decision making is striking. At no point in

---

Direct Guidance—
What New Testament Examples Show

- Direct, supernatural guidance for specific decisions was the exception to the rule.

- Direct guidance was given to people who played a strategic role in the drama of world evangelization.

- Direct guidance was provided only at critical points during the formative years of the church.

- Direct guidance was always communicated by means of supernatural revelation.

Figure 13

Scripture do we read of a believer asking, "What is God's individual will for me in this matter?" Much of the terminology found in presentations of the traditional view is absent, either in vocabulary or in concept, from the pages of the Bible. One does not read of the "specific will," "center of God's will," "right decision," "putting out a fleece," or even "finding God's will."

But even more startling is the fact that no decision is ever explained on the basis that it was "God's individual will." Today we commonly hear people say, "I did thus and such because I knew it was God's will for me." Or, "I felt in my heart God wanted me to do it." The apostles often gave reasons for their decisions, but never in such terms.[5] If their decisions were based upon God's individual will, it seems remarkable that they never mentioned it. What is so common and essential to the traditional view is passed over in silence in the New Testament.

What we have shown, then, is that there are no normative examples of ordinary believers making decisions in the manner outlined by the traditional view. Proponents of that view have had to "water down" the patently supernatural examples to support what they contend is normative guidance. Such an approach to biblical interpretation is highly questionable, to say the least.

To take an example, we read in Acts 8 that God gave supernatural guidance to Philip leading him to explain the gospel to the Ethiopian eunuch. Is it valid, on that basis, to deduce that God will similarly put impressions in the heart of the believer to point out individuals to whom they should witness? Unless there is some specific teaching of Scripture that promises such guidance (and we contend there is none), such a deduction hardly seems warranted. The difference between "an angel of the Lord" who spoke to Philip (Acts 8:26) and an inward impression in the heart of a contemporary believer is just too great.

Sometimes the life of Christ is cited as an example of individual guidance. All will agree that Christ is unique, being the God-man. But even with this uniqueness, guidance came to Christ through the Scriptures or through direct revelation. And direct revelation was fitting with Christ since He is Prophet, Priest, and King.[6]

To sum up, a survey of some of the biblical examples of detailed guidance has shown that they do not prove the existence of an individual will of God for every believer. What such examples show is that God has broken into history at infrequent times to reveal detailed guidance through supernatural revelation to selected people usually for the purpose of evangelism. The exceptional proves only the exceptional. Such guidance is not normative according to any viewpoint. Nor is it necessary for normal decision making in the Christian life.

Although the examples do not prove an individual will of God, in fairness to the traditional view it must also be said that they do not disprove it either. The direct teaching of the Word of God must act as the final arbitrator.

Notes

1. Our established definitions for the terms *individual will* and *sovereign will* of God must be carefully observed here. Each star in the universe is one "individual" part of God's *sovereign plan;* but there is no *individual will* of God for each star, as defined by the traditional view. This distinction applies in the same way to people. Every person has an "individual" part in God's sovereign plan. But that is not what is meant by the traditional view when it speaks of God's individual will for a person.

2. In our evaluation of the evidence from experience for an individual will, we have assumed (for the sake of discussion) a definition of "spiritual success" that equates it with some positive and identifiable response to ministry. That is, when people respond to the proclamation of God's Word in repentance and faith, we tend to label such ministry "successful."

But in Scripture, spiritual success is described as faithfulness to the commands of God (cf. 1 Corinthians 4:2; 2 Corinthians 2:14-17; Hebrews 11:32-39). For faithful service always glorifies God and matures God's servant — whether the outcome is a great revival or a slammed door.

On the other hand, there have been situations where God has sovereignly chosen to reap a spiritual harvest through the efforts of men who were motivated by wrong attitudes (cf. Philippians 1:12-18; Jonah 3-4). Spiritual results? Certainly. Obedience to God's will? Hardly. For God's will encompasses both action and attitude (cf. Philippians 2:3; Romans 2:8).

Since faithfulness in ministry does not always yield "positive" results, and since sinners are sometimes brought to repentance through the agency of carnal heralds, *any* argument from experience is of dubious value. For it is simply impossible to judge the "success" of an action or a ministry strictly on the basis of its observable outcome.

3. The actual processes by which the apostles determined most of their decisions are analyzed at length in chapters 11 and 14. Additional illustrations from the New Testament are interspersed throughout the applicational chapters of Part 4, "Deciding the Big Ones."

4. For completeness it should be noted that examples outside the book of Acts could be cited that seem to show detailed guidance in common, everyday decisions. Such examples might include the Shunamite woman who received specific directions to move in order to avoid a famine (2 Kings 8:1-2); Saul, who received guidance in finding his donkeys (1 Samuel 9:20); the wandering Israelites, who experienced guidance in daily travel from a pillar of cloud (Numbers 9:15-23); and the twelve disciples, who received direction from Christ on where to lodge and how to serve the 5,000 (John 6:10-12).

But even these additional cases do not alter our point. To show that normative guidance provides specific direction for each decision, the traditional view must offer much more than a few sporadic examples.

Furthermore, though they concern everyday matters, the examples do not purport to indicate the nature of normative guidance. The Shunamite's guidance, for instance, demonstrated the prophetic authority of Elisha who was miraculously enabled to predict the famine. It also showed God's care for the woman who had earlier aided His prophet (2 Kings 4:8-17). Even in this example, the guidance did not specify the location to which she should move. It was left to her to go "wherever you can sojourn" (2 Kings 8:1). Evidently, Philistia was her selection (2 Kings 8:2).

The direction that enabled Saul to find his donkeys was not provided as normative guidance, but as evidence of Samuel's authority as a prophet. For Samuel was preparing to anoint Saul as king. The finding of the donkeys was one in a series of signs that were given to prove that God had chosen Saul to be Israel's first king (1 Samuel 10:1-13).

The pillar of cloud was provided as evidence of God's special care for Israel so that the people would learn at the inception of the nation to trust Him. When Israel entered the land of Canaan, the cloud was removed. It was a temporary provision which was no longer needed (Joshua 5).

The guidance received by the twelve disciples of Jesus from time to time can hardly be considered normative. Christ was God-in-the-flesh, and the disciples were appointed to a unique office. Yet even in their daily life with the Son of God, the Twelve were not specifically told what they should do in every decision.

5. The actual processes by which the apostles determined most of their decisions are analyzed at length in chapters 11 and 14.

6. The example of Christ is often used to support the idea of following an individual will of God. Traditional writers refer to the life of Christ, but they never give a detailed explanation of those areas where Christ's example is normative. Everyone agrees that Christ's life was not normative for Christian experience at every point. His relationship with the Father is different from that of everyone else. God is "His own Father" which means that He is "equal with God" (John 5:18). It is not normative experience for the believer to follow the example of Christ by being equal with God, or regularly performing miracles, or speaking authoritatively on every interpretation of Scripture, or receiving worship, or calling for absolute allegiance, or reading the thoughts of opponents, or giving others the authority to do miracles, or exercising any other prerogative of deity.

The non-normative character of Christ's life is further underscored by His office as a prophet (Deuteronomy 18:15, 18; Matthew 11:21; John 6:14; Acts 3:20-23). As a prophet, He would regularly receive direct revelation from God—a privilege not experienced by everyone else.

Christ did perfectly obey God's will for His life. He said, "'My food is to do the will of Him who sent Me, and to accomplish His work'" (John 4:34). He also said "'"Behold, I have come...to do Thy will, O God"'" (Hebrews 10:7). Jesus repeatedly said that the work He did was the work which the Father had for Him to do (John 5:19, 30, 36; 6:38; 8:28-29, 42; 10:37-38; 12:49-50; 14:31; 15:10; 17:4). The question is, what was the content of the "will of God" for Jesus Christ?

It must have included the moral will of God revealed in the Bible for all men — for He was a true man (John 9:4). It must have included, in particular, all those passages specifically written for the Messiah to fulfill (Luke 4:18-21). It must have included any commands He received by direct revelation from God as His Prophet. It must have included all communication between Father and Son from eternity past until the incarnation which concerned the words and works of the Son when He became the Messiah. Finally, the will of God for Jesus must have included the direct revelation that passed between Father and Son *during* Christ's incarnation on earth. The content of this last category of communication is known only to the Godhead, but it did include whatever Christ said He was seeing and hearing the Father do (John 5:19, 30). There is nothing to preclude the possibility that the communion of God with God touched every detail of Christ's life. In other words, it is entirely possible that God the Father did have an individual will for the details of the life of His only begotten Son — an individual will that coincided perfectly with His moral will and His sovereign will.

But the uniqueness of Christ is so pervasive, it would behoove us to be cautious in suggesting those points at which Christ's life provides a normative example for the believer today. In the epistles, Christ is declared to be our example. But the extent to which He is our model is not open-ended. He is our example in specific ways. Whenever the Bible calls God, or Christ, our example, it delineates the area of likeness. Those areas cited include: humble service (John 13:1-15), holiness (1 Peter 1:15-16), righteousness (1 John 3:7), purity (1 John 3:3), love (Ephesians 5:1-2), forgiveness (Colossians 3:13), compassion (Ephesians 4:32), endurance (Hebrews 12:2-4), submission (1 Peter 2:21-24), humility and obedience (Philippians 2:5-8), kindness (Luke 6:35), and generosity in giving (2 Corinthians 8:1-9).

Significantly, the areas in which believers are told to imitate Jesus Christ *concern the manner in which He fulfilled the moral will of God.* Just as Jesus obeyed His Father's will, so the sons of God should obey their Father's will. The difference is this: For the only begotten Son of God, His Father's will was revealed through a variety of means; for the born anew sons of God, their Father's will is fully revealed in His Word — the Bible.

Chapter 6

Does Scripture Teach the "Dot"?

Note to the Reader: Since this chapter involves discussion of the biblical text, an open Bible will be very helpful. You will find that this chapter will require more concentration than earlier chapters or those which follow it. This is because of the extreme importance of a clear and detailed understanding of pertinent Scriptures on God's will.

*V*irtually all evangelical Bible teachers agree that while reason and experience can support a doctrinal position, they cannot prove it. Likewise, scriptural examples can add strong support if they are shown to be normative. But in the final analysis, it is the straightforward teaching of Scripture itself which must determine and establish one's viewpoint on any issue. And so our question is, what does God's Word teach with respect to an individual will of God? Can an ideal plan for each individual be proved from the sacred text?

The approach of this chapter will be to consider the Scripture passages most often quoted by the traditional view as teaching an individual will. For the person who assumes that God has an individual will for each life, each of these passages will, upon first reading, appear to confirm that presupposition. However, closer scrutiny of these verses in context will show that, in most cases, it is more likely that the writer is referring to the *moral* will of God. And in all of the passages cited, the idea of the moral will fits the context well. What we expect this chapter to establish, then, is that these key passages do not prove an individual will of God for each person; rather a stronger case can be made for understanding them in terms of the moral will of God.

97

PROVERBS 3:5-6

Trust in the LORD with all your heart, and do not lean on your own understanding. In all your ways acknowledge Him, and He will make your paths straight.

This passage may contain the most frequently quoted verses in discussion of God's will. Usually, it is the King James Version that is noted, for the translation ". . . and He shall direct thy paths" gives a vivid picture of personal leading according to an individual plan.

Still the interpreter must ask what the original writer meant by that expression. In order to answer that question, it is important to first of all determine the most correct translation of the original Hebrew statement, and then to note other usages of that same expression by the same writer to get additional light on its meaning.

Hebrew lexicons and commentaries on the Psalms and Proverbs agree that the correct translation of Proverbs 3:6b is: ". . . and He shall make your paths straight, (or) smooth, (or) successful."[1] The noun "path" is frequently employed in the Psalms and Proverbs. But it does not have the idea of an individual will of God. Hebrew writers use it to describe the general course or fortunes of life (see Proverbs 4:18-19; 15:19). When the verb "make straight, make smooth" is connected with the noun "paths," the meaning of the statement is, "He shall make the course of your life successful." This meaning is clearly indicated in Proverbs 11:5: "The righteousness of the blameless will *smooth his way,* but the wicked will fall by his own wickedness." This verse contrasts the righteous man who experiences true success in life with the wicked man who brings trouble upon himself by his own devious behavior. This is a common theme in Proverbs (4:18-19; 11:5; 15:19; 22:17-21).

The point of Proverbs 3:5-6, then, is that those who trust God, and trust in His wisdom rather than their own worldly understanding, and acknowledge God in each part of their life, will reap a life that is successful by God's standards. This understanding fits the larger context precisely. Proverbs 3:1-10 is a series of two-verse couplets. Each couplet describes the internal or external blessings which come to the person who acknowledges God. A summary of each couplet would look like this:

Keep my commandments and have long days and peace
(1-2).
Keep kindness and truth and find favor and good repute
(3-4).
Trust in the LORD and He will make the course of your
life successful (5-6).
Fear the LORD and it will bring healing to your body
(7-8).
Honor the LORD with your wealth and your barns will be
filled with plenty (9-10).

The way one acknowledges God in all his ways is by believing
and obeying the Law of God rather than trusting and following
man's finite, worldly philosophy for success and happiness. With
this elucidation of the writer's meaning it can be seen that Proverbs
3:5-6 is not dealing with specific guidance into an individual "path"
marked out by God. This fact is confirmed by Dr. Bruce Waltke:

All of us have had the shock of discovering that a
favorite verse in the King James Version was inaccurate,
and hence that we had been led into an inauthentic experience. I recall the astonishment of one of the committee members assigned to translate the Book of Proverbs
for the New International Version when he discovered
that Proverbs 3:5 [-6] had nothing to say about guidance.
He had taken as his life text: "In all your ways
acknowledge Him and He will direct your paths." But
when confronted with the linguistic data he had to admit
reluctantly that the verse more properly read ". . . and He
will make your path smooth."[2]

The true intent of Proverbs 3:5-6 is to set forth a pattern to be
followed to experience true success in life—a pattern in which one
demonstrates his trust and obedience of God by following the
directions of God's moral will.

PSALM 32:8

I will instruct you and teach you in the way which you
should go; I will counsel you with My eye upon you.

In the King James Version, the second clause is translated: "I will guide thee with mine eye." The verb translated "guide" has the sense of "counsel" as it is rendered by the New American Standard Bible above. Such counsel is given in the form of instruction and teaching which represents a kind of guidance. The traditional view understands the speaker to be the Lord who is promising specific guidance in a particular "way" — i.e., the individual will of God.

The speaker could be God. But some respected commentators believe that it is David himself who is speaking. The reason for such an idea stems from the relation that Psalm 32 bears to Psalm 51. Psalm 51 is a prayer for forgiveness and restoration offered by David after his sin with Bathsheba was exposed by God's prophet. In that prayer, David promised that if God forgave him, he would teach transgressors God's way (Psalm 51:10-13). Psalm 32 records David's response when he received word that God's forgiveness had been granted. What David had promised in Psalm 51:13, he fulfilled in Psalm 32:8.[3]

Again, the "way which you should go" refers to the course of life one should follow. This is the way of righteous living which the Law revealed and David taught.[4] Even if God is viewed as the speaker, He is seen teaching His way of righteousness. This customary usage fits the context, so an individual will is not in view.

Virtually all commentators struggle with the last phrase "with My eye upon you." The best explanation seems to be that David is giving counsel to sinners as his eye of concern is upon them.

In all likelihood, if the word "guide" had not been used in the rendering of the King James Version, this verse would never have been used in presentations on guidance. For it is simply reiterating the message of so many other Old Testament passages that describe instruction in the life of righteousness provided by the Law, the moral will of God.

ISAIAH 30:20-21

Although the Lord has given you bread of privation and water of oppression, He, your Teacher will no longer hide Himself, but your eyes will behold your Teacher. And your ears will hear a word behind you, "This is the way, walk in it," whenever you turn to the right or to the left.

This passage is often quoted by proponents of the traditional view as describing the inward work of the Holy Spirit giving specific guidance into God's individual will. It is suggested that whenever a believer strays from the pathway of God's will for his life, the Spirit will communicate that fact and give directions for return to the proper road.

In this case, the translators of the New American Standard Bible made an interpretive decision with which we disagree. In capitalizing the word "Teacher," and adding the italicized "He" (a pronoun not in the original text), they indicated their conclusion that the teacher who gives the directions is the Lord.[5] But there is a better explanation. It is more likely that the teacher was a prophet sent to teach the people.[6] For since the time of wicked King Ahaz, the prophets had to be in hiding for their safety. This fact is even mentioned in the near context (Isaiah 30:8-11).

This being the case, the "eyes" and "ears" in this passage should be taken literally. The promised blessing was that when Israel repented (Isaiah 30:19), God would bring the prophets out of hiding. When He did that, they would see their teacher with their eyes, and hear him with their ears.[7] (If the teacher was the Holy Spirit, it is difficult to grasp in what way He could be seen with the eyes. Literal interpretation, which fits the context well, removes that difficulty.)

This understanding suits the larger context as well. In Isaiah 30:1-17, God declared His judgment against wayward Israel. Then in verses 18-26, He listed the blessings that would come upon the repentant nation. One of those blessings would be the needed return of the teaching prophets.

The message of the prophets is significant: "This is the way, walk in it." It is true that some of the prophets predicted future events. But the primary prophetic function was that of appealing to the nation to return to the Lord and live in obedience to His moral Law. The prophets were to teach and preach the precepts of the Law so that the people could repent and avoid God's certain judgment.

"The way" is the way of God's Law, whether the speaker in this passage is the Lord or a prophet. This is the consistent meaning of the term throughout the Old Testament. And frequently, full obedience to the Law was described in negative terms as "not turning to the left or to the right" (Deuteronomy 5:31-33; 17:18-20; 28:13-14; Joshua 1:7; 23:6). For example, in Deuteronomy 5:31-33, "the way" is defined as "all the commandments and the statutes and the judgments..." From this teaching Israel was commanded "...you shall not turn aside to the right or to the left." Clearly, "the way" was the righteous way of the Law.

Now this voice that the people of Israel would hear was not described as an inward voice of the Spirit,[8] but as a voice *behind them.* The word "behind" probably indicates the idea that if Israel did depart from the way of the Law, the people would be turning their backs on God's commands, and the prophets would call to them from behind to return to the pathway of righteousness. In any case the description of the voice better fits the teaching of the prophets than the inward impressions of the Holy Spirit.

The point of Isaiah 30:20-21 for us is that one of the great blessings of God is teachers who clearly instruct us in the way of God's moral will and call us to return to the path of righteousness when we stray as Israel did. There is danger to the right and to the left, but God's way of righteousness is the way of success (Joshua 1:7-8).

COLOSSIANS 1:9

For this reason also, since the day we heard of it, we have not ceased to pray for you and to ask that you may be filled with the knowledge of His will in all spiritual wisdom and understanding.

Whenever the phrase "God's will" appears in the text of Scripture, the reader must determine in which sense it is being used.[9] Did Paul pray that the Colossians might know God's sovereign will, His moral will, or His individual will? Sovereign will can be immediately ruled out because it is hidden and cannot be known in advance. Whatever sense of His will is presented in this verse, it can be known. Furthermore, such knowledge is desired for Christian living, and that knowledge could be missed. So far, these characteristics apply to both the moral and individual wills. On what basis can a judgment be made for correct interpretation?

In this case, the context of the verse proves decisive.[10] Verses 10 through 12 read as follows:

> ...so that you may walk in a manner worthy of the Lord, to please Him in all respects, bearing fruit in every good work and increasing in the knowledge of God; strengthened with all power, according to His glorious might, for the attaining of all steadfastness and patience; joyously giving thanks to the Father, who has qualified us to share in the inheritance of the saints in light.

The first indication that Paul was praying for knowledge of God's *moral* will follows from the stated purpose for the knowledge of that will. The purpose was that believers might *walk worthy* of the Lord and *be pleasing* to Him. When Paul used that same terminology in other passages, he was referring to the *moral* will of God. In Ephesians 4:1, the worthy walk is described in terms of obedience to the general moral commands that immediately follow in the context. In fact, Ephesians 4:1 introduces the section of that epistle that is devoted to moral commands concerning Christian behavior. A "worthy walk" would conform to all of the exhortations in chapters 4, 5, and 6 of Ephesians!

Paul uses the same terminology in his writing to the Thessalonians (1 Thessalonians 2:12; 4:1-3). His directions on how they should "walk and please God" are termed "commandments" (4:2) and "the will of God" (4:3). The will of God in this context is clearly God's *moral* will.[11] So what we have seen is that Paul's concept of a Christian "walk" that is "worthy of the Lord" and "pleasing to the Lord" is consistently connected with God's moral will. (See also 2 Corinthians 5:9-10; Romans 14:18; Ephesians 5:10, 17; 6:6; and 1 John 3:22).

Returning to the immediate context of Colossians 1, we find further evidence that "His will" means His moral will. For in the clauses that follow verse 9, God's will and the worthy walk are further defined in terms of a series of actions. Do these things that follow from the knowledge of God's will fit the concept of an individual will of God, or do they fit the more general goals of God's moral will? The list includes: bearing fruit in every good work, growth in the knowledge of God, strengthening by God's power, steadfastness, patience, joy, and thanksgiving. God's moral will encompasses every item on that list. God desires those things to be true of every believer. And in 1 Thessalonians 5:18, thanksgiving is specifically declared to be God's moral will for believers. Ephesians 1:16-19, a parallel passage that elaborates on the proper content of the Christian's knowledge, adds further support to this interpretation that it is God's moral will that must be known.

The point of Colossians 1:9 is very important for Christian living. It is vital that the believer be filled with the knowledge of God's moral will. For such knowledge is foundational to a worthy walk that pleases God! One might legitimately develop an applicational paraphrase of Paul's request to this effect: "I pray that you might study the Word so that your mind will be filled with knowledge of His revealed will as the basis for all spiritual wisdom and understanding. May God give us pastors who faithfully and accurately teach the Scriptures. May you develop a hunger for His truth that compels you to seek out spiritual insights and principles by which to govern your daily walk."

On the basis of the consistent teaching of Paul throughout his epistles, and the immediate context of this exhortation, it seems clear that in Colossians 1:9 the moral will of God is in view as that which must be known as the basis for godly living.

COLOSSIANS 4:12

Epaphras, who is one of your number, a bondslave of Jesus Christ, sends you his greetings, always laboring earnestly for you in his prayers, that you may stand perfect and fully assured in all the will of God.

Again, the identification of "the will of God" is the issue of importance. The request that the Colossians "...may stand perfect and fully assured" does not appear to fit the sovereign sense of God's will. But either of the other two categories would make sense within the immediate context. For purposes of accurate interpretation, it is not enough that a potential meaning "makes sense." One must determine if there are other factors that indicate the superiority of one interpretation over any others.

With respect to this passage, the evidence points to the moral will. First, such an understanding would be consistent with Paul's usage of the phrase in 1:9. In both passages, the reference to God's will occurs in the context of intercessory prayer. It would be strange if Epaphras, in his prayer for these people, meant something entirely different from what Paul intended by the same expression.

Second, the request that the Colossian believers "may stand perfect and fully assured" is almost an echo of Paul's statement concerning the goal of his ministry made in Colossians 1:28: "...that we may present every man complete (or perfect) in Christ." In other words, what Paul was striving for, and what Epaphras was praying for, were the same — the perfection, the maturity of the saints. The means by which Paul hoped to accomplish his goal is significant here: "And we proclaim Him (Christ), admonishing every man and teaching every man with all wisdom,..." Paul was bringing the moral will of God to bear upon the lives of those to whom he ministered to bring them to maturity. That being the case, Epaphras' prayer that the believers might stand perfect and fully assured in all the will of God would be a request that the moral will of God would accomplish its purpose in those believers' lives.

Further substantiation comes from a similar use of the phrase "full assurance of understanding" in Colossians 2:2.[12] This understanding would be a grasping of God's mystery in contrast to the tradition and philosophy of men (2:8). Again this supports the idea that it is God's moral will, in 4:12, that establishes what is to be believed as the ground for assurance.

Finally, there are indications from the wider context of Paul's teaching throughout the entire epistle that God's moral will is in view in the prayer of Epaphras. Paul's concern in the letter was to refute heretical teaching that was a composite of Jewish and Gnostic elements. His antidote for such poison was a correct understanding of and faith in a correct doctrine of the Person and work of Christ (2:16-23). This wider context dovetails perfectly with our understanding of Epaphras' prayer. The Colossians were being influenced by false beliefs and practices, but Epaphras was striving in prayer that they would be mature and fully assured in the true doctrine of the Word of God, that is, His revealed moral will.

Therefore, even though the immediate context of the verse is not determinative about which sense of God's will is intended, the wider context of the epistle indicates that the moral will better corresponds to the flow of Paul's thought.[13]

ROMANS 12:1-2

I urge you therefore, brethren, by the mercies of God, to present your bodies a living and holy sacrifice, acceptable to God, which is your spiritual service of worship. And do not be conformed to this world, but be transformed by the renewing of your mind, that you may prove what the will of God is, that which is good and acceptable and perfect.

This passage is used frequently by proponents of the traditional view to show that one must prove or find God's individual will, and that personal surrender is a prerequisite to finding it. God's sovereign will does not fit the context, but the moral will and the individual will both do. The verb "prove" can also mean "approve after proving," but in either case the idea of "prove" or "discern" is involved.[14] And the verb will fit either the moral or individual senses of God's will. There are, however, some positive indications that the moral will is in view in this passage.

The 12th chapter of Romans marks the beginning of the second major section of the epistle. The first eleven chapters contain a closely argued exposition of doctrine. Chapters 12 through 16 follow through with exhortations regarding appropriate behavior that corresponds to the doctrine taught. In Romans 12:1, Paul is saying on the basis of God's mercies, which have just been explained in detail, surrender your body to God for obedient living. Then, beginning with verse three, and extending on into the next four chapters, he spells out the commands that ought to be obeyed. In other words, as soon as he completes his exhortation to "prove what the will of God is," he begins giving specific examples of that will. Significantly, they are moral commands addressed to all believers. The immediate context says nothing about such things as finding one's vocation, choosing one's mate, or anything else that is so specific as to be part of God's individual will. Rather, there are commands concerning the use of one's gift (12:6-8), love (12:9), devotion to other believers (12:10), diligence in serving the Lord (12:11), rejoicing (12:12), hospitality (12:13), blessing persecutors (12:14), and so on. These obviously reflect the moral rather than the individual will of God.

Second, the three words that qualify "the will of God"—"good, and acceptable and perfect"—closely resemble a similar three-fold description employed earlier in the letter with reference to the Law of God, which was His moral will (7:12).[15]

Third, the moral will best fits the general contrast between conformity to the world and transformation of the mind. For in other passages of Scripture, it is specifically the Word of God (His moral will) that effects that spiritual metamorphosis. For instance, in 2 Corinthians 3:18, Paul uses the same verb, "transformed," in a context where exposure to the mirror of God's Word is the key element in the transforming process (2 Corinthians 3:14-18; see also James 1:25).[16]

The one other place where renewal of the mind is discussed specifically is Ephesians 4:22-24. The process is not described in that context. The idea seems to be that believers who are properly taught (4:20-21) adopt a radically different approach to life — an approach that is governed by a new perspective or mentality. How this new way of seeing life is brought about is not precisely spelled out. But it is part and parcel with putting on "the new self, which in the likeness of God has been created in righteousness and holiness of the truth." In the verses that follow (25-32), Paul gives some direct commands that those who are being "renewed in the spirit of [their] mind[s]" (4:23) will obey. The commands are general, universal, and expressive of the moral will of God.

Now in these verses in Ephesians 4, Paul offers teaching "in which are some things hard to understand" (2 Peter 3:16). But some specific conclusions may be detailed. Namely, that the renewal of the mind has a strong relationship to "the truth" (4:21,24). Those who have been taught the truth understand the imperative of being renewed in the spirit of their minds. And those who are so renewed have "put on" a "new self" that was created by God with a view to obeying the truth in holy living. Though the wording is different, the results of mind renewal in Ephesians 4 are the same as the results of mind renewal in Romans 12. And the centrality of the moral will of God in both passages is evident.

In Ephesians 5:10 there is a similar use of the word "prove" in the expression "trying to learn [lit., proving] what is pleasing to the Lord." In that context, the means by which that is to be accomplished is by walking in light, goodness, righteousness, and truth (Ephesians 5:8-9) — namely, the moral will of God. The vocabulary of Romans 12:2 occurs again in Ephesians 5, most notably in verse 17 where "the will of the Lord" appears to be directly related to a list of moral commands (Ephesians 5:18-21, see below). This is consistent with Paul's use of the term "His will" earlier in Romans (2:18) where the sense of moral will is clearly indicated.

Again, the meaning of Romans 12:1-2 is important for believers to understand. Christians are urged to surrender themselves wholly to God as a living sacrifice. They are to work this self-dedication out through resistance to worldly conformity and conscious involvement in a divine process of transformation. The process of transformation is carried out as the mind is renewed by the Word of God, thereby enabling the believer to prove what God's moral will is. Thus the believer knows that God's moral will is good, acceptable, and perfect for his life. Romans 12:1-2 does not summarize a process for discovering detailed guidance for specific decisions, but rather urges a basic approach to the entirety of one's Christian life — an approach in which the moral will of God plays a central and transforming role.[17]

EPHESIANS 2:10

For we are His workmanship, created in Christ Jesus for good works, which God prepared beforehand, that we should walk in them.

This verse is not often emphasized by traditional view writers. This is surprising for it offers stronger possibilities for their position than many of the verses that are used. Those who do employ it point out that this verse establishes that God has prepared in advance certain good works for a believer to do. It is appropriate, then, that the Christian should seek the leading of the Lord to learn what good works God has chosen for him to do. Such an interpretation makes good sense.

There are, however, two other possible interpretations of the verse that also make good sense. And neither of them requires an individual will which must be discovered. One such interpretation is that the works referred to in this passage are only described in general terms. There is no article or adjective qualifying "good works." Since good works are one of the purposes for which Christians are created, the idea could be that God prepared those works "beforehand" by providing what was needed for their existence.

That is, He created new creatures with new hearts capable of producing good works. Then He gave those creatures the Holy Spirit for enablement, and gave clear instructions in the Word of God to direct them in the use of His power to accomplish good works.[18] All of these provisions precede the good works, and so by His equipping of saints with divine power and instruction He "prepared beforehand" the good works.

A second alternative interpretation would view the good works "prepared beforehand" from the perspective of God's sovereignty.[19] In Romans 9:23, the only other verse in the New Testament where the expression "prepared beforehand" is used, Paul is obviously referring to God's sovereign plan. The concept is very close in meaning to Paul's description of that plan in Ephesians 1:4-5, a similarity that is even more apparent in Greek than in English.[20]

Such an understanding would also fit well with the verses that immediately precede Ephesians 2:10, for they speak of God's sovereign work in our salvation. The point of the well known Ephesians 2:8-9 passage is that salvation is by God's grace and is not of ourselves, nor is it the product of our good works. The idea is reinforced in verse 10 when believers are called "His workmanship" and described as "created in Christ Jesus." It is that same sovereign grace that has prepared in advance good works in which the believer will walk. Just as salvation is of God, so also are the good works which flow from it. Believers are involved in both, but the ultimate cause or source is God. He sovereignly "prepared beforehand," in eternity past, that we should walk in good works (even possibly in specific good works) through which we will help to carry out His sovereign plan. Within this interpretation the elements of enablement and instruction would also be incorporated as part of God's means in His sovereign work.

While we have a definite preference for the third interpretation, we concede that the three alternatives come closer to being equal than any of the others discussed thus far. The most that can be said, then, is that either side could use this verse in support of their position, but neither side could use Ephesians 2:10 to *prove* their position.

EPHESIANS 5:15-17

Therefore be careful how you walk, not as unwise men, but as wise, making the most of your time, because the days are evil. So then do not be foolish, but understand what the will of the Lord is.

Here is a command to understand the will of God. So the sovereign will is immediately ruled out. The alternatives once again are the moral will and the individual will. The question we are asking, then, is this: If we are to make the most of our time in these evil days, and avoid living foolishly, what aspect of God's will are we to understand? Is it necessary for the believer to understand God's individual plan for his life if he is to buy up every opportunity? Or will his grasp of God's moral will give him the direction he needs for wise living?

Even a casual reading of the 5th chapter of Ephesians should answer our question. The context, both preceding and following this passage, points without ambiguity to the moral will of God. In verses 1-14 of this chapter, there is a general contrast between the believer's walk in light and the unbeliever's walk in darkness. The intent of the contrast is to highlight the differences between a life style of goodness, righteousness, and truth, which "is pleasing to the Lord" (5:6, 9-10). As was established earlier, this whole exhortation can only be seen as an appeal to follow the moral will of God.

Further confirmation of this viewpoint comes from a side-by-side comparison of the relevant portions of verses 8-10 and 15-17:

"walk as children of light... trying to learn what is pleasing to the Lord" (8, 10).	"...walk...as wise [men].... do not be foolish, but understand what the will of the Lord is" (15, 17).

There can be little doubt that Paul was giving the same message, in different terms, in the two segments.[21] This equation of "what is pleasing to the Lord" with "the will of the Lord" (both referring to the *moral* will of God) corresponds to what is indicated elsewhere in the New Testament (see 1 Thessalonians 4:1-2; 2 Corinthians 5:9-10; Romans 14:18; 1 John 3:22; Hebrews 13:21).

The context that follows verse 17 gives added confirmation of this position. Immediately after the command to understand the will of the Lord, there follows a series of examples. These examples of the Lord's will include being filled with the Spirit (5:18), spiritual singing (5:19), giving of thanks (5:20), and mutual subjection (5:21). The theme of submission is applied to the various relationships within the believer's household (5:22-6:9). Of specific interest is the exhortation to slaves (6:5-8), where these believers are told to do "the will of God from the heart" (6:6). Such compliance includes obedience, respect, sincerity, and diligent labor, "as to the Lord" (6:7). Such statements show that God's will throughout this context means God's moral will.

The instruction of Ephesians 5:15-17 would follow these lines: Christians are to avoid foolish living. Wise living understands the folly of immorality and the value of doing whatever is pleasing to the Lord. The days are so evil, and the need for properly functioning, serving Christians is so great, wise Christians will make good use of their time, taking opportunities for ministry as they come. Knowledge of the moral will of God will not only give discernment between good and evil, but between what is wise and what is foolish.

The passages of Scripture discussed in this chapter are very helpful for the guidance of the believer. They are not, however, proof for guidance by means of an individual will of God. In each case the context does not require the interpretation of the traditional view. Rather there is better evidence that "God's will" indicates His moral will. These passages underline the vital place the *moral will* of God, *not* an *individual will*, has in directing the believer. It is in fact essential for us to know the moral will of God so that we might "walk in a manner worthy of the Lord, to please Him in all respects" (Colossians 1:10).

Scripture Does Not Teach the "Dot"

Our study of the biblical support for the traditional view raises a logical question: If a contextual interpretation of the key passages fails to substantiate the concept of an individual will for each decision, why has that idea been taught and *accepted as biblical* by so many for so long?

Without being dogmatic, we would suggest that the basic reason is imprecise hermeneutics. It would appear that the definition of the "individual will of God" stems from a synthesis of biblical teaching and biblical examples. Using two representative verses by way of example, we could diagram that synthesis in the following manner:

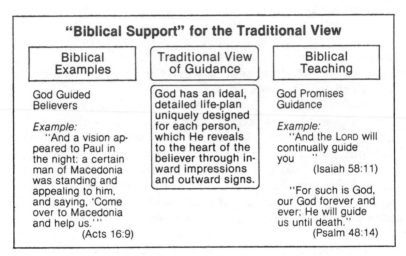

"Biblical Support" for the Traditional View

Biblical Examples	Traditional View of Guidance	Biblical Teaching
God Guided Believers *Example:* "And a vision appeared to Paul in the night: a certain man of Macedonia was standing and appealing to him, and saying, 'Come over to Macedonia and help us.'" (Acts 16:9)	God has an ideal, detailed life-plan uniquely designed for each person, which He reveals to the heart of the believer through inward impressions and outward signs.	God Promises Guidance *Example:* "And the LORD will continually guide you " (Isaiah 58:11) "For such is God, our God forever and ever; He will guide us until death." (Psalm 48:14)

Figure 14

A superficial reading of the passages does provide a foundation for the traditional view that is scriptural. But closer scrutiny reveals that foundation to be inadequate. For in order to arrive at the conclusion of the traditional approach, it is necessary to water down the biblical examples and spice up the biblical teaching.

What we have demonstrated is that careful exegesis of the relevant passages fails to support the basic premise of the traditional view.

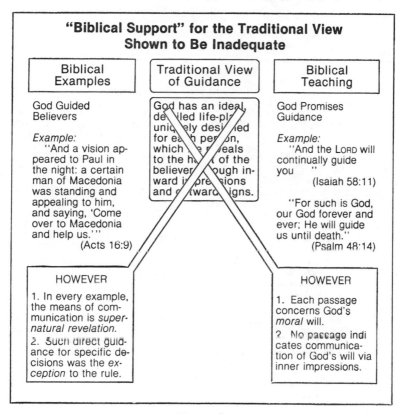

Figure 15

Accordingly, in response to Bill Thompson's second question, "Does God have a plan for my life?", we would say this: If God's plan is thought of as a blueprint or "dot" in the "center of God's will" that must be discovered by the decision maker, the answer is no. On the other hand, we affirm that God does have a plan for our lives — a plan that is described in the Bible in terms that we can fully understand and apply. But more on that in Part 3.

Notes

1. Frances Brown, S.R. Driver, and Charles A. Briggs, *A Hebrew and English Lexicon of the Old Testament*, s.v. " יָשַׁר ". See also: C.F. Keil and F. Delitzsch, *Commentary on the Old Testament*, 10 vols. (Grand Rapids: Wm. B. Eerdmans Publishing Co., 1950), vol. 6: *Proverbs, Ecclesiastes, Song of Solomon*, by F. Delitzsch, trans. by M.G. Easton, p. 232. Delitzsch gives this translation and cites Proverbs 3:6 as a parallel example of this usage; Crawford H. Toy, *A Critical and Exegetical Commentary on the Book of Proverbs*, The International Critical Commentary (Edinburgh: T. & T. Clark, 1899), p. 222; John Peter Lange, ed., *A Commentary on the Holy Scriptures*, 25 vol. (Grand Rapids: Zondervan Publishing House, n.d.), vol. 10: *Proverbs, Ecclesiastes, Song of Solomon*, by John Peter Lange, trans. by Philip Schaff, p. 58.

2. Bruce K. Waltke, "Dogmatic Theology and Relative Knowledge," *CRUX* 15, no. 1 (March 1979).

3. Keil and Delitzsch, *Commentary on Old Testament*, Vol. 2: *Biblical Commentary on the Psalms*, by F. Delitzsch, trans. by Francis Bolton, p. 398; Joseph Addison Alexander, *The Psalms: Translated and Explained* (Grand Rapids: Baker Book House, 1975), p. 139.

4. Charles Augustus Briggs and Emile Grace Briggs, *A Critical and Exegetical Commentary on the Book of Psalms*, The International Critical Commentary, 2 vols. (Edinburgh: T. & T. Clark, 1906), 1:281.

5. By way of contrast, note the preferable translations of the King James Version and the New International Version:

"And though the Lord give you the bread of adversity, and the water of affliction, yet shall not thy teachers be removed into a corner any more, but thine eyes shall see thy teachers: and thine ears shall hear a word behind thee, saying, This *is* the way, walk ye in it, when ye turn to the right hand, and when ye turn to the left" (KJV).

"Although the Lord gives you the bread of adversity and the water of affliction, your teachers will be hidden no more; with your own eyes you will see them. Whether you turn to the right or to the left, your ears will hear a voice behind you, saying, 'This is the way; walk in it'" (NIV).

6. Joseph Addison Alexander, *Commentary on the Prophecies of Isaiah* (Grand Rapids: Zondervan Publishing House, n.d.) 2:481; the plural form attributed to the context by Delitzsch in Keil and Delitzsch, *Commentary on Old Testament*, Vol. 7: *Biblical Commentary on the Book of the Prophet Isaiah*, 2:35.

7. Edward J. Young, *The Book of Isaiah: The English Text, with Introduction, Exposition, and Notes* (Grand Rapids: Wm. B. Eerdmans Publishing Co., 1969), 2:356-57; Delitzsch, *Isaiah*, 2:35.

8. This understanding excludes guidance by subjective impressions, but does not exclude the biblical teaching that inward convincing of the Spirit will accompany the outward proclamation of the Word. John Calvin, *Commentary of the Book of the Prophet Isaiah*, trans. by William Pringle (Grand Rapids: Wm. B. Eerdmans Publishing Co., 1948), 2:371-72; E.H. Plumptre, "Isaiah," *Ellicott's Commentary on the Whole Bible: A Verse by Verse Explanation*, ed. by Charles John Ellicott, vol. 4: *Job—Isaiah* (Grand Rapids: Zondervan Publishing House, 1959), p. 499.

9. There are several Greek words that are translated as "will" in the New Testament phrase "will of God." Unlike other Greek synonyms, the distinctions in meaning are not determined by the specific vocabulary words so much as they are by the context. Both the *boulomai* word group and the *thelō* word group can refer to the desired (moral) or determined (sovereign) will of God. As a result, for nearly every word in these two groups, examples of God's moral will and His sovereign will can be found. In each case, the context must determine in which sense the Greek word is being used. (However, a case can be made that when *boulē* is used of God in the New Testament, it invariably denotes His sovereign will. See Luke 7:30; Acts 2:23; 4:28;

13:36; 20:27; Hebrews 6:17; Ephesians 1:11.) Cf. John Murray, *The Epistle to the Romans,* The New International Commentary on the New Testament (Wm B. Eerdmans Publishing Co., 1965), 2:115. He gives a list of references that demonstrate two uses of the term "God's will." His titles are "will of determinate purpose" and "will of commandment." The older theologians often use the similar titles of decretive will and preceptive will.

10. T.K. Abbott, *A Critical and Exegetical Commentary on the Epistles to the Ephesians and to the Colossians,* The International Critical Commentary (Edinburgh: T & T Clark, 1897), p. 202.

11. John Calvin says, "The knowledge of *the divine will,* by which expression he rejects all inventions of men and all speculations foreign to the Word of God. For His will is not to be sought anywhere else than in His Word." John Calvin, *The Epistles of Paul the Apostle to the Galatians, Ephesians, Philippians and Colossians,* Calvin's Commentaries, trans. T.H.L. Parker, ed. David W. Torrance and Thomas F. Torrance (Grand Rapids: Wm. B. Eerdmans Publishing Co., 1965), p. 304.

12. William Hendrickson, *Exposition of Colossians and Philemon,* New Testament Commentary (Grand Rapids: Baker Book House, 1964), p. 191. He feels Paul is using the perfect participle "fully assured" in the sense of the cognate noun in Colossians 2:2.

13. Charles John Ellicott, *A Critical and Grammatical Commentary on St. Paul's Epistles to the Philippians, Colossians and to Philemon, with a Revised Translation* (Philadelphia: Smith, English, and Co., 1976), p. 60; R.C.H. Lenski, *The Interpretation of Colossians and Philemon* (Columbus, Ohio: Wartburg Press, 1937), p. 203; Clark paraphrases, "That ye may stand firm, perfectly instructed, and fully persuaded of the truth of those doctrines which have been taught you as the revealed will of God." Adam Clark, *Clark's Commentaries: Romans-Revelation* (Nashville: Abingdon, n.d.), p. 300.

14. William F. Arndt and F. Wilbur Gingrich, trans, *A Greek-English Lexicon of the New Testament and Other Early Christian Literature,* 2nd. ed., (Chicago: University of Chicago Press, 1979), s.v. "δοκιμάζω."

15. Murray, *Romans,* 2:115. Murray notes the parallel between the two passages. He takes the three as substantival usage.

16. Ibid., 2:114. Murray calls 2 Corinthians 3:18 a fuller explanation of the same process of transformation.

17. That the moral sense of God's will is intended here is also supported by Murray, *Romans,* 2:115-116; C.K. Barrett, *A Commentary on the Epistle to the Romans,* Harper's New Testament Commentaries, gen. ed. Henry Chadwick (New York: Harper and Bros., Publishers, 1957), p. 233; John Calvin, *The Epistle of Paul the Apostle to the Romans and to the Thessalonians,* Calvin's Commentaries, trans. Ross MacKenzie,ed. by David W. Torrance and Thomas F. Torrance (Grand Rapids: Wm. B. Eerdmans Publishing Co., 1960), p. 265; William G.T. Shedd, *A Critical and Doctrinal Commentary upon the Epistle of St. Paul to the Romans* (New York: Charles Scribner's and Sons, 1879), p. 359; R.C.H. Lenski, *The Interpretation of St. Paul's Epistle to the Romans* (Columbus: Lutheran Book Concern, 1936), p. 758.

18. William Hendricksen, *Exposition of Ephesians,* New Testament Commentary (Grand Rapids: Baker Book House, 1967), p. 124.

19. S.D.F. Salmond, "The Epistle to the Ephesians" in *The Expositor's Greek Testament,* 5 vols. (Reprint ed., Grand Rapids: Wm. B. Eerdmans Publishing Co., 1974), 3:290.

20. The reference is simply to the similar *pro* as a prefix to *proorisas* (Ephesians 1:5) and *proetoimasen* (Ephesians 2:10).

21. Francis Foulkes, *The Epistle of Paul to the Ephesians: An Introduction and Commentary,* The Tyndale New Testament Commentaries, R.V.G. Tasker, gen. ed. (Grand Rapids: Wm. B. Eerdmans Publishing Co., n.d.), p. 150.

Chapter 7

More Doubts About the "Dot"

*T*o this point in Part 2 of this book, we have responded to the first two questions of Bill Thompson's outline. To the question "What does God's will mean?", we have expressed our essential agreement with the traditional view that the sovereign and moral aspects of God's will are scripturally valid. We do not agree, however, that the Bible reveals an individual will for each person. Our reasons were presented in chapters 5 and 6 through a critique of the arguments cited by the traditional view in support of an ideal plan for each life—arguments based on reason, experience, biblical example, and biblical teaching.

Consequently, to Pastor Thompson's second question, "Does God have a plan for my life?", we gave a qualified negative. *Scripture does not teach the "dot."* God's plan for our lives must be understood in a manner that is fundamentally different from the traditional view.

Now we can consider the third question in the outline: "How can I discover God's will?" Of course, in Pastor Thompson's presentation, "God's will" meant the *individual* will. If we are correct in our conviction that there is no such thing as an individual will, then it follows that one cannot discover it. There is simply no point in looking for something that does not exist.

Having determined that, we may also express our confidence that such an ideal individual will is *not necessary* for making good decisions in the Christian life. Looking at the matter from one angle, if God has only revealed the actuality of His sovereign will and the content of His moral will, we may expect them to be fully adequate for our decision-making needs. That this is indeed the case will be established and explained in Part 3, "The Way of Wisdom."

From another viewpoint, one would expect that if the individual will does not exist, believers who are looking for it will necessarily encounter frustration. As a matter of fact, such frustration has indeed been experienced in different ways and in varying degrees as Christians have attempted to pinpoint that elusive "dot" in the "center of God's will."

In seminars that I have conducted on the subject of God's will, people with whom I have talked have readily admitted that they have often been unsure of God's individual will before making decisions. Furthermore, a good number have testified that they are *never* 100 percent certain of God's individual will. Of course if there is no individual will to be found, this common experience can be easily explained.

Mum's the Word

There was a time, though, when such confessions were few and far between. Before I began my study of God's will many years ago, I was convinced that everyone else was successful in finding this "dot" that so often eluded me. Whenever someone would give a testimony of God's specific detailed guidance of which they were 100 percent certain, I would nod my head along with everyone else. I never stood up to testify that I had a hard time finding God's will all the time. No one else did either. We all just nodded at the testimony and said to ourselves, "Yes, that is the way it should be." Mum was the word.

That silence is not hard to explain. The traditional view was taught by all the godly speakers we heard. The approach was never challenged or brought into question by any reputable Bible teachers. Who were we to question speakers whom we really respected? Furthermore, we sincerely believed that our frustrations must have been the result of sin or insincerity in our hearts. For we continually heard, "God will always clearly reveal His will to the sincere seeker."

Recently, a woman told me that she had abandoned the traditional view years ago. But she never told anyone of her defection lest she be regarded as a heretic. It was only when she was exposed to an alternative approach to Christian decision making that she felt free to express her previous sense of frustration.

When Sincerity Begets Anxiety

For a small segment of believers, the situation is more than just frustrating—it is critical. One woman who adopted an alternative position to the traditional view said that when she did, she began enjoying her Christian life for the first time. That sounded like an overstatement, until she explained. In her sincerity to seek God's individual will, she was continually plagued with feelings of guilt as well as frustration. She earnestly looked for indications of God's plan, but she had to admit to herself that she was never 100 percent certain that she had found it. The result was feelings of anxiety before every decision, and feelings of guilt following every choice she made. Since life is filled with decisions that must be made, she was not able to enjoy her Christian life. When she learned that "finding the dot" was not the essence of Christian decision making, she was set free from the frustration and guilt. In their place, she found the joy that she knew Christians were supposed to have in Christ.

A dedicated man now in seminary testifies that the same issue was formerly critical for him. Being convinced of the traditional view, he believed that God had one particular place for him and his wife to live. As hard as he tried, however, he could not get clear guidance on where that place was. His anxious uncertainty soon resulted in a loss of sleep as each night he was haunted by this matter of where God wanted him to live. The problem was acute, for he had to live somewhere, and he needed his sleep. The extremity of his frustration motivated him to consider an alternative to the traditional view. Now he is no longer plagued by an illusive search for God's individual will. In particular, he and his wife experienced genuine satisfaction in the decision-making process that culminated in his going to seminary. (See pp. 349 ff. for an extended account of this man's personal testimony.)

In this chapter and the next, we are going to expose some of the practical difficulties that arise from efforts to consistently apply the traditional approach to decision making. In doing so, we shall not be disproving the concept of an individual will of God. That has *already been done* by our examination of Scripture. What we shall see is that the conclusion we have come to from our study of God's Word is confirmed by experience. For deficient doctrine normally betrays itself by deficient practice.

THE PROBLEM OF "ORDINARY" DECISIONS

There are a number of practical problems experienced by those who try to consistently live out the traditional view in everyday life. The first, put quite simply, is that it cannot be done. At some point, *everyone* abandons the traditional view's approach to making decisions. That may sound like a bold statement, but you can check it yourself quite simply with this little test: During the past week, in what percentage of the decisions that you made did you have certainty of knowing God's individual will in advance? While you are computing, don't overlook such choices as which route you took to work, which pew you sat in at church, which shoe you put on first each morning, and which particular fruit you selected at the grocery store.

Such decisions, and hundreds of others like them, are made each week. Speakers or writers on God's will often say, "God's will for your life is detailed, so you can expect guidance from Him in every decision of life." And that statement is perfectly consistent with the total position of the traditional view. But in the small, seemingly unimportant decisions, specific guidance does not seem to materialize. Those sincere Christians who have conscientiously attempted to seek God's direction for every minute decision have either given up after a few hours, or ended up in some mystical fringe group.

It is these small decisions that most obviously reveal the inadequacy of the traditional view approach. In practice, all believers are forced, either consciously or unconsciously, to relegate "finding God's perfect will" to those decisions categorized by Bill Thompson as "Presidential Problems." We quickly learn from experience that certainty of God's will in every daily decision is a practical impossibility. As a result, in the small, nonmoral decisions of life, virtually all Christians habitually make those decisions on the basis of what seems best to them at the time. It is the only livable approach, but it does not square with the teaching of the traditional view.

Drawing the Line

What is required, then, is that people believe one way and live another. Each person must draw a horizontal line through the decisions of life (Figure 16). All decisions above the line are "important," and thus require knowledge of God's individual will before a choice is made. All decisions below that line are "mundane" or "common" and must be made to the best of one's ability without lengthy deliberation. Such a line may prove helpful, but it is not taught by the traditional view or by Scripture.

Life's Decisions

- **Important Decisions:**
  I Must Know
  God's Will!

  Shall I marry?
  Whom shall I marry?
  Should I go to school?
  Which school?
  Where should I live?
  What vocation?
  Which car should I buy?

- **Ordinary Decisions:**
  I Must Use
  Good Judgment
  Without Wasting
  Time.

  What shall I wear today?
  What should I have for
  lunch?
  How shall I get to work?
  Where shall I sit in class?
  Where should I buy gas?
  When should I have
  devotions?
  Which cologne shall I wear?

Figure 16

The inconsistency is not normally discussed in books or lectures on the will of God. It may just be an oversight, but usually, while the applicability of God's individual will to every decision is maintained, all of the illustrations normally deal only with important decisions. But if the doctrine proves to be unworkable at the level of small decisions so that it must be abandoned in practice, something is clearly wrong. It would seem that an alternative viewpoint is needed, for the traditional view cannot consistently deal with the small as well as the large decisions of life.

Applicational Difficulties of the Traditional View

1. Ordinary Decisions: The decision-making process must be abandoned in the "minor" decisions of life.

THE PROBLEM OF EQUAL OPTIONS

A second situation that presents difficulties for the traditional view is the matter of equal alternatives. In many of the choices one faces, two or more of the options seem to be equal in value, making a decision all the more complicated. The traditional view teaches that in such cases the equality is only apparent. One option, and one only, is God's will. If every road sign seems to point equally to two decisions, the signs are not being properly read. To be consistent to its position, the traditional view cannot recognize truly equal alternatives.

Again, it is the small decisions that most clearly indicate the weakness of what is claimed. The reason is simply that with smaller decisions, the options are more nearly and more often equal. Consider the matter of getting dressed in the morning. "Which pair of shoes should I wear today—the brown slip-ons or the brown oxfords? Which of three pairs of brown socks should I wear? Which shoe should I put on first?" and so it goes. Are the options equal? They sure seem to be. Does the final choice really matter? Probably not. But to be consistent, the traditional view has to say that, in principle, it does matter.

While this inability to explain and deal with equal alternatives is most obvious in small decisions, it also affects those that are more important. For there are situations, like my own choice between two schools described in the introduction, where the options in a major decision appear equivalent. In such cases, the person who is convinced of the traditional view is stymied, and the frustration level soars. Instead of rejoicing that he has more than one good opportunity rather than none, he is worried because he is afraid he will choose the wrong one and miss God's will.

Applicational Difficulties of the Traditional View

1. Ordinary Decisions: The decision-making process must be abandoned in the "minor" decisions of life.

2. **Equal Options: Insistence upon only one "correct" choice generates anxiety over "missing the dot" rather than gratitude for more than one fine opportunity.**

THE PROBLEM OF IMMATURITY

A third practical difficulty with the traditional view is its inability to reckon with immaturity on the part of the decision maker. What does one say, for instance, to the two young believers who meet on a weekend college retreat and announce at its conclusion that God has revealed in their hearts that He wants them to get married? What counsel can be given to the young man who is about to drop out of Bible school in the middle of his second semester because he feels that the Lord has called him into a full-time ministry of evangelism? Neither of those decisions is antibiblical, but more mature Christians might have good reason to be apprehensive about their long-range consequences. In fact, concerned friends would probably feel compelled to approach such young people and counsel them to wait awhile before following through on their respective courses of action. Good reasons could be given in support of wiser plans. But if the final, determining factor in making the decision is based on the conviction that "God told me to do it," little more can be said.

The reason for such a dilemma is not hard to see. The traditional view teaches that there is one ideal choice to be made in every decision. And it holds that any sincere believer can discover this ideal individual will. Furthermore, God gives final guidance in each decision only to the specific person involved. So as long as the decision that is made is within the moral will of God, it is not open to refutation by others who may be more mature. If God has indicated His verdict, there can be no higher court of appeal—unless, of course, one is prepared to challenge *His* wisdom!

But the fact of the matter is that sincere Christians *do* make foolish decisions. Immature believers tend to make immature decisions—at least with a higher degree of frequency than more mature saints. And the problem is not lack of sincerity. Often, it is the enthusiastic "babe in Christ" who is most anxious to do whatever God wants him to do. If he becomes convinced that the Lord has directed him to dive into a thimble, he will run for his swimming trunks and snorkel! The observer might wonder, "Did God really intend for him to do such a foolish thing?" But if the act is not forbidden in Scripture, and the believer is convinced of the Lord's guidance, there is little room for discussion.

Clearly something is wrong. If it is true that God has really made the decision in question and has revealed it to the young believer, then the decision should be "ideal," not immature. Yet, one suspects that somehow the signals got crossed. Or else God has an immature individual will for immature believers.

Can't Argue with God

Furthermore, the problem becomes compounded when Christians justify foolish behavior to others by announcing that it was God's decision—not theirs. And so, inadvertently, the traditional view tends to actually encourage immaturity. For it provides a means of defending unwise behavior that can be neither verified nor critiqued by the scrutiny of others.

There are, in addition, several other ways in which immaturity is promoted by the traditional view. It is often taught that one should not make a decision until there is certainty concerning the Lord's direction. One must be careful not to "run ahead of the Lord" in such matters. Now it is true that one ought not be hasty—especially in making important decisions. Often the long waiting is because the decision maker is not 100 percent certain of God's individual will. While the traditional view calls this "waiting on the Lord," it soon begins to look like common indecisiveness.

Unnecessary delay may have at least two undesirable consequences. The first is loss of valuable time. In some cases, time is an important factor in the execution of a particular decision that has been made. Time wasted in making the decision subtracts from the time available to carry it out.

The second, related consequence is that circumstances come to dominate the decision to a greater and greater degree. With the passing of time, some alternatives may be eliminated. Or the circumstances surrounding the decision may become altered, forcing the decision maker to make additional adjustments that would not have been required had he acted earlier.

Redeem the Time

The mature believer learns that some decisions should be made earlier than is absolutely necessary, provided there is a sufficient basis for making a choice. The immature believer, on the other hand, may actually find comfort in "having the decision made for him" circumstantially. But in taking such an approach to decision making, he loses the ability to engage in long-range planning. Indecision due to lack of certainty may crowd the decision-making process to the point where there is no longer any decision to be made, or it may significantly reduce the full potential of an opportunity due to lost time or changed circumstances. Any or all of these undesirable consequences may be experienced by the Christian who is stymied by lack of a clear go-ahead on a particular decision.

The traditional view of God's will lies behind other questionable approaches taken by sincere believers. Some very dedicated Christians, when confronted with two seemingly equal options, have been known to select the one that was personally less appealing. The motivation in such cases does not necessarily stem from a distorted view of God. Such a choice is often prompted by the desire to guard against self-centered ambitions. In other words, as the deadline for making a decision arrives, the person who is unsure about God's ideal will in the matter selects the less desirable alternative. He may remain uncertain as to whether the choice was the "right" one or not. But at least he knows that he did not select his own selfish will over against God's choice. The reasoning is based on a sincere effort to maintain pure motives, but it promotes immaturity and results in Christian experience that is thereby robbed of potential joy.

If She Answers on the First Ring . . .

Then there is the "phone fleece" method of dating. I used to be quite good at it. On those occasions when I did not know which girl the Lord might want me to take out on a particular date, I would set up these "providential signs" in advance: If no one answered the phone, that meant God wanted me to call back later; a busy signal was a closed door—I shouldn't call back (maybe some other fellow was asking her out); if she answered but turned me down, then God did not want me to take her out (nor did the girl); if she answered the phone and accepted my invitation, she was the one!

I once thought that my "phone fleece" method of dating was a private arrangement between me and the Lord until I began encountering a number of fellows who followed the same procedure. One day I confessed my approach by way of illustration in a seminary theology class, much to the delight of the students. Then I added, "You're laughing, but I bet some of you used to do that same thing in your sincerity to find the 'dot' of God's will." Some were sheepishly nodding when a voice said, "What do you mean *used* to do it?" God appreciates such sincerity, no doubt, but I imagine that a few of the angels must get a good chuckle when they see some of the things we have done in the process of finding the elusive "dot."

The Traditional View Promotes Immature Decisions

- By permitting believers to justify unwise decisions on grounds that "God told me to do it."
- By fostering costly delays because of uncertainty about God's individual will.
- By influencing people to reject personal preferences when faced with apparently equal options.
- By encouraging the practice of "putting out a fleece"—letting circumstances dictate the decision.

Figure 17

In this chapter we have seen various practical problems that are created by the traditional view in its search for an individual will of God. First, in the "ordinary" decisions that one makes all day, every day, the approach suggested by the traditional view must be abandoned. Second, the traditional view has no room for "equal options." And third, the traditional view tends to promote immature approaches to decision making.

Applicational Difficulties of the Traditional View

1. Ordinary Decisions: The decision-making process must be abandoned in the "minor" decisions of life.
2. Equal Options: Insistence upon only one "correct" choice generates anxiety over "missing the dot" rather than gratitude for more than one fine opportunity.
3. **Immaturity: In some instances, the logic of the traditional view tends to promote immature approaches to decision making.**

A fourth applicational difficulty is the problem of subjectivity. Because we view this as the most significant applicational difficulty of the traditional view, we have devoted the following chapter to its discussion.

Chapter 8

Impressions Are Impressions

*W*hile engaged in a ministry to high school students in eastern Oklahoma, I once began a youth meeting with the following declaration: "This afternoon, I have a message from the Water Tower Monster." I had immediate attention as curiosity peaked. "The Water Tower Monster is an awesome specter who lives beneath the water tower just outside of town beside Highway 59. His message is this: He wants everyone in town to believe in him. He says that if there are any unbelieving residents remaining at the end of one year, he will destroy the whole town. When you believe in him, you will experience an unmistakable shiver in your liver. The stronger your faith becomes, the more he will reinforce your faith through communication with your inner being. Are there any questions?"

After a few moments of restless silence, one student decided to humor me. "I live pretty close to that tower. Why haven't I ever seen this monster?"

"The Water Tower Monster is only visible to believers," I replied.

Another spoke up. "Then you have personally *seen* the monster with your own eyes?"

"Oh, yes," I replied. "Not, however, with my physical eyes. I see him with the eyes of my heart."

"The eyes of your heart?"

"Right. As I grow closer to the Water Tower Monster, the liver shivers become stronger and his presence is more clearly confirmed within."

One boy looked especially perplexed. "Wait a minute. Are you talking about the eyes of your heart, or the eyes of your liver?"

"That's right," I said.

A girl probed further. "Has anyone else ever felt these liver shivers?"

"Of course. All true believers have them."

"But how do you know the difference between a genuine 'liver shiver' and liver disease?" she continued.

"When you experience the real thing," I explained, "there is no doubt about it. The inner message is as distinct as if the Water Tower Monster were speaking audibly."

Finally, one of the kids could stand it no more. "This is ridiculous!" he exploded, to the obvious approval of all present.

"Tell me," I replied. "Is your belief in God substantially different from such faith in the Water Tower Monster?"

What followed was a lively discussion of the bases of Christian faith. And many of those young people came to appreciate more than ever that their faith was built not upon a wholly subjective foundation, but upon the solid rock of God's entrance into human history and His objective revelation to man.

THE PROBLEM OF SUBJECTIVITY

The problem of nonverifiable subjectivity touches many aspects of religious experience. People with widely divergent, even contradictory convictions testify to personal experiences that seem to be alike. And yet the reputed cause of the experiences differs according to the religious perspective of the individual reporter. What is needed is an objective standard by which these claims may be evaluated. In the area of decision making and the will of God, it is the *lack of such an objective source of knowledge* that, to my mind, constitutes the greatest applicational weakness of the traditional view.

In this chapter, we will be using the word "subjective" in the technical sense of an opinion that cannot be substantiated by an objective source of truth. By way of illustration, let us say that two men witness an accident in which an automobile strikes a pedestrian. Both are called to testify at the trial of the driver. At issue is the question of whether the car was exceeding the speed limit of 25 miles per hour when it hit the person.

The first man, who saw the accident from the street corner, testifies for the prosecution. When asked to judge the speed of the car prior to impact, he replies, "I believe the car was going at least 35 miles per hour."

In the cross-examination, the defense attorney wants to discredit that testimony. So he says, "My client insists that he was traveling no more than 25 miles per hour. What makes you so sure that he was doing 35?" To which the witness replies, "I can tell the speed of a car, and I'm sure that vehicle was doing at least 35—maybe faster."

The other witness, who saw the accident from his own car, testifies for the defense: "I was following the car in question for several blocks. Just prior to the accident, I remarked to my traveling companion how hard it is to keep one's speed at or below the speed limit in residential areas. I was saying that if it wasn't for the car in front of me, I would probably be going too fast. We both glanced at my speedometer and noted that we were traveling just under 25 miles per hour. Then the accident occurred."

In this illustration, the jury would undoubtedly disregard the testimony of the former witness on the grounds of subjectivity. By contrast, the testimony of the second man has credence because his judgment was based on an objective standard (the speedometer) by which the truth could be reliably determined.

God has provided two objective sources for certain knowledge of His will: His Word and direct revelation from Himself. But the traditional view does not claim that God's individual will may be learned from either of these sources. The Bible only reveals God's moral will, but His ideal will is more specific. And direct revelation (i.e., verbal communication by God to the individual) is not to be sought or expected. So when someone holding the traditional view says, "I have discovered God's will concerning which school I should attend," he is not claiming to have received supernatural revelation, nor did he find such leading from a direct statement of Scripture.

What we shall see is that the traditional view relies almost entirely on subjective elements in determining God's individual will for a specific decision. And that creates a tremendous dilemma: How can the traditional view obtain certain knowledge of God's individual will without an objective source of knowledge?

Interestingly enough, that question corresponds precisely with the fourth and final question in Bill Thompson's outline: "How can I know God's individual will for sure in a specific situation?" Our answer, which we shall develop in this chapter, is that you cannot. For if the source of one's knowledge is subjective, then the knowledge will also be subjective—and hence, uncertain.

Consider the Source

Let's look again at the means put forth by the traditional view for discerning God's will. How is God's individual will communicated? The key ingredient in the entire process is the indwelling Spirit of truth (John 16:13). One of his ministries in the life of the believer is that of "leading" (Romans 8:14; Galatians 5:18). The means by which He does this is variously described within the traditional view: the still small voice, inner voice, inward pressure, inward urging, guiding impulse, inner impression, and so on.

It is important to reiterate that such inner impressions are not equated with supernatural revelation by the traditional view. The divine revelation received by Ezekiel or Paul was much more definitive and authoritative than guidance received by individual believers today. In fact, the traditional view instructs Christians to test the inner impressions by the other "sign posts" to confirm their significance. Because much of the time, the inner impressions that are so crucial to the entire process are downright vague.

This lack of clarity has been experienced by everyone who has approached decision making in this manner. And the sense of ambiguity is in no way dispelled by labeling such impulses "impressions of the Holy Spirit." For the first question usually uttered by the sincere seeker of God's will is: "How can I tell whether these impressions are from God or from some other source?"

This is a critical question. For impressions could be produced by any number of sources: God, Satan, an angel, a demon, human emotions (such as fear or ecstasy), hormonal imbalance, insomnia, medication, or an upset stomach. Sinful impressions (temptations) may be exposed for what they are by the Spirit-sensitized conscience and the Word of God. But beyond that, one encounters a subjective quagmire of uncertainty. For in nonmoral areas, Scripture gives no guidelines for distinguishing the voice of the Spirit from the voice of the self — or any other potential "voice." And experience offers no reliable means of identification either (which is why the question comes up in the first place). And yet the traditional view requires that the source of those impressions must be identified if the believer is to discern God's guidance. Tremendous frustration has been experienced by sincere Christians who have earnestly but fruitlessly sought to decipher the code of the inward witness.

Inner impressions are not a form of revelation. So the Bible does not invest inner impressions with authority to function as indicators of divine guidance. Impressions are real; believers experience them. But impressions are *not authoritative.* Impressions are impressions. Call them "spiritual," or attribute them to the Holy Spirit, and they are still the same — just impressions. Impressions by any other name confuse the issue and confound the believer in the process of decision making.

An Impressive Commentary

By way of illustration, there is one area where an appeal to inner impressions is deemed to be invalid in decision making. Virtually no one admits to such an approach in *biblical interpretation* — the science of hermeneutics. There are many accepted principles for the study of God's Word, but tuning in to inward impulses is not one of them.

When a Christian studies the Bible, he is required to make a number of decisions about the meaning of the text. Most of the time, the meaning is not difficult to discern — especially if the reader is a careful, prayerful student. But some passages are difficult to understand. And, in such cases, while the author had a single meaning, the text is often interpreted in more than one way.

Bible commentaries have been prepared by knowledgeable scholars to assist the student at such points. A thorough commentator will usually explain the plausible views on the passage in question before stating his own interpretation. At the same time, he will state the reasons why he has adopted one viewpoint while rejecting others — reasons that may be evaluated by the reader by the standard of accepted principles of hermeneutics.

If a commentator were to adopt the traditional view of decision making and apply it to matters of biblical interpretation, he might write something like this:

> Having just explained the five possible interpretations that Bible scholars have suggested for this text, this writer confesses that this is a very difficult passage to understand. In such cases, the Holy Spirit must be the final Guide. In response to my prayer for guidance, the Spirit has indicated to my heart through His still small voice that the correct interpretation is the last one listed above.

Surely such a rationale would raise red flags in the mind of the reader. What about the scholars who hold the other four positions? Are we to assume that they didn't ask for similar guidance? Or should we assume that they misunderstood the leading they were given? How do we know that this writer isn't the one who garbled the message? How is a layman to decide which commentator is correct? Should he follow the opinion of the man he considers to be the most spiritual? Or should he add up the number of scholars supporting each view and go with the majority (or, in the absence of a majority, a plurality!)?

Of course the entire hypothetical situation is absurd. A commentator might write such an opinion as the one suggested above. And he would be consistent with the traditional view.[1] But his book would probably never make it into print. For it would be rejected by any reputable publisher (and rightly so) on grounds of improper methodology and irresponsible scholarship. If such an approach was permitted in the field of hermeneutics, there would be nothing to prevent scholars who espouse opposing views from making the same claims to divine guidance. That, in turn, would make a mockery of genuine biblical scholarship, and impugn the Spirit of truth as the Author of confusion. Instead, claims to speak *ex cathedra* on matters of biblical interpretation are rejected as being nonauthoritative at best, and contrary to Scripture itself at worst.

The fact that the traditional view of decision making is declared to be invalid when applied to questions of biblical interpretation supports our denial of its applicability to other nonmoral areas. The reasons for rejecting that approach in all such spheres are the same. Impressions may be good commentaries of one's present feelings; but they are not trustworthy guides for determining proper interpretation of Scripture or finding specific guidance from God.

Pick a Sign, Any Sign

A proponent of the traditional view might reply: "I know that I cannot prove clear guidance on the basis of inner impressions alone, but there are other signs that point the way to God's will."

That is a remarkable statement. For it is a tacit admission of the very point that we have been making. If the inner impressions, which reportedly provide the most personal and direct indication of God's will, are really from the Holy Spirit, why is there any need of confirmation from other signs? It seems that if God were to choose to reveal His will in that manner, His communication would be crystal clear. His voice might be "still" and "small," but it would certainly be understandable.

On the other hand, if we grant the validity of multiple signs for the sake of discussion, the problems are hardly resolved. For the other signs are subject to the same difficulties encountered with the inward impressions.

Consider, for example, the sign of circumstances. Do circumstances give clear direction of God's will? God *is* sovereign over circumstances; but is He trying to tell us something specific through them?

We will develop this subject at greater length in chapter 12, "God Only Wise," but for now it will suffice to observe some of the difficulties encountered by the traditional view with respect to circumstances. In order for circumstances to give direction, they must be interpreted. And, again, Scripture gives no guidelines for reading providence. And so the subjective element creeps back in.

When, for instance, does a circumstance constitute a "yes" sign? How does one distinguish between an "open door" and one that is only ajar? If one is presented with an "open door," must that opportunity be taken? Would the believer who decided not to go through such an open door be disobeying God? On the other hand, is an opportunity really an indication of God's leading, or might it not be an easy way into "God's second best?" And who opened that door—God, or Satan, or neither of them? Conversely, when one encounters an obstacle in pursuit of some goal, is that obstruction to be viewed as a roadblock, a closed door, or a test of faith? Circumstances are complex, seldom pointing conclusively in a single direction. And the traditional view has not provided an objective means for interpreting them. The result, once again, is uncertainty.

Subjectivity and consequent ambiguity characterize every one of the so-called signs. The traditional view appears to give a significant role to *counselors*. But it undermines the value of such advice with the warning that human beings are fallible, and the reminder that God's will is revealed ultimately only to the individual seeking it. *Common sense* must also be exercised, it is said. However, one must also be open to guidance that may not, at first glance, seem so logical. After all, what would have been accomplished by Noah, Joshua, Gideon or Namaan the Syrian if they had followed the dictates of common sense? So does the traditional view promote the exercise of common sense? Well, yes and no.

Time and time again, the traditional view points to the road signs. But the instructions and warnings about the reading of these signs underscore the difficulty experienced in determining an accurate interpretation. Certainly such factors as circumstances, counselors, and common sense ought to have an important bearing on our decisions. But when they must be read as a "yes" or "no" indicating God's individual will, they cannot yield the desired certainty.

Compounding the Uncertainty

At this point someone might respond: "All right. I can see that an individual sign by itself is subjective, but *agreement* of the signs will produce guidance that is objective."

But will it? What happens if a believer, whose perspective becomes distorted either by zeal or sin, incorrectly reads several of the signs as indicating "yes?" Does such "agreement of the signs" yield a positive indication of what God wants him to do? Of course not.

And how often does one find incontestable unanimity among the signs? If one is "pretty sure" that the circumstances are positive, and "quite sure" that the inner impressions give the go-ahead, the combination of the two can never rise above "pretty" or "quite sure." If anything, the addition of the two reduces the level of certainty.

How many of the signs must agree? Most presentations of the traditional view stress the importance of agreement among the Big

Three: the Word, circumstances, and the inner voice. But whether one must reconcile three signs or twenty-three, the problem remains the same: If the elements which make up the whole are uncertain, the whole will also be uncertain. Uncertainty plus uncertainty yields uncertainty. As one adds more signposts to the equation, the subjective factor is multiplied and the degree of uncertainty is magnified.

Of all the signs, the only one which provides the desired objectivity is the Bible. It can clearly disqualify an option that violates moral standards. But it gives no positive indicators in nonmoral areas. To specific questions of vocation, marriage, or education, for instance, the Bible cannot say "yes." It can only indicate what is, and is not, permissible. The traditional view must appeal to the other signs for more specific direction, thereby denying the decision maker the confidence that only an objective source of knowledge can give.

Testing the Signs

And so the traditional view is able to list several sources of guidance pointing to God's individual will. But the person who is attempting to read these "road signs" finds that he must answer a host of questions about the *road signs themselves* before he can use them. Such questions include:

1. Do I sense inward urgings that might be pointing the way to God's individual will?
2. What is the source of those impressions?
3. What is the meaning or message of the impressions?
4. Are there any other signs that will either confirm or correct my inner impressions?
5. What is the message of the other signs?
6. Is the message that I am "receiving" authoritative?

That last question brings us to the heart of the problem. If God tells a person to do something, is that person obligated to obey? Absolutely. Any direction of God is binding for the one to whom it is given. And disobedience is sin. It follows, then, that if God makes His will known to an individual, the only remaining decision to be made is whether to obey or disobey.

It is the logic of that conclusion that has made the traditional approach to decision making so agonizing for many. For how can one obey God if he is uncertain about His direction (cf. Romans 14:23)? And how can one be certain of God's will if the indicators are incapable of providing objective guidance?

Too Many Cooks Spoil the Broth

The uncertainty is compounded not only by adding more signs to the equation, but by adding more people. Many decisions, such as those made by a church board or the congregation of a local church, are group decisions. When two, ten or two hundred people must all have the same inward leading, the process grows increasingly complicated. Should a church require unanimity of thought before proceeding with a decision? The work would grind to a standstill. And so most churches make decisions on the basis of a majority or two-thirds vote. But that does not square with the theology of the traditional view. By definition, a nonunanimous vote signifies that a segment of the decision-making group somehow missed God's leading.

This fact creates a real tension in the minds of some people. I once sat in on a congregational meeting of a church which I was attending, though I was not a member. That church had to make a difficult decision, and the members had given the matter much thought, discussion, and prayer. However, they could not form a consensus. Godly men and women lined up on opposite sides of the issue.

In the course of that meeting, one lady stood up and said, "We can't vote now." When asked why, she replied in total sincerity: "I have talked with several others here who are earnestly seeking God's perfect will in this matter. Apparently, the Holy Spirit has told some of us to vote 'yes' and some of us to vote 'no.' How can we resolve the question when the Holy Spirit is telling us two different things?"

She was longing for unity in the church. But she was frustrated by the necessity of discovering which choice God had made. And the official reply that the church would follow the procedure outlined in the church constitution comforted her not one bit.

What we have seen, then, is that the element of subjectivity that is an inescapable factor in the traditional approach rules out any possibility of attaining certain knowledge of God's individual will. When we add that deficiency to the problems discussed in the previous chapter, we are reminded of at least four areas of frustration encountered by those who follow the traditional view (Figure 18).

Applicational Difficulties of the Traditional View

1. Ordinary Decisions: The decision-making process must be abandoned in the "minor" decisions of life.

2. Equal Options: Insistence upon only one "correct" choice generates anxiety over "missing the dot" rather than gratitude for more than one fine opportunity.

3. Immaturity: In some instances, the logic of the traditional view tends to promote immature approaches to decision making.

4. Subjectivity: Certainty that one has found God's individual will is impossible apart from an objective source of knowledge.

Figure 18

THE LEADING OF THE HOLY SPIRIT

If this chapter were a discussion, at some point the most pertinent question of all would be raised by the traditional view: "Doesn't the Bible teach that one of the ministries of the Holy Spirit is to lead believers?"

The answer, of course, is yes. The issue, however, is not *whether* God leads, but *how*. We have already examined the primary passages cited by the traditional view in support of the concept of an individual will of God (chapter 6). It remains for us now to investigate the key passages on the leading of the Holy Spirit.

Romans 8:14

For all who are being led by the Spirit of God, these are sons of God.

This verse is often quoted as proof of the idea that the Holy Spirit leads believers through inner impressions into the ideal will of God. The word "led" certainly looks like guidance, and the Agent of leading is the Holy Spirit. The context, however, deals a death blow to such an understanding of this passage.

Negatively, there are three considerations. First, the context is not dealing with daily decision making in nonmoral areas. Second, neither the verse itself nor the near context give any indication that the *means* of the leading is by inward "impressions." Furthermore, there is no hint that the *goal* of the leading is directed toward the individual will of God. Not one of the distinctive features of the traditional view is present in Romans 8:14 or its context. The word "led" is a common, nontechnical word which does not in itself indicate either the goal or the means of the leading.[2]

What the apostle Paul *is* discussing in this passage is righteous living.[3] The answers to the problems of slavery to sin (raised in Romans 7:7-25) are given in chapter 8:1-17. The issue in question is not anything like the choice between two possible home sites or the decision to buy a new suit. The issue is set forth in a series of vivid, mutually exclusive contrasts: good versus evil (7:19); the law of sin and death versus the law of the Spirit of life (8:2); life according to the flesh versus life according to the Spirit (8:5); being hostile to God versus pleasing God (8:7-8); being in the flesh versus being in the Spirit (8:8-9); being indwelt by the Spirit versus not having the Spirit of Christ (8:9); and, finally, living according to the Spirit versus putting to death the deeds of the body (8:13, which is the immediate context). What Paul is talking about is experiential conformity to the *moral* will of God.[4]

In this context, "being led by the Spirit of God" is another way of describing life "according to the Spirit" in which the Christian is "putting to death the deeds of the body."[5] The leading is guidance into the moral will of God to do what is pleasing to Him. Obedience to that will would be impossible apart from the life-changing presence and empowering of the Holy Spirit (8:6,13). While the means of the Spirit's leading is not emphasized, the goal of His direction is the clearly revealed, moral will of God (7:12, 14, 22; 8:3-4).

Romans 8:14 must not be interpreted apart from its context.[6] Even considered alone, the verse would not prove guidance through inner impressions indicating an individual will of God. But in context, the meaning is transparent: Sons of God are those who are led by the Holy Spirit to put to death the deeds of the flesh and accomplish the moral will of God.

Galatians 5:18

> But if you are led by the Spirit, you are not under the Law.

This verse, which is very similar to Romans 8:14, is often cited with it in support of the traditional view of guidance. But the context of Galatians 5 is even more decisive in ruling out such an interpretation.

In this passage, Paul described the conflicting pulls of the flesh on the one hand, and the indwelling Spirit on the other. The key to overcoming the lust of the flesh and fulfilling the desire of the Spirit consists in walking by the Spirit (5:16) and being led by the Spirit (5:18). Failure to do so will result in deeds of immorality (5:19-21). However, being led by the Spirit will result in love, joy, peace, patience, kindness, goodness, faithfulness, gentleness, and self-control (5:22-23).[7]

In addition, the Spirit leads the way in fulfilling the Law to love one's neighbor as oneself (5:13-14). This is great guidance! But this passage cannot be construed as a proof-text for the traditional view. For this leading is unquestionably related to the moral will of God as revealed in Scripture.

Besides examining these verses in their immediate context, it is helpful to see them within the overall framework of total biblical revelation. Accordingly, we affirm that Scripture does teach that God has, on certain occasions, given direct guidance to selected individuals through supernatural means. Second, Scripture also teaches that the Holy Spirit is actively, personally involved in the lives of believers, leading them in the fulfillment of His moral will. The Bible does not, however, teach a synthesis of those two facts—namely, that the Holy Spirit is providing direct guidance for believers in nonmoral decisions through some sort of inaudible, inner "voice." It is a fallacy to superimpose Paul's "Macedonian Call" onto his comments regarding "being led by the Spirit." Yet that is apparently what many have done. The distorted perspective that has resulted from such a synthesis must be corrected.

John 16:12-14

> "I have many more things to say to you, but you cannot bear them now. But when He, the Spirit of truth, comes, He will guide you into all the truth; for He will not speak on His own initiative, but whatever He hears, He will speak; and He will disclose to you what is to come. He shall glorify Me; for He shall take of Mine, and shall disclose it to you."

Because of Christ's promise of the guiding ministry of the Holy Spirit, some have cited these verses in support of the traditional view. "All the truth" could appear to encompass knowledge needed to make even nonmoral decisions according to God's individual will. It is usually suggested that this guiding ministry is effected through the inward impulses of the Spirit.

The text, however, will not permit such an interpretation. In context, "all the truth" must refer to spiritual truth such as the teaching they had been receiving from Jesus (in John 14-16)[8] This is required by verses 12 and 14. Further, any broader interpretation must make the expression exhaustive in scope—all the truth whatsoever. But no one takes it that way. Rather, Jesus is promising guidance into spiritual understanding.

Second, there is no hint in the passage that this guidance will be provided through inner impressions.

Third, the "you" to whom the promise was made refers to the men to whom Jesus was speaking—the apostles. It is difficult to determine with certainty the nature of the promise. One view is that Christ was here making provision for future revelation—truth that would be written down and passed on in the pages of the New Testament.[9] Another good possibility is that Jesus was promising these men future illumination to grasp the necessity and significance of His imminent death and resurrection.[10]

If this passage has a direct application to believers today, it would be on the order of the ministry of illumination as described in 1 John 2:20 and 27. The promise would be that of enablement in recognizing and understanding spiritual truth.

The above explanations are in harmony with the context and the New Testament doctrine of the Holy Spirit. He did reveal truth to the Church through the apostles and He does indwell the believer to illumine that truth to him. This is clearly guidance by the Spirit into God's moral will, whether by revelation or illumination, rather than inward leading in nonmoral decisions.

THE PEACE OF CHRIST

For many who follow the traditional view, there is one final factor that either indicates God's stamp of approval or His red flag of warning—the peace of God. Since peace is a fruit of the Spirit (Galatians 5:22), it is viewed by many as one of the means at His disposal to communicate His will to the believer. To quote Pastor Bill Thompson, the inward witness of the Holy Spirit may be defined as "that ministry of the Spirit in which He guides the believer through personal impressions and *inner peace within the heart* to reveal God's individual will."

Appealing to the Umpire

This concept is based primarily on the exhortation of Colossians 3:15: "And let the peace of Christ rule in your hearts...." The explanation is that this peace functions as an umpire that "calls" each decision in question.[11] So long as the believer is living within the center of God's will, he experiences an inner quietness of heart "which surpasses all comprehension" (Philippians 4:7). Through this peace the Umpire is calling "Safe!" But if the Christian begins to move in the wrong direction, he experiences increasing restlessness and inner anxiety—an indication that he is about to step "out of bounds."

It is not difficult to see the logic of this explanation, and it corresponds beautifully with the other aspects of the traditional view of guidance. Unfortunately, it does not correspond with the rest of the passage of which it is a part, and we suspect that the apostle Paul would be surprised to learn that his statement to the Colossians was being explained in such a way. For he was not writing about God's provision for decision making, but rather a moral life style that is consistent with the believer's position in Christ.

The statement "let the peace of Christ rule in your hearts" is part of a paragraph that runs from verses 12 through 17 in Colossians 3. That paragraph begins with an exhortation for believers to "put on" certain virtues: compassion, kindness, humility, gentleness, patience, forbearance, forgiveness, and above all, love, "which is the perfect bond of unity" (3:14). These virtues are to replace discarded vices such as immorality, greed, anger, abusive speech, lying, and the like (3:5-11). Such evil manifestations of "the old self" are the cause of the tremendous divisions that we see in the world. But the tensions that exist between "Greek and Jew, circumcised and uncircumcised, barbarian, Scythian, slave and freeman" are not to exist in the church. Rather, believers are to be characterized by unity—a unity that will grow spontaneously as Christians put on the garments of love (3:12-14), submit to the peace of Christ (3:15), share the word of Christ (3:16), and do all things with thanksgiving in the name of the Lord Jesus (3:17).

A Matter of Harmony

Commenting on the expression "peace of Christ," Abbott correctly notes: "The immediate reference here is not to inward peace of the soul; but to peace with one another, as the context shows."[12] To put it differently, peace may be defined negatively as the *absence of anxiety within a person* (as in Philippians 4:6-7), or as the *absence of hostility between persons*. In Colossians 3:15, it is clearly the latter.

To sum up, the whole appeal of Colossians 3:12-17 is for believers to manifest Christlike attitudes and virtues that will result in an experiential unity among believers. Such harmony reflects a supernatural change that replaces hatred and animosity with love and peace. Any interpretation of Colossians 3:15 that explains it in terms of inner guidance in nonmoral decision making is absolutely foreign to the context.

Disturbing the Peace

In addition to the exegetical problem described above, the traditional view has a secondary, experiential problem with its appeal to the peace of God. It is the same problem that has emerged like a monotonous refrain throughout this chapter: the inherent subjectivity in accounting for the experience of peace—or more precisely, the lack of it.

For the sake of argument, we shall return to the traditional view's definition of peace as inner quietness of heart, or the absence of anxiety. Now when a believer experiences "lack of peace" in the process of decision making, the question that must be asked is, what is the source of the anxiety? Is it always an indication of the Spirit's guidance, or could it be explained by other factors?

A moment's reflection will yield several potential disturbers of the peace. One likely suspect in certain cases is the conscience. If the Christian begins to pursue a course of action in violation of God's revealed moral will, the Spirit-sensitized conscience will produce the first symptoms of guilt. This disruption of peace is designed to be an alarm system warning the believer to change his direction and get back on the path of righteousness (cf. Ephesians 4:25-32). Of course, in such instances, it is obedience to the moral will of God that is in question.

However, even in the face of nonmoral decisions, Christians often experience a lack of peace. Again, the potential causes are numerous: insomnia, illness, concern for a loved one, occupational stress, an approaching deadline, nagging uncertainties, timidity, a new experience, and so on.

There Goes the Groom

I was once the best man for a friend who was getting married in North Dakota. In order to get to our position "backstage" without being seen, we had to crawl through the church baptistry. Doubling as the unofficial photographer, I took a picture of the groom as he crawled through the baptistry. Then the camera focused on Mike as he sat by the entrance door biting his fingernails with the wide-eyed look of a condemned convict.

The pose was made in jest. But suppose that he had looked up at me at that moment and said, "Garry, I've prayed a lot about marrying Chris. But right now I feel so unsettled inside, I think the Lord must be telling me not to go through with it." What should I have done? Should I have stopped the wedding? Isn't that what best men are for?

Of course, he didn't say that. And I didn't stop the wedding. Nor would I have—not without a more legitimate reason. If all marriages were called off because of nervous grooms, there would be no weddings. Such "lack of peace" is normal when one faces a major new step in life.

Some people experience lack of peace because of immaturity. Decisions entail responsibilities and result in consequences. An immature person may be unwilling to accept new responsibilities. That individual may resist even making the decision. And he will experience considerable anxiety. Such turmoil is not produced by the Holy Spirit saying "no" to a decision; it is the result of simply facing a difficult decision. Such inner anxiety reveals the need for emotional growth; it is not specific guidance from God.

Again, as we have already noted, some Christians experience a lack of peace as a result of trying to apply the traditional approach to decision making. The individual who cannot discern God's individual will in a decision becomes increasingly concerned. Believ-

144 The Case of the Missing "Dot"

ing he must make the "right" decision, he seeks 100 percent certainty of God's inward leading. If doubts persist, and they often do, the anxiety can become acute. Such lack of peace is the result not of God's guidance, but of faulty theology. And the more sincere the believer is, the greater his frustration becomes.

Our point is that a disturbance of one's quietness of heart can be accounted for in all sorts of ways. Further, there is no instruction in Scripture explaining the criteria by which one may distinguish the negative leading of the Spirit from other disquieting influences. And it will not work to dismiss the whole discussion with the assertion that God's peace "surpasses all comprehension" (Philippians 4:7). For it is not the presence of God's peace we are seeking to understand in this case, but rather the reasons for the lack thereof.

As important as God's peace is in the life of the believer, our conclusion is that its presence or absence is not to be construed as a sign of God's leading in *nonmoral* decisions. It cannot function as such, nor was it so designed.

In summary, the problem with the traditional view is not that it recognizes the reality of inner impressions, but that it requires too much of them. Since it is impossible to define with certainty either their source or their meaning, it is also impossible to derive from them objective guidance pointing to one "right" decision. God's Word does not invest subjective sources of knowledge with divine authority. We must not either.

Behold the Forest!

Lest we lose our way among the individual "trees" of our presentation, let us pause momentarily to review where we have been. Then we should be able to see where we need to go. Based on the seminar presentation in Part 1, the distinctive features of the traditional view are as follows:

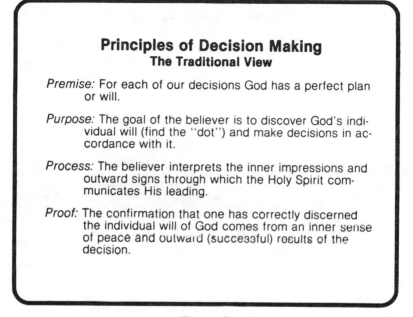

Principles of Decision Making
The Traditional View

Premise: For each of our decisions God has a perfect plan or will.

Purpose: The goal of the believer is to discover God's individual will (find the "dot") and make decisions in accordance with it.

Process: The believer interprets the inner impressions and outward signs through which the Holy Spirit communicates His leading.

Proof: The confirmation that one has correctly discerned the individual will of God comes from an inner sense of peace and outward (successful) results of the decision.

Figure 19

As we promised, Part 2 has been essentially critical. In these chapters, we have worked to establish a single major point, and a secondary corollary. The *major point* is this: God does not have an ideal, detailed life-plan uniquely designed for each believer that must be discovered in order to make correct decisions. The concept of an "individual will of God" cannot be established by reason, experience, biblical example, or biblical teaching (chapters 5 and 6).

The *secondary consequence* is this: Attempts to find a "dot" that does not exist have generated needless frustration in the process of decision making. We have shown, for instance, that practitioners of the traditional view are forced to abandon the process in the "minor" decisions of everyday life. Second, the traditional view provides no adequate means for dealing with genuinely equal options. Third, the traditional view tends to promote immature approaches to decision making. And finally, since the traditional view can appeal only to subjective sources of knowledge, the seeker of guidance is denied the possibility of objective certainty that he has found God's will (chapters 7 and 8). Not only is the individual will of God not found in Scripture, but the suggested process for finding it is absent as well.

Thankfully, the Christian is not left to his own devices when he must make decisions. God's provisions are abundant and practical. It is into that portion of our theological forest — the doctrine of the nature of guidance — that we may now proceed.

Notes

1. By "consistent with the traditional view" we do not mean that proponents of the traditional view actually do it or espouse it. We do mean that it is consistent with the method of decision making presented by the traditional view. We would assume in the illustration that the interpretation did not contradict other Scripture and that it was not illogical, showing agreement of the "signs." I am convinced that in actual practice quite a few immature believers do in fact follow such a procedure.

2. William F. Arndt and F. Wilbur Gingrich, trans., *A Greek-English Lexicon of the New Testament and Other Early Christian Literature,* 2nd ed. (Chicago: University of Chicago Press, 1979), s.v. "ἄγω."

3. John R. W. Stott, *Men Made New* (Downers Grove, Ill.: InterVarsity Press, 1966), p. 93.

4. W. H. Griffith Thomas, *St Paul's Epistle to the Romans: A Devotional Commentary* (Grand Rapids: Wm. B. Eerdmans Publishing Co., 1946), p. 215; John Murray, *The Epistle to the Romans,* The New International Commentary on the New Testament (Grand Rapids: Wm. B. Eerdmans Publishing Co., 1959), 1:293-95.

5. Stott, *Men Made New,* pp. 92-93.

6. The context includes a verse construed by some to show the use of subjective impressions spoken directly to the heart of man. Romans 8:16 says, "The Spirit Himself bears witness with our spirit that we are children of God." The message here is not daily decision making. The phrase "with our spirit" refers back to 8:15. There the believer's spirit is described as one of adoption which cries out, " 'Abba! Father!' " With this witness of the human regenerated spirit is added the witness of the Spirit. The Spirit witnesses to the believer that he is a child of God. As Murray says, "Particularly it is made manifest in sealing to the hearts of believers the promises which are theirs as heirs of God and joint-heirs of Christ and the generating in them of the assurance of the great love the Father has bestowed upon them that they should be called children of God (cf. 1 John 3:1)." This witness of the Spirit is in perfect harmony with the objective revelation of the Word of God. See Murray, *Romans,* 1:297-98.

7. John R. W. Stott, *The Message of Galatians* (Downers Grove, Ill.: InterVarsity Press, 1968), p. 152.

8. Leon Morris, *The Gospel According To John,* The New International Commentary on the New Testament (Grand Rapids: Wm. B. Eerdmans Publishing Co., 1971), p. 700, n. 30.

9. Merrill C. Tenney, *John: The Gospel of Belief* (Grand Rapids: Wm. B. Eerdmans Publishing Co., 1948), pp. 238-39.

10. Charles Caldwell Ryrie, *The Ryrie Study Bible* (Chicago: Moody Press, 1979), p. 1632.

11. The idea of umpire comes from the fact that *brabeuō* was used for the umpire who "ruled" over an athletic game. The traditional view would understand the word to mean more than overall supervision, but to mean making specific decisions in

specific cases. However, the context of Colossians 3:15 favors the general sense of "rule" or "control."

12. T.K. Abbott, *A Critical and Exegetical Commentary on the Epistles to the Ephesians and to the Colossians,* The International Critical Commentary (Edinburgh: T. & T. Clark, 1897), p. 289. See also F.F. Bruce, "Commentary on the Epistle to the Colossians," in *Commentary on the Epistles to the Ephesians and the Colossians,* the New International Commentary on the New Testament (Grand Rapids: Wm. B. Eerdmans Publishing Co., 1957), p. 282.

PART 3
The Way of Wisdom
The Wisdom View Explained

Chapter 9

Thy Word Is Truth

*T*he expression *will of God* is used in the Bible in two ways. God's *sovereign will* is His secret plan to determine everything that happens in the universe. God's *moral will* consists of the revealed commands in the Bible that teach how men ought to believe and live.

To these biblical usages, a third has been added. It is commonly taught that for each person, God has an *individual will* — an ideal, detailed life-plan for each person. In this traditional view, the key to decision making is to discover God's individual will, and then do it. Accordingly, the burden of most books on guidance is to explain how God's specific leading is to be discerned in each situation.

By contrast, the emphasis of Scripture is on God's moral will. In fact, the Bible reveals nothing of an "individual will" governing each decision. Rather, the teaching of Scripture may be summarized by these basic principles:

1. In those areas specifically addressed by the Bible, the revealed commands of God (His moral will) are to be obeyed.

2. In those areas where the Bible gives no command or principle (nonmoral decisions), the believer is free and responsible to choose his own course of action. Any deci-

151

sion made within the moral will of God is acceptable to God.

3. In nonmoral decisions, the objective of the Christian is to make wise decisions on the basis of spiritual expediency.

4. In all decisions, the believer should humbly submit, in advance, to the outworking of God's sovereign will as it touches each decision.

These four principles comprise the thesis of this section and summarize the "way of wisdom" that will be developed, explained, and illustrated throughout the chapters of Part 3.

In chapter 2, "Hitting the Bull's-eye," Bill Thompson gave a necessarily brief but accurate explanation of the sovereign will and moral will of God. Since these concepts are foundational to the Christian's decision-making process, it is appropriate at this point to establish in greater detail both the genuineness and character of each of these biblical senses of God's will. Then we will be prepared to recognize the important bearing that each has on our decisions.

THE REALITY OF GOD'S MORAL WILL

I had studied long and hard, and I felt that I had a good grasp of the material. The exam was taxing, but it was a fair test of how much we had learned. I knew I had done well; the only question was whether I would get an "A" or a "B."

I lived with the suspense for a week or so. At last, the graded exams were returned—the moment of truth had arrived. Or had it? What was the letter in the upper right-hand corner? It was neither an "A" (as in "astute"), nor a "B" (as in "brilliant"). It was a "D" (as in "dumbbell")! How could that be?

I quickly paged through the exam, finding that I had done even better than I expected on pages one, two, and three. But page four was a disaster. I had missed nineteen out of nineteen "true or false" questions. I could have done better flipping a coin! Then I saw the problem: I had put a "T" or "F" in each answer blank while the instructions had specifically directed me to spell out "True" or "False." The penalty never did seem completely fair to me, but I did learn a valuable lesson: Before you begin an exam, read *all* of the instructions carefully.

The same principle applies to our spiritual lives. God's instructions are always fair, and they bear careful reading. Those instructions, which are clearly set forth in the Bible, comprise the *moral will* of God.

Bookworm's Delight

God's moral will is the perfect and complete guide for the Christian's faith and practice. Most Christian books are concerned with God's moral will. Bible commentaries interpret God's moral will as it is presented in the text of Scripture. Books on theology and doctrine organize God's moral will into various subjects and categories. Ethics books wrestle with proper application of God's moral will to complex, real-life situations. Devotional books inspire us to follow God's moral will in daily living.

As was demonstrated in chapter 6, "Does Scripture Teach the 'Dot'?," this moral aspect of God's will was a common subject of biblical writers. One clear example is found in Romans 2:18. Addressing the unbelieving Jew, the apostle Paul said, "...[you] know His will,...being instructed out of the Law,...." In this statement, Paul could not have been speaking of God's sovereign will (which cannot be known), nor His individual will (which is neither revealed in the Law nor ever discovered by unbelievers). Rather, Paul was speaking of God's moral will.[1] For in the Law, God's moral laws and requirements are revealed to all Jews, believing and unbelieving alike.

Again, in 1 Thessalonians, Paul directly equated God's will with specific moral commands. For instance, sanctification of life, including sexual purity, is called "the will of God" (4:3). And, "in everything give thanks; for this is God's will for you in Christ Jesus" (5:18). (In context, "God's will" may actually encompass the whole list of terse commands which immediately precede the directive to give thanks [5:12-17].)

THE NATURE OF GOD'S MORAL WILL

The moral will of God is *the expression,* in behavioral terms, *of the character of God.* Perhaps the most succinct statement of divine expectation is Peter's quotation of the Old Testament imperative: "You shall be holy, for I am holy" (1 Peter 1:16; Leviticus

11:44-45). Now how is one to guide his life so as to "be holy...in all...behavior" (1 Peter 1:15)? By obeying the moral will of God, which, like God Himself, is "holy and righteous and good" (Romans 7:12). Put differently, God's children are to manifest the family likeness by obeying the Father's will (Ephesians 5:1; 1 John 5:3).

Like Father, Like Son

Ironically, what Satan sought to usurp (" 'I will make myself like the Most High' " [Isaiah 14:14]), and tempted Eve to pursue (" 'you will be like God' " [Genesis 3:5]), has been part of God's design for mankind from the very beginning. Created in the image of God, Adam and Eve were already "like God." His purpose for them was that they would reflect the Creator's likeness on the finite level (Genesis 1:26-31).

No lesser purpose defines God's "new creation" (2 Corinthians 5:17), which, through the redemptive and re-creative activity of the Godhead, is being progressively renewed and will ultimately conform precisely to the Creator's image (Colossians 3:10; Romans 8:29). The capacity and the resources needed by men to manifest the character of God have been granted by His grace (2 Peter 1:3-4). Consequently, one of the most frequent and fundamental motivations for godly living in the New Testament is the reminder of what God is like. Specifically, the following traits are among those that are to characterize the believer *for the reason that they characterize the Godhead:* holiness (1 Peter 1:15-16), righteousness (1 John 3:7), purity (1 John 3:3), love (Ephesians 5:1-2), forgiveness (Colossians 3:13), compassion (Luke 6:36), endurance (Hebrews 12:2-4), submission (1 Peter 2:21-24), humility and obedience (Philippians 2:5-8), kindness (Luke 6:35), and generosity in giving (2 Corinthians 8:1-9).

If the moral will of God is the expression of His character, then one would expect that it would encompass much more than legislation governing merely external behavior. In point of fact, the imperatives of God's moral will *touch every aspect and moment of life.* This is so because they prescribe the believer's goals and attitudes, as well as his actions. To put it differently, God is not concerned simply with *what* we do; He's equally concerned with *why* we do what we do, as well as *how* we do it. The purpose, the process, and the product are all directed by His moral will.

The End Just as the Means

These generalities are more clearly seen via specifics, so we will look more closely at the guidance God has given us in Scripture concerning our goals, our attitudes, and our means for achieving our objectives.

Goals, by their nature, are more general than behavioral commands. In Scripture, the believer's primary goals reflect God's purposes for His children during their earthly lives.

A good example of God's will for our goals is found in 1 Peter 4:10-11:

> As each one has received a special gift, employ it in serving one another, as good stewards of the manifold grace of God. Whoever speaks, let him speak, as it were, the utterances of God; whoever serves, let him do so as by the strength which God supplies; so that in all things God may be glorified through Jesus Christ, to whom belongs the glory and dominion forever and ever. Amen.

Here, the believer's ultimate goal is to glorify God in all things (1 Corinthians 10:31; cf. 2 Corinthians 5:9; Colossians 1:10). Toward that ultimate end, intermediate objectives are established. They include ministering to others ("serving one another"; cf. 1 Corinthians 10:23; Romans 14:19), and fulfilling God-given responsibilities ("as good stewards"; cf. Ephesians 5:22-6:9; Galatians 6:9-10).

Other important assignments given elsewhere include evangelization of lost people (1 Corinthians 10:31-33; 2 Peter 3:9), and production of spiritual fruit and good works (John 15:8; 1 Corinthians 6:12; Ephesians 2:10; Colossians 1:10).

Such directives plainly state God's moral will for our lives. When the Christian adopts those imperatives as his own personal goals, he has concrete guidance that is applicable even to situations that may not be directly addressed by Scripture. When considering an opportunity, for instance, the believer can often clarify his options with this evaluation question: If I take this opportunity, will it help or hinder me in accomplishing my goals? Similarly, a choice between two or more options should raise the question: Which choice will maximize the fulfillment of my objectives?

A second category of life in which we receive guidance from God's revealed moral will is that of *attitudes.* Scriptural exhortations appealing for God-honoring attitudes are legion. The chart below represents only a portion of these directives, and is offered as a "pump-primer" for the reader's own personal study.

God's Will for Our Attitudes		
Is...	**Not...**	**Key Passages**
Love	Lust	Mark 12:28-31; Romans 14:13-19; 1 Corinthians 13:1-3 Romans 13:14
Reliance	Independence	Proverbs 3:5-6; Galatians 5:16;
Humility	Pride	James 4:6; Philippians 2:5-8
Gratitude	Presumption	Colossians 3:17
Clear Conscience	Guilt	Romans 14:22-23
Integrity	Irresponsibility	Colossians 3:17, 22
Diligence	Laziness	Colossians 3:23
Eagerness	Compulsion	1 Peter 5:2
Generosity	Selfishness	1 Timothy 6:17-19
Submission	Self-advancement	1 Peter 5:5-6
Courage	Cowardice	John 16:33; Matthew 10:26-28
Contentment	Greed	Hebrews 13:5; Philippians 4:11

Figure 20

A third area that is governed by God's moral will is the *means* Christians use to accomplish their goals. Most nonmoral decisions that people make, and most questions about decision making and the will of God, actually concern means to ends. For very few of our activities are done for their own sake. They are part of an overall process by which we strive to fulfill our plans. In that sense, such disparate choices as which shoes to put on and which person to marry are means-related decisions. Both have to do with the fulfillment of personal objectives.

The moral will of God for appropriate means for our goals may be summed up in two broad principles: First, our means must be biblically *lawful*—that is, they may not be outside of the revealed moral will of God (cf. Ephesians 5:1-14); second, our means must be *wise*—that is, the believer may not make a decision he knows to be foolish (Ephesians 5:15-17; cf. Luke 14:28-32). These principles will be developed further in subsequent chapters.

The moral will of God is *fully revealed in the Bible,* and is our final and complete authority for faith and practice (2 Timothy 3:16-17; Hebrews 1:1-2). It was authoritative for Jesus Christ (Matthew 4:4-10; 5:18; 22:29), and His apostles (2 Peter 1:19-21).

Since it expresses God's own character, touches every aspect and moment of life, and contains God's complete revelation pertaining to faith and life, the Bible is *able to equip believers for every good work.* This is explicitly stated by the apostle Paul:

> All Scripture is inspired by God and profitable for teaching, for reproof, for correction, for training in righteousness; that the man of God may be adequate, equipped for every good work (2 Timothy 3:16-17).

By contrast, human traditions do not have this authority and often divert people away from God's moral will by encouraging a violation of it (Matthew 15:1-6; Colossians 2:8, 16-23).

The Nature of God's Moral Will

- It is the expression, in behavioral terms, of God's character
- It touches every aspect and moment of life: goals, attitudes, and means (why, how, and what).
- It is fully revealed in the Bible.
- It is able to equip believers for every good work.

Figure 21

The Most Important Decision

It is the moral will of God that each person believes on Christ and has eternal life. It is possible that your genuine interest in spiritual things has caused you to read this book, but you are not certain of eternal life. Believing in God's existence is not enough. Heart trust in Christ is all that is needed. The difference is like that of believing in doctors over against trusting your doctor in major surgery. The first is commendable, the second is lifesaving.

God does not have a low self-image which needs a boost from a lot of people affirming that He exists. God's existence will not be altered by the percent of Americans who believe or disbelieve in His existence. The issue is man's sin. God's holiness has been violated, and the just penalty is God's wrath. God's love has not ignored His holiness, but satisfied it by paying the price of sin. The price was death, and the perfect Christ paid it in full. As a result of Christ's sacrifice, God can offer forgiveness and eternal life as a gift — a gift purchased with a precious price. It is God's moral desire that all men accept this gift.

> This is good and acceptable in the sight of God our Savior, who desires all men to be saved and to come to the knowledge of the truth. For there is one God, and one mediator also between God and men, the man Christ Jesus, who gave Himself as a ransom for all,... (1 Timothy 2:3-6).

In fact, God's judgment against sin has been "postponed" so that all men will have time to respond.

> The Lord is not slow about His promise, as some count slowness, but is patient toward you, not wishing for any to perish but for all to come to repentance. But the day of the Lord will come...(2 Peter 3:9-10).

No excuse for rejecting Christ is excusable. A pastor friend of mine likes to put it this way, "If you refuse Christ, be sure that you have a real good excuse thought up, because it's the excuse you will give when you stand before God on judgment day." It is the moral will of God that men trust Christ. It is the sovereign will of God that those who do will certainly have eternal life.

> For this is the will of My Father, that everyone who beholds the Son and believes in Him, may have eternal life; and I Myself will raise him up on the last day (John 6:40).

THE BELIEVER'S RESPONSE TO GOD'S MORAL WILL

The moral will of God has been well illustrated as the area enclosed by a circle. The interior of the circle contains all commands and principles which are morally binding upon the believer.

Any thought, attitude, or action that conforms to the scriptural imperatives is acceptable and pleasing to God. But any thought, attitude, or action that falls outside of that circle is sin (1 John 3:4). Thus, it is of supreme importance that the believer learns where the perimeter of that circle runs. Jesus told His disciples, " 'If you know these things, you are blessed if you do them' " (John 13:17). The blessing of obedience is impossible apart from fulfillment of the first "if" — "if you *know* these things."

Accordingly, the Christian's first responsibility is to *gain a good understanding* of what is included within God's moral will. The source of such knowledge, as we have emphasized, is God's Word. The process for gaining such an understanding includes reading (1 Timothy 4:13), careful consideration (2 Timothy 2:7), search and inquiry (1 Peter 1:10-11), diligence in study (2 Timothy 2:15), meditation (Psalm 1:2; Joshua 1:8), memorization (Psalm 119:11), and learning from gifted Bible teachers in oral and written form (Philippians 4:9; 1 Corinthians 12:28-29; Galatians 6:6). This process obviously requires time and effort! Furthermore, the Bible student should strive to progress in his understanding, moving on from the "milk" of God's truth (as is appropriate for infants) to the "meat" of the Word (which is enjoyed only by the more mature) (1 Corinthians 3:1-4; Hebrews 5:12-14).

The believer can expect that God will be at work within him to give understanding as he studies. Paul exhorted Timothy, "Consider what I say, for the Lord will give you understanding in everything" (2 Timothy 2:7). The Holy Spirit of truth does not work apart from our diligent study of the Bible to illuminate its meaning, but rather works through it.

Your Wish Is My Command

As the Christian grows in his understanding of God's moral will, he must also *grow in his obedience* of it. Such obedience is one of the most important responsibilities believers have during this life. In the early years of the church, there was a great debate over whether a Gentile believer should become circumcised or remain uncircumcised. In the minds of many, it was an earthshaking issue. But the apostle Paul wrote: "Circumcision is nothing, and uncircumcision is nothing, but *what matters is the keeping of the commandments of God*" (1 Corinthians 7:19).

Such obedience has always been of paramount importance to God's people. Moses summarized the whole point of propositional revelation with this statement:

"And now, Israel, what does the LORD your God require from you, but to fear the LORD your God, to walk in all His ways and love Him, and to serve the LORD your God with all your heart and with all your soul, and to keep the LORD's commandments and His statutes which I am commanding you today for your good?" (Deuteronomy 10:12-13)

In this declaration, Moses stated a theme that is reiterated again and again throughout Scripture: Whatever outward response one makes to God's declared will must be a genuine expression of the heart to be acceptable to God (1 Samuel 16:7; Mark 12:28-31). Just as God's moral will addresses the inner man at the level of his goals and attitudes, so the believer's obedience is to be an activity of the soul as well as the body. Consequently, it is the spirit of the Law, not the letter, that is of supreme importance to God. And so it should be for the believer.

You Can't Know the Players Without...

The keeping of the moral will of God is so significant that believers are distinguished from unbelievers on the basis of their response to God's commands. Jesus said that those who do the moral will of God will enter the kingdom of heaven; while those who do not, will not (Matthew 7:21; 21:31). Using different terms, Christ said that those who obey God's will are part of His spiritual family (Matthew 12:50).

In his first epistle, the apostle John made a vivid contrast:

Do not love the world, nor the things in the world. If anyone loves the world, the love of the Father is not in him. For all that is in the world, the lust of the flesh and the lust of the eyes and the boastful pride of life, is not from the Father, but is from the world. And the world is passing away, and also its lusts; but the *one who does the will of God abides forever* (1 John 2:15-17).

John expected that the one born of God will give evidence that he is a new creature with overall obedience to the moral will of God as a pattern of life. Throughout the epistle, he specified what will characterize such a life style: keeping the commands of God (2:3-6), a life of love (4:7-8), and belief in true doctrine (2:21-23; 4:1-3; 5:1). Such distinctives are not the basis for one's salvation, but are rather the *evidence* of it. We are saved by grace through faith (Ephesians 2:8-9), but genuine saving faith can never be separated from good works which follow from it (Acts 26:20; Ephesians 2:10; James 2:14-26). Obedience to the moral will of God is of supreme value. It is not optional.

Significantly, it is that very obedience which is the key ingredient in successful living. When Joshua was commissioned by God to lead the nation of Israel into the Promised Land after the death of Moses, he was given this divine prescription for success:

> This book of the law shall not depart from your mouth,
> but you shall meditate on it day and night, so that you
> may be careful to do according to all that is written in it;
> for then you will make your way prosperous, and then
> you will have success (Joshua 1:8).

The promise made to Joshua was declared to be a universal principle, applicable to all of God's people, by the psalmist:

> How blessed is the man who does not walk in the counsel
>   of the wicked,
> Nor stand in the path of sinners,
> Nor sit in the seat of scoffers!
> But his delight is in the law of the LORD,
> And in His law he meditates day and night.
> And he will be like a tree firmly planted by streams of
>   water,
> Which yields its fruit in its season,
> And its leaf does not wither;
> And in whatever he does, he prospers (Psalm 1:1-3).

Certainly Moses reflected this same understanding when he told Israel that God's commandments were "for your good" (Deuteronomy 10:13), and the apostle John affirmed from experience the beneficial nature of God's moral will when he wrote:

"For this is the love of God, that we keep His commandments; and His commandments are not burdensome" (1 John 5:3).

Eat, Drink, and Be Mature

The importance and value of obeying God's will received equal emphasis in the teaching of our Lord. Early in His public ministry, Jesus used two elements that are basic to physical life, food and water, to instruct a thirsty woman and hungry disciples about spiritual necessities. To the woman at the well, He offered the ultimate thirst-quencher: His salvation, which would cover her sins and supply the dynamic gift of eternal life (John 4:10, 13-14). The disciples, on the other hand, had already been satisfied at Christ's salvation-fountain. To them He explained that the purpose of believers is to do the moral will of God. Furthermore, such service has the same nourishing effect on the soul that eating does for the body. Jesus said, " 'My food is to do the will of Him who sent Me, and to accomplish His work' " (John 4:34).

Do you desire the spiritual success described in Joshua 1:8 and Psalm 1:2-3? Is your greatest goal in life to please the heart of God? If you are His child through faith in Jesus Christ, the process is clear: Learn, love, and obey the moral will of God. If you read only this far in this book, you will know how to become a person like King David, of whom God said, " 'I have found David the son of Jesse, a man after My heart, who will do all My will' " (Acts 13:22).

How did this "man after God's heart" regard God's moral will? Reflect on these words of David. For when you perceive and respond to God's Word as David did, your life, too, will be pleasing to God.

The law of the LORD is perfect, restoring the soul;
The testimony of the LORD is sure, making wise the simple.

The precepts of the LORD are right, rejoicing the heart;
The commandment of the LORD is pure, enlightening the eyes.

The fear of the LORD is clean, enduring forever;
The judgments of the LORD are true; they are righteous altogether.

They are more desirable than gold, yes, than much fine
  gold;
Sweeter also than honey and the drippings of the
  honeycomb.

Moreover, by them Thy servant is warned;
In keeping them there is great reward.

Psalm 19:7-11

Principles of Decision Making
The Way of Wisdom

1. In those areas specifically addressed by the Bible, the revealed commands and principles of God (His moral will) are to be obeyed.

Notes

1. John Murray, *The Epistle to the Romans,* New International Commentary on the New Testament (Grand Rapids: Wm. B. Eerdmans Publishing Co., 1959), 2:82; Charles Hodge, *A Commentary on Romans* (Carlisle, Pa.: The Banner of Truth Trust, 1972), p. 61.

Chapter 10

Free to Choose

"THE FIRST SUPPER"
(WITH APOLOGIES TO MOSES BEN AMRAM)*

*A*dam was hungry. He had had a long, challenging day naming animals. His afternoon nap had been refreshing, and his post-siesta introduction to Eve was exhilarating, to say the least. But as the sun began to set on their first day, Adam discovered that he had worked up an appetite.

"I think we should eat," he said to Eve. "Let's call the evening meal 'supper.'"

"Oh, you're so decisive, Adam," replied Eve admiringly. "I like that in a man. And 'supper' has a nice ring to it. I guess all the excitement of being created has made me hungry, too."

As they discussed how they should proceed, they decided that Adam would gather fruit from the garden, and Eve would prepare it for their meal. Adam set about his task and soon returned with a basket full of ripe fruit. He gave it to Eve, and went to soak his feet in the soothing current of the Pishon River until supper was ready. He had been reviewing the animals' names for about five minutes when he heard his wife's troubled voice.

"Adam, could you help me for a moment?"

"What seems to be the problem, dear?" he replied.

"I'm not sure which of these lovely fruits I should prepare for supper. I've prayed for guidance from the Lord, but I'm not really

---

*The narrator of the original Garden account

sure what He wants me to do. I certainly don't want to miss His will on my very first decision. Would you go to the Lord and ask Him what I should do about supper?"

Adam's hunger was intensifying, but he understood Eve's dilemma. So he left her to go speak with the Lord. Shortly, he returned. He appeared perplexed.

"Well?" probed Eve.

"He didn't really answer your question," he answered.

"What do you mean? Didn't He say anything?"

"Oh yes," replied Adam. "But He just repeated what He said earlier today during the garden tour: 'From any tree of the garden you may eat freely; but from the tree of the knowledge of good and evil you shall not eat.' I assure you, Eve, I steered clear of the forbidden tree."

"But that doesn't solve my problem," said Eve. "What should I prepare for tonight?"

From the rumbling in his stomach, Adam was discovering that lions and tigers are not the only things that growl. So he said, "I've never seen such crisp, juicy apples. I feel a sense of peace about them. Why don't you prepare them for supper? Maybe while you're getting them ready, you'll experience the same peace I have."

"All right, Adam," she agreed. "I guess you've had more experience at making decisions than I have. I appreciate your leadership. I'll call you when supper is ready."

"OK," replied Adam, relieved. "I'll get back to my easy-bank."

Adam was only halfway to the river when he heard Eve's call. He was so hungry that he jogged back to the clearing where she was working. But his anticipation evaporated when he saw her face.

"More problems?" he asked.

"Adam, I just can't decide what I should do with these apples. I could slice them, dice them, mash them, bake them in a pie, a cobbler, fritters, or dumplings. Or we could just polish them and eat them raw. I really want to be your helper, but I also want to be certain of the Lord's will on this decision. Would you be a dear and go just one more time to the Lord with my problem?"

Since he didn't have any better solution himself, Adam did as Eve requested. When he returned, he said, "I got the same answer as before: 'From *any* tree of the garden you may eat *freely;* but from the tree of the knowledge of good and evil you shall not eat.' "

Adam and Eve were both silent for a moment. Then Adam said, "You know, Eve, the Lord made that statement as though it ought to fully answer my question. I'm sure He could have told me what to eat and how to eat it; but I think He wants us to make those decisions. It was the same way with the animals today. He just left their names up to me."

Eve was incredulous. "Do you mean that it doesn't matter which of these fruits we have for supper? Are you telling me that I *can't* miss God's will in this decision?"

Adam explained: "The only way you could do that is to pick some fruit from the forbidden tree. But all of these fruits are all right. Why, I suppose we could eat all of them." Adam snapped his fingers and exclaimed, "Say, that's a great idea! Let's have fruit salad for supper!"

Eve hesitated. "What's a salad?"

THE PRINCIPLE OF FREEDOM AND THE NATURE OF LAWS

The principle of freedom of choice within revealed limits was clearly part of the Creator's design from the very beginning. And it is a principle that continues to be applied routinely in everyday situations. For instance, on public beaches it is not uncommon to find posted regulations for swimmers. These signs inform everyone of the restrictions that must be observed for the sake of safety. Each swimmer rightly assumes that he may do anything else not forbidden. He may build a sand castle, fill a pail with water, splash a friend, float on his back, do the sidestroke, and so on. He does not have to ask the lifeguard for permission to do things that are not on the list. Freedom of activity within the declared limits is assumed by all.

Before You Ask, the Answer is "Yes"

As a teacher, I frequently prepare assignments for my students. Most of the time, my directions assume a freedom of choice, which I then regulate and restrict. For instance, my instructions for a written research paper might include these directions: This paper must deal with one of the topics listed on the syllabus; it must be typed, double-spaced, and be eight to ten pages long.

Such an assignment both assumes and restricts freedom. I must present it this way or it would take reams of paper to explain a single assignment! The student who does not realize that he is given freedom of choice in areas not addressed by the instructions often asks unnecessary questions: "May we use erasable paper? May I do my paper on the fifth topic listed on the syllabus? May I use outside sources from the public library? Is it alright to number each page in the upper right-hand corner?" The potential questions not directly answered by the instructions are innumerable. Simplicity and conciseness demand that I assume an area of freedom and then restrict and regulate that freedom where I think necessary. It is as if I were saying, "You may do anything you want on this paper, with these restrictions..."

What these two examples illustrate is that *effective* lawmaking requires the assumption of freedom of choice and activity within the designated limitations. That is not to say that the more exhaustive approach has not been tried. In fact, one of the major differences between the Mosaic Law and other legal codes of the ancient Near East is that the surrounding nations attempted to legislate all the details of life. But when the Lord God gave His Law to Israel at Sinai, rather than attempting to cover every conceivable situation that might arise, He first gave ten absolute principles that were sufficiently concise to fit on two transportable tablets of stone. Then He explained how to apply those commandments in various situations. The specific issues addressed were to serve as models of application. Consequently, in contrast to the famous Code of Hammurabi, which predates Exodus by at least 200 years, the Law of Moses is the model of simplicity and conciseness.

Historically, there have been two basic approaches to lawmaking: *casuistic law,* such as that developed by the pagan nations of the ancient Near East, and *normative law,* which governed the nation of Israel.[1] The approach taken by God to guide the people of Israel in their social, civil, and religious affairs was to give laws that both assumed and regulated freedom.

"If a Little is Good, Then..."

A similar contrast may be seen between the respective approaches of Pharisaic Judaism and Christ. By the time of Jesus' birth, Jewish life was rigidly governed by a minutely detailed body of tradition. The scribes and Pharisees had achieved the ultimate in casuistry. The requirements for "holy living" had become so complex, common people despaired of even learning them, much less observing them. "Righteousness" became the private property of the professionals.

But Jesus repudiated the Pharisaic approach to religion. He rebuked the legalists for burying the Law of God beneath a mountain of minutiae. He condemned their mentality of externalism and the attitude of self-righteousness that accompanied it (cf. Matthew 23; Luke 11). In His own teaching, Jesus focused on revealing the spirit of the Law, explaining how God had always intended the Law to be understood. In so doing, He returned to a normative approach where stated principles were illustrated by concrete examples (cf. Matthew 5-7).

One of the significant features of the Church Age was the lifting of the regulations that were appropriate to the national life of Israel and the period that anticipated the culmination of God's revelation in Christ (Acts 10:9-16; 11:1-18; 15:5-29; Romans 6:14; 7:6). More than ever before, the people of God are to govern their lives by personal application of revealed principles. Just as a wise father trains his children toward maturity by granting increased freedom and responsibility throughout their development, so God has progressively prepared His people to live responsibly within the relatively greater freedom of apostolic revelation (Galatians 4:1-7).

The point of this discussion is this: Whether God has spoken directly (as to Adam), through His prophets, through His Son, or through His apostles, His approach has been uniform. He has given laws which reveal His moral will. And those laws assume freedom of choice within the stated limitations. In fact, as revelation has become more complete, the areas of freedom and responsibility have grown.

If a Horse and Chariot Were Good Enough for David...

Proper understanding of the nature of laws can serve as a corrective to a common error in decision making. There are sincere Christians who refuse to participate in certain activities or utilize any human inventions unless they can find some specific warrant in the Bible. Of course, the Bible says nothing about eyeglasses, padded pews, pipe organs, electric appliances, automobiles, or any number of things devised since the first century. And so these saints are obliged to either deny themselves any of the products of human progress, or seek for veiled biblical allusions to such things by which permission for their use may be obtained.

Accordingly, Dr. Francis Schaeffer concludes his chapter on "Form and Freedom in the Church" with this observation:

> It is my thesis that as we cannot bind men morally except with that which the Scripture clearly commands (beyond that we can only give advice), similarly, *anything the New Testament does not command in regard to church form is a freedom to be exercised under the leadership of the Holy Spirit for that particular time and place.*[2]

Then, in a footnote, he adds:

> It seems clear to me that the opposite cannot be held, namely that only that which is commanded is allowed. If this were the case, then, for example, to have a church building would be wrong and so would having church bells or a pulpit, using books for singing, following any specific order of service, standing to sing, and many other like things. If consistently held in practice, I doubt if any church could function or worship.[3]

THE PRINCIPLE OF FREEDOM AND THE NATURE OF SIN

Biblical explanations of the nature of sin support the concept of freedom of choice within revealed limitations from a second perspective. Sin is defined as breaking God's law: "Everyone who practices sin also practices lawlessness; and sin is lawlessness" (1 John 3:4). The reverse is also true: "where there is no law, neither is there violation" (Rom. 4:15). As a result, the only way a person can sin against God in a decision is to break one of God's laws—i.e., make a decision outside of the moral will of God. As we have seen, such an offense could involve a wrong purpose or attitude, as well as a wrong action.

However, if a particular decision is not addressed by God's commands, and one's goals and attitudes are right, then one cannot sin with regard to the decision in itself. For instance, the Bible says nothing about where a student ought to go to college. So that student's choice of a school cannot in itself be sinful. If no biblical principles are violated in the process, such a decision lies within the area of moral freedom.

Nevertheless, some Christians experience feelings of guilt after making a decision that is not specifically addressed by Scripture. Why? They fear that they have missed God's individual will. In the absence of clear leading, they went ahead and made a choice. Now they feel guilty because they are not certain they have done what God wanted them to do. For some, the feelings are compounded by the belief that failure to perceive God's guidance is an indication of spiritual insensitivity or carnality. So they feel guilty on two counts: blocking out God's signals, and possibly missing His will.

Such guilt is not intended by God. If His moral will has not been violated, there has been no sin. If there has been no sin, there should be no guilt. It's as simple, and profound, as that. In decisions where God's law does not restrict, the believer has moral freedom to decide. Where there is no moral law, there can be no moral sin. Where there is no moral law, there is moral freedom to decide.

Relief is Spelled F-R-E-E-D-O-M

It may interest the reader to know that the most common response to the teaching of this chapter has been one of relief. As the truth of the principle of freedom within the moral will of God has sunk in, many have experienced a sense of release, as though they were being set free from some kind of burden. The reason is not hard to understand. An automatic tension develops when one's experience does not conform to one's beliefs. (We have already seen that there are several points at which the traditional view breaks down in practice.) If the stress is great enough, the individual is motivated to scrutinize the two potential causes of the tension: either his beliefs are erroneous, or his practice is faulty. If, after further investigation, he remains convinced of the truth of his belief, the only remaining possibility is that there is something wrong with the way he is living it out. But if he cannot further identify the specific problem in his life, he is forced to just live with unresolved tension.

To complicate matters further, the Christian has to also contend with a hostile outside agent. Our archenemy, Satan, is "the accuser of our brethren" (Revelation 12:10). He knows that unresolved guilt is a great incapacitator. In some ways, false guilt is more effective for his purposes than appropriate guilt because it is harder to identify and dispel. There can be no doubt that he preys upon ignorance and confusion to compound the frustrations of believers, thereby reducing their effectiveness in the spiritual warfare.

A sense of release is experienced by those sincere believers who recognize that their floating guilt feelings are not God's conviction. The inner turmoil can end when the God-given area of freedom within the moral will is recognized. This then eliminates false guilt and answers the slanderous accusations of our enemy. The God-breathed revelation of Scripture is indeed "profitable. . . for correction" (2 Timothy 3:16).

THE PRINCIPLE OF FREEDOM IN DIRECT STATEMENTS OF SCRIPTURE

That being so, it is appropriate to conclude by adding to our arguments from the nature of laws and the nature of sin the clinching evidence for this principle: namely, specific statements of Scripture. For there are numerous instances in which the freedom that is always assumed is actually declared.

"The First Supper" Revisited
The first case in point is the very first command given by God to a man:

> And the LORD God commanded the man, saying, "From any tree of the garden you may eat freely; but from the tree of the knowledge of good and evil you shall not eat, for in the day that you eat from it you shall surely die" (Genesis 2:16-17).

This first direct commandment conforms perfectly to God's original design for mankind. For when God created man, He made him in His own image (Genesis 1:26-27). That image accounts for man's great value to God and distinguishes human beings from all other earthly creatures. Only man was outfitted with the determinative features of personality: intellect, emotion, and will. Only man was assigned a position of responsibility requiring the exercise of those attributes of the soul. If man were to make his decisions as a function of instinct, he would be no different from the animals. If he required direct input from the Creator for every choice, he would be no more than a manipulated robot. By God's design, only the image-bearer approaches decisions *in the same manner as the Creator.* Within boundaries prescribed by God's own character, man analyzes, evaluates, judges, and freely determines his choices. Only man was given the competence to make free judgments. And only man was given the dignity of bearing full responsibility for the consequences of his choices.[4]

It is a demonstration of God's goodness that He *began* His first commandment with a declaration of the extent of Adam's *freedom* of choice: "From *any* tree of the garden you may eat *freely."* Then He added the single restriction with a clear explanation of the consequence of violation.

In this very first commandment, the freedom which was thereafter assumed was clearly stated, revealing God's graciousness and refuting in advance Satan's allegation that God is a tyrant (Genesis 3:1-5).

The introduction of sin into human nature and experience did not require that the principle of freedom within revealed limits be revoked. It did require a more extensive revelation of God's moral will and character. For the fallen heart is deceitful (Jeremiah 17:9), and man's nature is now oriented away from God rather than toward Him (Romans 8:7-8). And so the area of freedom became more restricted as the limits of God's will were spelled out.

Nevertheless, as was noted above, the principle of freedom remained in force as a distinctive feature of the Mosaic Law. Examples abound. In Leviticus 11 and Deuteronomy 14, very definite limits were placed upon which animals could be eaten by the Israelites and which ones were forbidden. "Unclean" animals were outside the circle of God's moral will for Israel. But from among the "clean" animals, the Hebrews could freely choose: " 'These are the creatures which you may eat from all the animals that are on the earth' " (Leviticus 11:2). There was moral freedom of choice as long as they were selecting from the approved menu.

The Nazirite vow (Numbers 6) was given to Israel as a special means of personal consecration. If a person made such a vow, he obligated himself to fulfill the terms of his commitment—terms that were clearly explained. But the decision to take such a vow was strictly voluntary. The man who took the vow and the man who chose not to take it were equally within God's moral will.

The Required Freewill Offering?

The same was true of the freewill offering (Leviticus 22:18). A man could ask, "Is it God's will for me to give a freewill offering today?" But if God answered, the gift would no longer be freewill! No, God wanted to give His people some ways that they could express their devotion to Him in voluntary displays of love. So He provided the option of the freewill offering, and explained what sacrifices would be acceptable for such purposes (Leviticus 22:18-25). Even that instruction delineated freedom within limits. For while the animal chosen for the burnt offering had to be a male without defect, it could be a bull, a ram, or a goat.

The Levite who wished to leave his hometown to work in the service of the temple could come *whenever* he desired and receive work (Deuteronomy 18:6-7).

The vow was another action which was acceptable to God but not required. It was a valid expression of worship to be offered voluntarily.

> "When you make a vow to the LORD your God, you shall not delay to pay it, for it would be sin in you, and the LORD your God will surely require it of you. However, if you refrain from vowing, it would not be sin in you. You shall be careful to perform what goes out from your lips, just as you have *voluntarily* vowed to the LORD your God, what you have promised" (Deuteronomy 23:21-23).

This particular expression of promise to God was left to the free choice of the believer, but once a vow was made the moral will of God required that it be kept (Ecclesiastes 5:4-5; Psalm 50:14; Nahum 1:15; Numbers 30:2). The vow was an example of a decision regulated by the moral will of God, but not determined by it.

The slave described in Deuteronomy 23:15-16 was free to live "'in the place which he shall choose in one of your towns where it pleases him.'" This freedom was assumed for everyone else. But it had to be spelled out in the case of the former slave. The text does not imply that only unbound slaves were free to choose where they wanted to live, while all others had to discover God's individual will for their lives. The point was that the former slave was free to live where he wanted—just like everyone else.

When we come to the gospels, Jesus' parable of "The Laborers in the Vineyard" (Matthew 20:1-16) serves to illustrate the principle of freedom of choice within God's moral will. Jesus told of a landowner who hired workers for his vineyard at different times during the day. At day's end, each worker was paid a full day's wage. This upset the laborers who had worked all day. They felt that since they had worked longer than the others they should be paid more. But the landowner said to one of them:

> "Friend, I am doing you no wrong; did you not agree with me for a denarius? Take what is yours and go your way, but I wish to give to this last man the same as to you. Is it not lawful for me to do what I wish with what is my own? Or is your eye envious because I am generous?" (Matthew 20:13-15).

This parable illustrates how God deals generously with all who enter the kingdom of God and receive eternal life in equal measure. It is clear that the landowner represents God. It is equally clear that what He did was not only just but more than just. There is no law against generosity! The landowner was obligated by the moral will of God to pay a fair wage. But he was free to pay more than fair wage if he chose to do so. The point of the parable hinges on the interpretation that what the landowner did was proper.

Freedom Inflation

Perhaps at this point it would be appropriate to entertain the question that might occur to some who are familiar with the traditional view. Might there not be a distinction between Old Testament saints and New Testament saints with respect to decision-making processes?

When we read New Testament passages related to decision making, we find that there is a continuity with what we found in the Old Testament. The principle of freedom remains in force; but the areas of freedom are much broader. Again, the examples are abundant. We will consider the matters of eating, circumcision, and giving.

The subject of food, which was so important in the Garden of Eden as well as in Israel, reappeared as a topic of discussion in the early Church. There were essentially two questions that arose in the predominantly Gentile churches: Is it permissible for Christians to eat meat (as opposed to vegetarianism, Romans 14:2), and is it permissible for Christians to eat meat that may have previously been offered to pagan idols (1 Corinthians 8:1)? The apostle Paul addressed both of these questions.

First, Paul dealt with how the issue of eating meat (or meat offered to idols) should be classified. Was this an issue about which God had given a direct command? No. Therefore, the decision to eat meat or abstain from eating fell within the area of moral freedom: "But food will not commend us to God; we are neither the worse if we do not eat, nor the better if we do eat" (1 Corinthians 8:8). One cannot choose wrongly concerning eating in itself. It is not a moral issue.

Paul used a variety of statements which underscore this freedom of choice. Eating, he said, was a "lawful" thing (1 Corinthians 10:23), a "right" (1 Corinthians 9:4), and a "liberty" or "freedom" (1 Corinthians 8:9; 10:29). In itself it was not an issue of conscience (1 Corinthians 10:25).

You are Cordially Required to Attend

The apostle then applied this principle to a specific situation. What should a Christian do if he is invited to supper by an unbeliever? And what should he do if he suspects that the main course is "idol meat"? Paul does *not* say: "If any unbeliever invites you over for dinner, pray about it and determine whether it is God's will for you to go. When you are sure what the Lord wants you to do, then answer the invitation following God's leading." Rather, Paul *does* say: "If one of the unbelievers invites you, and *you wish to go, eat anything* that is set before you, without asking questions for conscience' sake" (1 Corinthians 10:27). The believer is free to accept or decline the invitation according to his desire. If he goes to dinner, he is free to eat anything served at the meal. He is not to probe the meal's pedigree or recent history for the sake of his conscience (1 Corinthians 10:29). Since there is no moral issue involved with the eating of meat in itself, the Christian is given the prerogative of choice.[5]

One of the hottest debates in the earliest years of the Church concerned the issue of circumcision: Was it required of converts to Christianity or not (Acts 15)? In the Old Testament, it had been the sign of God's covenant with the people of Israel. Beginning with

Abraham, it was the outward sign of faith in the covenant (Genesis 17; Romans 4:11). But at the Jerusalem Council, it was determined that since salvation came through faith in Jesus Christ, circumcision was no longer a condition of the covenant relationship with God. Accordingly, when Paul addressed the issue for the Corinthian church, he observed: "Circumcision is nothing, and uncircumcision is nothing, but what matters is the keeping of the commandments of God" (1 Corinthians 7:19). Circumcision was no longer a moral question. It just didn't matter what a man might choose for himself (Galatians 5:6; 6:15).

I Already Gave at the Office

When an opportunity is presented to give money to some aspect of the Lord's work, or when a Christian brother is in financial need, how should the believer determine how much money to contribute to the offering that is being received? Should he go to the Lord in prayer and request a divine impression indicating a specific amount?

When the Corinthian Christians were gathering funds to send to their impoverished brethren in Judea, the instruction they received from the apostle Paul was: "Let each one do *just as he has purposed in his heart;* not grudgingly or under compulsion; for God loves a cheerful giver" (2 Corinthians 9:7). Here is freedom of choice within the moral will of God. In this case, the emphasis of the moral will was not so much on the *act* of giving as it was on the *attitude.* Consequently, the amount, which is left totally up to the individual to determine, is not as significant as the spirit of the giver. What is God's will for our giving? Generosity, enthusiasm, and faith are imperative; a reluctant spirit that forks over money only under pressure is forbidden. The actual amount is a personal decision, freely made.[6]

The question of whether to marry and whom to marry constitutes a major decision that will alter more practical aspects of daily life than any decision short of salvation. The New Testament gives no clue that God's individual will determines these decisions. Rather, when these subjects are touched, the area of freedom allowed by God includes both whether to marry and whom to marry (1 Corinthians 7). Marriage in fact is probably the classic example of the principle of freedom within the moral will of God.

Two entire chapters will be dedicated to a close look at decision making and marriage in Part 4, chapters 17 and 18.

To sum up: The reader will recall that the distinctive element of the traditional view is the individual will of God. It is often visualized as a "dot" in the center of God's will. The key to decision making in the traditional approach is to "find the dot"—discover God's individual will for that decision.

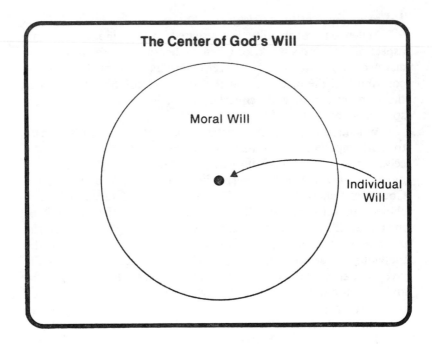

By the way of contrast, Scripture indicates that the dot should be replaced by an area of freedom where genuine opportunity of choice is granted to the believer.

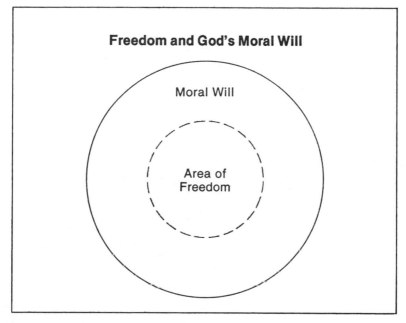

Figure 22

For God's children, all things within the moral will of God are lawful (1 Corinthians 6:12; 10:23), clean (Mark 7:19; Luke 11:41; Romans 14:14, 20), and pure (Titus 1:15). In decisions that are made within that moral will, the Christian should not feel guilty about his choice; neither should he fear that his decision is unacceptable to God. God has made it clear what He wants: His plan for His children is for them to enjoy the freedom that He has granted. It is a freedom that is clearly established in Scripture from the nature of laws, the nature of sin, and direct statements of the Bible.

Principles of Decision Making
The Way of Wisdom

1. In those areas specifically addressed by the Bible, the revealed commands and principles of God (His moral will) are to be obeyed.

2. **In those areas where the Bible gives no command or principle (nonmoral decisions), the believer is free and responsible to choose his own course of action. Any decision made within the moral will of God is acceptable to God.**

Notes

1. The simplicity represented in Israel's law is often described as apodictic (normative) legislation in contrast to casuistic legislation which is characterized by exhaustive detail. See William Dyrness, *Themes in Old Testament Theology* (Downers Grove, Ill.: InterVarsity Press, 1979), pp. 132,138-39; R. Alan Cole, *Exodus: An Introduction and Commentary*, Tyndale Old Testament Commentaries (Downers Grove, Ill.: InterVarsity Press, 1973), pp. 149-50; John J. Davis, *Moses and the Gods of Egypt* (Grand Rapids: Baker Book House, 1971), p. 196.

2. Francis A. Schaeffer, *The Church at the End of the Twentieth Century* (Downers Grove, Ill.: InterVarsity Press, 1970), p. 67.

3. Ibid.

4. John White, *The Cost of Commitment* (Downers Grove, Ill.: InterVarsity Press, 1976), p. 8.

5. The subject of eating meat, or eating meat offered to idols, and the central passages (Romans 14-15; 1 Corinthians 8-10) are developed in greater detail in chapter 23, "Wisdom When Christians Differ."

6. The subject of giving and the central passage (2 Corinthians 8-9) are developed in greater detail in chapter 22, "Giving and Wisdom."

Chapter 11

Competent to Choose

*I*t was observed earlier that the most common response to the teaching on freedom within God's moral will is a sense of release or relief. But that is only the primary response. For every conscientious Christian is fully aware that freedom brings responsibility. Put differently, if the believer is free to choose, he is also *required* to choose. If there is no divinely-determined "right" choice that the Christian must find in order to make a decision, then it follows that he may not shift the responsibility for the decision or its consequences onto someone else. Responsibility presupposes accountability.

It should not surprise us, then, to encounter this sober reminder given by the apostle Paul in the context of a discussion on decision making:

> Let each man be fully convinced in his own mind...For we shall all stand before the judgment seat of God...So then each one of us shall give account of himself to God (Romans 14:5,10,12).

These realities beget a single question: *On what basis is the believer to make his decisions* in nonmoral areas? That crucial question assumes that if God has granted the privilege of choice, and the dignity of accountability, He has also given appropriate instructions for the exercise of our responsibility. The assumption is correct.

To sharpen our perspective, let's reflect once again on the approach taken on such choices by the *traditional* view. It is instructive to note how people commonly explain the decisions they have made. For instance, a college freshman might say, "I am really glad that I came here for my first year of college. God *showed* me that He *wanted* me here and I know that I am *exactly* where I *should* be." An engaged man might say, "Barbara and I both prayed independently about our future, and we both felt that God was *definitely telling* us to get married." A common prayer request is expressed: "Pray that I will find *God's will* concerning the *right* summer job God *wants* me to have." The announcement of a church business meeting might include this exhortation: "Pray that we will be able to *discern the Lord's mind* as to whether we should relocate." The fulfilled Christian worker testifies, "God very definitely guided us to this ministry and we are enjoying the blessings of living in the *very center of His will.*" A pastorless church will often pray, "Lord, help us to recognize the man you have *called* to be our pastor."

Such terminology reflects the conviction that the key to making the "right" decision is discernment of God's ideal plan. What is so striking, as one searches the pages of the New Testament, is the glaring absence of such expressions. The apostles often explained the reasons for their decisions, but they never gave the kind of explanations cited above. What they did say reflects a much different mentality. Thankfully, the Spirit of God saw fit to include such mundane explanations by the apostles in the canon of the inspired text. For the pattern that they established in practice has become one of the most fruitful sources of insight into principles of decision making.

APOSTOLIC EXAMPLES

The Thessalonian Connection

On his second missionary journey, Paul founded a church in Thessalonica, but was driven out by jealous Jews (Acts 17:1-8). Paul went on to Berea, but was pursued by the Thessalonian Jews who forced him out of that town as well (Acts 17:10-15). So Paul moved on to Athens, and the Jews went back home.

Being mindful of the certainty that the believers in Thessalonica would be tested by persecution (1 Thessalonians 3:4) without benefit of experienced leadership (1 Thessalonians 3:5), Paul, Silas, and Timothy agreed on a plan whereby the church could be encouraged and strengthened:

> Therefore when we could endure it no longer, *we thought it best* to be left behind at Athens alone; and we sent Timothy, our brother and God's fellow worker in the gospel of Christ, to strengthen and encourage you as to your faith" (1 Thessalonians 3:1-2).

How was their decision made? "We thought it best." It was their decision. And there were good reasons for it. They were concerned about their converts (3:1,5), so they chose a course of action whereby they could strengthen those converts' faith. As far as they could tell, sending Timothy was the *best* means to accomplish their spiritual goals.

The Case of the Homesick Minister

As Paul awaited his trial before Caesar in Rome, he enjoyed the company of a number of men, one of whom was Epaphroditus. Epaphroditus had come from Philippi bearing a love-gift from the church there to Paul (Philippians 4:10,14). In the carrying out of his mission, Epaphroditus became ill and perilously close to dying. But God preserved his life and restored his strength. So Paul decided to send him home, and gave this explanation:

> But I *thought it necessary* to send to you Epaphroditus, my brother and fellow worker and fellow soldier, who is also your messenger and minister to my need; because he was longing for you all and was distressed because you had heard that he was sick (Philippians 2:25-26).

In this decision, Paul "thought it necessary" to send Epaphroditus back to Philippi, not because he had been directly instructed by God to do so, but because of the exigencies of the situation. He stated the reasons that compelled him: He wanted to dispel the Philippians' anxiety with joy, thereby reducing his own concern for them (2:28); and Epaphroditus was anxious to get home to let everyone know that he was all right (2:26). Additionally, there were some important things that Paul wished to communicate to the Philippians in this "thank you letter." Epaphroditus would function as a messenger on his return trip as well.

On what basis did Paul make this decision? It was the best way to accomplish important spiritual goals.

Blest be the Offering that Binds

The Gentile churches of Greece, Macedonia, and Asia Minor had agreed to collect an offering to send to the Jewish believers in Judea who were in dire straits (Romans 15:25-26). For his part, Paul would put his apostolic seal on the gift by sending out the messengers with personal letters of introduction. In fact, he told the Corinthians he might even accompany the gift himself. How would he decide?

> And when I arrive, whomever you may approve, I shall send them with letters to carry your gift to Jerusalem; and *if it is fitting* for me to go also, they will go with me (1 Corinthians 16:3-4).

Would Paul join the messengers with the gift? He would "if it is fitting." What did he mean? Paul did not say. Most commentators feel that the issue was the size of the gift.[1] If it turned out to be small, such a gift would hardly warrant the apostolic presence—his letters of introduction would suffice. If, however, the gift was very substantial, it would be a tangible demonstration of the unity of Jews and Gentiles in Christ, which was a dominant theme in Paul's theology (Ephesians 2:11-22). The financial gift might also serve as a sort of down payment on the spiritual debt that the Gentiles (and Paul himself) owed to the Jewish Christians (Romans 15:27; 1 Corinthians 15:9, 1 Timothy 1:13).[2] If this analysis is correct, Paul intended to wait and see how large the gift was before making his decision. In this case, one particular unknown circumstance would be the deciding factor. There is no indication that Paul thought of it as a "fleece." He was simply calculating how to make best use of his time and energy for the Lord.

On the Care and Feeding of Widows

During the earliest days of the Church, one of the first internal problems was a complaint of discrimination against the food service. The Hellenistic Jews felt that their widows were being overlooked in the daily distribution of food (Acts 6:1). The matter was dealt with as follows:

> And the twelve summoned the congregation of the disciples and said, *"It is not desirable* for us to neglect the word of God in order to serve tables. But select from among you, brethren, seven men of good reputation, full of the Spirit and of wisdom, whom we may put in charge of this task. But we will devote ourselves to prayer, and to the ministry of the word" (Acts 6:2-4).

The plan that was adopted was designed to alleviate a situation that was "not desirable." The apostles were being distracted from accomplishing the priorities that Christ had given to them. And so something had to be done. They analyzed the problem, reviewed their assignments, and came up with a wise, practical plan that would meet all of the relevant needs.

At no point did they stop to seek the "ideal will of God" either for the solution to the problem, or for their choice of men to carry it out. Rather, they established qualifications that were appropriate for a task that would require spiritual insight and personal sensitivity. Then they left the choice of the men to the people. The plan that was chosen was wisely formulated to give all concerned the time and opportunity to exercise their gifts and fulfill their responsibilities. Because it accomplished those objectives, it proved to be a good decision.

The Circumcision Schism

A second problem that was encountered during the early years of the Church was more serious. At stake was the doctrine of justification by grace through faith apart from works. The threat to the doctrine was presented by a Judaistic faction that was insisting that all Gentile believers must be circumcised. In essence, they were saying that Gentiles had to become Jewish proselytes before they could be saved through faith in Christ (Acts 15:1).

The issue was discussed at a council in Jerusalem. There was much debate (15:7). Peter reviewed the historical work of the Holy Spirit to bring salvation to the Gentiles through the grace of the Lord Jesus (15:7-11). Barnabas and Paul related the confirming ministry of the Holy Spirit who produced supernatural signs and wonders through them as they preached the gospel to the Gentiles (15:12). And James cited relevant Scripture passages stating that God was "taking from among the Gentiles a people for His name" (15:14-18).

By then, the solution to the issue was obvious: Circumcision was not required for salvation. The council decided to draft a letter to the Gentile churches declaring the judgment that had been reached. In it, the Gentile believers were asked to refrain from practices that would be especially abhorrent to their Jewish brethren. The letter was concluded as follows:

> For *it seemed good* to the Holy Spirit and to us to lay upon you no greater burden than these essentials: that you abstain from things sacrificed to idols and from blood and from things strangled and from fornication; if you keep yourselves free from such things, you will do well. Farewell (Acts 15:28-29).

The expression, "it seemed good" appears three times in Acts 15 (vv. 22, 25, 28). In the third instance only, the Holy Spirit was included as a coauthor of the decision. Does that mean that the conclusions of the council were supernaturally dictated by God? He certainly did give special guidance on other occasions in Acts. But in this case, in the absence of any direct statement to that effect, a better explanation would be that the Holy Spirit had *already given* His guidance before the council ever met. That is, He had worked through Peter to bring salvation to Gentiles apart from circumcision (15:7-11); He had miraculously confirmed the evangelistic ministry of Barnabas and Paul among the Gentiles (15:12); and He had inspired the writers of Scripture to foretell the inclusion of Gentiles among the people of God (15:15-18). For these reasons, the church leaders could write that their decision "seemed good" to the Holy Spirit as well as to them.

The decision of the Jerusalem Council was not the result of discovering God's individual will. If they discovered anything, it was God's moral will which had already been revealed. The actual decision-making process involved debate, application of Scripture, and a determination of what "seemed good" to do. The final decision was first described as the "judgment" of James (15:19), and then of the whole group (15:22,25,28). The request that the Gentiles exercise restraint with respect to Jewish sensibilities was not the product of divine revelation, but reflected a reasonable desire to promote unity in the Church.

Evidently this decree was temporal, for when it was no longer considered relevant, it faded from use.[3] The evidence for this is Paul's later discussion of the issue in which no reference is made to this decision by the Jerusalem Council (1 Corinthians 8-10). Apparently, the decision came to be seen as the best way to deal with a specific, but temporary situation.

THE PRINCIPLE OF SPIRITUAL EXPEDIENCY

The question to which we are seeking a biblical answer is: In nonmoral areas, on what basis is the believer to make his decision? Observation of apostolic decision making has revealed that they did *not* attempt to discover God's individual will for such decisions. Their explanations for their plans are couched in phrases such as: "We thought it best," "I thought it necessary," "If it is fitting," "It is not desirable," "It seemed good," and simply "I have decided" (Titus 3:12). (Luke explained a decision Paul made with respect to an itinerary with the words, "for he was hurrying" [Acts 20:16].) Clearly these men were exercising their freedom of choice within God's moral will. But on what basis?

Perhaps the principle could be stated this way: *In nonmoral decisions, the goal of the believer is to make wise decisions on the basis of spiritual expediency.* In this statement, some definitions are important. "Spiritual" means that the ends in view, as well as the means to those ends, are governed by the moral will of God. In nonmoral decisions, as in every other aspect of life, the Christian's aim is to glorify and please God. In that sense, every goal and procedure is to be "spiritual." "Expediency" refers to the quality of being suitable or advantageous to the end in view. Put simply, it means what works best to get the job done—within God's moral will, of course. And finally, Dr. J.I. Packer's definition of "wisdom" is right on target: "Wisdom is the power to see, and the inclination to choose, the best and highest goal, together with the surest means of attaining it."[4] Wisdom is the ability to figure out what is spiritually expedient in a given situation.

It should be noted, by way of further clarification, that not all of the passages cited in this chapter make direct reference to wisdom. The verses speak of decisions that were "good," "fitting," "desirable," and so on. In each case, the descriptive term explains the reason for the decision. And in each case, the explanation was that, in the judgment of the responsible decision maker, the choice made (or the counsel given) appeared to be the best way to accomplish some worthy objective. In our effort to find the common elements in these decisions and formulate a consistent principle, we chose the word "wise" to describe the goal and character of the overall process. And Dr. Packer's definition of wisdom fits precisely with that aspect of biblical wisdom which we are considering.

APOSTOLIC EXHORTATIONS

To this point, we have illustrated the principle of spiritual expediency in the practice of the apostles, and composed a statement of that principle. The culminating proof is exhibited in the instructions given by the apostles to the Church. Are the apostles' exhortations consistent with their example? The answer is yes.

A Vacancy on the Bench

In 1 Corinthians 6, Paul declares his conviction that Christians, of all people, ought to be competent to make wise decisions:

> Does any one of you, when he has a case against his neighbor, dare to go to law before the unrighteous, and not before the saints? Or do you not know that the saints will judge the world? And if the world is judged by you, are you not *competent* to constitute the smallest law courts? Do you not know that we shall judge angels? How much more, matters of this life? If then you have law courts dealing with matters of this life, do you appoint them as judges who are of no account in the church? I say this to your shame. Is it so, that there is not among you *one wise man* who will be *able to decide* be-

tween his brethren, but brother goes to law with brother, and that before unbelievers? (1 Corinthians 6:1-6).

In this rebuke of the Corinthians, Paul was maintaining that there ought to be at least one man among them who could be trusted to make fair judgments and settle disputes. Perhaps he was thinking of King Solomon, of whom it was said, "the wisdom of God was in him to administer justice" (1 Kings 3:28). The administration of justice requires the making of decisions, some of which are moral (discernment of right and wrong, guilt and innocence), and some of which are nonmoral (such as determining the best means to execute an equitable judgment).

It is noteworthy that in the Church, there is no single King Solomon who has been uniquely endowed by God with "an understanding heart." Rather, "ordinary" Christians (such as those at Corinth!), who will one day judge the world and fallen angels, are deemed competent to judge the more mundane "matters of this life." Furthermore, those who possess a greater measure of wisdom are recognized as being able to make the better decisions.

Good, Better, Happier

Probably the classic chapter of instruction on decision making within the moral will of God is 1 Corinthians 7. In that chapter, the apostle Paul answered a number of questions related to singleness and marriage. For some of the questions, the moral will of God is determinitive. For instance, married believers are not to abstain from fulfilling their sexual responsibilities to one another (7:3-5); nor are they to get divorced (7:10-11). Other issues, however, fall within the area of freedom where the decision is left up to the individual believer. To those questions, Paul gave his *advice* (rather than command), together with reasons showing the wisdom of his counsel.

The two adjectives that most often qualify his advice are "good" and "better." Should a believer get married? There is no command from Scripture one way or the other. So how should one decide? Paul said it is "good" for a man not to touch a woman (7:1). It is "good" for the unmarried to remain single (7:8). It is "good" in view of the present distress for a man to remain in his present state (7:26). Now Paul is not speaking of "good" in contrast to "evil." He is using it in the sense of "advantageous."[5] So what would be advantageous about remaining single? Two things: First, in Paul's view, the circumstances of that period of time brought great stress upon families — pressure that would not be nearly so acute for a single person (7:26, 28); and second, single people are freer to serve the Lord without the distraction of family commitments (7:7, 32-35).

On the other hand, Paul recognized it is "better" to be married than to be consumed with passion (7:9). If a single person lacks self-control, or has not been specifically gifted by God to live without a partner (7:7), he certainly will not be able to give "undistracted devotion to the Lord" (7:35). For such a person, marriage would be "better." For in spite of whatever problems marriage might bring, the potential for holy living would be greatly enhanced (7:2).

Paul's advice to men with unmarried daughters was similarly expressed. The question was whether these fathers should permit their grown daughters to marry.[6] Paul first declared that such a decision belonged within the area of freedom: "Let him do what he wishes, he does not sin" (7:36). He did have a practical preference: "So then both he who gives his own virgin daughter in marriage does well, and he who does not give her in marriage will do better" (7:38). In each instance, Paul's counsel reflects a recognition of spiritual priorities. In his advice, he urged Christians to establish relationships and conditions that will prove to be the most conducive to the accomplishment of spiritual goals.

It is in this same vein that we find some of Paul's most surprising terminology:

> A wife is bound as long as her husband lives; but if her husband is dead, she is free to be married to whom she wishes, only in the Lord. But in my opinion she is *happier* if she remains as she is; and I think that I also have the Spirit of God (1 Corinthians 7:39-40).

In his answer to the question concerning the remarriage of widows, Paul once again established the principle of freedom within the revealed will of God. The believing widow is free to be married. The man that she marries must be a Christian ("only in the Lord"). But she may marry *whichever* Christian man she *wishes*.

However, for the reasons noted above, Paul felt that she would be happier if she did not remarry.[7]

It is certainly a measure of the greatness of God's love that the matter of one's own happiness is permitted as a valid consideration in the process of decision making! Obviously, it is not the *only* consideration; nor is it to be the *primary* factor (cf. Matthew 6:19-33). But one's experience of happiness is certainly significant, and must not be discounted in the decision-making process. For enjoyment in the outworking of a decision promotes an attitude of eagerness and gratitude. And that kind of motivation is pleasing to God (Colossians 3:17, 23). Consequently, when one faces a decision in an area of freedom, it is valid to ask, "What decision would lead to my greatest happiness?" It is not the only question to consider, but it is clearly a biblical one.

Every Day In Every Way

The principle of wise decision making according to spiritual expediency is most clearly stated in Ephesians 5:15-16, and the parallel passage of Colossians 4:5:

Therefore be careful how you walk, not as unwise men, but as wise, making the most of your time, because the days are evil (Ephesians 5:15-16).

Conduct yourselves with wisdom toward outsiders, making the most of the opportunity (Colossians 4:5).

These two passages have three parallel words or phrases which, in the Greek text, are the same. The first is the verb "walk" or "conduct yourselves." In Ephesians, the word is translated to show the literal denotation "walk"; in Colossians, "conduct yourselves" indicates the sense. Paul was telling Christians to live every aspect of their lives in a certain way.

That certain way is described by the words "wise" and "wisdom." And those words are further qualified by the expression "making the most of your time" or "opportunity." The word "wisdom" has a great breadth of meaning in Scripture. In Ephesians 5:17, it is directly related to understanding "what the will of the Lord is." In context, that would seem to refer to understanding the truth that God has revealed in His Word. But in both passages, wisdom is also linked to "making the most of" specific opportunities that come up from time to time. Wisdom, in short, is spiritually opportunistic.

Follow the Leader

While wisdom is an appropriate goal for all believers in every decision, such wisdom is especially essential for those decisions that affect the lives of many others. Accordingly, practical wisdom and sound judgment are required qualifications for those who would lead God's people. In the Old Testament, Moses gave this charge to the people of Israel: " 'Choose wise and discerning and experienced men from your tribes, and I will appoint them as your heads' " (Deuteronomy 1:13). In Acts 6, the apostles specified that the first deacons must be " 'men of good reputation, full of the Spirit and of wisdom' " (Acts 6:3). And in both lists of qualifications for elders, Paul affirmed that the leaders of local churches must be "prudent," and "sensible" (1 Timothy 3:2; Titus 1:8).

To sum up: The pattern that we observed in examples of apostolic decision making appears with equal clarity in their instructions to the saints. Together, these examples and exhortations comprise the biblical foundation and validation for this principle: In nonmoral decisions, the goal of the believer is to make wise decisions on the basis of spiritual expediency.

Acquire Wisdom

For the sincere Christian who is committed to glorifying God through wise decisions, one further question begs to be answered: How does one get the requisite wisdom for such decisions? The biblical answer to that question has several parts. But the core truth is, wisdom is gained by those who *seek for it:*

> "I [wisdom] love those who love me;
> And those who diligently seek me will find me"
> (Proverbs 8:17).

The key to obtaining wisdom, then, lies in knowing *where* to find it, and *how* to look for it. And both aspects are spelled out in Scripture.

For the believer, the question of wisdom's source is hardly difficult. For "wise" is what God is in His essence—every bit as much as He is love, or truth, or holiness (Job 9:4; 12:13; Isaiah 40:28;

Daniel 2:20). In fact, in Him alone can wisdom be found in its fullness (Romans 16:27). And so whatever wisdom is to be found is to be obtained from God:

> For the LORD gives wisdom;
> From His mouth come knowledge and understanding (Proverbs 2:6).

But such wisdom is not given to just anyone, even if they know where it comes from. It is granted only to those who value it enough to pursue it:

> If you seek her [wisdom] as silver,
> And search for her as for hidden treasures;
> Then you will discern the fear of the LORD,
> And discover the knowledge of God (Proverbs 2:4-5).

Indeed, such seeking must be done properly if the "treasure" is to be uncovered. The "how" of this important endeavor concerns two fundamental aspects of the believer's search: his attitude and his approach.

The Christian's *attitude* is to reflect, first of all, his awareness that no man, himself included, is naturally wise in himself (Proverbs 3:7); and therefore, if he is to gain wisdom, it must come from some other source. Equally, his attitude must mirror his conviction that the ultimate source of wisdom is God alone. Those who refuse to acknowledge these basic realities are self-deceived fools (Romans 1:21-22). But the posture of the one who would find wisdom is that of bowing.

Accordingly, God grants wisdom to those who manifest certain spiritual characteristics:

Reverence—

> The fear of the LORD is the beginning of wisdom,
> And the knowledge of the Holy One is understanding (Proverbs 9:10).

Humility—

> When pride comes, then comes dishonor,
> But with the humble is wisdom (Proverbs 11:2).

> The fear of the LORD is the instruction for wisdom,
> And before honor comes humility (Proverbs 15:33).

Teachableness—

> Give instruction to a wise man, and he will be still wiser,
> Teach a righteous man, and he will increase his learning
> (Proverbs 9:9).

> He whose ear listens to the life-giving reproof
> Will dwell among the wise (Proverbs 15:31).

> Listen to counsel and accept discipline,
> That you may be wise the rest of your days
> (Proverbs 19:20).

Diligence—

> 'I love those who love me;
> And those who diligently seek me will find me'
> (Proverbs 8:17; cf. 2:4-5).

Uprightness—

> He [the Lord] stores up sound wisdom for the upright;
> He is a shield to those who walk in integrity
> (Proverbs 2:7).

Faith—

> But if any of you lacks wisdom, let him ask of God, who
> gives to all men generously and without reproach, and it
> will be given to him. But let him ask in faith without any
> doubting, for the one who doubts is like the surf of the
> sea driven and tossed by the wind. For let not that man
> expect that he will receive anything from the Lord, being
> a double-minded man, unstable in all his ways
> (James 1:5-8).

In the pursuit of wisdom, the believer must not only have the right attitude, but he must adopt the proper *approach*. In Scripture, there are at least five avenues of investigation opened to the man who would find wisdom.

First, he must *ask God for it* (James 1:5-6; cf. Colossians 1:9-10). The search for wisdom is never impersonal. Even if research, study, inquiry, and reflection are required, the process is not strictly academic. It is true that God *has given* wisdom through

His Word. But He also *gives* it through a variety of channels. And so the search for wisdom begins by asking for it.

James's counsel (1:5-6) includes an exhortation and a promise. The promise is that God will generously give wisdom to the one who asks for it in faith. That promise is straightforward. But its implications merit careful thought. James is not promising, for instance, that God will give instant omniscience to the supplicant. Nor is he suggesting that wisdom is divinely injected "intravenously" apart from a regular diet of God's revealed wisdom, the Bible. The trials of real life are not like those portrayed in a television drama where hopelessly complex problems are unraveled and resolved one hour and ten commercials later. James 1:5 is not a promise of instant solutions to every problem. Such interpretations are simply not permitted by the rest of Scripture.

James's promise was given in answer to an implied question. In the opening sentences of his epistle, he challenged believers to accept their trials with joy because of the character development that would result. Such a response, however, is not the most natural one. And so the reader might be expected to ask: How can I develop a proper perspective toward my trials? How can I know how to respond in a way that will produce positive effects in my life? To which James replied: Ask God for wisdom.

In that context, the needed wisdom would probably be multifaceted: it could include the ability to see the situation from God's perspective and recognize its potential values; it could include a recognition of ways to bring relief and/or avoid unnecessary pain where possible (cf. Paul's wisdom in 1 Corinthians 7:28ff.); it could include the recollection or discovery of relevant Bible passages that would reveal divine viewpoint; it could include the ability to apply specific biblical principles to the immediate situation; and it could include the perspective needed to wait on the Lord.

The single condition of unadulterated faith addresses the stance of the believer's heart in the face of trials. From the perspective of faith, the Christian realizes that God has neither abandoned him, nor turned against him — even though he has come upon hard times. Faith recognizes that the crucibles of life are divinely appointed, and seeks to cooperate with the Refiner's purposes. Faith does not reserve the right to reject God's wisdom after it is given, but submits in advance to the higher ways and thoughts of the heavenly Father. Faith realizes that wisdom, like every other benefit of temporal experience, is given progressively as a concomitant of spiritual growth. Faith is committed to gaining wisdom, not only *for* the trial at hand, but *through* the present trial—for future application. And faith rests confidently in the assurance that the One who promises wisdom will give it in perfect measure (Matthew 7:7-8; James 4:2-3).

As one asks for wisdom in prayer, it is appropriate to seek for it in the *pages of Scripture.* For in those pages, God has spoken. His gift of wisdom has, in large measure, been given.

The superlative value of Scripture as the revelation of God's wisdom is the theme of Psalm 119. Concerning this Psalm, Dr. Charles C. Ryrie observes: "The psalm conveys the thought that the Word of God contains everything a man needs to know."[8]

On wisdom and God's Word, the psalmist wrote:

> O how I love Thy law!
> It is my meditation all the day.
> Thy commandments make me wiser than my enemies,
> For they are ever mine.
> I have more insight than all my teachers,
> For Thy testimonies are my meditation.
> I understand more than the aged,
> Because I have observed Thy precepts
>   (Psalm 119:97-100; cf. Psalm 19:7; 2 Timothy 2:7;
>   3:15-17; 2 Peter 1:19).

The third avenue provided in the search for wisdom is *outside research* where such is appropriate. One biblical example is provided by Nehemiah, whose surreptitious inspection of Jerusalem's broken walls supplied the necessary data for a plan to rebuild them (Nehemiah 2:11-16). General Joshua's dispatch of two intelligence agents to Jericho would be another example of extrabiblical research for the purpose of making wise decisions (Joshua 2).

Many contemporary writers and speakers recognize the importance of research in the process of decision making. It is often suggested that it is a good idea to take a sheet of paper and list all of the potential assets and liabilities connected with each option. That is sound advice! For one cannot make a wise decision without the facts (cf. Luke 14:28-32).

The book of Proverbs stresses the value of *wise counselors* to the decision maker:

> Where there is no guidance, the people fall,
> But in abundance of counselors there is victory
>   (Proverbs 11:14).

> He who walks with wise men will be wise,
> But the companion of fools will suffer harm
>   (Proverbs 13:20).

> Without consultation, plans are frustrated,
> But with many counselors they succeed
>   (Proverbs 15:22).

In obtaining advice, one should seek out two kinds of counselors. Of those who possess deep *spiritual insight,* the question should be asked: "Are you aware of any biblical principles that touch upon my decision?" To those who have gone through relevant *personal experiences,* the query should be: "When you went through a similar experience, did you gain any insights that would be of value to me?"

The fifth source of wisdom is *life itself.* One should become a student of life as well as of Scripture. Agur, author of Proverbs 30, makes that point from one perspective:

> Four things are small on the earth,
> But they are exceedingly wise:
> The ants are not a strong folk,
> But they prepare their food in the summer;
> The badgers are not mighty folk,
> Yet they make their houses in the rocks;
> The locusts have no king,
> Yet all of them go out in ranks;
> The lizard you may grasp with the hands,
> Yet it is in kings' palaces (Proverbs 30:24-28).

His point would seem to be that God has built His wisdom into nature and men would do well to reflect on the practical habits which animals perform by instinct (cf. Proverbs 6:6-11).

The writer to the Hebrews applies the same principle to one's own spiritual life:

For though by this time you ought to be teachers, you
have need again for someone to teach you the elementary
principles of the oracles of God, and you have come to
need milk and not solid food. For everyone who partakes
only of milk is not accustomed to the word of
righteousness, for he is a babe. But solid food is for the
mature, who *because of practice have their senses trained
to discern* good and evil (Hebrews 5:12-14).

Maturity, of which wisdom is a component part, is gained by
experiential application of learned truth. It is the product, humanly
speaking, of in-depth Bible study and conscientious obedience of
God's Word. It is the "practice" of the truth that expands one's
capacity for a greater depth of wisdom through maturity.

What One Must do to Acquire Wisdom

- Have the right ATTITUDE:
  - —Reverence
  - —Humility
  - —Teachableness
  - —Diligence
  - —Uprightness
  - —Faith

- Take the right APPROACH:
  - —Ask God for Wisdom
  - —Seek Wisdom in the pages of Scripture
  - —Seek Wisdom through personal research
  - —Seek Wisdom through wise counselors
  - —Seek Wisdom from life itself

Figure 23

To sum up: The ultimate Source of the wisdom that is needed
in decision making is God. Accordingly, we are to ask Him to provide what we lack. God mediates His wisdom to us through His
Word, our personal research, wise counselors, and the applied
lessons of life.

Principles of Decision Making
The Way of Wisdom

1. In those areas specifically addressed by the Bible, the revealed commands and principles of God (His moral will) are to be obeyed.

2. In those areas where the Bible gives no command or principle (nonmoral decisions), the believer is free and responsible to choose his own course of action. Any decision made within the moral will of God is acceptable to God.

3. **In nonmoral decisions, the objective of the Christian is to make wise decisions on the basis of spiritual expediency.**

Notes

1. Archibald Robertson and Alfred Plummer, *A Critical and Exegetical Commentary on the First Epistle of Paul to the Corinthians,* International Critical Commentary (Edinburgh: T. & T. Clark, 1911), p. 387.

2. Frank E. Gaebelein, gen. ed., *The Expositor's Bible Commentary,* vol. 10: "2 Corinthians," by Murray J. Harris (Grand Rapids: Zondervan Publishing House, 1976), pp. 311-12.

3. Charles A. Hodge, *An Exposition of the First Epistle to the Corinthians* (Grand Rapids: Wm. B. Eerdmans Publishing Co., n.d.), pp. 135-136; Locality rather than the temporal aspect is another possible explanation. See F.F. Bruce, *The Epistle of Paul to the Romans* (Grand Rapids: Wm. B. Eerdmans Publishing Co., 1963), p. 248.

4. J.I. Packer, *Knowing God* (Downers Grove, Ill.: InterVarsity Press, 1973), p. 80.

5. The word "good" is *kalos.* For the idea of beneficial see Matthew 17:4; 18:8-9; 1 Corinthians 9:15; and Charles Hodge, *First Corinthians,* pp. 108-109.

6. Hodge, *First Corinthians,* p. 132.

7. The subject of marriage and singleness and the central passage (1 Corinthians 7) are developed in greater detail in chapters 17 and 18.

8. Charles Caldwell Ryrie, *The Ryrie Study Bible* (Chicago: Moody Press, 1978), p. 911.

Chapter 12

God Only Wise

Most of the biblical teaching concerning decision making relates the believer's choices to the moral will of God. God's moral will not only dictates what men must and must not do, but it also defines the sphere within which Christians have freedom and responsibility of choice.

But what of God's sovereign will? What bearing does it have on the activity of decision making? That is the question to which this chapter is devoted.

THE NATURE OF GOD'S SOVEREIGN WILL

Does God have a sovereign will? Does He have a "predetermined plan for everything that happens in the universe"? Man has always recognized that he is not the ultimate determiner of what happens. So what is? Is it blind chance? Is it an impersonal force or fate? Is it a wicked god or goddess? Such questions have challenged the intellects of philosophers and theologians for centuries. But the nature of the mystery is such that, at best, finite minds are limited to speculation.

There is One, though, who is not so limited. He knows the answers; and He has made them known. That One is "the blessed and only Sovereign, the King of kings and Lord of lords"

(1 Timothy 6:15). He is the Ultimate Determiner of everything that happens. He does have a sovereign will.

What does Scripture reveal about God's sovereign will? First, it declares that it will *certainly be fulfilled.* It will not be frustrated by men, angels, or anything else (Daniel 4:35). The sinner who tries to defy God's plan may shake his fist to the heavens, but God will determine how many times he shakes it and whether that man will live to shake his fist tomorrow (James 4:15). Satan is God's strongest enemy, but God sets the limits on the extent to which the devil may express his evil intents (Job 1).

The Ultimate Test Case

The ultimate proof of the certainty of God's sovereign will was presented at Calvary. Far from frustrating God's plan, the most wicked act ever committed—the willful murder of God's Son and Israel's Messiah—actually accomplished the central requirement in God's glorious plan of redemption! Contrary to misled opinion, the crucifixion did not force God into "Plan B." A Savior was foreknown before the foundation of the world (1 Peter 1:20) and promised while the core of the fruit was still in Adam's hand (Genesis 3:15). The crucifixion was prophetically described in detail (Psalm 22) and the death of Messiah divinely interpreted as an offering for sin some 600 years before the event (Isaiah 53). Judas' betrayal was prophesied (Matthew 26:24; Acts 1:16) and expected by Jesus at the Last Supper (Luke 22:21). The time of the "cutting off" of the Messiah was predicted by Daniel (9:26).

In his Pentecost sermon, Peter declared that the very criminals who carried out the farcical proceedings of six separate trials accomplished God's "predetermined plan" (Acts 2:23). Peter names Herod, Pontius Pilate, the Gentiles, and the people of Israel as those who gathered against Jesus "to do whatever Thy hand and Thy purpose predestined to occur" (Acts 4:27-28).

The final verdict is in. No one can frustrate the sovereign will and plan of God. To Paul's challenging question: "Who resists His will?" (Romans 9:19), we are humbly compelled to agree, "No one!" (Romans 9:6-29). God's sovereign will is indeed certain.

God Determines Who Lands on "Park Place"

The second thing the Bible indicates about God's plan is that it is *exhaustive.* It includes the germ as well as the galaxies. Specifically, Scripture teaches that God's sovereign will ultimately determines which of our plans find fulfillment (James 4:13-15), the existence of creation (Revelation 4:11), the president's personal plans (Proverbs 21:1), the numbers that come up when dice are thrown (Proverbs 16:33), the suffering which believers undergo (1 Peter 3:17), and our personal salvation (Romans 8:29-30; 2 Thessalonians 2:13-14). In a word, the sovereign God "works *all things* after the counsel of His will" (Ephesians 1:11). His sovereign will is exhaustive as well as certain.

The third thing we learn about God's plan is that it is *secret*. God hides it from us until it happens. Many of the older theologians referred to God's sovereign will as His "secret will," contrasting it to His revealed will in the Bible. One can know God's sovereign will, but only after it happens. Would you like to know His sovereign plan for the past? Find a good history book and curl up with it on a rainy day. If something happened, it was part of the plan. Would you like to know God's sovereign will for next Tuesday? Wait until next Wednesday. Only God knows what will happen in advance, and He's not telling. (Deuteronomy 29:29; Psalm 115:3; Romans 11:33-34; James 4:15).

No Exceptions Except...

There are two exceptions to the secrecy of God's plan. One of them is prophecy (Amos 3:7). In the foretelling of specific future events, God gives us a sneak preview, as it were, of some of the details of His yet-to-be-fulfilled plan. For instance, we know that Christ is coming back (Matthew 24:30), that there will be a great time of tribulation in the future (Revelation 6-19), and that there will be wars on earth right up to the end (Matthew 24:6-7). What are the chances that these things will happen just the way they are described? 100 percent! The outcome of God's future plan is as certain as the things that have already happened.

The other thing that God has revealed about the future concerns the ultimate destiny of the saved and the lost. If you are trusting in Jesus Christ as your Savior, you have been given everlasting life and you will spend eternity with Christ in heaven (John 3:16; 14:3). If you reject Christ and the salvation He has provided, you can be certain of your reservation in the burning fire of hell (John 3:16; Revelation 20:11-15; 21:8).

Revelations of prophecy and the destinies of mankind are the two exceptions to the rule. Most of God's sovereign will, which we have seen to be both certain and exhaustive, is also hidden until it happens.

To any thinking person these truths raise some important questions. For instance, if God has determined in advance everything that happens, doesn't that make God responsible for sin? The Bible does not accept that logic. It rather affirms the absolute holiness of God (Isaiah 6:3) and declares: "The LORD is righteous in all His ways, and kind in all His deeds" (Psalm 145:17). God is truly sovereign, even over sinful acts of men (Acts 2:23), but He is not Himself a sinner (James 1:13).

No explanation of how this can be is given in Scripture, even when the issue is raised by one of God's prophets (Habakkuk 1:3). Because of this, God's justice is often brought into question (Romans 3:5; 9:14). But through the Apostle Paul, such objections are ruled out of court. "How dare you impugn the righteous character of your Creator!" is the apostle's incredulous reply (Romans 3:4-6; 9:14, 20-21).

How can God sovereignly control sin, yet be perfectly righteous in all He does? This is probably one of the "secret things" (Deuteronomy 29:29) that may simply be beyond the grasp of finite minds. Still, I am helped by an illustration suggested by Jonathan Edwards.

The Sun Turned Me Cold
Imagine a planet in space which has no inherent capability to generate heat. It is by nature a cold and desolate sphere. Yet, because of its proximity to the sun, its actual environment is warm and comfortable. Now suppose that, for reasons of its own, the sun decided to move away from that planet toward another one. The consequences for the first planet would be devastating. The former climate so conducive to life would give way to frozen desolation.

Now here is the question: Did the sun make the planet cold? The answer is yes *and* no. Yes, the sun ultimately determined the frigid condition of that planet by moving and leaving that orb to its own nature. But no, the sun could not be "morally guilty" for the coldness of the planet. Only a fool would say that the sun and its rays actually produced the frozen atmosphere of the planet. In a similar way, God ultimately determines all things, including sinful acts. Yet He cannot be called the author of sin.

A second question that is commonly raised is this: If God sovereignly determines everything that happens, how can human decisions have any meaning? Isn't fatalism the natural, logical conclusion of sovereignty?

Once again, the Bible does not concur with such thinking. Scripture presents man as being a free moral agent who is responsible for his decisions. God is not a Cosmic Puppeteer, and we are not marionettes that jump when He jerks our strings. No man can say of his actions, "God made me do it," or "the devil made me do it," or even "my mother-in-law drove me to it." A man's decision constitutes a real cause that produces an effect for which he is held accountable. He is not the ultimate cause; God is. But the man produces real secondary causes with his decisions and actions.

How God works this out is another mystery. But here is a suggestion that might help. God never violates our responsibility because He never works contrary to our nature, nor forces our wills. He works within our wills and in harmony with our nature to bring about His determined end.

We have an example of this in the case of Judas Iscariot. In his betrayal of the Lord, Judas displayed treachery which was perfectly consistent with his greedy, fallen human nature. He willingly carried out his betrayal without compulsion or force. Yet his act was certain from eternity past. God worked within situations and within Judas' will to determine exactly how Judas would express his evil desires. And he voluntarily acted in the precise way that fulfilled God's sovereign plan. It was possible that Judas could have bailed out earlier when he saw that his days of pilfering the "petty cash" were over. He could have handed in his resignation as an apostle and tried to start a new movement. He could have simply gone home, yelled at his wife, and kicked the dog. God, however, determined that Judas would act willingly, according to his own nature, by betraying Christ with a kiss for thirty pieces of silver. It was certain, but Judas was certainly responsible (Matthew 26:24; Luke 22:22).

Only Your Wife Knows for Sure

An illustration given by one of my favorite professors may help to further illustrate this idea. Prior to his marriage, he assumed that he was acting voluntarily in courting his wife. The decision to propose to her was his own. He acted freely in accordance with his nature and desires. He was certain that he was in control of the whole situation as the initiator.

After they were married, however, his wife informed him that he only thought he was in total control. Actually, she had considerable influence over his actions and decisions. She desired his courtship and willed his proposal of marriage. So she moved to make him willing. She did not hold a gun to his head, but acted in more subtle ways—ways she claims a man would not understand—to mold his will. As a result, she was the one who determined they would marry.

Who is right? I trust that they both are. If so, the illustration shows in a limited way that while a man is not a puppet, God does ultimately write the script. God's sovereignty and man's responsibility are asserted side-by-side in Scripture (Acts 2:23; 4:27-28). Whether we can put them together in our minds or not, we must accept both truths and respond appropriately to both.

What we have seen, then, is that God does have a sovereign will that is certain, exhaustive, and hidden from human view. Yet God is not the author of sin, and man is not absolved of responsibility for his decisions and actions.

There is one final characteristic of God's sovereign will to consider before we look at the implications of God's plan for decision making. God's sovereign will is *perfect*. It is perfect in the sense that it will ultimately lead to God's greatest glory. No other plan could be as perfect. In fact, there never was another plan (Ephesians 1:4). But would not a plan that excluded sin be better? Apparently not. God's glory is not always immediate, but it is certain. He will be glorified for His holiness, for His defeat of Satan, for His righteous judgment, and for His grace to redeemed sinners (Revelation 5). This glory must have a backdrop of sin to be realized. The cross is followed by resurrection, and His victory over the grave brings Him glory (John 12:32-33). The first sin is followed by the promise of a Redeemer, and God is glorified for His grace (Genesis 3:15; Romans 5:20). The temporal rejection of the Savior by sinning Israel results in the reconciliation of the world and God is glorified for His wisdom (Romans 11:15, 30-33).

All Is Not Well that Ends Well

We often quote Romans 8:28 and receive comfort from the truth that "God causes all things to work together for good to those who love God." The basis for the truth of that statement is the sovereign will of God, as indicated in the verses that follow (Romans 8:29-30). We must be careful to note that God does not say that all things *are* good, for they are not. Rather, all things work together for good. They work together to make us conformed to Christ (Romans 8:29) and thus glorify God through His people. Even a flat tire, a crying child, or a disabled washing machine work "together for good" to conform one to Christ's quality of endurance (James 1:2-4).

We know that God's plan is perfect because God is perfect. Our knowledge of that fact is grounded in faith, not sight. According to the human eye, the world often seems chaotic, controlled by the sovereign rule of Satan. The person who walks by sight will not be equipped to face and cope with tragedy when it comes to him. Such a person sees external circumstances from the same perspective as an unbeliever, and is more inclined to curse his bad luck or become bitter toward God for His failure to intervene than to glorify God even in adversity. But the Christian who has a mature understanding and trust in God's sovereign plan is spiritually prepared for anything. He may not fully understand why he had to endure some difficulty, but he will know that his experience was part of the sovereign plan of an all-wise and loving God. In tragedy, one can never unscrew the inscrutable and explain why something happened. All our "why" questions ultimately must have the same answer—our loving God in His sovereign wisdom willed it so. His plan is perfect. That is all we know, but that is enough.

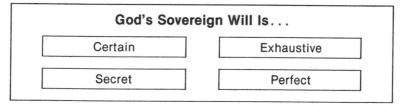

Figure 24

To sum up: God's sovereign will is of certain fulfillment, exhaustive, hidden from human view, and perfect. In the outworking of His plan, God is never the author of sin; all men are held accountable for their decisions and actions. Those who, through study of God's Word, gain humble appreciation for the wonder of God's sovereign will find themselves echoing in their hearts the doxology of the apostle Paul: "Oh, the depth of the riches both of the wisdom and knowledge of God! How unsearchable are His judgments and unfathomable His ways!" (Romans 11:33).

Chapter 13

God's Sovereign Will and Decision Making

*H*aving surveyed the biblical data on the nature of God's sovereign will, we may now consider the ways in which sovereignty affects the believer's decision-making process.

In doing so, we will see how the Bible relates God's sovereignty to such important considerations as planning, circumstances, "open doors," and "fleeces."

SOVEREIGNTY AND PLANNING

One logical question often raised in connection with God's sovereign will is this: If God controls everything that happens, what point is there in making any plans?

One passage of Scripture, in particular, expounds the viewpoint of the Holy Spirit on that question.

> Come now, you who say, "Today or tomorrow, we shall go to such and such a city, and spend a year there and engage in business and make a profit." Yet you do not know what your life will be like tomorrow. You are just a vapor that appears for a little while and then vanishes away. Instead, you ought to say, "If the Lord wills, we shall live and also do this or that." But as it is, you boast

in your arrogance; all such boasting is evil
(James 4:13-16).

All through his epistle, James used a verbal paint brush to illustrate his points. One moment the reader visualizes the wave of
the sea (1:6), then the flowering grass (1:10). The image of a man
studying his reflection in a mirror (1:22-25) gives way to the
somewhat comical picture of the man putting a bridle on his tongue
(1:26).

In the paragraph above (4:13-16), James portrays a group of
successful, confident, self-made Jewish merchants. They are hover-
ing over a map discussing plans. One of the men points to a city on
the map and declares, "That's the place to go. If we do business in
Sucha City for a year, we are certain of substantial profit. Let's
leave with our merchandise today, or tomorrow at the latest."

James, however, interrupts their discussion with a stern
rebuke. He condemns arrogant, self-confident planning which does
not recognize God or His sovereignty. James attacks their boastful
presumptuousness for "all such boasting is evil" (4:16). His sar-
castic "Come now" (4:13) indicates to the reader that the merchants
are displaying a self-confidence born of pride. Each detail of the
plan that is added underscores the attitude of arrogance and self-
sufficiency.

The Best Laid Plans of Merchants and Mice

In verse 14, James points out the absurdity of such boasting.
Life is like a temporary vapor. No man can say what his life will be
like tomorrow. He cannot even be certain that he will be alive
tomorrow! So to make such a confident assertion concerning the
certainty of profit a year hence is foolish presumption. The high-
pressure life insurance salesman has a point when he says, "If you
don't want to buy a policy now, think about it tonight and call me
in the morning—if you wake up." Life is uncertain and short.

Furthermore, the merchants make no mention whatsoever of
God in their planning. Such an omission makes their self-trust all
the more evident. (For a similar warning using graphic imagery,
read Jesus' parable of "The Rich Fool" in Luke 12:16-21.)

However, it is noteworthy that there is one aspect of the merchants' proceedings that James does not condemn. He never
reproves their practice of planning. In fact, apart from their at-

titude, no other individual detail of their planning is rebuked. James apparently accepts their short-range planning ("today or tomorrow"), their long-range planning ("spend a year"), their site selection ("such a city"), and their formulation of a goal ("make a profit"). James has no complaint with planning as such. It is the godless, self-assured attitude he deplores.

"If"—the Motto of the Humble

In verse 15, James submits his corrective. He commands that believers adopt a humble attitude in planning—an attitude that properly recognizes God's sovereignty. The vapor-like nature of human life is part of the Christian's reality as well. So he must recognize that his planning is always finite and "iffy." The most ungodly, immoral, foolhardy plan always has an "if" attached to it. The same is true of the plan that is godly, moral, and wise. So Christians should *not* say, "We have diligently prayed about this plan and we know the Lord is going to bring it about." Others may be impressed with such an expression of faith, but James would say, "What happened to the 'if'?" Spiritual plans are commendable, but even they are not 100 percent certain.

The believer is to express his humility in planning not only with an "if," but further with "if the Lord wills." Proper planning recognizes that God's sovereign will is the final determiner of the outcome. This understanding was absent from the considerations of the ungodly merchants. They did not take into account that it is God who determines what one's life will be like tomorrow, or whether one will even see a tomorrow. It is a mystery why God does not will to bring certain godly plans to fruition, while allowing certain wicked plans to find a successful end. We are certain, however, that no plan, whether good or bad, comes to pass unless God sovereignly wills it.

Finally, James says that when all contingencies have been duly acknowledged, *planning is appropriate:* "...we shall...do this or that" (4:15). God's sovereign determination of all things in no way diminishes the need or importance of wise planning. Christians should simply express their intentions in the future tense of resolve. A good plan should probably include all of the elements noted before: a starting time, a location, a goal, and a target date for completion (4:13).

To sum up, James condemns arrogant planning which does not recognize God or His sovereignty. He commends planning which submits in advance to the outworking of God's sovereign will.

What was taught by James was modeled by the Apostle Paul who characteristically made both short-range (Acts 20:16; 1 Corinthians 4:19) and long-range plans (Acts 18:21; 19:21; 1 Corinthians 16:5-7). In practice, Paul did not often use the phrase "if God wills" or the equivalent. Yet he often expressed his plans in the book of Acts or in his epistles. This indicates that a slavish repetition of the phrase is not necessary or expected with every declaration of intention. It is the attitude of humility and recognition of God's sovereignty that is required.

There are occasions when it is especially appropriate to qualify a statement of resolve with the words "Lord willing." For instance, Paul included the phrase, "if the Lord wills" in 1 Corinthians 4:19 in the middle of a very strong declaration of purpose, probably to avoid communicating the attitude of arrogance he sensed in others. There are, in addition, a variety of synonymous expressions found in Scripture that appropriately express the proper attitude in planning. "By God's will" or "through God's will" are phrases that emphasize the determinative role that divine sovereignty plays in bringing plans to fulfillment (Romans 1:10; 15:32). The expression "if the Lord permits" acknowledges that God puts limits or boundaries on the plans of men (1 Corinthians 16:7).

It is interesting to note that most of Paul's plans did come to pass (Acts 18:21; 1 Timothy 1:3), just as most of our well-laid plans are accomplished. Each time a carefully devised plan is successful, two truths are reinforced: the importance of wise, orderly planning (Proverbs 24:6); and the effectiveness of God's sovereign will in accomplishing the plans of men and God (Romans 1:10; 15:32).

The failure of a plan should prompt one to reevaluate the intended strategy with a view to correcting it if appropriate (Proverbs 20:5). Such lack of success should also motivate the believer to thank God that He is working in all things, even our incompleted or aborted plans, to accomplish His divine purposes for good (Romans 8:28; 1 Thessalonians 5:18). Any outcome, whether successful or not, should remind the Christian that finite, human plans work only "if the Lord wills" (James 4:15).

God's Sovereign Will and Decision Making

1. God's sovereignty does not exclude the need for *planning;* it does require humble submission to His will.

SOVEREIGNTY AND CIRCUMSTANCES

Some presentations of the traditional view teach that the believer should "read providence" as a means of determining direction from God in a particular decision. It is not uncommon to hear a Christian say, "The Lord led me to do thus and such." When asked about the means and details of such leading, he explains the series of specific circumstances that clearly pointed the way to God's will.

If there is no individual will of God, as we have established, such an approach to decision making is automatically ruled out. But it must also be added, for complete clarification, that circumstances are not designed to "give hints" about God's future sovereign will or about His moral will either. His sovereign will is hidden, and His moral will is already revealed in its entirety in the Bible.

Telegram from the Blue

The only time that circumstances can be "read" is when a divine interpretation is placed upon them by supernatural revelation. Apart from such revelation, circumstances may be taken to mean almost anything. Just listen to this imaginary but believable discussion concerning the "message" God was trying to convey when lightning struck a church steeple.

"God is telling us to relocate in the suburbs."

"Oh no, I think it's quite obvious He's saying 'no' to our expansion plans."

"Maybe the Lord is telling us that there is sin holding back the work in our church."

Solomon made it clear that watching providence makes life seem futile (Ecclesiastes 1:1-11). It often appears that God favors the wicked rich and resists the downtrodden righteous (Psalm 37:1). Apart from revelation concerning God's work in history, the raw data of circumstances is mysterious to say the least.

It should not be surprising, therefore, to read in Scripture that those who attempted to interpret providence failed in their efforts. The natives who saw a viper bite Paul concluded that he must be a murderer (Acts 28:4). When he remained unaffected by the venom, they determined that he must be a god (Acts 28:6). In answer to His disciples' question concerning the spiritual state of a blind man, Jesus declared that the blindness was unrelated to any sin the man, or his parents, might have committed (John 9:2-3). Similarly, the Lord corrected popular opinion when He explained that a group of Galileans killed by Pilate were not greater sinners than others (Luke 13:1-3). Nor was there any special guilt in the eighteen who perished when the tower of Siloam unexpectedly collapsed (Luke 13:4-5). For practical living, some things should simply be viewed as happening "by chance," just as the Bible does (Ruth 2:3; 1 Kings 22:34; Luke 10:31). Such events are determined by God, to be sure, but they are not to be viewed as "signs" to be read.

Even Hindsight Isn't 20-20

God has His wise and sovereign reasons for each event, but He does not regularly give man a running commentary of His reasons. Even Paul did not pontificate on the sovereign reasons behind the escape of Onesimus, Philemon's servant:

> For *perhaps* he was for this reason parted from you for a while, that you should have him back forever, no longer as a slave, but more than a slave, a beloved brother, especially to me, but how much more to you, both in the flesh and in the Lord (Philemon 15-16).

When the believer observes such "chance" happenings, he can still apply wisdom appropriate to his lack of knowledge:

> Just as you do not know the path of the wind and how bones are formed in the womb of the pregnant woman, so you do not know the activity of God who makes all things. Sow your seed in the morning, and do not be idle in the evening, for you do not know whether morning or evening sowing will succeed, or whether both of them alike will be good (Ecclesiates 11:5-6).

Probably the classic interpreters of providence were Job's "comforters"—Eliphaz, Bildad, and Zophar. The most helpful thing they did was to sit silently with the afflicted Job for seven days, thereby showing their empathy for him (Job 2:13). When they finally felt compelled to speak, God let them talk for nine chapters with their expositions of providence. In their interpretations of Job's situation, they were wrong nine chapters out of nine! Only God really knew what was going on. When did Job finally receive the divine interpretation of his troubles? He never did. During his earthly life, the most he could say was, "The LORD gave and the LORD has taken away. Blessed be the name of the LORD" (Job 1:21).

Fathoming Famines

An event cannot communicate a message apart from divine revelation. There are many instances in which such explanations are given in Scripture. Israel's crop failures and plagues were often the result of God's judgment—judgment announced *in advance* by the Lord's prophets (Deuteronomy 11:17; Amos 4:6-8). The prophet Joel declared that an invasion of locusts was not a tragedy of chance (Joel 2:1-10), but an act of discipline from the Lord designed to bring Israel to repentance (Joel 2:11-17). Without such divine commentary, locusts are just locusts. A famine is just a famine. Even in the New Testament, when the prophet Agabus predicted a coming famine, he did so, not to explain its meaning, but to warn the saints so they could adequately prepare (Acts 11:27-30).

Another kind of event which Scripture indicates is capable of communicating truth is the divinely-wrought miracle. The miracles of Christ attested that He was from God (John 5:36) and manifested His glory (John 2:11). A miracle is not open to subjective interpretation. It clearly indicates supernatural intervention by Satan or God, and God gives revelation to distinguish the source (Deuteronomy 13:1-5; 18:20-22).

Apart from the two kinds of exceptions indicated above, attempts to read messages from God through circumstances are invalid. For God's sovereign plan presently includes both good and evil. It permits Gabriel and Lucifer, Jesus and Judas to exist side by side. A day is coming when God will judge all evil and reward all good. In that day we will be able to read God's goodness and justice in His providence. In that day there will be no distinctions between His sovereign will and His moral will. Until then, we are instructed to pray that God's moral "will be done, on earth as it is in heaven" (Matthew 6:10).

God's Sovereign Will and Decision Making

1. God's sovereignty does not exclude the need for *planning;* it does require humble submission to His will.

2. ***Circumstances* define the context of the decision and must be weighed by wisdom . . . not "read" as road signs to God's individual will.**

SOVEREIGNTY AND "OPEN DOORS"

But doesn't Scripture speak of "open doors?" What are they if not circumstantial indications from the Lord concerning a direction He wants us to take?

The term "open door" is a natural figure for access to something or an opportunity to do something. One hot Texas summer, I was engaged in efforts to start a local church by door-to-door evangelism. Having grown up in the cooler climes of the north, it was a major adjustment for my parched body to get used to temperatures ranging from 90 to 105 degrees. On such days, my zeal to enter an air-conditioned home to witness increased remarkably. Residents were not inclined to talk at the front door lest all the cool air escape. So as I knocked, I literally prayed, "Lord, give me an open door." I was praying both for access into the coolness of the air-conditioned house as well as for an opportunity to present the gospel.

The expression "open door" is found in a few places in the New Testament. The nature of the access or opportunity available is determined by the context. For instance, in Acts 14:27, Paul and Barnabas reported how God "had opened a door of faith to the Gentiles," meaning that the Gentiles had been given an opportunity to hear the gospel and believe. Most New Testament occurrences of the expression relate to some opportunity for gospel ministry. The nature of such open doors is important for a discussion on the subject of guidance, for their very existence implies that a decision must be made concerning them. Does an "open door" constitute direction from the Lord that must be obeyed (assuming the compatability of other "road signs")? Or is it an opportunity or way of access that may be taken or bypassed with the decision being left to the judgment of the believer?

In addition to the reference in Acts 14:27, the expression "open door" is found in one form or another in 1 Corinthians 16:9; 2 Corinthians 2:12; Colossians 4:3; and Revelation 3:8. Of those four instances, the usage in Revelation 3:8 is least clear. It speaks of an open door that the risen Lord placed before the Philadelphian church. The precise meaning is admittedly obscure. It may refer to entrance into the Messianic Kingdom (on the basis of the reference to "the key of David" in the preceding verse). It may also refer to an open opportunity for effective missionary work. In either event, all that can be indisputably determined from this passage is that such an open door is desirable. The usages by the apostle Paul will prove more fruitful.

Opportunity and Opposition

In 1 Corinthians 16:8-9 Paul wrote:

> But I shall remain in Ephesus until Pentecost; for *a wide door* for effective service *has opened* to me, and there are many adversaries.

At the time of this writing, Paul's short-range plans called for him to remain in Ephesus for approximately two months. Navigation from Ephesus would then be open. In the interim, the people in Corinth would have time to digest and properly respond to this particular epistle. And such a schedule would permit Paul to stay longer in Corinth when he did come — something Paul was hoping the Lord would permit (1 Corinthians 16:7).

Additionally, verse 9 reveals two other very important reasons for Paul to stay in Ephesus awhile longer. On the positive side, "a wide door for effective service" had been opened for him; on the negative side, there were "many adversaries" trying to close that door. In short, Paul stayed to utilize the opportunity and neutralize the opposition.

Now the "door" in this case was an opportunity for effective and widespread gospel ministry. The adversaries in question were seeking to hinder the potentially large harvest. It is instructive to see how Paul regarded this situation. He did not, on the one hand, seem to look upon the "door" as a "sign" commanding him to stay in Ephesus. He was not under moral compulsion; he was spiritually opportunistic. Nor did Paul view the adversaries as messengers from God telling him to move on to more productive fields of service. Rather, to Paul, the presence of opposition signalled the need for reinforcements, and Paul was an excellent soldier (2 Timothy 4:7). The combination of opportunity and opposition provided Paul with good spiritual reasons for an extended ministry in Ephesus. He was making the most of his time and his opportunities (Ephesians 5:16) while combatting the enemy with the shrewdness of a serpent (Matthew 10:16).

The Apostle Paul can be likened to a man searching for jewels while trying to cover a large plot of ground. When he sees a good-sized jewel, he does not pass it up because he has so much ground to cover. He gets down and digs to utilize the opportunity to the fullest. Paul's "jewel" was to minister for Christ using opportunities, when available, to the fullest.

Get Me a Soapbox

In his epistle to the Colossians, Paul wrote:

> Praying at the same time for us as well, that God may *open up* to us *a door* for the word, so that we may speak forth the mystery of Christ, for which I have also been imprisoned (Colossians 4:3).

The one who seeks opportunities to minister for Christ is motivated to pray for such opportunities and to seek partners in such prayer. That is what Paul was doing — recruiting the Colossian believers as prayer partners in this request. Since he was writing from prison, this verse could be an expression of Paul's hope that he would be released after his hearing before the Roman tribunal. Such a release would open his prison door and allow him to resume preaching with complete freedom. It is even more likely that the prayer was simply a request for abundant opportunities to share the gospel — a request that was subsequently answered in a wonderful way (Philippians 1:12-18). There were occasions, recorded in the book of Acts, when prayer for opportunity to minister the Word resulted in the opening of literal doors!(Acts 5:19; 12:6-11; 16:26).

With respect to our subject of decision making, Paul was not praying for guidance, but rather for opportunity. He needed no providential "sign" to encourage him to preach in a certain place. He was a "preacher's preacher" who prayed for an empty pulpit and filled pews. On the basis of such an example, those who have been given a ministry of substantial giving should also pray for such opportunities. Teachers should pray for excellent opportunities to teach. Helpers should seek out and pray for God-given occasions for service.

The Door Not Taken

Our final Pauline reference is 2 Corinthians 2:12-13:

> Now when I came to Troas for the gospel of Christ and when *a door was opened* for me in the Lord, I had no rest for my spirit, not finding Titus my brother; but taking my leave of them, I went on to Macedonia.

Behold, here is an "open door" from which the apostle walked away! The reason for such a decision can only be understood in light of the historical context. Apparently, Paul had written a "severe letter" to the Christians at Corinth, and had sent Titus to deliver it personally (2 Corinthians 2:4; 7:8). At a later time, Paul was to leave Ephesus (1 Corinthians 16:8) and stop in Troas (2 Corinthians 2:12-13) en route to Corinth. The plan was that he would meet Titus there, and hopefully get a report from him concerning the Corinthians' response to his letter. The situation that Paul had addressed in his "severe letter" was extremely serious. In his estimation, the future of that church might well depend on the nature of their response to what he wrote.

When he got to Troas, Paul waited anxiously for Titus to arrive with the verdict. He waited, and waited, and waited. While he waited, he became aware of an open door for gospel ministry. However, he was so concerned about the situation in Corinth that he left Troas, open door and all, and went looking for Titus. It was a search fraught with fear and conflict (2 Corinthians 7:5). But it ended happily with the rendezvous in Macedonia with Titus and the report that the Corinthians had responded to his letter with sorrow and repentance (2 Corinthians 7:6-12). From Macedonia, Paul joyfully penned another epistle (2 Corinthians) to acknowledge his receipt of Titus's report and to prepare further for his personal arrival in Corinth.

Why did Paul leave an "open door"? If an open door constitutes a "sign" written by God through providence which the believer is to read and obey, Paul's action is inexplicable. But if an open door is an opportunity to be considered and weighed by the decision maker, then the explanation is not difficult. Normally, Paul would take advantage of such an open door for ministry (1 Corinthians 16:9; Colossians 4:3). He would only pass up such potential if something more important demanded his attention. And that was precisely the case in this situation. Rather than build a new house with available land and materials, Paul ran to put out the flames that threatened the existence of a house he had already built.

There are, in addition, other considerations which may have had a bearing on Paul's decision. It is likely that his restless spirit of concern for the Corinthians would have hindered the effectiveness of his work in Troas had he stayed. There was also deep concern in Paul's mind that some in the Corinthian church might reject his authority as an apostle, for 2 Corinthians is filled with multiple defenses of that authority (4:7-15; 5:11-13; 6:1-12; 10:7-18; 11:4-33; 12:1-21; 13:7-10). If such potential rejection materialized and spread, tremendous harm could come to the entire apostolic church. A final consideration might have been the possibility of a return to Troas to pursue the open door at a later time. Some Bible scholars think that he did, in fact, return and establish a church in Troas which he later visited in passing (Acts 20:6).

Evaluating Doors

On the basis of these passages, we can make the following conclusions concerning the place of "open doors" in guidance and decision making: (1) the term "door" refers to an opportunity, usually related to the effective ministry of the Word; (2) opportunities, like everything else, come through God's sovereignty; (3) the nature of such opportunities, as well as the common practice of Paul, indicate that most of the time "open doors" should be utilized as part of wise, resourceful living for the Lord (Ephesians 5:15-16); (4) if a greater opportunity or more pressing work is at hand, it is acceptable and proper to pass by the open door; and (5) an "open door" is not a direct providential sign from God telling the believer to go in a certain direction. A door is used, not because it is a sign, but because doors facilitate entrance. It is foolish to climb through a back window or tear down a wall when the front door is open.

As a postscript to this discussion, it seems appropriate to make some comments with respect to "closed doors." Interestingly, though Christians today speak of doors that are "closed," Scripture does not. The need for open doors certainly implies the existence of some that are closed. But that doesn't seem to be the mentality of Paul. If he were sovereignly prevented from pursuing a plan, and yet the plan itself was sound, he simply waited and tried again later. He did not view a blocked endeavor as a "closed door" sign from God that his plan was faulty. He accepted the fact that he could not pursue that plan at that time. Yet he continued to desire, pray, and plan for the eventual accomplishment of the goal. This approach is clearly demonstrated in Paul's attempts to visit Rome, as he explains in Romans 1:10-13. This passage will be discussed in detail in the next chapter.

God's Sovereign Will and Decision Making

1. God's sovereignty does not exclude the need for *planning;* it does require humble submission to His will.

2. *Circumstances* define the context of the decision and must be weighed by wisdom   not "read" as road signs to God's individual will.

3. **Open doors are God-given opportunities for service. . . not specific guidance from God requiring one to enter.**

SOVEREIGNTY AND "FLEECES"

One approach to decision making that is invariably discussed by writers and speakers on the subject is the practice of "putting out a fleece." Both the expression and the technique are based on the experience of Gideon:

> Then Gideon said to God, "If Thou wilt deliver Israel through me, as Thou has spoken, behold, I will put a fleece of wool on the threshing floor. If there is dew on the fleece only, and it is dry on all the ground, then I will know that Thou wilt deliver Israel through me, as Thou hast spoken." And it was so. When he arose early the next morning and squeezed the fleece, he drained the dew

from the fleece, a bowl full of water. Then Gideon said to God, "Do not let Thine anger burn against me that I may speak once more; please let me make a test once more with the fleece, let it now be dry only on the fleece, and let there be dew on all the ground." And God did so that night; for it was dry only on the fleece, and dew was on all the ground (Judges 6:36-40).

"Putting out a fleece" is a method of determining God's individual will in a given situation by determining in advance a circumstantial sign by which God can indicate the right decision. Author John White gives this description:

> Gideon's fleece has become the basis of a practice among some Christians which is called "putting out a fleece." In essence, when you put out a fleece you say to God, "If you really want me to carry out plan A, then please make the telephone ring at 9:10 p.m., then I will know that plan A is what you want." (You can make the "fleece" anything you wish, just so long as it can serve as a "sign" to you.)[1]

The concept is not inconsistent with the traditional view of decision making. But it cannot be supported by the passage on which it is based. To understand why, we must first review the historical setting as described in Judges 6.

Gideon was told by an angel that he would defeat Israel's enemy, Midian (6:11-16). In response to Gideon's request for a confirming sign, God consumed his offering by fire (6:17-24). The Spirit of God came upon Gideon giving him the ability to gather troops (6:33-35). Gideon then asked for the two signs involving the fleece to further substantiate the promise that God would bring victory by his hand (6:36-40, quoted above). The Lord granted his request and the battle was miraculously won (Judges 7).

The Fleece that Wasn't a "Fleece"

At a number of points, this event fails to authenticate the contemporary practice of "putting out a fleece." In the first place, Gideon's fleece was not simply a circumstantial sign, but rather a miraculous display of supernatural power. Gideon's request for the fleece sign would hardly be less than an insistence on a miracle since he had already received several supernatural demonstrations; the angel claimed to be God (6:21); his offering was consumed by fire from the rock (6:21); God spoke to him (6:23-26); and the Spirit of God came upon him giving him enablement (6:34). After such supernatural manifestations, it is inconceivable that Gideon would ask for a sign that was merely "circumstantial." The reversal of the fleece sign completely precludes such a possibility.

Second, Gideon was not employing the fleece to ascertain guidance, but to gain confirmation of guidance *already given*. And the guidance already given came by means of supernatural revelation. So Gideon was not seeking the right decision, but enough faith to believe that God's deliverance would come through him. Even Gideon's own words express his understanding of the purpose of the sign: "'...then I will know that Thou wilt deliver Israel through me, *as Thou hast spoken*'" (Judges 6:37).

Third, rather than being an example of a proper approach to receiving guidance, Gideon's demand for further signs was really an expression of doubt and unbelief. God's instructions to Gideon were clear, as he himself indicated (6:37). Apparently, God graciously acceded to Gideon's lack of faith because of the severe circumstances which tested him. As understandable as his fears might have been, Gideon's perpetual testing of the Lord was not appropriate. For God's attitude toward those who demand signs in unbelief is expressed in Christ's rebuke of the scribes and Pharisees (Matthew 12:38-39) and demonstrated in the silencing of the priest, Zacharias (Luke 1:11-20). Gideon's apologetic tone in asking for the second fleece sign shows that even to him "it looked so like a peevish humorsome distrust of God and dissatisfaction with the many assurances he had already given him."[2]

What we have seen, then, is that the practice of "putting out a fleece" cannot be established by the scriptural passage on which it is based. For Gideon was not seeking a circumstantial sign, but a miraculous one; he did not use the fleece to obtain guidance, but to confirm guidance already given; and his motivation was not a desire to do God's will, but rather his reluctance to follow God's guidance because of his own doubts.

As Bill Thompson noted (see chapter 3), there are many proponents of the traditional view who agree that a proper understanding of Judges 6 completely invalidates the appropriateness of "putting out a fleece." Significantly, this conclusion is confirmed by the absence of any teaching or example in the New Testament that even hints at such an approach to decision making.[3] For the Christian, that fact should be decisive.

Wisdom in Sheep's Clothing

There is, however, a practical question that needs to be answered. If the practice of putting out a fleece is improper, why does it sometimes bring good results? The answer, quite simply, is that on some occasions the fleece that is chosen is really wisdom in disguise.

The distinguishing feature of this whole process is that the *decision maker chooses the circumstantial sign* (as opposed to an "open door" of opportunity provided by God.) Since the individual names the fleece, the character of fleeces varies greatly. A fleece that demands a miracle for fulfillment (like Gideon's sheepskin) will automatically receive a negative "answer." That kind of fleece is of no value whatsoever in coming to a decision, and may result in harmful consequences if valid criteria for decision making are ignored.

Further, the person who chooses a bizarre fleece or a sign unrelated to the decision also risks being fleeced. Here are two examples: "I will know God is telling me to change jobs if I see a 1957 Chevy run a stop sign today"; "I will know God wants me to go to Bible school if the Detroit Tigers win their game today." These fleeces range from improbable to a 50-50 chance of fulfillment. But a flip of a coin would have the same degree of reliability. Decisions made on the basis of such circumstances are determined by chance.

But there are some fleeces that lead to good decisions in spite of themselves. These are the fleeces that reflect wisdom. Let us say, by way of illustration, that a man is thinking of selling his car and has determined that $2,000 would be a good, fair selling price. If the owner follows the traditional view, he might set up this fleece: "If someone offers me $2,000 or more for my car, I will take that as a positive sign that God wants me to sell it." If someone subsequently offered $2,000 for the car, he would sell it and the result would be a good decision. The reason that particular fleece might work is not because the practice itself is valid, but because the man was applying wisdom to his decision—even if he didn't think of it that way.

Let's look at that same situation from the perspective of the wisdom view. In this case the owner might say to himself: "I would like to sell my car. If I can't get at least $2,000 for it, I would be better off keeping it. So if someone offers me at least $2,000, I will sell it." Then he would pray for a buyer and advertise his car. This believer would be consciously seeking to manifest wisdom and good stewardship in his decision. But he would be under no illusions that he was getting a "sign" from God. If the car sold, he would thank God for giving him the wisdom to set a good price and for the provision of a buyer. Furthermore, if someone offered him $1,999, he would be able to accept the payment as "close enough" since the $2,000 figure was not a sign.

God's Sovereign Will and Decision Making

1. God's sovereignty does not exclude the need for *planning;* it does require humble submission to His will.

2. *Circumstances* define the context of the decision and must be weighed by wisdom   not "read" as road signs to God's individual will.

3. *Open doors* are God-given opportunities for service   not specific guidance from God requiring one to enter.

4. **"Putting out a *fleece*" is an invalid practice that sometimes works when it is really wisdom in disguise.**

Figure 25

The Difference Is in the Attitude

In conclusion, the question with which we have been concerned in this chapter is: What bearing does the sovereign will of God have on the process of decision making? The essential answer has two parts:

1. Since God's sovereign will determines the outcome of all decisions, the believer should humbly submit in advance to the outworking of God's plan.

2. Since God's sovereign plan cannot be ascertained in advance, it has no direct bearing on the actual consideration of options or formulation of plans. God's sovereign will governs circumstances and provides open doors, but His moral will and wisdom are the determinative factors in the making of the decision itself.

In short, while God's sovereign will has no direct bearing on the *activity of* decision making, its reality should govern the believer's *attitude in* decision making. Humble planning is the proper response to the sovereign will of God.

Principles of Decision Making
The Way of Wisdom

1. In those areas specifically addressed by the Bible, the revealed commands and principles of God (His moral will) are to be obeyed.

2. In those areas where the Bible gives no command or principle (nonmoral decisions), the believer is free and responsible to choose his own course of action. Any decision made within the moral will of God is acceptable to God.

3. In nonmoral decisions, the objective of the Christian is to make wise decisions on the basis of spiritual expediency.

4. **In all decisions, the believer should humbly submit, in advance, to the outworking of God's sovereign will as it touches each decision.**

Notes

1. John White, *The Fight* (Downers Grove, Ill.: InterVarsity Press, 1976), p. 165. White does not advocate putting out a fleece. In fact, his very next statement is, "Forget about fleeces. If you've never used them, don't start. If you have, then quit."

2. Matthew Henry, *An Exposition of the Old and New Testaments,* vol. 2: *Joshua to Esther* (London: James Nisbet, and Co., 1884), p. 163.

3. There are two Old Testament passages which tell of believers employing circumstantial signs to determine God's specific leading. The first of these, Genesis 24, is discussed in detail in chapter 18. There it is demonstrated that the process whereby Abraham's servant selected a bride for Isaac was not normative then, and offers no support for utilizing "fleeces" now.

The second passage is 1 Samuel 14:6-15. Though not normally cited by the traditional view in support of the validity of using circumstantial fleeces, it appears to be an example of the method. In the narrative, Jonathan determined that if the Philistines invited him up to their battle site, he would take that as a sign that he should go up and fight them. They did and he did. The result was a miraculous victory in which Jonathan killed twenty of the enemy (14:14) and put a trembling spirit in the rest of the Philistine army. When the Israelites perceived the fear of the Philistines, they attacked and won a great battle (14:15-30.)

As was the case with the selection of Isaac's bride, the explanation for this unusual incident lies in the nature of God's covenant with Israel. Israel's conflict with the Philistines is categorized as "holy war." In a holy war, God was fighting *His* enemies through the army of Israel. For such warfare, God provided supernatural guidance for His earthly king through revelatory dreams, the Urim and Thummim, or a prophet (1 Samuel 28:6). When the army obeyed God's commands, victory was certain. In such cases, supernatural guidance was normative. That direct revelation was anticipated in the crisis of a holy war is evidenced in the near context where Saul sought direction for specific battle plans through the Urim and Thummim in the ephod (14:36-37). Also, he later employed lots, just as Joshua did to implicate Achan (Joshua 7:13-21), to identify those who disobeyed his command to fast (1 Samuel 14:41-42).

In this instance, however, Israel's King, Saul, was "out of fellowship" with God. By contrast, his son Jonathan loved and obeyed the Lord. In view of his father's disobedience, Jonathan went out with only his armor bearer to secretly fight for God. In doing this, Jonathan was cut off from the "normal" sources of supernatural guidance. For he had no prophet with him, and the Urim and Thummim in the ephod were with Saul (14:3). And if God revealed a plan to Saul through a dream, Jonathan had no way of learning it.

Though cut off from the usual channels of divine guidance, Jonathan nevertheless thought that "perhaps" the Lord would lead him through circumstantial signs (14:6). And, in contrast to Gideon, the motivation of Jonathan was that of courage, faith, and the desire to preserve God's honor. That the Lord consented to go along with Jonathan's unorthodox approach is evident from the miraculous victory that was accomplished through Jonathan's initiative.

Finally, it might be argued that the casting of lots was a form of guidance through a circumstantial "fleece." It should be noted, first of all, that the traditional view does not recommend the flipping of a coin or the rolling of dice as a valid method of decision making. There were situations in which God communicated specific facts through the casting of lots in the Old Testament. But that approach is not viewed as being appropriate to the Church Age.

The only New Testament example occurs in Acts 1, when the disciples cast lots in the selection of Judas' replacement — Matthias (Acts 1:24-26). Commentators correctly note that that episode took place prior to the inception of the Church Age, so it cannot be considered normative for the present economy. There is considerable doubt as to whether the action taken on that occasion was recognized by God or the Church as being valid. Jesus had declared that in the Kingdom, the apostles would judge from "twelve thrones" (Matthew 19:28). While Matthias is never mentioned again as carrying out the apostolic office, Paul's claim to apostleship is well established.

Chapter 14

Guidance: A Biblical Model

*I*n our development of the biblical data on the will of God, we have seen that Scripture utilizes that expression in two ways: God's *sovereign will* is His secret plan that determines everything that happens in the universe; and His *moral will* consists of the revealed commands in the Bible that teach how men ought to believe and live.

Some of the contrasts between these two senses of God's will may be noted in this comparative chart:

Comparing and Contrasting God's Sovereign and Moral Wills	
Sovereign Will	Moral Will
1. God's secret plan that determines everything that happens in the universe.	1. God's revealed commands in the Bible that teach how men ought to believe and live.
2. Mostly hidden	2. Totally revealed
3. Cannot be learned in advance	3. Should be learned for guidance
4. Cannot be "missed"—should be humbly accepted	4. Can be "missed" through ignorance or disobedience
5. Indirectly Ideal Plan: Though it includes evil acts and foolish decisions, it will ultimately lead to God's glory.	5. Directly Ideal Pattern: Includes only those behaviors and attitudes that conform to God's character thereby glorifying Him.

Figure 26

In addition to establishing the genuineness of these two biblical aspects of God's will, we have set aside as scripturally invalid a third, commonly accepted concept — the *individual will* of God. As a result, we have discarded the idea that the primary objective in nonmoral decisions is to discover God's individual will among the options available. The Bible does not teach that the Holy Spirit seeks to perceptibly direct the believer to an ideal will through inward impulses and outward signs.

BIBLICAL GUIDANCE DEFINED

In what sense, then, may it be said that the Holy Spirit leads or guides God's people? Based on the biblical revelation covered to this point, there are four distinctive ways in which God guides. These four kinds of divine guidance are defined in the chart below (Figure 27).

Four Distinctive Ways God Guides			
Moral Guidance	**Wisdom Guidance**	**Sovereign Guidance**	**Special Guidance**
Sphere: In moral conduct	In nonmoral decisions	In all things	In unique cases
Nature: God *directly* guides believers	God *mediately* guides believers	God *secretly* guides believers	God has *supernaturally* guided believers
Means: By revealed commands and principles	By acquired wisdom	By sovereign control over all events	By divine voice, angel, dream or miracle
Governing Principle: According to His moral will (Bible)	According to spiritual expediency	According to His sovereign will	According to special revelation

Figure 27

When viewed from this perspective, God's guidance is seen to be abundant indeed! Furthermore, the kind of guidance provided corresponds exactly to our particular needs. Once again, the wisdom and love of God are manifested through His gracious gifts to His children.

A few additional observations about the definitions will help us to recognize some of the relevant implications for our own decisions:

1. The four kinds of guidance are not only distinct from one another, they are distinctive *at every point* in each definition. That is, the sphere, nature, means, and governing principle of each type of guidance are different from any of the other definitions.

2. In two kinds of guidance, the means is *direct* (moral and special); in one, the means is *indirect* (wisdom); and in one, it is *imperceptible* in advance of the decision (sovereign).

3. In two kinds of guidance, the believer has an *active* role (moral and wisdom); and in two he has a *passive* role (sovereign and special).

4. The definition of special guidance is deliberately worded in the past tense. That is not because God is incapable of communicating by special revelation; rather, special guidance is not normative. Virtually all teachers and writers on the will of God agree that Christians should neither seek nor expect special guidance of this kind in making their decisions.

BIBLICAL GUIDANCE DESCRIBED

How, then, may these various types of guidance be brought to bear upon our daily decisions? That is the question toward which this entire book has been directed. We are now prepared to bring our several conclusions together.

Figure 28 represents an attempt to visually demonstrate the relationships between the various aspects of God's will. In the illustration, the large circle to the left represents the sovereign will of God; the large circle to the right designates God's moral will; and the smaller, broken-line circle indicates the sphere of moral freedom within the moral will. The numbers located throughout the diagram represent the distinct classes of action, attitude, or motive, and will be explained below.

As we have noted, God's sovereign will encompasses all events that have or will come to pass, whether good or evil (Ephesians 1:11). God's moral will encircles all human activities done in fulfillment of commands or prohibitions expressed in the revelation of God's Word. It also includes all activities done in harmony with the biblical imperatives.

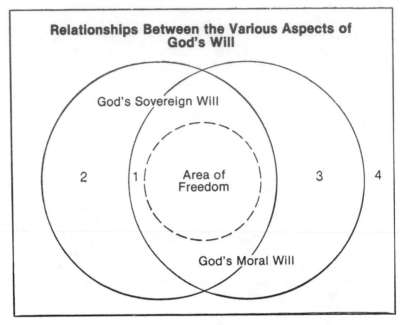

Relationships Between the Various Aspects of God's Will

God's Sovereign Will

Area of Freedom

2   1

3   4

God's Moral Will

Figure 28

Category 1 represents any action done in fulfillment of both the sovereign will and moral will of God. That is, God's Word commanded it, and someone actually obeyed it (Joshua 11:15).

Category 2 identifies actions that are outside of God's moral will, yet they have fulfilled God's sovereign will. For instance, the crucifixion of Christ, which was a heinous violation of God's moral will, actually fulfilled God's sovereign plan (Matthew 26:24; Acts 2:23; 4:27-28).

Categories 3 and 4 designate possible events in the past or the future which *will not* come to pass, for both lie outside of God's sovereign will. They are included in the diagram to remind us of the extent of God's attribute of omniscience. For His knowledge is so "omni" that He even knows every potential eventuality. For example, Jesus was able to declare what the citizens of Tyre and Sidon *would have done* if they had been given a different kind of revelation (Matthew 11:21-24).

So, Category 3 represents anything desired by God (in His moral will) that has not or will not come to pass. For instance, 2 Peter 3:9 declares that the Lord is "...not wishing for any to perish, but for all to come to repentance." That is God's moral will. But such universal repentance is not, apparently, within His sovereign will. For not everyone will come to repentance (Matthew 25:41-46; Revelation 20:15).

Category 4, then, stands for any potential, sinful action that does not come to pass (Genesis 20:6).

The broken-line circle within the moral will of God marks off the area of moral freedom. It delineates actions done in harmony with the moral will of God, but not directly commanded or prohibited by it (1 Corinthians 8:8). When such a nonmoral action comes to pass, it is part of the sovereign will of God, and is encompassed within His moral will.[1]

The believer's decision-making process is touched by each circle, and there are considerations to be made with respect to each type of guidance.

First, one asks, what bearing does God's sovereign will have on my decision? Negatively, we are reminded that God's sovereign will is *secret* — it cannot be known in advance. So the Christian is warned against trying to "read providence" or perceiving an "open door" as a command for what God "wants" him to do. In short, for all practical purposes, *sovereign guidance has no direct bearing on the conscious considerations of the decision maker.*

However, since the outcome of any decision is ultimately determined by God's sovereign will, the believer ought to humbly submit both his plans and their results, in advance, to God. Perhaps the best way to express this attitude concretely is through prayer.

Second, one asks, what bearing does God's moral will have on my decision? Are any of my options directly commanded or prohibited by Scripture? One important thing to remember at this point is that the moral will of God encompasses much more than one's actions. Goals, motives, attitudes, and means to ends are all governed to some degree by God's moral guidance. In fact, as we observed in chapter 9, "Thy Word Is Truth," many decisions that are nonmoral in themselves have several moral considerations. To be pleasing to God, a given decision must reflect obedience to His moral will at every point. The goal, the attitude, and the means to the goal must all aim to glorify God.

If the decision falls within the area of moral freedom, the goal of the believer is to choose the alternative that will best expedite and promote the revealed will and purposes of God. To accomplish that objective, he should seek for wisdom from the channels God has provided: prayer, Bible study, research, counselors, past experience, and personal reflection. The amount of time and energy invested in such a search should be in proportion to the importance of the decision (Ephesians 5:15-16)! If one option is recognized as being the most spiritually expedient, it should be chosen. If two possible alternatives appear to be equally expedient, either may be selected. In fact, in the latter case, if the believer has a personal preference, that is the one he should choose.

The final decision should be explained and defended on the basis of moral guidance ("God's Word says...") and wisdom guidance ("It seemed best..."). The decision should be shown to be in harmony with the moral will of God in all its details. Then the decision maker should demonstrate that the decision is thought to be a spiritually expedient alternative for promoting God's moral will.

BIBLICAL GUIDANCE DEMONSTRATED

A significant and thorough application of these very guidelines appears in Paul's epistle to the Romans. This great theological treatise is so freighted with mind-boggling concepts, the present day reader is apt to overlook the wealth of insight contained in the seemingly incidental comments at the letter's beginning and end. But if the Roman believers had been wondering about such practical matters as principles for decision making, this letter would have provided welcome instruction. That instruction was contained in Paul's explanation of his plans to visit them:

First, I thank my God through Jesus Christ for you all, because your faith is being proclaimed throughout the whole world. For God, whom I serve in my spirit in the preaching of the gospel of His Son, is my witness as to how unceasingly I make mention of you, always in my prayers making request, if perhaps now at last by the will of God I may succeed in coming to you. For I long to see you in order that I may impart some spiritual gift to you, that you may be established; that is, that I may be encouraged together with you while among you, each of us by the other's faith, both yours and mine. And I do not want you to be unaware, brethren, that often I have planned to come to you (and have been prevented thus far) in order that I might obtain some fruit among you also, even as among the rest of the Gentiles (Romans 1:8-13).

Paul the Planner

The first thing that the Romans would have noticed from Paul's explanation is the *appropriateness of making plans* (1:13). They may have known that on two or three specific occasions Paul had received special guidance concerning his geographic field of ministry (Acts 16:6-10); but no such revelation is mentioned here. God neither commanded Paul to go to Rome, nor forbade such a journey.[2]

Second, Paul *prayed* about his plans (1:8-10). He asked that they might be accomplished. Apparently, there had been several plans to go to Rome (1:13), and Paul was asking that the Lord would bring this one to pass, hopefully soon (1:10).

Third, through his prayers, Paul *submitted* himself and his plans to *God's sovereign will.* The wording of his petition reveals his conviction that if he ever made it to Rome, it would be "by the will of God" (1:10). To that point in time he had been "prevented" (1:13). And though he did not yet indicate the direct cause of the hindrance, it was certainly clear that, as far as Paul was concerned, the ultimate cause was God's sovereign will. Accordingly, he was able to accept delay without experiencing undue frustration.

Ready...Aim...

The fourth thing the Romans would have noted is that Paul's plans were based on spiritual goals. In fact, though they were not stated first, the goals were certainly established first. For the plans were formulated as means to achieve the goals.

And what were Paul's goals?

1. To provide spiritual ministry to the Roman believers (1:11).
2. To further establish and encourage the church in Rome (1:11-12).
3. To receive encouragement from them (1:12).
4. To win unbelievers to Christ (1:13-15).

Some believers in the Roman church might have wondered why Paul was planning to come to Rome, as opposed to some other worthy destination where the same goals might be accomplished. If so, they had to wait until almost the end of the epistle to find out.

> And thus I aspired to preach the gospel, not where Christ was already named, that I might not build upon another man's foundation; but as it is written, "They who had no news of Him shall see, and they who have not heard shall understand." For this reason I have often been hindered from coming to you; but now, with no further place for me in these regions, and since I have had for many years a longing to come to you whenever I go to Spain — for I hope to see you in passing, and to be helped on my way there by you, when I have first enjoyed your company for awhile — but now, I am going to Jerusalem serving the saints. For Macedonia and Achaia have been pleased to make a contribution for the poor among the saints in Jerusalem. Yes, they were pleased to do so, and they are indebted to them. For if the Gentiles have shared in their spiritual things, they are indebted to minister to them also in material things. Therefore, when I have finished this, and have put my seal on this fruit of theirs, I will go on by way of you to Spain. And I know that when I come to you, I will come in the fulness of the blessing of Christ (Romans 15:20-29).

"We're Number Four, We're Number Four"

If Paul's initial explanation of his plans in chapter 1 generated a sense of excitement among the Roman Christians, these further details may have initially had the opposite effect. For it was only in chapter 15 that Paul's full intentions were revealed. And what the Romans learned is that they were not at the top of Paul's priority list.

Nor were they second.

They weren't even third.

They were fourth!

Why?

Because Paul had goals that were even broader and more ambitious than the ones he had stated earlier. While he had specific objectives for a visit to Rome, they were subordinate to the greater strategy of which they were but a part.

The point that should not be lost on observers of Paul's decision making process is that Paul *arranged his goals according to priorities*. Since he did not know how much time he had, he determined which things needed to be accomplished first, and which projects could wait.

Paul, Your Priorities Are Showing

The immediate priority was to complete the task of evangelizing Greece. Ever since Jesus Christ commissioned Paul as "an apostle of Gentiles" (Romans 11:13), Paul followed a policy of taking the gospel to regions where people had never heard of Christ (2 Corinthians 10:16). In explaining this policy to the Romans (Romans 15:20-21), Paul mentioned again the "hindrance" that prevented his coming to them (15:22). In all likelihood, it was his unfinished work in Greece that had prevented his coming before now (15:23). It was just taking longer than he had expected to establish reproducing churches in that region. And Paul recognized the wisdom of finishing one job before moving on to another.

But now, it looked like he would soon be able to move on to his second priority—a trip to Jerusalem (15:25).

Wait a minute. Jerusalem? Why, that's in the opposite direction!

True. But it *was* number two on the list. Why? Paul's explanation in verses 26 and 27 is that he wanted to accompany the financial gift being sent from the churches of Greece, Macedonia, and Asia Minor to the beleaguered saints in Judea.[3] It is apparent from a number of New Testament references that Paul considered this gift to be highly significant (see chapter 11 where 1 Corinthians 16:3-4 is discussed). In Romans 15:27, Paul explained the gift from two perspectives: it was a gift of love ("they were pleased to do so"), and it was the down payment on a spiritual debt ("they are indebted to them"). But for Paul, the most important thing, the one factor that warranted his presence in Jerusalem, was that the gift symbolized the experiential reality of the truth he had been declaring and defending: the unity of Jewish believers and Gentile believers in one Body—the Church (Ephesians 2:11-22). Paul may well have anticipated that this act of love by the Gentiles would help his Jewish brethren to understand and accept the truth of this wonderful "mystery" which God had revealed through His apostle to the Gentiles (Ephesians 3:1-10).

"Pit Stop"—Rome

That accomplished, Paul would head west. To Rome? Well, yes. But ultimately to Spain. As Paul envisioned it, Rome was going to be a sort of "pit stop" on his journey to "the uttermost part of the earth." In addition to the goals listed in Romans 1, Paul now made it clear that he was hoping to "raise his support" for Spain while he was in Rome (Romans 15:24).

Was Spain more important to Paul than Rome? Probably. For Paul was the consummate missionary. Rome had the gospel; Spain did not. It was as simple as that. Did God command Paul to go to Spain? No, not specifically. He had specified that Paul's primary ministry would be to the Gentiles as a group (Acts 9:15; 26:17); and He had announced that He would send Paul "far away" to reach lost people (Acts 22:21). But it was Paul who made it his own life-goal to reach "all the Gentiles" (Romans 1:5; 2 Timothy 4:17). His plans were calculated, apart from special revelation, to reach the world in his lifetime.

Thus did Paul spell out his priorities: Greece, Jerusalem, Spain, and, in passing, Rome.

Were the Roman believers disappointed in Paul's itinerary, or offended by their position on his list of priorities? Obviously, we don't know. But it is worth observing that Paul's full declaration of his personal plans was withheld until he had given his most complete exposition of the gospel and its far-reaching ramifications. It seems likely that, having learned of the glories of the gospel, the Roman church would have been eager to assist in the spread of this good news in any way possible.

The postscript to this discussion is that Paul did eventually make it to Jerusalem, Rome, and possibly even Spain—in that order. He did have to modify his plans somewhat along the way. For the two-year stopover in the Caesarean jail, and the shipwreck at Malta had not been included in Paul's original projections. Nor did Paul just visit the Romans "in passing." His confinement under house arrest delayed his plans for westward advancement for at least two years.

On the plus side, Paul's transportation from Palestine to Rome was provided courtesy of Caesar, who also furnished a military escort for his protection. And the period of imprisonment was used by Paul to pen a major portion of what was to become the New Testament.

Because he responded properly to God's guidance in its various forms, Paul became a model of one who engaged in *long-range planning* on the one hand, and *snatched up present opportunities* on the other. Interruptions became occasions for personal growth and ministry. It is just such a balance that believers today should seek to maintain.

Steps in Paul's Decision-Making Process

- PURPOSES: Paul adopted spiritual goals that were based on divine revelation.

- PRIORITIES: He arranged his goals into wise priorities determining what should be done first, second, third, etc.

- PLANS: Next, he devised plans that gave him a strategy for accomplishing his objectives.

- PRAYER: Through prayer, he submitted himself and his plans to the sovereign will of God. (No doubt, he also prayed for wisdom in the formulation of his plans, though not mentioned in this context.)

- PERSEVERANCE: When providentially hindered from accomplishing his plans, he assumed that the delay was God's sovereign will. This conviction freed him from discouragement. Since his plans were sound, the only thing he adjusted was the timetable.

- PRESENTATION: Paul explained his decisions on the basis of God's moral will and his own personal application of wisdom.

Figure 29

Notes

1. Strictly speaking the diagram omits a depiction of those acts in the area of freedom which do not come to pass. Paul's earlier attempts to go to Rome fit this category (Romans 1:13). Such a trip was in harmony with but not commanded by the moral will of God either in its destination or time schedule.

Also the diagram could include some representation of special guidance. Special revelation has been used by God to command a believer to do something normally within the circle of moral freedom. For instance, the apostle Paul was normally free to take the gospel message anywhere he personally chose. But there were occasions when God overruled Paul's use of his freedom through special guidance (Acts 16:6-10). For the individual who receives such guidance, the sphere of moral freedom is thereby reduced, and the area of moral obligation is expanded.

It is not impossible to visually represent these two additional concepts, but the resulting diagram becomes too complicated to be helpful.

2. Later, God did guarantee Paul's safe arrival in Rome, but that was well after the plans had been made and Paul was en route (Acts 23:11; 27:23-24). From the outset, the idea and the plan were Paul's (Acts 19:21; Romans 1:13; 15:22-29).

3. Some commentators conclude that the reason behind Paul's trip to Jerusalem was disobedience to the clear guidance of God. The main support for this position is Acts 21:4.

> And after looking up the disciples, we stayed there seven days; and they kept telling Paul through the Spirit not to set foot in Jerusalem (Acts 21:4).

This verse describes what happened in Tyre on Paul's way to Jerusalem. Was Paul disobedient in this journey?

There is no hint of such disobedience in Romans 1 or 15. Nor is there any other direct comment in the book of Acts that shows Paul as traveling in disobedience. Luke seems favorable in his comments with the possible exception of Acts 21:4.

It is best to consider the Jerusalem trip as free of disobedience, but full of risk to Paul. The trip itself was the result of Paul's planning after leaving Ephesus on his third journey. He "purposed in the spirit to go to Jerusalem" (Acts 19:21). This is best understood as Paul's human spirit since the text gives no evidence of direct revelational guidance from the Spirit, and Romans 1 and 15 describe it as Paul's spiritual planning. At the end of the third journey Paul hurried past Ephesus to try to get to Jerusalem by Pentecost (Acts 20:16). In his human spirit he had made a firm decision that he would make this trip (Acts 20:22).

However, all along the way to Jerusalem the Spirit spoke through prophets revealing that "bonds and afflictions" awaited him in Jerusalem (Acts 20:23). This happened in Tyre (Acts 21:4-5) as well as Caesarea (Acts 21:10-14). The fullest account of how the warnings came to Paul comes in Caesarea with the prophet Agabus. He took Paul's belt, bound his own feet and hands, and said,

> "This is what the Holy Spirit says: 'In this way the Jews at Jerusalem will bind the man who owns this belt and deliver him into the hands of the Gentiles'" (Acts 21:11).

At this prophecy Paul's companions and local residents urged him to cancel his trip to Jerusalem. Paul answered them and their fears by saying,

> "What are you doing, weeping and breaking my heart? For I am ready not only to be bound, but even to die at Jerusalem for the name of the Lord Jesus" (Acts 21:13).

When further persuasion failed to dissuade Paul they quietly said, " 'The will of the Lord be done!' " (Acts 21:14).

Soon after Paul arrived in Jerusalem the prophecy was fulfilled. God's word to Paul after his arrest and the uproar before the Jewish council was " 'Take courage; for as you have solemnly witnessed to My cause at Jerusalem, so you must witness at Rome also' " (Acts 23:11).

The majority of the evidence supports the view that Paul was not disobedient to God's guidance. The trip itself was neither commanded nor forbidden. Paul could make the trip within the moral will of God if he considered it spiritually expedient. Paul had good reason for going since he desired to accompany the Gentile gift to needy Jewish believers. Furthermore, Paul wanted to testify once more to his unbelieving countrymen.

The prophecies were warnings of what would happen if he went, not commands prohibiting the trip. This is best seen in the most complete description of the warnings at Caesarea through Agabus. The prophecy predicted but did not forbid. The people in loving concern for Paul urged him to turn from Jerusalem because of the prophecy. "Afflictions" were certain, but Paul was ready to die if necessary to give this final appeal to the Jews (Acts 21:13). Acts 21:4 should be understood in light of this more detailed description through Agabus. " 'They kept telling Paul through the Spirit not to set foot in Jerusalem' " (Acts 21:4) should be interpreted as a parallel to the Agabus account. The Spirit warned Paul of bonds and afflictions. Through hearing this prediction, the people urged Paul for his own safety not to set foot in Jerusalem. The decision ultimately was Paul's. So when the dissuading failed they turned the matter over to the sovereign will of God saying, " 'The will of the Lord be done!' " (Acts 21:14).

Paul was courageous to go, not sinful. The people were concerned in urging him away from Jerusalem, not sinful. This conclusion, however, is not necessitated by the wisdom view. The proponent of the wisdom view of guidance may consistently hold to his theology whether he concludes that Paul was disobedient or not. The proponent of the traditional view may also hold to either view of the Jerusalem trip and be consistent with his view of guidance.

Chapter 15

Guidance Is Personal

*I*t is not unusual, when a person gains new insight into Scripture, for him to "overcorrect" his previously held position. This has happened to some believers as they have begun to apply principles of the wisdom view to their decisions. They have unintentionally found themselves on the opposite stroke of the pendulum's swing. One student commented, "I feel like a deist when it comes to guidance." Another said, "Wisdom guidance seems so impersonal to me. I feel as though God is no longer involved with me as a person."

Swing Back, Sweet Pendulum

To some observers, our emphasis on God's already revealed will and human wisdom appears to be rationalistic. By contrast, one apparent strength of the traditional view is the sense that God's leading is personal and direct. We are emotional beings who often crave the mystical experience in which our inner spirit "walks with God." This seems to happen regularly in the traditional view. God is thought to be working in the Christian's heart to reveal each decision that is made. Such communication may lie outside the realm of objective proof; but, says the believer, "I know in my heart that it's real."

THE WAY OF WISDOM IS NOT IMPERSONAL

The most common misconception of the way of wisdom is that it is impersonal — that God is excluded from the decision-making process. Our contention that this is a misconception, rather than a bona fide flaw in the position, is based on a couple of spiritual facts.

I Call the Apostles to the Witness Stand

The first is that the apostles did not consider the wisdom approach to be impersonal. They never defended their decisions on the basis of inward impulses which led them to God's "perfect will"; nor did they teach such a method. Yet they are illustrations of the Christian life in action. The apostles frankly explained the decisions they made and usually gave the attending reasons. But they did not regard that process as being carnal, rationalistic, or impersonal. The apostles clearly trusted God for guidance, but not in the manner expected by the traditional view of today. Their decision making was in harmony with the way God said He would guide. Therefore, we can affirm that making decisions in accordance with God's instructions is never impersonal.

Furthermore, the apostles were comfortable with the form of guidance available to them in spite of the fact that it was much less specific than that received by the Old Testament saints. Somehow we have the notion that to be "personal," God must give the determinative leading for *each* of our decisions. But the trend in Scripture is in the opposite direction.

Less Is Best...in Specific Guidance

God's guidance in the Old Testament reached down into the details of daily life while His guidance in the New Testament is expressed in more general commands and principles. And yet the New Testament writers evidence no apprehension that God is withdrawing from personal involvement in the lives of His people. In fact, as we shall see, the relationship of the New Testament believer with God is characterized by the greater level of intimacy.

It is instructive to compare more closely the nature of God's guidance in the Old and New Testaments respectively. The first thing we observe is how much more *specific* the Old Testament directives were.

God's guidance for the people of Israel regulated such details as: which persons were to be their spiritual leaders; exactly where they were to camp; how far they were to travel each day; when they were required to go to Jerusalem; which foods they could and could not eat; when they were to go to battle as a nation; when they must bathe; which cities their spiritual leaders must live in; how much offering to give as a minimum; the exact location and dimensions of the "church building"; the precise words their prophets were to deliver; how the new year was to be celebrated; who would inherit a man's land; how long land was available for sale; which years the people must work, and which ones they must rest; how punishment was to be meted out to the convicted thief, murderer, homosexual, idolator, and rebellious child; what uniforms the religious leaders must wear; when all male Israelites must be circumcised; how interest rates were to be regulated; and even the manner in which the corner of each garment was to be adorned! (For a more complete list, start with Leviticus and Deuteronomy.)

God's provisions for guidance in the Church Age are of a different character. Most of the specific regulations that constituted God's moral will for the Israelites have been moved into the "area of freedom" for Christians. We are free and responsible to decide for ourselves what to eat, what to wear, where we will live, which church we will attend, and so on. And all decisions are to be governed by the general commands that comprise God's moral will as revealed in the New Testament. The inescapable conclusion is, "less specific" does not equal "less personal."

Personal Father, Not Pillar of Fire

The second most important difference we observe in God's methods of guidance is that His leading in the Old Testament was more *empirical*—that is, more immediately *perceptible* to the senses. The Lord revealed His presence through a variety of supernatural manifestations that were observable to the entire nation: the thunder, lightning, and voice from Mt. Sinai; the pillar of cloud and fire; the daily provision of manna; and so on.

Christians, however, do not behold a pillar of fire for assurance of God's presence. Nor do they consult the Urim and Thummim for His direction. Instead, they rely on the Word of God for both.

So we see that God's provisions for our guidance are less *specific* and less *empirical* (oriented to our physical senses) than the guidance that He gave to Israel. Does that mean that God has become less effective in His guidance? Does it mean that He has lost interest in His people? Does it mean that God has withdrawn and become "less personal" than He used to be? No. No. No. In His wisdom, God saw fit to guide Old Testament saints as "immature children" who had a limited understanding of His nature and will. But those who have the benefit of receiving the revelation of Jesus Christ and the empowerment of His Spirit, God treats as "grown-up children." New Testament believers are equipped to relate to their Father on an "adult" level without requiring the kind of detailed parental supervision that was appropriate to childhood (cf. Galatians 4:1-7).[1]

The fact that God guides Christians as a father guides his sons is proof of His personal concern for us. This is demonstrated at the level of human relationships. In my own case, as I was growing up, my parents were training me so that I could learn to make decisions for myself. They taught me to distinguish right from wrong; they taught me biblical values and principles that I could apply to specific decisions. The older I got, the less they told me what to do.

When it came time for me to choose which college I would attend, my parents were very helpful. As we discussed the options together, their loving concern was evident. But they refrained from suggesting what I should do. As I agonized over that decision, there were times when I wished they would tell me which school to choose. But they would not. Instead, they assured me that I was mature enough to come to a good decision myself. And I was encouraged by the knowledge that they were praying for me.

Were my parents withholding guidance? No. For nearly twenty years they had provided guidance that I could appropriate for this decision. Were they unloving, disinterested, or impersonal? Quite the contrary. Their insistence that I come to my own conclusion was evidence of their love. In making their wisdom available to me, they were personally involved. In a similar manner, our Heavenly Father personally guides His children.

THE PROPER PLACE OF EMOTIONS

What we have seen, then, is that the kind of guidance we have described is not regarded as impersonal by the New Testament. It remains for us to explain *why some people feel as though God is cut out of the decision-making process.*

An Impressive Feeling

Perhaps the problem is that, at first glance, there seems to be nothing in the way of wisdom that corresponds to the sense of intimacy with God that is usually identified with the inward impulses. When a person has spent his life responding to inner impressions as though "this is God speaking to me in my spirit," it is very difficult to conceive of a personal relationship with God that is experienced in some other way. Even when the believer accepts with his mind that those impressions are not communications from God, and he mentally understands that God has revealed 100 percent of His moral will for the believer's guidance, he may feel a void in his heart. He may find he cannot escape the notion that he has had to exchange present tense direction for past tense revelation. It can ooom that God is at least 1900 years away, while the believer is left by himself to sort out God's guidance "by the Book."

What we are talking about here is the involvement of the emotional aspect of our being. For that's what inner impressions are—feelings. We even speak of them that way: "I feel that we should stay right where we are for the time being"; "I have a feeling that if we don't buy it today, we may never have another chance."

Emotions: Your Initiators or Your Responders

There are two things we must bear in mind about our emotions. The first is that they can be greatly influenced by a host of things: our health, our upbringing, fatigue, medication, the weather, our diet, our hormonal balance, a news report, the feelings of others—in sum, everything that influences our immediate perception of reality.

The second factor is that emotions can affect our lives in one of two ways. They can function either as initiators or as responders. They can be the means whereby one determines "reality," or they can be the means whereby one responds to truth. When a person makes decisions on the basis of how he feels at any given moment, his emotions are governing his life and his decisions are only as reliable as his emotional state. But when a person makes decisions on the basis of objective truth, he is on solid ground, and his emotions find their proper place in expressing his response to reality.

One of our criticisms of the traditional view is that it tends to put the emotional cart before the intellectual horse. That is the problem of subjectivity—making decisions on the basis of one's interpretation of inward impulses (feelings) and other "road signs" that cannot be objectively verified. While the emotional element is real, it is misinterpreted because the process has been turned inside out. Those inner impressions are not the "still small voice" of God; they are the emotional "voice" of the person himself. One's own feelings are not an authoritative source of direction for making decisions. But because they are mistakenly taken as divine guidance, they are often regarded as being authoritative.

Furthermore, the believer who evaluates his walk with the Lord primarily on the basis of his subjective feelings is vulnerable to spiritual "seasickness"—the cumulative effect of being "like the surf of the sea driven and tossed by the wind" (James 1:6). Such an individual may experience euphoric "highs" and despondent "lows" with neither extreme being directly related to God's work in his life. It is entirely possible for such a person to feel "out of fellowship" with the Lord for no valid reason; it is equally possible for him to "feel good" about his relationship with God even though he is living in disobedience.

The wisdom view gives our emotional makeup its rightful place. Our feelings are designed to express our response to objective reality. If a person loses a loved one, it is appropriate to feel sorrow and grief. If the individual achieves a major accomplishment, joy is a fitting emotion.

The question is, how are we to determine what is real and true? The answer is, God has told us in His Word. Most of the time, our five senses are reliable interpreters of reality, for God designed them to be trustworthy. But whenever there is a conflict between one's own perception of reality and what God says is true, the wise believer trusts God's Word (cf. 2 Kings 6:15-17). For often, in the midst of hostile circumstances, one's inner impressions are casting doubts on God's wisdom, love, and/or power, while God's Word affirms that He is at work in all things to accomplish what is good on behalf of the believer (Romans 8:28-29). At such points, the Christian has to overrule the pull of his emotions and adopt the perspective of faith (cf. Matthew 6:25-34). When he does, he not only has a more solid foundation for making decisions, he is also able to bring his emotions under control. For they will eventually follow what his mind has determined to be true. Such a process enables the believer to be in control of his emotions rather than permitting his feelings to dominate him.[2]

WALKING BY FAITH, NOT SIGHT

From the perspective of the way of wisdom, the formula for experiencing the fullness of one's relationship to the Lord is succinctly expressed in 2 Corinthians 5:7: "we walk by faith, not by sight." In the context of this discussion, to walk by sight would be to require perceptible proof of God's presence and ongoing direct communication of His will. But that approach amounts to testing God (Deuteronomy 6:16), which He rejects (Matthew 4:7). On the other hand, to walk by faith is to act on the basis that what God has said is true (Romans 4:20-21).

To spell this out further, there are three specific steps that can be identified in the process of cultivating a personal relationship with God. *Intellectually,* one must *learn* what God has declared to be true and real. *Volitionally,* one must take God at His word and *accept* His pronouncements as being true. Then one can *respond emotionally* in accordance with God's moral will.

Let's look at these three steps separately. First, what has God declared to be true? Here are some "for instances." He is the Sovereign Lord over history and creation. He has provided redemption for rebellious man through the death and resurrection of His Son, Jesus Christ. He has decreed that those who turn from their sin and come to God through faith in Jesus are forgiven and brought into an eternal relationship of sonship to God. To those who thus become His children, God has promised His personal, continual, indwelling presence. He has promised to cause all things to work together for good in the process of conforming believers into the image of Jesus Christ. To those who are dependent upon Him in the pursuit of His purposes, He has promised the spiritual power necessary to obey His moral will. And He has promised to personally respond to the prayers of His children in a way that will meet their needs, reflect His character, and glorify His name.[3]

Well, I Reckon So

As far as the Christian's will is concerned, the operational term is "reckon" (Romans 6:11). To reckon is to consider something to be true and act on the basis of it. This is faith applied: "God said it, I believe it, that settles it, so I'm going to do it."

The intellectual and volitional steps set the stage and establish the objective content for the emotional response. Significantly, just as God's moral will governs the believer's actions, attitudes, motivations, means, and goals, it also directs his personal response to God. According to Scripture, God is to be loved (Matthew 22:37), praised (Psalm 135:1; 150:1-6), blessed (Psalm 135:20), worshipped (Psalm 99:5), exalted (Psalm 99:5), feared (1 Peter 1:17), hoped upon (1 Peter 3:5), trusted (1 Peter 4:19), rejoiced in (Psalm 149:2), extolled (Psalm 145:1), and thanked (Psalm 140:13). (The reader would do well to consult the Psalms for a "personal relationship with God" that finds appropriate emotional expression.)

By now, the contrast between the subjectivity of the traditional view and the emotional response of the way of wisdom should be evident. "In my heart I know God wants me to quit my job, for He surely has something better to take its place." That is unacceptable subjectivity, for that conclusion cannot be verified by an objective source of truth. "My heart exults in God, my Savior." That is a proper, emotional response to the character and work of God as revealed in the objective Word of God. God *is* our Savior, and as such He merits our praise, thanksgiving, worship, and adoration. The believer's emotional energy should be channeled into biblically mandated responses to divinely defined truth. When these commands relate to the person of God, the believer's experience of his personal relationship to the Lord is legitimately lifted to the highest possible level of enjoyment.

Once we understand the proper pattern of emotional expression (learn—reckon—respond), we are in a position to recognize that in reality, the relationship of New Testament saints with God is characterized by an intimacy Old Testament believers would never have dreamed was possible.

Far Then, Father Now

In the Old Testament, God spoke from the mountain, He spoke from the cloud, He spoke from His throne "lofty and exalted" (Isaiah 6:1). But for all of His visible and audible manifestations, it would never have occurred to an Israelite to come boldly before the throne of God. He was the Holy Sovereign. "Again and again it was stressed that man must keep his place, and his distance, in the presence of a holy God. This emphasis overshadowed everything else."[4]

But with the advent of Christ, and the revelation of God through Him, an entirely new order of relationship between God and the believer was opened up. J.I. Packer gives this superb explanation:

> What is a Christian? The question can be answered in many ways, but the richest answer I know is that a Christian is one who has God for his Father....
>
> The revelation to the believer that God is his Father is in a sense the climax of the Bible, just as it was a final step in the revelatory process which the Bible records....
>
> ...If you want to judge how well a person understands Christianity, find out how much he makes of the thought of being God's child, and having God as his Father. If this is not the thought that prompts and controls his worship and prayers and his whole outlook on life, it means that he does not understand Christianity very well at all. For everything that Christ taught, everything that makes the New Testament new, and better than the Old, everything that is distinctively Christian as opposed to merely Jewish, is summed up in the knowledge of the Fatherhood of God. "Father" is the Christian name for God.[5]

No Pity Parties Allowed

The Bible declares that God is my Father. There may be days when I don't feel like God is my Father. But that doesn't change the truth one iota. On those occasions, I can either believe my inner impressions and feed the self-pity that attends my imaginary state of orphanhood; or I can refute my initial feelings with the truth, and bring my attitudes into alignment with the reality that my heavenly

Father is actively involved in my life. His love promotes my highest good; His wisdom determines how to achieve it; and His power accomplishes what His love and wisdom have ordained. That is all fact. I can count on it. I can act on it. And I can express my love, gratitude, confidence, and dependence from the depths of my heart when I bow in His presence and say "Abba! Father!" (Romans 8:12-17, 28-39).

To sum up: In response to the misunderstanding that the wisdom view of guidance cuts God out of the process, we have noted, first of all, that the apostles did not regard that approach as impersonal. Rather, they explained that God's method of guidance for Christians, though less specific and less empirical than that given to Israel, is exactly suited to our status as sons of God.

Further, we have seen that a major part of the problem can be attributed to confusion regarding the role of our feelings in the cultivation of our relationship with God. Rather than functioning as a subjective source of knowledge concerning the "perfect will of God," our emotions should find expression in responding to the objective truth of God's revelation. When one learns to walk by faith rather than by sight, he learns that his fellowship with God is very genuine and personal indeed.

WALKING BY FAITH IN DECISION MAKING

It now remains for us to see how these observations relate to the process of decision making in particular. How is God involved in this important aspect of our lives? And how do we respond to Him as we apply the principles of His moral will and wisdom to our decisions?

God at Work

According to the Bible, God is involved in our decision making at several levels. First, He has provided the resources for making decisions that are acceptable to Him. He has revealed His moral will in its totality. He has instructed us in His Word to seek wisdom for making decisions, and has informed us how to do it. Further, He has given us a new nature which makes obedience of His moral will possible. As a loving Father, He has equipped us with everything we need to make decisions that are pleasing to Him.

As we work through the process of arriving at a decision, God is continually present and working within us. The words of Paul remind us that "it is God who is at work in you, both to will and to work for His good pleasure" (Philippians 2:13). Specifically, His grace enables us to trust in Him (Acts 18:27). He gives the believer the desire to obey His will. By His Spirit, He provides the enablement to keep His commandments. So every single act of obedience is proof of God's personal involvement in our lives (cf. Romans 8:5-8).

Furthermore, it is God who sovereignly opens doors of opportunity for us. When we ask for wisdom, He gives it through the channels He has established for our benefit. He also answers the related prayers we offer concerning our decisions. And He brings to successful completion those of our plans that are within His sovereign will.

Along the way, He utilizes the circumstances and the very process of decision making to change our character and bring us to maturity. As we depend on Him, He blesses our obedience to His moral will and produces His spiritual fruit in our lives. Finally, He works through our decisions to accomplish His purposes — not only in us, but through us.

My primary response to these objectively revealed truths is to be one of trust in God. Trust is actualized by thinking, feeling, and acting as though everything God said about Himself is true.

Trusting God's Work in Guidance

Such trust is expressed in a variety of ways. It is expressed in my confidence that God exercises control over all things. It is manifested in my prayer for open doors, and my expectation that He is working all things together for good. This is my response to His *sovereign guidance.*

I demonstrate faith when I conscientiously obey what I understand of God's moral will, and seek to apply the principles of God's Word to my decisions. I express trust when I take seriously God's intention that decisions within the area of freedom are to be made by me. This is my response to His *moral guidance.*

Trust is expressed in my prayer for wisdom as I approach the decision at hand. And my careful pursuit and evaluation of the wisdom sources He has provided reflect my confidence in the reliability of the pattern He has prescribed. This is my response to His *wisdom guidance.*

I also trust God that if anything more is needed for my guidance — such as an audible voice, an angelic messenger, or some other form of supernatural revelation — He will supply it just as He has when it was necessary in times past. This is my response to His *special guidance.*

Finally, I express trust when I thank Him in advance for what He is going to accomplish through the decision-making process as well as in the outcome of the decision itself. This is my response to the reality of His presence and involvement in my life.

In conclusion, the most common misunderstanding of the wisdom view of guidance is that it is impersonal — that God is not directly involved in the process of our decision making. The cause of that misconception is not the way of wisdom itself — for we have seen that God *is* thoroughly involved at every level of the process. The cause is either an incorrect perception of how God manifests Himself and His will to the believer; or it is an incomplete understanding of the extent and nature of God's participation in the believer's life.

The resolution lies in recognizing that "we walk by faith, not by sight" (2 Corinthians 5:7). First, one must understand that inner impressions are not authoritative messages about God's presence or the content of His will. Second, one must comprehend fully God's complete role in the decision-making process. And third, one must respond in faith to the truth that God has revealed about Himself and His guidance.

The result will be full enjoyment of one's relationship with God authentically expressed in an emotional response that conforms to His moral will.

> The conclusion, when all has been heard, is: fear God and keep His commandments, because this applies to every person (Ecclesiastes 12:13).

Notes

1. James Montgomery Boice gives the following explanation of the imagery in the first paragraph of Galatians 4:

"The English reader will miss the flavor of these verses unless he realizes that the moment of growing up was a very definite one in antiquity and that it involved matters of great religious and legal importance. . . .

"Under Roman law there was. . .a time for the coming of age of a son. But the age when this took place may not have been as fixed as is often assumed (cf. Lightfoot), with the result that the father may have had discretion in setting the time of his son's maturity. . . . A Roman child became an adult at the sacred family festival known as the *Liberalia,* held annually on the seventeenth of March. At this time the child was formally adopted by the father as his acknowledged son and heir and received the *toga virilis* in place of the *toga praetexta* which he had previously worn. . . .

"This is the general background. . .of Paul's words in these verses.

"When the child was a minor in the eyes of the law—it is this word that Paul actually uses—his status is no different from that of a slave, even though he was the future owner of a vast estate. He could make no decisions; he had no freedom. On the other hand, at the time set by his father the child entered into his responsibility and freedom. The application of the illustration is obvious as Paul applies it to the inferior condition of a person under law, both a 'minor' and a 'slave,' and to the new freedom and responsibility that come to him in Christ."

Frank E. Gaebelein, gen. ed., *The Expositor's Bible Commentary* (Grand Rapids: Zondervan Publishing House, 1976), vol. 10: "Galatians," by James Montgomery Boice, p. 471.

2. Cf. Frank B. Minirth and Paul D. Meier, *Happiness Is A Choice: A Manual on the Symptoms, Causes, and Cures of Depression* (Grand Rapids: Baker Book House, 1978), pp. 174-76. These authors stress focusing on behavior in order to control emotions; i.e., do what is right in order to feel right.

3. This list could include every attribute of God, every promise He has made, and another book full of related truths. But since that "other Book" has already been written, we won't seek to duplicate its contents here!

4. J.I. Packer, *Knowing God* (Downers Grove, Ill.: InterVarsity Press, 1973), p. 183.

5. Packer, *Knowing God,* pp. 181-82.

Chapter 16

Making a Good Thing Better

*T*hroughout the last seven chapters, our aim has been to construct a biblical approach to decision making. We believe that we have established both the scriptural validity and practical relevance of "the way of wisdom."

Principles of Decision Making
The Way of Wisdom

1. In those areas specifically addressed by the Bible, the revealed commands and principles of God (His moral will) are to be obeyed.

2. In those areas where the Bible gives no command or principle (nonmoral decisions), the believer is free and responsible to choose his own course of action. Any decision made within the moral will of God is acceptable to God.

3. In nonmoral decisions, the objective of the Christian is to make wise decisions on the basis of spiritual expediency.

4. In all decisions, the believer should humbly submit, in advance, to the outworking of God's sovereign will as it touches each decision.

Figure 30

In Part 2, "The Case of the Missing 'Dot,' " the biblical and experiential deficiencies of the traditional view were examined in detail. Our purpose in this chapter is to review those weaknesses in light of the above principles. What we intend to show is that the way of wisdom incorporates the valid aspects of the traditional view while providing the needed correctives to the shortcomings we have identified. The emphasis, of necessity, will be on the changes that are called for in the perspective of the decision maker. But the result will be a positive clarification of the wisdom approach to decision making.

RESOLVING INTERPRETIVE DIFFICULTIES

As we observed in chapter 5, "Does God Have Three Wills?," the traditional view encounters a major problem when it appeals to *biblical examples* for evidence of an individual will of God. For the historical illustrations say too much, and the statements of doctrine say too little.

Historical examples, such as Paul's "Macedonian Call" and Peter's vision of the "unclean" animals, cite instances of supernatural revelation. Direct guidance was provided, but the means always entailed divine intervention (revelatory vision, angelic messenger, physical miracle, audible voice, or prophetic declaration). The traditional view must dilute the examples to get them to illustrate inward leading. For there is no record of any direct guidance communicated through an inner impression.

On the other hand, while the general statements recorded in the epistles speak of being led by the Holy Spirit, they say nothing about God revealing His will to the heart of the believer on each decision. To those promises of guidance, the traditional view must "add spice," explaining details that are absent from the text.

The way of wisdom is not compelled to add either water or spice to the biblical record. The incidents of divine revelation are recognized as being supernatural provisions in exceptional circumstances. And the general promises of guidance into God's moral will are accepted and appreciated for what they are—provisions of guidance mediated through God's revealed Word.

The same situation exists with regard to *biblical teaching*. In chapter 6, "Does Scripture Teach the 'Dot'?," we examined the key passages most frequently cited in support of the traditional view. In every case, our conclusion was that the concept of an individual will was not required by the text. In most instances, God's moral will is clearly indicated. Furthermore, God's moral will is all that is needed.

When all is said and done, the traditional view lacks a single, definitive proof text. The wisdom view, on the other hand, emerges out of a thorough, natural interpretation of the biblical record.

RESOLVING APPLICATIONAL DIFFICULTIES

In chapters 7 and 8, we identified a number of experiential problems that people encounter because of the flaws in the traditional interpretation of guidance-related passages. By way of review, we grouped those problems under four main categories. The way of wisdom resolves each of those difficulties and the frustration that often attends them.

Applicational Difficulties of the Traditional View

1. Ordinary Decisions: The decision-making process must be abandoned in the "minor" decisions of life.

2. Equal Options: Insistence upon only one "correct" choice generates anxiety over "missing the dot" rather than gratitude for more than one fine opportunity.

3. Immaturity: In some instances, the logic of the traditional view tends to promote immature approaches to decision making.

4. Subjectivity: Certainty that one has found God's individual will is impossible apart from an objective source of knowledge.

An Unneeded Dichotomy Dissolved

In practice, those who follow the traditional view find that they simply don't have time to conscientiously seek God's will for every decision. If they tried, it would take all day just to get dressed. And so they reserve the prescribed decision-making process for "significant" matters. In the ordinary decisions, they try to exercise good judgment, without wasting time.

This pragmatic necessity results in an experiential dichotomy between the "big" and "little" decisions of life. The traditional view consistently maintains that God's individual will applies to every detail of our lives. But in practice, the theology is selectively discarded, being too cumbersome for the demands of real life.

The wisdom view teaches what the traditional view is forced to practice at the level of ordinary decisions — good judgment. But it also takes the same approach to the more important matters. Whatever the decision, the criteria are the same: What is moral and what is wise? Those factors are equally relevant to one's choice of a menu and one's choice of a spouse.

Wisdom does not deny that some decisions are more significant than others. On the contrary, wisdom recognizes that the more important a decision is, the more time and energy should be devoted to it. Insignificant decisions should be made quickly. Such an approach makes good use of time—an important element in walking in wisdom (Ephesians 5:15-17).

Applicational Solutions of the Wisdom View		
	Traditional View	Way of Wisdom
Ordinary Decisions:	The decision making process must be abandoned in the "minor" decisions of life.	**One should exercise good judgment and not waste time.**

Equal = Equal

As long as the traditional view has to find the "dot," the center of God's will, it must maintain that in any given decision, there can be only one "correct" choice. That rules out the possibility of "equal options." When the decider is able to recognize the superiority of one alternative among several, there is no problem. But when two or more possibilities evidence the same degree of promise, and no clear winner emerges, the anxiety level begins to climb.

The wisdom view eliminates that tension. In nonmoral decisions, we can say, "six of one, half dozen of the other." And we have the theology to back it up. It really doesn't matter which shoe one puts on first. If you are ambidextrous, use either hand.

In the area of freedom, equal options are more likely than not. Realizing that fact enables one to be grateful when God, in His sovereign grace, opens two or more doors of opportunity. The choice may not be any easier (a decision still must be made!), but the individual does not have to worry about "missing the dot." When alternatives that are equally wise appear within the moral will of God, that is a "no lose" situation. The believer can make his choice with the full confidence that God will work out His purposes through whichever decision he makes!

Applicational Solutions of the Wisdom View		
	Traditional View	Way of Wisdom
Ordinary Decisions:	The decision making process must be abandoned in the "minor" decisions of life.	One should exercise good judgment and not waste time.
Equal Options:	Insistence upon only one "correct" choice generates anxiety over "missing the dot" rather than gratitude for more than one fine opportunity.	**One should thank God for the opportunity to select from acceptable alternatives, and choose one's personal preference.**

Immaturity Exposed

The traditional view is unable to account for the fact that immature Christians tend to make immature decisions while more mature believers usually evidence greater wisdom in their decisions. The traditional position maintains that God's individual will is perfect; it also holds that that perfect will is fully available to each Christian — regardless of his level of growth.

The wisdom view better corresponds to reality. It recognizes that wisdom is gained progressively. God has not promised to whisper "perfect plans" or omniscience into the mind of any believer who asks. Accordingly, the apostles counseled that when a decision is required, those who are "full of...wisdom" (Acts 6:3) and "prudent" (1 Timothy 3:2) will do the best job. The church has not been told to identify those who are best at picking up and decoding inner impressions, but those who are mature and wise (1 Corinthians 6:5).

Not only is the traditional view unable to account for an "immature will of God," it actually tends to promote immature approaches to decision making in certain circumstances. In chapter 7, "More Doubts About the 'Dot,' " we identified four ways this happens. The way of wisdom provides the needed corrective to each of these improper approaches.

First, since the way of wisdom requires the believer to defend his decisions with sound reasons, an individual is not permitted to hide his motives behind a vague "the Lord led me." If the decision in question is reckless or foolhardy, a more mature believer has a basis for counseling his brother. By gently exposing the fallacies in the foolish plan, he can direct the less mature believer away from

---

The Traditional View Promotes Immature Decisions

- By permitting believers to justify unwise decisions on grounds that "God told me to do it."
- By fostering costly delays because of uncertainty about God's individual will.
- By influencing people to reject personal preferences when faced with apparently equal options.
- By encouraging the practice of "putting out a fleece"—letting circumstances dictate the decision.

---

potentially harmful consequences. He can do that because he is not intimidated by any "final word" that supposedly came from the Lord.

Furthermore, the explanation of reasons behind a decision by a mature Christian can become an occasion of training and growth for others. For when younger believers watch a godly man work through a complex problem, the process of seeking wisdom is modeled for them. That's one reason we are so thankful for the numerous explanations given by the apostle Paul for his decisions.

"I Felt Led"

This idea of explaining the reasons for difficult decisions is one that merits careful consideration on the part of pastors in particular. When the determination has been made to move from one place of ministry to another, it is very common (and perhaps expected) for the pastor to announce, "I feel that the Lord has called me to a new place of service." That explanation sounds very spiritual, and is usually accepted at face value by many in the church, including the pastor himself. But a few can't help thinking, "I wonder what the real reasons are." And in many cases, the real reasons are so painful, the pastor is thankful he can hide behind the "Lord's will." As a result, the problems that prompted the decision to move (if that was the case) remain camouflaged until a new pastor stumbles onto them. At the very least, the departing pastor misses a golden opportunity to model wise decision making before his flock. While there may be occasions in which silence is the better part of wisdom, there are many others in which the church would benefit if the pastor manifested greater candor in explaining his decisions.

Second, where the follower of the traditional view might waste valuable time seeking an unmistakable message from the Lord, the wisdom view would encourage decisiveness. For one of the prime characteristics of a wise decision is good use of time, as we have already established. The decision maker should allow adequate time to gather facts and acquire wisdom, but there is no need to wait for some inner signal to proceed.

Third, where the applicant of the traditional view might choose the less appealing of two equal options (to guard against self-centeredness), the one who follows the way of wisdom would probably do just the opposite. For he would understand that, all other things being equal, he is perfectly free to choose the alternative he prefers (cf. 1 Corinthians 7:39-40). In fact, wisdom recognizes that following one's personal inclination will make it easier to carry out the decision with eagerness and gratitude—attitudes that are part of God's moral will.

Fourth, rather than "putting out a fleece" and expecting God to reveal His plan circumstantially, the way of wisdom carefully evaluates possible eventualities and considers their potential side-effects on the decision. The decision maker who is seeking wisdom would determine which circumstances would render a given option

---

Applicational Solutions of the Wisdom View

	Traditional View	Way of Wisdom
Ordinary Decisions:	The decision making process must be abandoned in the "minor" decisions of life.	One should exercise good judgment and not waste time.
Equal Options:	Insistence upon only one "correct" choice generates anxiety over "missing the dot" rather than gratitude for more than one fine opportunity.	One should thank God for the opportunity to select from acceptable alternatives, and choose one's personal preference.
Immaturity:	In some instances, the logic of the traditional view tends to promote immature approaches to decision making.	**One should apply maturity by gathering and evaluating data, devoting sufficient time to the process, giving personal desires their proper place, and basing the decision on sound reasons.**

wise, and which ones would make it unwise. But he would not view those circumstances as being a message from the Lord.

For instance, a pastoral candidate might determine in advance that he would accept a call to a church if the congregational vote was at least 95 percent in his favor. Such a vote would be an indication of unity and support, elements that a pastor would consider to be highly desirable at the outset of a new ministry. But wisdom would not regard that vote as God's stamp of approval guaranteeing the future success of that ministry. It would be an objective indication of potential compatability, not a green light from heaven.

What we are demonstrating is that the way of wisdom resolves the applicational difficulties of the traditional view. To this point we have seen how wisdom effectively corrects the problems concerning ordinary decisions, equal options, and immature approaches to decision making.

The Goliath of Subjectivity

The way of wisdom also eliminates the major applicational difficulty of the traditional view — subjectivity. In chapter 8, "Impressions Are Impressions," we saw how subjectivity permeates the traditional approach. The decision maker has to: (1) evaluate the signs to determine whether they are indicating some direction from God; (2) discern what the message is; (3) decide whether it is confirmed by other signs; and (4) determine whether the leading is clear enough to be considered authoritative. And he must do all of that without having access to any biblical standard by which such judgments should be made. Scripture is helpful in that it sets the moral limits on the options. But it is not specific enough to point to God's individual will for a particular decision. God could break through with supernatural revelation, but that kind of direction is not to be sought or expected. Without an objective source of knowledge, the decider is denied the certainty that he needs in order to obey God's individual will. As a result, while the traditional view requires the believer to know God's will in order to make correct decisions, it does not offer an objective source of truth to discover it.

Certainty at Last

In the wisdom view, there is no individual will of God that must be discovered, and no ambiguous system for sorting it out.

Christian decision making is grounded on the objective truth of God's *moral* will. According to the Bible, the only aspect of God's will that must be known, the only aspect that can be known, is God's *moral* will. And 100 percent of God's moral will—not 80 percent, not 90 percent, but 100 percent—has been revealed in the Bible. The believer already has at his disposal everything that God is going to tell him about his decision. There will be no further hints, clues, nudges, or hunches to try to decipher—they just aren't needed.

The moral will of God is objective, complete, and adequate. If we needed more revelation, God would give us more. But the Bible says that what God has told His children is sufficient for every area of life.

> All Scripture is inspired by God and profitable for teaching, for reproof, for correction, for training in righteousness; that the man of God may be adequate, equipped for every good work (2 Timothy 3:16-17).

And Peter added that God's "divine power has granted to us everything pertaining to life and godliness . . ." (2 Peter 1:3).

Not only does the Bible contain all of God's moral will, it also instructs the believer regarding the application of God's will to decision making. God's Word does not tell one *what* to decide in every situation; it teaches *how* to come to a decision that is acceptable to God. It is from Scripture that we learn the necessity of determining those choices that are both *moral* and *wise*. It is the Bible that tells us to acquire wisdom and apply it to our decisions. It is the Bible that tells us where wisdom is to be found. It is the Bible that tells us of God's involvement in giving us wisdom. It is the Bible that establishes the objective standard by which we may define and recognize what is moral and wise.

Furthermore, it is assumed in Scripture that knowledge of God's moral will and the necessary wisdom for good decision making are attainable. Whether the passages contain a promise (Romans 10:9; James 1:5), a command (Ephesians 5:17; Colossians 4:5), a statement of purpose (Romans 12:2; Proverbs 6:6), or a prayer (Colossians 1:9; James 1:5-7), the goal is always viewed as reachable.

The Reality of Growth Incorporated

It is important to note here that the wisdom view acknowledges growth in the process. The Bible indicates that one's depth of wisdom and knowledge of God's moral will will increase progressively over a period of time. God never requires either absolute knowledge of His moral will or perfect wisdom (omniscience) of the decision maker. Nor does He promise it. The believer is expected to study the Word sufficiently to become personally convinced of its meaning (2 Timothy 2:15). On the basis of that understanding, he is to develop spiritual convictions (Romans 14:5). If the decisions he makes are consistent with the explicit commands of Scripture (1 Thessalonians 4:1-3) and his own carefully derived convictions, they are acceptable to God (Romans 14:3, 22). As he grows in spiritual insight and understanding of God's Word, his convictions will be appropriately revised, his judgment will mature, and his decisions will reflect greater wisdom. But at any

Applicational Solutions of the Wisdom View		
	Traditional View	Way of Wisdom
Ordinary Decisions:	The decision making process must be abandoned in the "minor" decisions of life.	One should exercise good judgment and not waste time.
Equal Options:	Insistence upon only one "correct" choice generates anxiety over "missing the dot" rather than gratitude for more than one fine opportunity.	One should thank God for the opportunity to select from acceptable alternatives, and choose one's personal preference.
Immaturity:	In some instances, the logic of the traditional view tends to promote immature approaches to decision making.	One should apply maturity by gathering and evaluating data, devoting sufficient time to the process, giving personal desires their proper place, and basing the decision on sound reasons.
Subjectivity:	Certainty that one has found God's individual will is impossible apart from an objective source of knowledge.	**Since God's moral will has been completely revealed and the means of acquiring wisdom has been explained, the knowledge required for decision making is fully attainable.**

Figure 31

given point, the believer can acquire a sufficient knowledge of God's moral will and an adequate level of wisdom to make a decision that meets God's approval. And the Bible tells him how.

What we are saying, then, is that the goal of the traditional view (certain knowledge of God's individual will) is unreachable, while the goal of the wisdom view (adequate knowledge of God's moral will and wisdom) is attainable. The reason why the traditional approach cannot reach its goal is because there is no individual will of God to be found and the method for finding it always yields uncertainty. The reason the way of wisdom can reach its goal is because the moral will of God has been objectively and completely revealed, and the means of acquiring wisdom is spelled out. Furthermore, God is personally involved in guiding believers into His moral will, increasing their knowledge of His moral will, and increasing their store of wisdom.

ADOPTING THE RIGHT PERSPECTIVE

We should add at this point that in all probability there are many who *think* in terms of the traditional view, but *act* more in accordance with wisdom. Though purist traditional theology holds out for certain knowledge of God's individual will, most practitioners are content with something less than "certain." They have an adequate basis for proceeding if they can say, "As far as I can tell, this seems to be the direction God is leading." In fact, some traditional writers will say, "If you come to a deadline without having certainty concerning God's will for that decision, don't worry about it. Make the best decision you can on the basis of what you know, and trust the outcome to the Lord."

Less Than Unanimous Is OK

Something of a similar nature occurs in many group decisions. From the traditional viewpoint, one would expect God to reveal His "perfect will" to the group in such a manner that there would be unanimity among the members of the group. But this does not always happen. And, as we noted in chapter 8, "Impressions Are Impressions," that fact has been disturbing to some individuals who are seeking to maintain consistency between their doctrine and practice. Most believers, however, accept differences of opinion as a fact of life. And so churches with congregational forms of government usually make decisions on the basis of a majority or two-thirds vote.

The wisdom view resolves the tension between principle and practice. When the goal of a group or committee is a wise decision, it is expected first of all that several opinions will be expressed in the process of gathering wisdom. Wisdom also anticipates that there is a good likelihood that some within the group will recognize the merits of one option while others may be more convinced of the advantages of another. That's because people have different perspectives, and most alternatives have their strengths and weaknesses. When, at last, a decision must be made, a less than unanimous vote is no cause for alarm. For the goal is not a "perfect will" but a wise decision.

Once a matter has been thoroughly discussed and the decision is made, each member is obliged to put away his personal preferences and join in a wholehearted effort to support the plan selected. For that is how unity is maintained. That unity, which Christ so desired for His Church, is not the product of uniformity of thought which determines an ideal will; it comes through the submission of each member to the authority of the local church by accepting and supporting the wisdom of the group.

Road Signs or Wisdom Signs

Similarities in practice between the traditional and wisdom views are perhaps most apparent in the evaluation of so-called "road signs." These similarities, which we will observe in a moment, are due to the fact that both viewpoints are searching for something specific; and both are working with the same data. But because the way of wisdom is seeking for wisdom rather than an individual will of God, the manner in which it perceives the "road signs" is significantly different. Rather than regarding them as pointers to the "perfect will of God, " they are regarded as "wisdom signs"—sources to be consulted in the acquisition of wisdom. The difference in perspective will be evident as we compare the respective approaches to the "road signs" of common sense, spiritual counsel, personal desires, circumstances, results, the Bible, and inward impressions.

Horse Sense Bridled

No one is against good ol' *common sense*. The traditional view commends its use as a pointer to God's individual will—usually. But specific biblical illustrations where God's individual will ran counter to common sense requires the traditional view to hedge. God must be given the freedom to lead in an "uncommon" way, as He did with Noah, Abraham, Joshua, Gideon, and Naaman. So in most cases, the traditional view utilizes common sense as an indicator of God's individual will—but not always.

With the wisdom view, the believer may confidently apply common sense to every single decision. For common sense is regarded as one form of wisdom that is part of God's gracious endowment to men. The opposite of common sense is naiveté, foolishness, or stupidity.

The only time common sense is to be set aside is when it contradicts God's revealed (moral) will. Man's perspective must always give way to God's moral will when the two come into conflict.

That principle accounts for Noah's ark, Abraham's sacrifice, and the military strategies of Joshua and Gideon. In every case, God revealed His moral will by divine revelation. In the same way, believers today must test and submit their common sense to the "divine sense" of God as revealed in the Bible. For common sense that opposes the wisdom of God is no longer sensible.

So important is common sense that Scripture commands that church elders must be "sensible" (Titus 1:8), and that older men, young women, and young men should learn to be "sensible" (Titus 2:2, 5-6). Much of the wisdom found in the book of Proverbs is just good common sense. This is evidenced by the fact that many of those proverbs have parallels in other cultures, as well as in our own.

So rather than being a road sign that one tries to read in order to find God's individual will, common sense is a source of wisdom that the believer is expected to follow as long as it harmonizes with the moral will of God. If that qualification is maintained, the source of the common sense does not matter. In fact, there are situations where unbelievers can be a valuable source of counsel for the Christian (cf. Luke 16:8). A local mechanic or a consumer magazine may offer valuable "common sense" that can help the believer make a wise decision.

Expanding the Frame of Reference

The traditional view takes seriously the scriptural admonitions to seek guidance from *spiritual counselors* (Proverbs 11:14; 24:6; et al.). But it has to add some words of caution. For the advice of counselors might conflict at some points, obscuring rather than clarifying the Lord's leading. Furthermore, since it is only the individual who can ultimately discern the Lord's ideal will for his decision, he must realize that the counsel of others must be carefully evaluated rather than simply adopted. As a result, one must exercise great care in reading this road sign. For some counsel could point down the wrong path.

The advisory nature of counsel creates no problems for the wisdom view. Counselors are viewed as one source of wisdom. They can supply facts and insight not otherwise available to the decision maker. But they are not viewed as omniscient or even determinative.

The searcher of wisdom not only asks for a counselor's opinion, but the reasons behind the viewpoint expressed. Thus, the inquirer is better able to judge the merits of the advice. In particular, there are two good questions that could be put to a godly advisor: "Do you know of any scriptural or biblical principles that apply to the decision I am making? Have you gained practical insight through your experience in making a similar decision that would be of value to me?"

Avoid Lemons with a Fruit Inspector

Wisdom seeks for competent advice where it is most needed. I am a dunce about anything under the hood of a car. So I do not shop for a car by myself. In fact, most of the cars I have owned were located and recommended to me by my father or some other mechanic friend. It is an application of wisdom for me to call my father and say, "This is your auto-ignorant son. I'm in the market for a car. I need something that will get at least 20 miles per gallon and cost no more than $3,000. Would you look for one for me?" I have yet to buy a lemon, and I don't think it has just been luck.

Counselors have real value in uncovering blind spots that are often overlooked under the pressure of a difficult situation. I regularly talk with students who are under great stress because they are unable to do all their school work. Often I learn that those students missed a week of classes because they caught some bug that was going around. In the process of counseling, I can say, "Is your goal to be faithful to God, or to get a certain grade in this course?" When they say, "I want to be faithful to God," the light begins to break through. I am able to point out that God expects them to be faithful in their use of whatever time is available to them—even if that results in a lower grade. If they are faithful with what they have to work with, God is pleased.

Under the pressure of grades, the students had unconsciously substituted an unreachable, human goal for the attainable objective established by God. By getting fresh insight from a counselor, the tension was legitimately eliminated, enabling them to function effectively again. That is a major value in good counsel. It can put matters into a proper and manageable perspective. And that kind of perspective is necessary if one is to make a sound decision.

Putting Desires in Their Place

The traditional view teaches that one's *personal desires* can be a road sign pointing to God's individual will. But once again, there is some difficulty in reading the sign. For believers have godly desires, sinful desires, foolish desires, proud desires, and any number that are hard to identify. Christians continually ask, "How can I distinguish a desire given by the Holy Spirit from one that springs from my own heart that would be satisfied with less than God's best?"

The wisdom view is not left with introspective guesswork. To begin with, it does not view any desire as authoritative. All desires must be judged by God's moral will and wisdom. Morally acceptable desires are approved by God and sinful ones are not—and the Bible explains which are which. Personal desires must also be judged by wisdom. Sometimes I feel like leaving my office to play some basketball in the gym next door. As I look at the work on my desk, I am forced to admit that it would be wiser to finish grading the Bible exams. If any time remains after that, I can run over to the gym for some exercise. My desire to continue as a faculty member overrides my desire to shoot a few baskets.

Personal desires that have been declared acceptable by God's moral will and by wisdom can be an excellent source of wisdom. For the Scripture says that we are to serve God eagerly with all our hearts. This command can be more easily obeyed if one's decisions are in harmony with one's personal inclinations. If third-grade girls give you the hives, and you are motivated by the challenge of giving some direction to junior high boys, accept the eighth-grade boys Sunday school class. If the options are genuinely equal, wisdom chooses that one that would be most enjoyable to carry out.

Spiritual growth will make a significant impact on one's personal desires over a period of time. For as one matures, he will have an increasing desire to live a life that manifests wisdom. Thus, as growth takes place, one's personal desires will more and more reflect what is wise.

It All Depends

Since God controls all *circumstances*, the traditional view concludes that He is inaudibly revealing His individual will through them to one who has learned to "read providence." In addition, the traditional approach looks for open and closed doors which are considered to be "yes" and "no" road signs indicating the direction of God's leading. The immediate problem with such a procedure is that of determining the message that the circumstances are supposed to be communicating. And, as we demonstrated in chapter 13, it is impossible to make a biblical case for "reading providence" as a means of gaining guidance for a personal decision.

That does not mean that circumstances are unimportant to the wisdom view. Quite the contrary. Since circumstances provide the context in which a decision is made, they are a key source of wisdom for the decision maker. They must be evaluated, not to determine some clue from God, but to help decide the advisability of a given course of action. "Circumstances" is a word that covers a multitude of specifics: cost, people available, time, mechanical problems, opportunities, and so on. Wisdom recognizes that every option "has its advantages and disadvantages." Circumstances indicate many of the pros and cons, but they carry no "yes" or "no" tags.

What about Jeremiah?

The traditional view often speaks of a decision being confirmed as God's will by the *results* that followed. But again, this road sign requires a tricky interpretation of circumstances. For one must answer the question: Which results equal confirmation? And no one is exactly sure. Human success is not an automatic proof or Jeremiah never was in God's will. Many of God's servants have been faithful in their ministries and have encountered nothing but difficulties and obstacles. Are they to be labeled as failures? Was their lack of "productivity" due to being out of God's will? That's not the teaching of Scripture. But the traditional view has no other basis for defining confirmation.

The way of wisdom views results from a different perspective. It is wise to gain wisdom from the results of previous decisions—whether those of others or our own. For those results may reveal factors that had not previously been taken into consideration. And the results of past decisions may indicate the potential outcome of a current decision. So it is good to ask questions of others who have been down similar paths: "How long did it take you to get to the church camp via Highway 30?"; "Was Bob effective as a teacher in Vacation Bible School?"; "How many miles to the gallon are you getting with your import?"

Results can reveal wisdom to the careful observer. But they must be viewed within the framework of God's sovereignty. Situations change and the impact of different factors varies. So the results that followed from a decision in the past do not guarantee the same results for an issue currently under consideration. Christian businessmen do well to analyze cause and effect relationships between marketing plans and actual sales. But they know that an unforeseen strike, a downturn in the nation's economy, or a sudden shift in consumer buying habits can make a shambles of a "proven" strategy. And so the believing businessman gains what wisdom he can from past successes and failures, sets his plans in motion, and leaves the outcome to the sovereign disposition of God.

The Bible Says

We have already discussed the respective perspectives of the two positions concerning *the Word of God*. The traditional view places a great emphasis on understanding the Bible, for a great deal of God's will for the individual has already been spelled out. The wisdom view would go farther and say that 100 percent of God's will has been revealed. God has said what He is going to say about how to make our personal decisions. That fact makes the understanding of God's Word the most important aspect of effective decision making.

Who Is This, Really?

Next to the road sign of the Bible, inner impressions are regarded by the traditional view as the most direct link between the believer and God. It is through these impressions that God is said to point the way to His ideal will for a given decision.

The wisdom view acknowledges the reality of inner impressions. In the course of making decisions, everyone experiences internal hunches that seem to point to some specific conclusion. What the wisdom view disavows is the significance attached to those inward impulses by the traditional view. (The reasons for this denial were detailed in chapter 8, "Impressions Are Impressions.") They may be summarized as follows: (1) there is no indication in *Scripture* that the Holy Spirit leads believers through inner impressions; (2) it is impossible to determine with certainty the *source* of the impressions; (3) it is impossible to judge with certainty the so-called *message* of the impressions; (4) the need for corroborative *verification* from the other signs discredits the genuineness of the supposed inner voice; and (5) since inner impressions cannot be considered to be revelation from God, they lack the necessary *authority* to compel obedience.

So how does wisdom respond to impulses? First, wisdom recognizes that impressions can come from a multitude of sources: God, Satan, the flesh, immaturity, past experience, gastric upset, euphoria, stress, insomnia, a TV commercial, and so on ad infinitum. And Scripture establishes no criteria for distinguishing sources. Second, wisdom emphasizes that no inner impression has the authority to function as an indicator of divine guidance. Third, inner impressions are *judged by the moral will of God and by wisdom.* And on the basis of that evaluation, the believer determines his response to the impressions.

Those impressions that conform to God's moral will and to wisdom may be followed. There are numerous occasions when an idea pops into a person's head apparently out of thin air. Subsequent reflection brings the individual to the conclusion that that impression is a first-rate plan. It promotes the accomplishment of one's goals and does so in an effective way. That impulse ought to be followed, not as an indicator of God's ideal will, but as a wise way to serve God.

On the other hand, those impressions that are either sinful or foolish ought to be ignored. Ideas that violate common sense, distract one from accomplishing other important tasks, or otherwise result in a waste of time can be confidently rejected. Bizarre impressions do not merit special attention. If God wants someone to do something that is not indicated in His revealed Word, He will tell them in plain words. But impressions do not have any authority requiring obedience.

A Key to Finding the Keys

By way of illustration, let's watch Bob who has lost his car keys. He goes through the house looking in all of the regular places—no keys. He goes through the house again, searching beneath cushions, under furniture, and any other spots where his keys might have fallen. Still no keys. Now he is beginning to realize the magnitude of his problem. The thought that he might not ever find his keys sends chills down his spine. In response to his increasing anxiety, he stops looking and prays, "Lord, I really need those keys. Please help me find them." Then he resumes the search.

Before long, he gets an impression: "Maybe they are in the trunk of the car."

Let's freeze the scene right there. Virtually everyone has experienced something of that sort, so we understand Bob's situation. If Bob were to remove the back seat of the car, climb into the trunk, and actually find his keys, he would rejoice for the rest of the day. In fact, he might go around saying, "I just knew they would be in the trunk. I asked God to help me find my keys, and He told me where they were."

But would that be the case? Let's return to the point of the impression. Bob now has a hunch that his keys are locked in the car trunk. He has to decide whether it is worth the trouble of dismantling the interior of his car to look there. Does he know that his keys are there? More to the point, is God's veracity at stake in the absence or presence of those keys? If he looks in the trunk and does not find the keys, should Bob tell his friends, "God lied to me today; He said I would find my keys in the trunk, but they weren't there"? The answer to all of these questions is no. Because impressions are impressions. They have no authority to impart divine revelation.

So what should Bob do? He should test his impression by the moral will of God and by wisdom. Will he violate God's revealed will if he looks in the trunk for his keys? No. What does wisdom indicate? Wisdom recognizes the plausibility of the hunch. If the impression had indicated that Bob's keys were in Yugoslavia, Bob would disregard it as being absurd. If the impulse had directed Bob to look in the attic where he had not been for three months, he would also rule that out as being a waste of time. But would it be a waste of time to look in the car trunk? Maybe not. There are some other things Bob could do first without using a lot of time. He could determine if he or any other member of the family had used the keys to open the trunk recently. He could look through other, more accessible parts of the car. If he remembered opening the trunk the night before, or learned that his wife had done so that morning, he could have a good basis for following that impression.

Adopting this perspective, if Bob finds his keys in the trunk, he will thank God for answering his prayer. But if he looks in the trunk in vain, he doesn't have to question his faith or God's trustworthiness. He can continue to look for his keys with the consolation that one legitimate possibility has been eliminated. If he later finds the keys in his "yard work pants," he will thank the Lord that his keys have been found, and learn a valuable lesson about keeping track of important items.

"I Just Don't Have Peace about It"

One aspect of inward impressions is the presence or absence of peace. We have shown that the way of wisdom does not consider peace or lack of peace as a direct message communicating specific guidance into the individual will of God. This does not mean, however, that the way of wisdom is oblivious to the importance of a believer's emotional state. Lack of Galatians 5:22 peace is a matter of sin which should be corrected by dependence upon the Spirit. But there are other times when lack of peace may indicate immaturity, fear of one's inability to keep a potential commitment, concern about the wisdom of a course of action, or uncertainty about one's judgment in the decision at hand. The way of wisdom judges the emotional makeup and momentary emotional state of the believer himself as one of the valid circumstances in the situation. That "concerned feeling" should be judged by wisdom. One's emotional makeup should be judged by wisdom. Certain jobs are not best accomplished by more emotional believers. Certain pressure situations should be avoided by those who cannot yet do them with emotional ease. Each believer has an emotional makeup which joins him in any decision. Wisdom considers the believer and his emotions as one of the valid circumstances in a potential course of action.

In the final analysis, every good thing comes from God (James 1:17). So any thought, impression, or feeling that is both moral and wise has its ultimate origin in Him. The believer should thank God for whatever wisdom He imparts through whatever means. But the Christian should always recognize wisdom for what it is—the perception of an effective way to accomplish spiritual goals. It is not a command from God; nor is it a guarantee of success.

To sum up: Everyone utilizes essentially the same sources of information in the process of decision making. So whether the believer is following the traditional view or the wisdom view, he will study input from common sense, spiritual counsel, personal desires, circumstances, results, the Bible, and inner impressions. The two views do not look at the data in the same way, but since the sources are the same it is not surprising that conclusions reached by the two approaches are often the same. The differences come in the final goal. The traditional view is looking for the individual will of God while the wisdom view is seeking a wise decision within the moral will of God. The differences also come in the way the sources are viewed. To the traditional view, they are "road signs" pointing to the individual will of God when interpreted properly. To the wisdom view, Scripture reveals the moral will of God and the other sources are "wisdom signs" corporately pointing to a moral and wise decision. So the earlier chart changes.

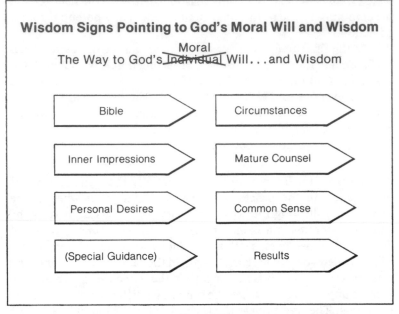

Figure 32

The title of this chapter, "Making a Good Thing Better," reflects our judgment that the traditional view offers a *good* approach to making decisions. The sheer volume of material devoted to critiquing that position may have obscured that fact. But we feel that much of what Pastor Bill Thompson presented in Part 1 is very accurate and helpful.

There are several reasons why Christians have received good service from the traditional approach. The primary reason is that the traditional view insists that all decisions must conform to the moral will of God. The Lord has promised to bless obedience to His Word. So decisions that promote such obedience are profitable.

The second factor behind many of the practical successes of the traditional framework is the maturity and wisdom of those applying it. When wise people search for God's ideal will, what they usually find, and apply, is wisdom. Wisdom by any other name still makes good decisions.

The only time people get into trouble with the traditional view is when they make a foolish decision. Usually, an unwise decision is the result of an immature reaction to one or more "road signs." The moral will of God prohibits us from following a course of action that we know to be foolish. But "foolish" (violating wisdom) is not as serious as "immoral" (violating God's moral will). And sometimes, even unwise decisions turn out all right because of God, who works all things together for good for those who love Him.

The third reason people have experienced success with the traditional view is because they have not tried to enforce its principles with the small decisions of life. Where it has proved unworkable, the traditional approach has been unconsciously set aside in practice.

As good as the traditional view is, *it is not good enough.* The way of wisdom makes this "good thing" better by bringing correction to the doctrinal deficiencies of the traditional position. On the foundation of a more accurate theology of guidance, the way of wisdom is also able to build a superstructure of principles that can be uniformly applied to all of life's decisions. The final product is an approach to decision making that is better doctrinally and applicationally.

It is to this—the application of the way of wisdom—that we now turn our attention. For any approach to decision making must show it knows how to face specific, difficult, and often perplexing choices in the arena of life. As we will discover, the way of wisdom is adequate for the task since God's teaching and grace are sufficient for the decisions we face today and will face tomorrow.

PART 4

Deciding the Big Ones

The Wisdom View Applied

Chapter 17

Singleness, Marriage, and Wisdom —

Should I or Shouldn't I?

*W*ithout question, Ted Bradford and Annette Miller qualified as the great match up of the year at Faith Bible College. They were attractive, intelligent, mature, compatible, and highly committed to Jesus Christ. And both were giving strong consideration to a vocation of service to the Lord. On campus it was a foregone conclusion that they would marry. They were perfect for each other.

Well, almost perfect. If it weren't for the Africa business.... If Ted had a clearer call to the ministry.... If only they could, in good conscience, follow the "almost perfect" will of God.

If Ted could have shared his innermost thoughts with the student body as he did with Pastor Thompson, his peers might have been initially surprised, and disappointed, to learn that there were any clouds on the horizon. But they would have understood. And they would have shared vicariously in the agony of working through the apparently conflicting commitments in the search for God's perfect will and His confirming peace. One doesn't have to walk in Ted's shoes to empathize with his feelings.

Indeed, if the counsel sincerely offered by Pastor Thompson is correct, the implications for Ted's marriage decision are very sobering:

1. In all the world, there is either no person or only one person who is eligible to be his wife.

2. If God wants him to remain single and he marries anyone at all, he is out of God's will.

3. If God has a particular wife chosen and he marries someone else, he is out of God's will.

4. If the woman God has selected for him marries someone else, he cannot enjoy God's will no matter what he does.

5. If either of the pair marry out of God's will, there is nothing they can do to reverse the decision and return to the center of His will. They are permanently stranded in the barren terrain of God's "second (third, fourth, . . .) best."

When the stakes are that high, most people would rather not gamble on anything less than a sure thing. But getting to the sure thing is precisely the problem.

The saddest part of this situation is that so much of the trauma experienced by Ted and Annette is unnecessary. That is not to say that one's decision about marriage is not overwhelmingly important. In terms of impact on the course of one's life, the determination concerning marriage probably ranks second only to one's decision to accept or reject Jesus Christ as Savior and Lord. The unnecessary stress is generated by the obligation to discover the one and only acceptable candidate among a field of millions.

There is a better way. It may not be easier, but it is certainly more enjoyable. It is the way of the Bible. It is the "way of wisdom." That wisdom will first be applied in this chapter to the decision of whether to marry and then in the next chapter to the selection of a mate.

Behold, the Trees

Before we stroll down the pathway to marital (or celibate) bliss, let's shinny up a flagpole for another glimpse of the terrain.

In this chapter and the ones to follow, we move from our development of general principles to a consideration of specific applications. We shall see how the way of wisdom approaches decisions pertaining to singleness and marriage, vocational opportunities, giving to the Lord's work, and matters where Christians disagree.

The specific topics addressed in these chapters have three common elements: (1) they are of *universal* interest, since virtually all believers face these particular decisions at some point; (2) they are *important* subjects, since the choices in question affect so much of one's life; and (3) there is significant *biblical teaching* directed to each of the issues in question.

Accordingly, we anticipate that these chapters will prove helpful in at least three ways. First, they will shed the light of God's Word on segments of our paths that are of vital concern to many. Second, they will validate the way of wisdom through consistent application of the guidance principles we have established. And third, these chapters will help to "flesh out" scriptural concepts of decision making through specific cases.

Returning to the subject of marriage, we find that the question has two parts: Should I marry? And, if so, who will become my spouse? The traditional view would say that God has already made both decisions as part of His individual will for each person's life. The goal of the believer, then, is to discover the choices God has made by reading and following the road signs that comprise the Spirit's guidance.

The way of wisdom would point out that since believers are given no imperatives commanding or forbidding marriage, these decisions fall within the area of freedom. From that perspective, the goal of the Christian is to make wise decisions — decisions that will best enable him to obey God's commands and fulfill God's stated purposes for his life.

The question that arises is: Are there any passages of Scripture on the subject of marriage that confirm and develop either of these views? The answer is yes.

THE TEACHING OF JESUS

Celebates for Jesus

With the recent proliferation of books on "How to Survive Life Without a Wife (or Husband)," it has become fashionable to point out that Jesus was a "single adult." Ironically, Christ's only recorded comments on singleness and marriage were occasioned by a question on divorce:

> And some Pharisees came to Him [Jesus], testing Him, and saying, "Is it lawful for a man to divorce his wife for any cause at all?" (Matthew 19:3).

The question was not academic. A wrong answer could alienate a significant segment of Christ's followers from Him. For the people of Israel were sharply divided on the issue of divorce. Some followed the stricter school of Shammai in holding that sexual immorality was the only legitimate grounds for divorce. But many agreed with Hillel that a man could divorce his wife if she displeased him "for any cause at all."

Rather than becoming embroiled in that dispute, Jesus reaffirmed God's original purpose — namely, that marriage was designed to join one man and one woman permanently. "'What therefore God has joined together,'" He concluded, "'let no man separate'" (Matthew 19:6).

It was a brilliant answer, undercutting all of the pious debate over what was merely permissible. But his enemies would not be deterred from their objective of compromising Jesus in the eyes of the people. "'Why then,'" they countered, "'did Moses command to 'give her a certificate and divorce her'?'" (19:7). Jesus' reply was complete:

> "Because of your hardness of heart, Moses permitted you to divorce your wives; but from the beginning it has not been this way. And I say to you, whoever divorces his wife, except for immorality, and marries another woman commits adultery" (Matthew 19:8-9).

That answer, which simultaneously refuted the position of Hillel and silenced the Pharisees, planted a serious question in the minds of His disciples. It was put in the form of a statement, but an answer from Jesus was surely expected: "'If the relationship of the man with his wife is like this, it is better not to marry'" (19:10).

This is one time when the disciples were perceptive enough to grasp the implications of their Master's teaching. It was conceivable, they reasoned, for a man to unwittingly marry a contentious woman who could make life miserable for him (Proverbs 21:9). If divorce was ruled out except for immorality, the man would be permanently locked into an intolerable situation. Unmarried deprivation would certainly be preferable to married desolation.

The Pharisees must have been delighted with the disciples' reaction. If Jesus agreed with the conclusion of His disciples' statement, He would be contradicting the Old Testament teaching concerning the blessedness of marriage and the attendent reward of a quiver full of children (Genesis 2:18; Psalm 127:3-5). But if He could not accept the ramifications articulated by His disciples, He would have to revise His position on divorce and adopt a more liberal stance.

The Lord had a way of dealing with apparent dilemmas that must have left people shaking their heads. This case was no exception. While it was obvious to everyone else that Jesus had to either agree or disagree with what His disciples had said, He did neither. What He said was this: "'Not all men can accept this statement, but only those to whom it has been given.'" He then went on to list three categories of men who, in fact, do not marry: (1) those who are unable to do so by reason of birth defect; (2) those who are rendered incapable of marriage at the hands of others; and (3) those who choose to remain single in order to more effectively serve the kingdom of heaven (Matthew 19:11-12).[1]

In effect, Jesus was agreeing that there would be some men for whom singleness would be preferable to marriage. But that was true not just because of the negative risks inherent in the bonds of marriage, but because of the positive potentials of service to God. On the other hand, His warning, "'He who is able to accept this, let him accept it'" (19:12), was a reminder that not all men can handle celibacy. For them, a wise marriage would be better.

In short, Jesus taught that singleness and marriage are both acceptable to God. Marriage is not commanded of anyone; neither is abstention from marriage, even for the sake of the kingdom of God. For some, as the disciples had said, "'it is better not to marry.'" But others could find celibacy too hard to take. For them, the ability to function effectively as a single person had not been given (19:11).

THE TEACHING OF PAUL

What Jesus declared in capsule form was amplified and developed in detail by the apostle Paul in 1 Corinthians 7. This is the central passage in the Bible on the subject of singleness. Paul's observations were made in response to a letter he had received from the believers in Corinth (7:1). Heading the list of questions included in that epistle were inquiries concerning the appropriateness of marriage for Christians.

If ever there was a place where one could expect biblical substantiation of the traditional view, that place is 1 Corinthians 7. Given the subject matter of the questions, one would expect the apostle to explain how believers should proceed to discover God's individual will for their lives in this crucial area. His insights would be expressed in his own characteristic style, of course. But one could anticipate that all of the distinctive features of the traditional view would be included.

By now, the reader will not be surprised to learn that, on the subject of singleness and marriage, Paul did not hold what has become the traditional view. It is probably for this reason that few contemporary books on God's will give very much attention to this passage despite its in-depth treatment of the issue. For while Paul has a lot to say about the pros and cons of celibacy and marriage, he makes no comment whatsoever about God's individual will. The reason for that will become apparent as we investigate the chapter.

Paul's discussion can be outlined in three main segments. In verses 1-7, he establishes the general principles that will be developed throughout the remainder of the chapter. In verses 8-24, he focuses on the problems of the married. And in verses 25-40, he discusses the problems of the unmarried.[2]

Regulated Freedom

Now concerning the things about which you wrote, it is good for a man not to touch a woman. But because of immoralities, let each man have his own wife, and let each woman have her own husband. Let the husband fulfill his duty to his wife, and likewise also the wife to her husband. The wife does not have authority over her own body, but the husband does; and likewise also the husband does not have authority over his own body, but the wife does. Stop depriving one another, except by agreement for a time that you may devote yourselves to prayer, and come together again lest Satan tempt you because of your lack of self-control. But this I say by way of concession, not of command. Yet I wish that all men were even as I myself am. However, each man has his

own gift from God, one in this manner, and another in
that (1 Corinthians 7:1-7).

Paul's opening statement reveals his preference for the celibate
state ("Touch a woman," being a euphemism for sexual inter-
course, is a striking equivalent for "marry." Accordingly, the New
International Version renders the statement: "It is good for a man
not to marry.")[3] However, Paul recognizes that those who are
single are especially vulnerable to sensual temptation. For that
reason, the divine institution of marriage provides the surest protection from sexual sin for most people. Again, neither celibacy nor
marriage is commanded (7:6). So even though Paul might have a
strong preference for his own state of singleness, each man has to
choose what is best for himself (7:7).[4] As Robertson and Plummer
summarize Paul's thought, "Celibacy is good, but marriage is
natural."[5] That is the first thrust of the paragraph.

The second major point is that those who choose marriage in-
cur certain obligations to their spouse. These obligations prohibit
intimate relations outside of marriage (7:2) or sexual fraud within
marriage (7:3-5). The one who marries is thereby bound to fulfill
his or her marital duties.

Right at the outset, Paul established a very important principle: One's decision about marriage is *regulated* and affected by the
moral will of God, but *not determined* by it. The commands of
God's Word are directed toward two aspects of the decision. The
first defines the acceptable group from which a mate may be
chosen. In these verses, Paul is assuming what he later states (7:39):
A Christian may only marry another Christian. That is God's moral
will and it must be obeyed. Second, biblical commands spell out the
believer's responsibilities once the marriage is in force.

But the decision to marry or remain single lies within the area
of freedom. The apostle had a definite preference for celibacy that
he "wished" all others could choose. But he knew he could not give
his desire the force of a command. For not everyone "has the gift."
God graces each believer differently. It is likely that Paul's meaning
is that some are "gifted" to enjoy singleness while others are
"gifted" to enjoy marriage with its extra responsibilities (7:7). One's
own make up must be taken into consideration in the decision, but
the choice is a personal one (7:6).

The principle that the marriage decision is regulated but not determined by God's moral will is reaffirmed throughout the chapter. Freedom to choose is declared in each of the following verses:

1 Corinthians 7:25: Now concerning virgins I have *no command* of the Lord,...

1 Corinthians 7:28: But if you should marry, you *have not sinned;* and if a virgin should marry, she *has not sinned.*

1 Corinthians 7:36: But if any man thinks that he is acting unbecomingly toward his virgin daughter, if she should be of full age, and if it must be so, let him *do what he wishes,* he does not sin; let her marry.

1 Corinthians 7:39: A wife is bound as long as her husband lives; but if her husband is dead, *she is free* to be married *to whom she wishes,* only in the Lord.

Again, all of those expressions of freedom of decision are circumscribed by the moral will of God. In addition to the imperatives already noted from the first seven verses, God's moral will prohibits: (1) divorce for two married believers (7:10); (2) remarriage of either a Christian wife or a Christian husband if they separate (7:11); (3) divorce by a believer of an unbeliever who is willing to continue the marriage (7:13-15). For the single person, God's moral will demands chastity (7:2, 9).

Weighing the Factors

At no point in this presentation does Paul suggest that the marriage decision is determined either by God's moral will or by His individual will. It lies in the area of freedom and believers are responsible for their own choices. Now if God's moral will and so-called individual will are not the basis for such a decision, it follows that *there must be some other criteria.* On what basis does Paul direct that this morally free decision is to be made?

In a variety of ways Paul explains that the choice of celibacy or marriage is based upon spiritual expediency. He does not use the word "expediency," but his expressions are well summed up in that term. His procedure is to enumerate some of the advantages and disadvantages that characterize both states. In short, he is sharing his wisdom "as one who by the mercy of the Lord is trustworthy" (7:25).

Paul's stress is upon the values of singleness. His reasons for this preference are as follows:

1. To avoid unnecessary worry (7:20-21)
2. To avoid needless troubles (7:28)
3. To make better use of limited time (7:29-31)
4. To be free from concern (7:32)
5. To be able to give undistracted attention to "the things of the Lord" (7:32)
6. To promote personal happiness (7:40).

Paul sums up the reasons for his recommendation of celibacy in 1 Corinthians 7:35:

> And this I say for *your own benefit*; not to put a restraint upon you, but to *promote* what is *seemly*, and to secure *undistracted devotion to the Lord*.

That is spiritual expediency!

I Don't Think I Have the Gift!

On the other hand, there are some real values to marriage that not only make it a good option, but for many, the more preferable one. In the first place, the temptation to sexual sin is greatly reduced by the holy state of marriage (7:2-5). Contentment with a condition of celibacy requires a "gift" from God which not everyone possesses (7:7). If a person lacking this gift were to try to serve the Lord as a single man, it is likely that he would be continually distracted by the barrage of sensuous enticements surrounding him (7:9). Marriage may place some limitations on what a man is able to do for the Lord; but such inconveniences are far preferable to the havoc that lust can raise. For the man lacking in self-control, the choice is between potential distraction (marriage) or potential destruction (celibacy).

On the positive side, marriage offers definite opportunities for ministry—especially to one's spouse and children (7:14-16). Further, it always pleases God whenever His children obey His commandments (7:19). And so the fulfillment of one's marital obligations conforms to the moral will of God (7:2-5). In short, marriage permits men and women to channel their God-given drives away from illicit behavior that destroys, and utilize them to realize God's original design for mutual fulfillment and completion.

A Mutual Appreciation Society

An illustration of these contrasts between singleness and marriage was occasioned by the writing of this book. I am single and Robin is married. And, for the record, we both enjoy our respective states. It was in working so closely together that we came to appreciate in a fresh way both the advantages of the other's status and the blessings of our own.

Garry: "During the summer of 1978, I stayed in the home of Robin and Louise Maxson for five weeks while Robin and I began our work on the manuscript for this book. At the beginning of the project, I was loaded for bear. I was away from my office, my classroom, and, above all, my telephone. As far as I was concerned, Klamath Falls, Oregon, was at the end of the world and I was delighted to be there. I was able to work all day without interruptions, get some exercise, eat supper, and put in another two or three hours at the typewriter before going to bed."

Robin: "I was excited to be involved in such a project, and I think my enthusiasm matched Garry's. It wasn't long, though, before I began to notice a difference in the level of our productivity. Garry was able to devote more time to the project than I could, since, in addition to my wife (who could have easily become a ' book widow '), we had an eleven-month-old baby girl who needed some attention from Daddy. From time to time, some of that attention was demanded in the middle of the night. And so there would be mornings when, as Garry left for the office bright-eyed and bushy-tailed, I was still recovering from my early morning visits with Rachel Beth. When he headed back to the office after supper, I stayed home to spend some time with my family.

"Both Garry and I understood that my responsibilities to my family had to take precedence over my work on the book. And normally that is a priority in which I find great delight. But in that situation, I had to consciously deal with the feelings of resentment that began to creep in because of my inability to match Garry's output on the manuscript."

Garry: "My apartment in Portland is a house, but not really a home. As I joined the Maxson family I felt the difference. Meals were occasions for fellowship, not just eating. I began to appreciate the value of companionship between husband and wife through the thick and thin of everyday living.

"Then there was my new love—Rachel Beth. She was just shy of being one year old, and barely shy of being able to walk. As she began to take her first steps, I saw a little of the miracle of watching a young life develop. I was almost as thrilled as Robin and Louise; I wanted a picture as badly as they did. It was nice being 'Uncle Garry' instead of 'Dr. Friesen' for five weeks. Each day I looked forward to getting 'home' from writing to play 'Where's Rachel?'—a variation on the peek-a-boo theme.

"Now Michael Benjamin has arrived. He looks like 'elder' material, though it is a bit early to tell. I'm an uncle twice! I'm content in my single state, but you won't hear me knocking marriage. God made it beautiful, just like Paul said in Ephesians 5."

Robin: "The frustration I experienced over not being able to match Garry's pace was new to me. We had worked on projects together before and our contribution had been more or less equal. But that was when we were in seminary and I was single, too!

"Did this experience make me long for the days when I was footloose and fancy-free? Sure it did—for about five seconds. That's how long it took my good sense (which goes on vacation from time to time) to return. The Lord has gifted me with a beautiful family and the ability to enjoy each one thoroughly. Yet I marvel afresh at God's wisdom in equipping some to live alone. I am a beneficiary of what such individuals are able to accomplish in their 'undistracted devotion to the Lord.' And I am grateful."

Bloom Where You Are Planted

In 1 Corinthians 7:17-24, Paul sets forth an overriding principle that applies to all Christians regardless of their state. To the married, the single, the divorced, the widowed, the circumcised, the uncircumcised, the enslaved, the free, Paul says: "Brethren, let each man remain with God in that condition in which he was called" (1 Corinthians 7:24). Make it the goal of your life not to change your status, but to serve God as effectively and energetically as possible in whatever state you are. The contemporary poster says it well: "Bloom where you are planted now!"

In declaring this principle Paul was not forbidding marriage for single people or freedom for slaves. If the opportunity comes along and it is expedient to take it, do so (7:21).[6] His point was that people tend to concentrate on the wrong things. They pour their energies into changing their condition for their own sake rather than into changing the world for Christ's sake.

So, how should one decide the issue of marriage? Weigh all the factors and make a wise decision. And what constitutes a wise decision? A wise decision is one which:

1. Is good, not in contrast to "evil" but in contrast to "unprofitable" (7:1, 8, 26)
2. Is better (7:9, 38)
3. Leads to peace (7:15)
4. Best helps one keep the commands of God (7:19)
5. Causes the least trouble (7:28)
6. Makes the best use of time (7:29)
7. Is most free of external concerns (7:33)
8. Is beneficial (7:35)
9. Promotes what is seemly (7:35)
10. Leads to undistracted devotion to the Lord (7:35)
11. Is necessary (7:36)
12. Promotes personal happiness (7:40).

The decision concerning one's choice of singleness or marriage thus is one which must be made according to spiritual expediency. Paul's detailed discussion urges that the believer carefully consider the advantages and disadvantages of each state for serving God. He is then free and responsible to choose the state which, in his judgment, will bring the greatest benefit to the Lord's kingdom as well as himself. Jesus said it and Paul developed it. For some, singleness is "better" than marriage; but for others, the natural state of marriage is "better." The objective for the believer is not to find the decision God has already made (as in the traditional view), but to make a wise decision.

Notes

1. Eunuch may be taken in a literal or figurative sense. It is best to take the first two cases in Matthew 19:12 as literal and the final case as figurative "of those who abstain fr. marriage, without being impotent." William F. Arndt and F. Wilbur Gingrich, trans. *A Greek-English Lexicon of the New Testament and Other Early Christian Literature*, 2nd. ed. (Chicago: The University of Chicago Press, 1979). s.v. "εὐνουχίζω" and "εὐνοῦχος."

2. S. Lewis Johnson, Jr., "1 Corinthians," *The New Testament and Wycliffe Bible Commentary* (New York: The Iverson-Norman Associates, 1971), p. 607.

3. Arndt and Gingrich, *A Greek-English Lexicon*, s.v. "ἅπτω."

4. Some people have construed Paul's remarks here as a deprecation of marriage. That such is not the case is proved by Ephesians 5:22-33, written by the same man. If a person were to read only Ephesians 5 with its obvious message that "marriage is beautiful," he might conclude that Paul considered the celibate state to be second-class. If that same person were to read only 1 Corinthians 7 with its assertion that "singleness has advantages," he might conclude that Paul considered the married state to be second-class. Reading both passages reveals Paul's true perspective: One must weigh the advantages and disadvantages of each state, and choose.

5. Archibald Robertson and Alfred Plummer, *A Critical and Exegetical Commentary on the First Epistle of St. Paul to the Corinthians*, International Critical Commentary (Edinburgh: T. & T. Clark, 1911), p. 130.

6. The NIV translates, "although if you can gain your freedom, do so." Some commentators take this phrase in an opposite sense to mean even if you can gain your freedom, rather use your slavery position and turn the freedom down. Such a translation is possible, but has weaker contextual support. Reasons for the view taken here are enumerated by Archibald Robertson and Alfred Plummer, *A Critical and Exegetical Commentary on the First Epistle of St. Paul to the Corinthians*, The International Critical Commentary (Edinburgh: T. & T. Clark, 1911), pp. 147-48; Frank E. Gaebelein, gen. ed., *The Expositor's Bible Commentary* (Grand Rapids: Zondervan Publishing House, 1976), vol. 10: "1 Corinthians," by W. Harold Mare, p. 235.

Chapter 18

Marriage and Wisdom —

Screening the Candidates

*T*he first part of the marriage decision concerns "whether." The second part, for the one who concludes that marriage is better, is really the bottom line — "Who?" In fact, in many cases the first question is swallowed up in the second. Some men, especially, seem to ignore the "whether" question until they find themselves in a close relationship with a specific "who." Such a circumstance tends to sharpen, if not complicate, the issues. In any event, the Christian who is committed to the authority of Scripture wants to locate and study those passages that provide direction for one's selection of a spouse. For this decision, proponents of the traditional view often refer to two beautiful stories in Genesis to support their approach. For in both instances, God chose the bride.

GOD'S WILL FOR ADAM AND EVE

A Matter of Limited Options

The first reference to marriage in the Bible is found in Genesis 2. That chapter described the creation of Adam (verse 7) and Eve (verse 22) and their subsequent marriage. That first "wedding" is narrated succinctly:

> And the LORD God fashioned into a woman the rib
> which He had taken from the man, and brought her to

the man. And the man said, "This is now bone of my bones, and flesh of my flesh; she shall be called Woman, because she was taken out of Man" (Genesis 2:22-23).

Some writers take this passage to indicate that for each man, God has prepared one woman who is perfectly suited to be his wife. Now Genesis 2 *does* set forth several normative principles for marriage. We know this because they are stated, and *declared to be normative*, in verse 24:

> For this cause a man shall leave his father and his mother, and shall cleave to his wife; and they shall become one flesh.

However, nothing whatever is said about mate selection. No promise is made, or implied, that God will similarly prepare and introduce men and women that He has chosen to be joined in marriage. Eve was part of God's *revealed* will for Adam because He created her and brought her to Adam to be his wife. The whole scenario was an extraordinary event never again repeated in biblical history. There could only be one first man and one first woman. That's what it took to start the human race.

Perhaps the safest deduction one could make from this passage concerning mate selection is this: If you ever discover that you are the only surviving representative of your sex in the world, and you come across your only existing counterpart, the two of you should consider marriage.

GOD'S WILL FOR ISAAC AND REBEKAH

One Hump or Two?

Without a question, the most frequently cited chapter supporting the concept of a divinely chosen spouse is Genesis 24. As a model of the traditional view of guidance, the account of the search for a wife for Isaac appears to be a classic.

The story is well known. Abraham sent his trusted servant to the city of Nahor in Mesopotamia to seek out a wife for his son Isaac from among Abraham's relatives. Upon arrival at his destination, the servant stopped by a well and made this request of God:

"O LORD, the God of my master Abraham, please grant
me success today, and show lovingkindness to my master
Abraham. Behold, I am standing by the spring, and the
daughters of the men of the city are coming out to draw
water; now may it be that the girl to whom I say, 'Please
let down your jar so that I may drink,' and who answers
'Drink, and I will water your camels also';—may she be
the one whom Thou hast appointed for Thy servant
Isaac; and by this I shall know that Thou hast shown loving kindness to my master" (Genesis 24:12-14).

Soon thereafter, Rebekah came to the well and fulfilled the
sign completely. The servant visited her family, Rebekah agreed to
become Isaac's wife, and the servant was able to take her back to
Canaan—mission accomplished!

This passage provides apparent support for three specific
aspects of the traditional view: (1) the granting of detailed guidance
beyond the moral will of God; (2) the validity of using a circumstantial "fleece" in discovering God's will in an important decision; and (3) the notion that God's individual will includes the
specific person a believer is supposed to marry. The evidence for
each of these aspects is obvious.

The problem with arguing these points from Genesis 24 is that
the experience of Abraham's servant is *not normative*. Virtually no
one is inclined to take it that way. This writer knows of no one who
would be willing to send out a servant to seek a wife for a son, and
then accept that servant's choice on the basis of a drink of water for
man and beasts.

But Does She Do Windows?

That is not to say that it could not be done. Making allowances
for differences in time and culture, a man could hire a representative from a Christian dating agency. He could send that agent on
a search to find a wife for his son. The agent could drive into a service station, offer a prayer, and sign up the first woman who meets
his request for a drink by filling his water jug and checking his
radiator! The whole idea sounds preposterous, but if Genesis 24 is
normative, it would be a legitimate approach to the same goal.

But Genesis 24 is not an example of how God customarily
works in the lives of His people. And that is so for several good
reasons. First, the Bible does not promise that every believer will

have a mate. But Isaac *had* to have one. Why? Because God had promised Abraham that he would have innumerable descendants (Genesis 15:5; 24:7). That promise first required the birth of a son. Then, necessarily, that son had to have a wife. Therefore, Genesis 24 does not depict the normal father using the normal method to pick a normal wife for his normal son. No, the account concerns Abraham, the recipient of God's covenant oath and the consequent promise of a great seed. "Isaac was not regarded as a merely pious candidate for matrimony, but as heir of the promise."[1] For this reason, the servant based his request on God's character as One Who is faithful to His promises (Genesis 24:7, 14, 27). And the wife that would fulfill the divine promise was appropriately described as the one "appointed" (Genesis 24:14) — not because God has selected a mate in His individual will for each person, but because God promised a wife for Isaac.

Furthermore, in this situation God had promised special guidance for the servant to guarantee the success of his venture. Specifically, an angel went ahead of the servant to make sure that the goal was accomplished (24:7, 40). Such a guarantee and such angelic assistance goes beyond the customary provisions for guidance of God's people.

When in Doubt, Check Things Out

With respect to the circumstantial "fleece," it is clear from the text that such a method of guidance was not normative even *then*. Having no other ideas on how to proceed, and being fully assured of God's guidance, the servant asked God to give the needed guidance through this method (24:12). He did not know for sure that the Lord would do what he asked; he simply asked, and then watched to see what would happen. Even when the sign was quickly fulfilled by a woman, he was still not sure that God was using his sign (24:21).[2] Even when her background was discovered to be acceptable (24:23-24), the matter was not concluded in the servant's mind until Rebekah indicated a willingness to return with him (24:58). He was careful to determine if her family would give their daughter to Isaac. If not, he would look to other families for the woman of God's choice (24:49). By his careful investigation subsequent to the fulfillment of the sign, the servant showed his awareness that such a procedure was highly unorthodox, and not to be fully trusted until all other conditions were met.

Genesis 24 does give an example of specific guidance in a particular decision, the use of a providential sign in the process, and the seeking and finding of an appointed mate. From the text it is clear that things happened that way because of the existence of a special covenant, the promise of angelic assistance guaranteeing success, and God's willingness to use a nonnormative method in response to the servant's prayer. This account of special guidance was recorded in detail not because it is descriptive of normative leading, but because it was an important step in the progressive fulfillment of God's promise to Abraham. God proved to be faithful to each part of the covenant, including the promise of a great seed—a promise that is central to the theme of the book of Genesis.

GOD'S WILL FOR BELIEVERS WHO MARRY

To find instructions concerning the choice of a spouse that are normative for Christians today, we must return to Paul's exposition in 1 Corinthians 7. The reader needs to be aware that in Paul's day, the cultural situation in Corinth (and most of the rest of the world, for that matter) was much different from our own. We are used to such important decisions being left up to the individuals involved. But 1 Corinthians 7:36-38 reflects a custom where the father made the arrangements for the marriage of (at least) his daughter.[3] The primary advantage of such an approach is that parents, who have the best interests of their children at heart, are able to bring maturity and good judgment to bear upon the decision. A father is not so vulnerable to the distorting effects of romantic involvement.[4] Nevertheless, in any culture the choice of a marriage partner must be made, and the decision is extremely important. On what basis is it to be made?

"Only in the Lord"

The first test question a believer should ask is: Are there any commands of Scripture that relate to this decision? The answer, as we have indicated, is yes. Believers may only marry believers.

This fact has been repeated so often by so many pastors, teachers, and writers, that many people accept it because of the overwhelming consensus that seems to exist on this point. And yet when push comes to shove, a remarkable number of Christians disregard the prohibition and marry unbelievers. After falling in love with non-Christians, they find supposed loopholes in the biblical statements, rationalize that in their situation the rules do not apply, and/or blatantly disobey the revealed will of God.

It will not suffice to establish a principle by the force of sheer repetition. The biblical foundation must be clearly established. And, in our judgment, one of the most transparent teachings of Scripture is: Believers may only marry believers.

In 1 Corinthians 7, it is assumed throughout that Christians should only marry other Christians, especially in verses 12-16 which deal with "mixed marriages" where one partner has become a Christian after the marriage. But the imperative is clearly stated, almost as an afterthought it seems, in 1 Corinthians 7:39: "A wife is bound as long as her husband lives; but if her husband is dead, she is free to be married to whom she wishes, *only in the Lord*."

First, the phrase "only in the Lord" means that the marriage partner must himself be "in the Lord," that is to say, a Christian.[5] For confirmation of this meaning, one has only to refer to verse 22 of this same chapter to find the phrase "in the Lord" used in the sense of becoming a Christian.

Second, it must be obvious that such a requirement is not simply restricted to Christian *widows*. The limitation of marriage prospects to Christians applies to Christian widows for the simple reason that it applies to Christians, period.

Pulling in Opposite Directions

The cross-reference most commonly cited is 2 Corinthians 6:14-16:

> Do not be bound together with unbelievers; for what partnership have righteousness and lawlessness, or what fellowship has light with darkness? Or what harmony has Christ with Belial, or what has a believer in common with an unbeliever? Or what agreement has the temple of God with idols? For we are the temple of the living God.

The opening statement employed an agricultural metaphor that called up a mental image of an ox and a donkey (Deuteronomy 22:10) being harnessed together in a double yoke.[6] No believer is to be so "mismated" with an unbeliever. The reasons given are set forth in five vivid contrasts: righteousness versus lawlessness, light versus darkness, Christ versus Belial (Satan), a believer versus an unbeliever, and the temple of God versus idols. The point is that not only are the believer's values, goals, standards, motivations, and means of enablement for living incompatible with those of an unbeliever; they *are diametrically* opposed! They are serving two different lords that are archenemies of one another.

If this passage does not apply to marriage, then it doesn't apply to anything, for marriage is much more than a "double yoke." It is a joining together of two individuals into a relationship that can only be described as "one flesh" (Genesis 2:24; Matthew 19:5; Ephesians 5:31). In Old Testament terms, marriage is more than a contract; it is a covenant—the most intimate relationship into which two human beings can enter. For a Christian to marry a non-Christian is to rule out the possibility of that marriage fully accomplishing its design; it is to sow the seeds of that marriage's conflict. For a believer and an unbeliever are fundamentally different, not on the surface, but at the very *core* of their lives.[7]

Who Is Lord?

But there is an issue that is of much greater importance than the eventual success or failure of the marriage—the issue of obedience. Christians are not left on earth to promote their own success; they are on assignment for the kingdom of God. To disobey a direct order from the King is to capitulate to the authority of the other side. Alice Fryling puts it well:

> Words cannot express the tragedy of this situation. The Christian is mocking God by reneging on his or her commitment to Him. A Christian is committing idolatry by falling down before someone other than God. And he or she is blatantly disobeying God, who said we are to marry only within the faith.[8]

On this point we are in total agreement with the traditional view. The only acceptable mate for a believer is another believer.

Apart from that single imperative, Scripture gives no other commands directly related to the selection of a marriage partner. As in all other decisions, however, the Christian is required to make the *wisest* possible choice. Accordingly, the first "woman" a Christian man should court is Wisdom! (Proverbs 2:1-6).

WISDOM SOURCES FOR MARRIAGE

God's provisions for wisdom in the choice of a mate are the same ones we have already described. The experiential starting point may be personal desires and inner impressions, but wisdom would begin with the *Word of God*. For it is the Bible that most completely answers the question: "What am I getting myself into?"

As we pointed out repeatedly, God's Word reveals many significant obligations that are God's job description for husbands and wives. Once a person marries, the list of imperatives that comprise God's moral will grows considerably. It would therefore behoove the unmarried Christian to find out what those requirements are. Some of the most important questions are:

1. What are the purposes of marriage?
2. What instructions has God given so that Christian husbands and wives can fulfill God's purposes in their marriages?
3. What are the responsibilities of the husband?
4. What are the responsibilities of the wife?

In Pursuit of Excellence

The relevance of such questions to the process of mate selection is easy to see. It would be wise for a man, for instance, to select a woman toward whom he could most easily and completely fulfill his commitments as a husband. And he would want to choose a woman whose first marital priority is the fulfillment of her God-given functions as a wife. That may sound obvious, but many people have come to grief in their marriage because they did not deliberately think these things through. A woman, observing that Scripture requires her to submit to her husband, should be asking in advance, "For what kind of man would submission come easily?", and so on. A man would want to observe whether the woman he is considering will be struggling between her loyalty to him and her pursuit of a career.

From a biblical perspective, the goal of the Christian is to establish a godly marriage that maximizes the potentials of God's purposes. That being the case, the Christian man or woman should be looking for a counterpart who is qualified and committed to fulfilling that goal. Who fits that description? In the most general terms, it is the most spiritually mature person who is willing to be joined in marriage. In short, when a Christian is thinking through the qualities he or she is seeking in a spouse, moral and spiritual characteristics should head the list.

The importance of finding a spouse who is characterized, above all, by spiritual excellence, is repeatedly underscored in the Old Testament. The segment of Proverbs that specifically addresses the issue of mate selection emphasizes that goal in the opening statement: *"An excellent wife*, who can find? For her worth is far above jewels"* (Proverbs 31:10). Accordingly, when Boaz told Ruth he wanted to take her as his wife, he explained, "for all my people in the city know that you are a *woman of excellence"* (Ruth 3:11). Spiritual excellence is the ultimate trait for marriageability.

Getting a Second Opinion

The second wisdom source that should be consulted is *spiritual counselors*. In our time, we have been blessed with an abundance of this kind of wisdom, and it is readily available to everyone. Even those who cannot have personal exposure to Christian counselors who specialize in marriage preparation, do have access to their wisdom in books, cassette tapes, and seminars. Godly men and women have shared their insights both in the elucidation of biblical principles and practical observations. Today it is literally possible for unmarried people to become theoretical experts on marriage before they marry. And while married couples might chuckle over such a statement, a single person considering marriage would be foolish not to learn as much as possible in advance.

There is no substitute, however, for personal counsel—especially when one is thinking about marrying a specific individual. A young person (anyone under 75 who is in love!) should give great weight to words of caution coming from mature counselors whom he or she respects. In this regard, the book of Proverbs emphasizes the counsel of parents, and those who reject such wisdom do so to their great peril.

Don't Confuse Me with the Facts

A third wisdom source, and one of the most valuable ones, is *common sense*. Unfortunately, among romantically involved couples it is a scarce commodity. Ted Bradford and Annette Miller are remarkable exceptions to that rule. And we made them up! Ironically, romance's rout of common sense is plainly observable to all but the participants. That is especially true in our Western culture where the romantic factor is declared to be ultimate. (If this paragraph appears to be characterized by overstatement, the truth of these statements can be confirmed by any pastor who has ever done premarital counseling!)

Common sense can, however, become a valuable source of wisdom for the individual who dares to say, "If I were not going with anyone at all, what are the questions I would ask about marriage and my prospective mate?" The list that would result from an objective response to that question would include such areas as age, finances, employment, education, personal goals, personality traits, birth control, principles of childrearing, health, hobbies, family background, socioeconomic background, and possessions.

In most decisions, *personal desires* become valuable indicators of the ease with which a person will fulfill his obligations. And that is an important aspect of spiritual expediency. But even more than other wisdom sources, personal desires must be judged by the Word of God and wisdom. For when it comes to marriage, many of our personal desires have been molded by our environment rather than by the Lord (Romans 12:2). Our notions of love, attractiveness, and ways of finding happiness can be profoundly influenced by the world rather than the Word. As a result, personal desires must first be evaluated as to their legitimacy before they can be trusted as sources of wisdom.

Beware of Football Nuts and Loose Shrews

Valid desires can enter into a constructive partnership with common sense. Take the respective cases of Fred and Sally. Fred loves football. If he marries someone who hates football, there is going to be tension in that marriage. It may not spell doom for the marriage, but every Monday night for five months, she is going to have to put up with something she hates or he will do without something he loves.

Sally loves Shakespeare. If she marries someone who is bored by drama and chafes in formal wear, there is going to be tension. Someone will have to go to the theatre alone, or someone will be bored for three hours.

These personal desires may seem trivial on paper. But in some marriages their importance grows to gigantic proportions. It is simple expediency for Fred Football to look for a wife who can at least tolerate a weekly diet of Cosell and the Cowboys. And Sally Shakespeare would be wise to look for a man who does not think the Elizabethan Arts are much ado about nothing. (Of course neither Fred nor Sally should be so immature as to insist that they must watch every football game or go to every play.) Common sense, and expediency, indicate that the fewer potholes there are in the pathway of adjustment, the smoother will be the journey to marital unity.

Sound Guidelines for an Important Decision

It is not the purpose of this book to provide the wisdom needed for a wise decision about marriage. We are simply trying to define some principles of approach, and point out some of the sources of wisdom that make up God's provision for our guidance. The content of this chapter and the previous one could be summed up in the following points:

1. The Christian who is thinking about marriage has to make two decisions: whether to get married, and whom to marry.

2. Scripture teaches that both of these decisions fall within the area of freedom. That decision is not determined either by God's moral will or a so-called individual will. God has given to the believer both the privilege and responsibility of making decisions that will most help that person obey the commands of God and fulfill His revealed purposes.

3. There are identifiable advantages and disadvantages with either marriage or celibacy. Many of these are enumerated in 1 Corinthians 7.

4. Whatever one's state, his primary objective is not to strive for a change in status but to learn to serve God effectively in his present condition.

5. While one's decision about marriage is not determined by God's moral will, it is regulated by it.

6. The moral will of God determines two aspects of the marriage issue. First, it defines the limits of acceptable candidates for marriage. A Christian may only marry another Christian. Second, it sets forth the obligations incurred by those who do marry.

7. The sources of wisdom provided by God are both abundant and adequate for the making of wise deci-

sions in this area. It is the job of the Christian to be
diligent in seeking them out.

For those who choose marriage, there are perhaps no more fitting words than those penned hundreds of years ago by King
Lemuel. While addressed to a man searching for a wife, they surely
have applicability as well to the Christian woman who wants a
godly husband:

An excellent wife, who can find?
For her worth is far above jewels.
The heart of her husband trusts in her,
And he will have no lack of gain.
She does him good and not evil
All the days of her life.

Her children rise up and bless her;
Her husband also, and he praises her, saying:
"Many daughters have done nobly,
But you excel them all."
Charm is deceitful and beauty is vain,
But a woman who fears the LORD, she shall be praised.
(Proverbs 31:10-12, 28-30).

Notes

1. C.F. Keil and F. Delitzsch, *Biblical Commentary on the Old Testament* (Grand Rapids: Wm. B. Eerdmans Publishing Co., 1951), vol. 1: *The Pentateuch*, p. 258, quoting Hengstenberg, *Dissertations*, 1:350.

2. H.C. Leupold, *Exposition of Genesis*, 2 vols. (Grand Rapids: Baker Book House, 1942), 2:669.

3. The "he" of 7:36 is probably the father (F.W. Grosheide, *The First Epistle to the Corinthians*, The New International Commentary on the New Testament [Grand Rapids: Wm. B. Eerdmans Publishing Co., 1953], pp. 182-84.), but could be the fiancé (Frank E. Gaebelein, gen. ed., *The Expositor's Bible Commentary* [Grand Rapids: Zondervan Publishing House, 1976], vol. 10: "1 Corinthians," by W. Harold Mare, pp. 236-37).

4. On the dangers of marrying solely for romantic reasons, Dr. James Peterson has written: "First, romance results in such distortions of personality that after mar-riage the two people can never fulfill the roles that they expect of each other. Sec-ond, romance so idealizes marriage and even sex that when the day-to-day ex-periences of marriage are encountered there must be disillusionment involved. Third, the romantic complex is so short-sighted that the premarital relationship is conducted almost entirely on the emotional level and consequently such problems as temperamental or value differences, religious or cultural differences, financial, oc-cupational, or health problems are never considered. Fourth, romance develops such a false ecstasy that there is implied in courtship a promise of a kind of hap-piness which could never be maintained during the realities of married life. Fifth, romance is such an escape from the negative aspects of personality to the extent that

their repression obscures the real person. Later in marriage these negative factors to marital adjustment are bound to appear, and they were not evident earlier. Sixth, people engrossed in romance seem to be prohibited from wise planning for the basic needs of the future even to the point of failing to discuss the significant problems of early marriage." Lyle B. Gangsei, ed., *Manual for Group Premarital Counseling* (New York: Association, 1971), pp. 56-57.

5. "But when he dies, she is free to marry anyone she chooses, so long as he is a Christian." Gaebelein, *Expositor's Bible Commentary*, p. 237. Cf. also S. Lewis Johnson, Jr., "1 Corinthians," *The New Testament and Wycliffe Bible Commentary* (New York: The Iverson-Norman Associates, 1971), p. 611; and Norman Hillyer, "1 and 2 Corinthians," *The New Bible Commentary* (Grand Rapids: Wm. B. Eerdmans Publishing Co., 1970), p. 1062.

6. Gaebelein, *Expositor's Bible Commentary*, vol. 10: "2 Corinthians," by Murray J. Harris, p. 359.

7. A thorough treatment of the principle, "marry only a believer," would require exposition of these relevant passages: Deuteronomy 7:1-6; 1 Kings 11:1-8; Nehemiah 13:23-27; Malachi 2:11; 1 Corinthians 9:5. The strong sanctions in the Old Testament against intermarriage with unbelievers were given for two primary reasons: (1) such intermarriage would compromise God's holiness (Deuteronomy 7:6); and (2) it would inevitably destroy the experiential holiness of God's people (Deuteronomy 7:4).

8. Alice Fryling, *An Unequal Yoke in Dating and Marriage* (Downers Grove, Ill.: InterVarsity Press, 1979), p. 14.

Chapter 19

The Ministry and Wisdom

*T*ed Bradford's dilemma was complex. He had come to a crossroads in his life where several major decisions had to be made. And the choices which confronted him were interrelated. An orderly list of the questions in Ted's mind would read like this:

1. Should I marry?
2. If so, should I marry Annette Miller?
3. If so, when?
4. Is God calling me to full-time vocational Christian service?
5. Is God calling me to become a foreign missionary?
6. Should I attend seminary?

There may have been other related questions, but those six were paramount.

Within the framework of the traditional view of guidance, it could be said that Ted was looking for six specific "dots"—the center of God's will for each of the six questions. Each separate decision would have a determinative impact on the rest of his life. Additionally, each separate decision would have a direct bearing on one or more of the other five. Missing one "dot" could result in missing all of them.

311

What difference would it make if Ted Bradford were to approach his decisions with the way of wisdom? His questions would still be important; they would still be interrelated. The main difference is that he would be freed from having to find six "dots." He would weigh the factors and make decisions that would promote the moral will of God in and through his life.

The question once again is: Which approach is taught in Scripture? We have already answered that question as it pertains to marriage (chapters 17 and 18). But what about one's vocation, one's career? Does the Bible direct the believer to discover the occupation God has already chosen? Or does this decision lie within the area of freedom?

THE CALL TO THE MINISTRY

In discussions pertaining to one's life-work, the traditional view employs a distinctive, biblical term: "called." Citing numerous instances in Scripture where God called a specific individual to a specific task, the traditional view teaches that the call of God is the indispensable factor in determining one's vocation. And that is said to be true even if one does not become a pastor or a missionary.

Since the concept of a personal "call" is the distinctive element in the traditional view on this subject, a study of the term as it is used in Scripture would be a good starting point. The verb *kaleo*, "to call," appears 148 times in the New Testament. (There are an additional 70 occurrences of related terms from the same root.)[1] Apparently the idea of calling or being called is significant.

You Are Cordially Invited...

There are three usages of the word that are theological in character. First, in the gospels, the term appears frequently in the words and parables of Jesus in the sense of "summon" or "invite."[2] The "invitation" was to come to repentance, faith, salvation, and service.[3] It was issued by Christ, not to the righteous, but to sinners (Matthew 9:13). It was a summons to enter the kingdom of God—an invitation that could be accepted or rejected by the individual (Matthew 22:2-14; Luke 14:16-24).

The second, more restricted doctrinal use of the term is found primarily in the writings of Paul. He employed the word "call" to describe God's gracious work within a sinner whereby He effectively brings that person to faith and salvation. (Theologians speak of this work as "effective grace" or "efficacious grace" in contrast to "common grace" which is given to all men but rejected by many.) God not only invites sinners to repent, but acts to secure a positive response to His summons.[4] For the apostle, "call" was an important theological vocabulary word in his development of the doctrine of sovereign grace and election (Romans 8:28-30).[5] Accordingly, in the epistles Christians are frequently designated as "the called."[6] That is, they are sinners who have not only heard God's invitation through the gospel but have responded to it in faith.

Obviously, neither of these two senses of the term is meant when the traditional view speaks of "being called." It is rather the third usage that is relevant to this discussion: the call to a specific function or office.

In the New Testament, there are three instances of this kind of call: (1) God's call of Paul to be an apostle (Romans 1:1; 1 Corinthians 1:1); (2) God's call of Barnabas and Saul to be the Church's first missionaries (Acts 13:2); and (3) God's call to Paul and his companions to take the gospel to Macedonia (Acts 16:9-10). However, careful examination of these examples along with the rest of the New Testament reveals that they are the exception rather than the rule.[7]

In the first place, in each case the *means of communication* was some form of *supernatural revelation*. When Saul of Tarsus received his call to apostleship, he heard the audible voice of the exalted Christ (Acts 26:14-20).[8] The command in Acts 13:2 to "'Set apart for Me Barnabas and Saul for the work to which I have called them'" is attributed to the Holy Spirit. How did the saints at Antioch receive this message? Either God spoke in an audible voice that could be heard by all (as in Luke 9:35); or, more likely, He spoke through one of the prophets in the church mentioned in Acts 13:1. And the "Macedonian Call" was communicated to Paul through a revelatory vision (Acts 16:9-10). In none of these cases, nor in any other in the New Testament, was such a call communicated through any sort of inward impression.

Few Are Called

Second, each "vocational call" was issued *only to certain individuals at certain times*. The book of Acts makes it clear that the Holy Spirit was carefully superintending the opening stages of the

Church's growth. Only at decisive moments and in decisive ways did God intervene supernaturally to commission a worker, chart a particular course, or point in a specific direction. The rest of the time, He accomplished His purposes through saints obeying the moral will of God.

The isolated, infrequent character of the Spirit's overt interventions is consistent with God's activity of "vocational calling" in the Old Testament. The only individuals in Israel who received such commissions from God were those who were called to a specialized, spiritual ministry: the high priest (Hebrews 5:4); judges (1 Samuel 3:4-10); prophets (Isaiah 6:1-8; Jeremiah 1:4-10); kings (1 Samuel 16:11-13); and certain artisans who had been supernaturally endowed to build the tabernacle (Exodus 31:1-6). In neither testament is such a call promised or required as part of God's provision for all believers.

Third, in every instance the special call of God was *unsought* and *unexpected*. God could give a vocational call to each believer. But there is no instruction directing Christians to seek out such leading. The examples in which God interrupted the normal flow of life to reveal His will emphasize the sovereign origin of such revelations.

Fourth, while the concept of "the call of God" is a prominent one in the New Testament, the vocational sense of the term occupies only a *minor place*.[9] And when it occurs, it is never presented as pertaining to all believers.

To sum up: The idea of a vocational call is consistent with the theological framework of the traditional view. There are instances recorded in Scripture where God did call certain men to special tasks. But those two facts are not sufficient to establish the reality of a vocational call for all believers. God could make such choices and reveal them as He has selectively done in the past. But the indication of Scripture is that God did not normally lead that way in Bible times; nor should we expect Him to do so today.[10]

BIBLICAL QUALIFICATIONS FOR CHURCH LEADERS

The traditional view of guidance so permeates evangelical thinking that the validity of a vocational call is not only assumed for all believers, it is actually required for "full-time ministers."[11] When a candidate is examined for ordination into the gospel ministry, the council usually questions him with respect to three key areas: (1) his experience of conversion; (2) his call to the ministry; and (3) his doctrinal positions.

The Ordination Ordeal

The appropriateness of testing a man in those three areas is obvious. But as I prepared for my own ordination exam, I knew I had a problem. I didn't anticipate any difficulty with the first or third questions. I was certain of my salvation. And I felt that ten years of formal Bible training had given me a good grasp of biblical theology. My doctrinal statement was the product of many hours of work, and I was prepared to explain and defend it. But what would I say to the question of my "call to the ministry"?

On the basis of my study of the Bible, I had come to the conclusion that God does not require of pastors today the same kind of bright light and voice that arrested Saul of Tarsus on the Damascus Road. Further, I had become convinced that Scripture does not require some kind of mystical experience whereby one "hears" God's "inward call." I did not anticipate that the ordination council would expect me to relate some "Damascus Road" experience; but I was fairly sure they would expect me to say something about a strong impression in my heart that God had told me to go into full-time ministry.

So on the evening before the examination, alone in my room, I did two things. First, I carefully reviewed the specific reasons for my desire to spend the rest of my life in Christian ministry. I would tell the council the truth. If they wanted to reject my reasons, they would do so with a clear understanding of what they were. Second, I spent the evening rereading the key biblical passages which set forth the qualifications for leaders in the church. If anything was recorded requiring either a "bright light" or a mystical call, I wanted to be certain I had not overlooked it.

The Case of the Missing Call

As I read through those passages, it was again confirmed to me that the Head of the Church has declared what kind of people should be set apart as spiritual leaders. The qualifications are given in 1 Timothy 3:1-7, Titus 1:5-9, and 1 Peter 5:1-4.[12] (Other passages could be cited, perhaps. But they add no additional requirements to the ones established in these primary passages.) A great deal could be said with respect to the qualifications for spiritual leaders,[13] but we will content ourselves with a brief, five-point survey.

First, leaders in the church must be *Christians*. If one is going to "shepherd the Church of God" (Acts 20:28), one must first be part of the Church of God.

Second, leaders in the church must be *men*. God's order in the church requires this (1 Timothy 2:12-14). Accordingly, the stipulations "husband of one wife" and "one who manages his own household well" (1 Timothy 3:2-4) assume male leadership.

Third, leaders in the church must have *two abilities*: to *lead* and to *teach*. To determine if a man can lead, the church is told to observe his family:

> He must be one who manages his own household well, keeping his children under control with all dignity (but if a man does not know how to manage his own household, how will he take care of the church of God?) (1 Timothy 3:4-5; see Titus 1:6).

The ability to teach cuts two ways:

> ...holding fast the faithful word which is in accordance with the teaching, that he may be able both to *exhort in sound doctrine* [positive thrust], and to *refute those who contradict* [negative thrust] (Titus 1:9; see 1 Timothy 3:2).

Fourth, leaders in the church must be characterized by a properly motivated *desire*. Paul wrote: "It is a trustworthy statement: if any man *aspires* to the office of overseer, it is a fine work he *desires* to do" (1 Timothy 3:1). Likewise, Peter warned against placing men in a position of oversight "under compulsion." Rather, the undershepherd is to be characterized by eagerness, serving voluntarily with the purpose of accomplishing God's will (1 Peter 5:2). Rather than waiting for some kind of inward voice, a man should cultivate an inward response to the challenge to serve God in the fullest manner possible. Certainly God will stimulate that desire, but the aspiration is said to belong to the man himself.

Fifth, leaders in the church must manifest *spiritual maturity*. This qualification seems to be emphasized more than all the others.

It is underscored in at least three ways. One is the negative require-ment: "Not a new convert" (1 Timothy 3:6). The second is the of-ficial designation: "elder."[14] This "title" applied to the office of church leader emphasizes a man's character—i.e., he is to be spiritually mature. The third way in which this qualification is underlined is by the nature of the characteristics in the lists. There is a clear stress on personal character qualities: "temperate, pru-dent, respectable, hospitable,...not addicted to wine or pugnacious, but gentle, uncontentious, free from the love of money," and so on (1 Timothy 3:2-3). Such qualities are not only to be confirmed by those in the church, but he "must have a good reputation with those outside the church" as well (1 Timothy 3:7).

To sum up: According to the New Testament, a church leader must be a *spiritually mature Christian man* who *desires* a position of leadership in the church, and is *able to lead* God's people and *teach* God's Word.

Examining the Examination

Since God Himself has established these qualifications, it seems that they should have a direct application to our process of "setting apart" (ordaining) men for the ministry. And they do, up to a point. For these passages affirm the validity of examining a man's experience of conversion (he must be a Christian) and his knowledge of Bible doctrine (he must be able to teach). It is curious, on the other hand, that Scripture emphasizes qualifica-tions that many ordaining councils overlook, while the councils stress a requirement that is not mentioned by Scripture.

Where, in our ordaining procedures, is a man tested with respect to his spiritual maturity and his ability to lead? If the apostles evaluated a man's level of growth as evidenced in his rela-tionships, his behavior, and his character, should not that same em-phasis be built into our screening processes as well? Prior to the or-dination examination, business associates, employers, roommates, family members, and friends could be interviewed. Attention would need to be given to securing observations from non-Christian acquaintances as well. It would be good to have concrete evidence that a man is progressing toward the ideals of spiritual leadership.[15]

Such scrutiny may occasionally require godly men to give hard counsel. A promising young candidate might need to be told,

"From our conversations with those who know you best, it is apparent that you presently have a real problem with your temper. Let's give you some time to develop greater patience and self-control before placing you under the stresses of caring for the flock of God."

If the ordination process should be adjusted to include evaluation of a man's character and ability to lead, it would be equally appropriate to bring the question about the call into alignment with Scripture. Where the traditional view speaks of a "call," the New Testament speaks of a "desire" or an "aspiration" for the pastoral office. Perhaps the question should be reworded: "Why do you desire to be set apart for the gospel ministry?"

With these observations, we come full circle. By now the reader must be wondering whether I was ever ordained.

Meanwhile, Back in the Coliseum

Here's what happened. About thirty pastors and church representatives arrived to sit on the examining council. As I prepared to face this questioning, one of the godly pastors of the association offered me these words of encouragement, "Just remember, son, it's the call of God that matters, the call of God." That's just what I needed to hear!

The actual examination began well. These men had all sat where I was sitting, and they were very supportive as the questioning started. I enjoyed narrating again the process by which I came to faith in Christ and the blessings of my life with Him.

Then came the inevitable Question Number Two: "Would you now describe your call to the ministry?" I began by explaining that I had never seen any bright lights nor heard any voices as did the apostle Paul. They assured me that they did not expect me to have such an experience. Then, in a manner that I hoped would reflect a submissive attitude, I asked if they would give me a definition of what they meant by "call." I also observed that it would be helpful if they could cite a specific passage of Scripture where such a call is required of ministers.

What followed was a very interesting discussion. Several descriptions of the inward call were offered. Expressions like "inward compulsion" and "strong inner feeling" were tossed around. Two things became clear: A precise definition was hard to nail down and the requirement of the inward call could not be found, but everyone was convinced that a call was needed. After one comment that defined the call as a strong feeling or compulsion, another pastor said, "If my ministry depended on my feelings, I would probably drop out about every two weeks." That remark elicited laughter and understanding nods.

Eventually the members of the council remembered who was supposed to be questioning whom. And so the focus came back to me. The questions I had raised made it apparent that I had problems with the concept of a call to the ministry. So the question was rephrased: "If you don't feel that you have had one of these 'calls' to the ministry, why do you want to be a minister?"

That, I thought, was the right question. My explanation was essentially a paraphrase of 1 Timothy 3:1: "I want to serve the Lord in the best and fullest way possible. God says that the office of pastor provides a good means for serving Him. So I have consciously aspired to become qualified for that position. The characteristics listed in 1 Timothy 3, Titus 1, and 1 Peter 5 have been my personal goals." That was an honest and candid answer.

Then I added, "It is possible that I experienced some kind of mystical impulse at some campfire service when I was younger. But if I did, I don't remember it very well. And even if I could recall it clearly, such an experience would not be the basis for my desire to enter Christian ministry."

The council showed balance in their reply to me. They agreed that my reasons for desiring ordination were good ones. But they also exhorted me to give careful, further consideration to the matter of my sense of a call. This I agreed to do. One of the men did warn that unless a man had more of a "call" than I had, he would quickly drop out of the ministry.

In the end, I was ordained.

DECISION MAKING AND THE MINISTRY

Hang in there, or Hang It Up?

The warning about dropping out of the ministry given to me at the ordination examination reflects the genuine concern of many who follow the traditional view of the call. I share that concern. Those who enter the ministry do experience extraordinary strains and pressures. And, as the other pastor noted in jest, the temptation to bail out comes up for review at least every two weeks.

But it seems to me that one's sense of a call, which was dubious scripturally and is highly subjective at best, lacks sufficient weight to function as the ultimate anchor in the heavy seas of Christian ministry. I can't help but wonder how many Christian workers have given up precisely because the force of an inward feeling faded with the passing of time.

I also wonder how many otherwise qualified people have refrained from pursuing a vocation of ministry because they haven't heard "the call." I know of at least one. After a teaching session, I was approached by a young youth worker with this question: "I have always wanted to serve Christ and share the gospel in a part of the world where people have never heard of Jesus. However, teachers and missionaries have told me to be certain that I have an inner call from God before I go. I've never really understood what they meant by a "call," but after listening to them, I am quite sure that I have not had one. Do you think I could go to the mission field without one of those calls?"

I asked her where the Bible required an inward mystical "call" to obey the Great Commission. She knew of none. I told her if she was qualified for the type of missionary work she would do, that God nowhere required a mystical call despite what is often taught. God does lay down qualifications for leaders for effective ministry, but she would look in vain for one that was holding her back.

The Call That Binds

We will return to the subject of missions, but first we should note other practical consequences stemming from the impact of the phantom call. For instance, how many Christians are plagued by guilt because they believe that God called them to some ministry at some time in the past, but they chose a "secular" vocation instead? How many pastors have responded to a supposed call only to experience frustration or even rejection because they lacked the revealed biblical qualifications? How many full-time Christian workers have discovered from painful experience that they just aren't suited for such a vocation, but won't change because they feel they would be disobeying God's call? For how many of God's men has a sense of failure been compounded by feelings of guilt because they were forced to "leave the ministry" to which they were "called"?

On paper, such questions are bound to be rhetorical. But for some of God's choice servants, they are very pertinent. If the circumstances of life have required you to serve God through a secular vocation, or if you have chosen such an occupation after evaluating your aptitudes, abilities, and opportunities, rest assured that *your work is acceptable to God* if you do it heartily as unto Him (Colossians 3:23-24). But more on that later.

The point that we are making here is that requiring a call does not solve the problem of attrition from the ministerial ranks. If anything, it complicates it. And it actually creates more problems than it purports to solve. Instead, believers should enter full-time Christian service for the reasons and with the qualifications established by the Bible. And decisions as to whether one should continue or change jobs should be made on biblical grounds as well.[16]

Notes

1. Colin Brown, ed., *The New International Dictionary of New Testament Theology*, s.v. "Call" (Grand Rapids: Zondervan Publishing House, 1975).

2. "We meet the meaning 'invite' for *kaleo* principally in the parables of the great banquet (Lk. 14:16-25), where it occurs 9 times." Brown, *Dictionary of NT Theology*, p. 274.

3. Everett F. Harrison, ed., *Baker's Dictionary of Theology*, s.v. "Call, Called, Calling" (Grand Rapids: Baker Book House, 1960).

4. Ibid.

5. See also 1 Corinthians 1:9; Galatians 1:15; 2 Thessalonians 2:13-15; 2 Timothy 1:9; Hebrews 9:15; 1 Peter 2:9; and 2 Peter 1:3.

6. See Romans 1:6-7; 8:28; 1 Corinthians 1:24; Jude 1; and Revelation 17:14.

7. Professor Charles R. Smith of Grace Theological Seminary correctly observes, "One of the most frequent causes of confusion with regard to God's will is the common failure to recognize the distinctiveness of God's dealings with those to whom and by whom He chose to reveal Himself in the sacred Scriptures. You are not a Moses! Nor are you a Joshua, an Abraham, Ezekiel, Daniel, Matthew, John or Paul! You are not to expect the kind of revelation they received. God's methods in dealing with them have not been His *normal* methods of dealing with believers in any age." Charles R. Smith, *Can You Know God's Will for Your Life?* (Winona Lake, Ind.: B.M.H. Books, 1977), p. 2.

8. The apostle Paul did not see his calling as providing a pattern for other ministers. Quite the contrary, in 1 Corinthians 9:16-18, he stresses the distinctiveness of his calling: He had been drafted into the Lord's service, while others were volunteers. A vivid contrast appears between Paul's situation and the exhortation for elders in 1 Peter 5:2. Whereas other undershepherds are to serve "not under compulsion, but voluntarily," Paul wrote that he preached "under compulsion" and "against my will" (1 Corinthians 9:16-17). For a fuller treatment of this passage and its relevance to this discussion, see Garry Lee Friesen, "God's Will As It Relates to Decision Making" (Th.D. diss., Dallas Theological Seminary, 1978), pp. 255-62.

9. J.I. Packer uses the word "subordinate" to describe the vocational use of the term "call." Harrison, *Dictionary of Theology*, pp. 108-09.

10. For the reasons cited, and for others to follow, we are inclined to agree with the suggestion of Dr. Charles Smith: "In view of the fact that young people are often confused by this terminology, and led to expect some supernatural revelation regarding their vocation, perhaps it would be wise to drop the term 'call' as a reference to such a conviction regarding our life-work." Smith, *Can You Know God's Will?*, p. 3.

11. We realize that *all* Christians are to be "full-time ministers" in the biblical sense of the term. But we must have some means of distinguishing between vocations where believers earn their living through their ministry (such as pastors and missionaries) and those jobs where people are not paid for such Christian service. For that purpose, throughout the remainder of this chapter, we will use terminology that recognizes a distinction between "sacred" and "secular" vocations.

12. That Paul intended his lists in 1 Timothy and Titus to be definitive is clearly indicated in the near-identical introductory words: "An overseer, then, *must be...*" (1 Timothy 3:2) and "For the overseer *must be...*" (Titus 1:7). Surely one could expect to find the normative qualifications for church leaders in such passages.

13. For an excellent treatment of leadership in the New Testament Church, see Gene A. Getz, *Sharpening the Focus of the Church* (Chicago: Moody Press, 1974), pp. 84-129, and Gene A. Getz, *The Measure of A Man* (Glendale, Ca.: G/L Publications, 1974).

14. The two principle "titles" for church leaders in the New Testament are "overseer" (or "bishop" which occurs six times in the New Testament in that sense) and "elder" (appearing fourteen times with that meaning). The two terms are interchangeable (see, for example, Titus 1:5 and 7). "Overseer" emphasizes the leader's responsibility; while "elder" stresses his character.

15. It is significant that several evangelical seminaries are now requiring much more extensive internship experiences for their students. Such extended on-the-job training gives opportunity for both practical training and evaluation of potential for pastoral ministry.

16. It is surely instructive that during the post-resurrection period of confusion for the disciples, the risen Lord held a vocational counseling session for Simon Peter, His fisherman-turned-shepherd (John 21:1-22). Even though Peter's original call to discipleship seems to be reaffirmed through the actions of Jesus, it is never specifically mentioned. Rather, the thrice-repeated question, "Do you love Me?" seems to point to the decisive factor in the staying power of the shepherd—i.e., the disciple's day-to-day response to the injunction, "Follow Me." It is a biblical principle that persistence in faithfulness to *any aspect* of one's stewardship is the product of spiritual maturity (1 Corinthians 4:2; 15:58; Galatians 5:22-23; 6:9; Hebrews 12:1-13). In the face of difficulties, what the minister needs in order to continue on is the grace of God (2 Corinthians 12:9-10) and the conviction that he is doing something that God wants done—His moral will.

Chapter 20

Missions and Wisdom

*F*or Ted Bradford, the vocational issue concerned not only whether he had been called to the ministry in general, but to the mission field in particular. Of course, much of the presentation in the previous chapter applies to the latter question directly. But the subject of the missionary vocation requires further treatment because the work of missionaries falls in a special category. If a call from God is required for any job, it must be that of a missionary.

There are at least two compelling reasons for this common assumption—one biblical and one practical. The biblical argument is that the very first missionaries in the church, Barnabas and Saul, were explicitly called by God to be missionaries (Acts 13:1-3). Those who were not called stayed put. A common inference from these facts is that those who are so called must become missionaries; everyone else gets to stay home and do what they choose.

The practical reason is that being a missionary is exceptionally hard work. In addition to all of the problems that normally attend Christian ministry, the missionary has to be able to adapt to a foreign culture and often a different language. Since God alone knows who can effectively handle such challenges, it is said that He handpicks the laborers for foreign fields.

MISSIONARY DECISIONS IN THE EARLY CHURCH

Now we have already touched upon the call of Barnabas and Saul. We noted that they were called precisely because they were to be the *first missionaries*. And their call came through supernatural means—either the voice of God, or the voice of a prophet (Acts 13:1-2). In the absence of confirming passages, it is going too far to construe from this unique event that all subsequent missionaries must be similarly called. (If one chooses to hold out for the necessity of a divine call, one should also insist on communication via special revelation.)

That is not to say that Acts 13 is irrelevant to contemporary decisions concerning missions. We should not look or listen for some dramatic call; but we should emulate the wisdom displayed by the Holy Spirit in His choice of missionaries and the timing of their commissioning. Note the following factors:

1. The men selected were qualified to do spiritual work, including evangelism and church planting (Acts 11:19-30).
2. Their ability to work together as a team had already been proven through their ministry at Antioch.
3. Their ability to work effectively among the Gentiles, which would be their primary target group (Acts 14:27), was already proven.
4. The sending church would not be spiritually impoverished through the loss of these two leaders (Acts 13:1). Others had become qualified to carry on the local ministry.

Having noted those valuable precedents and the wisdom demonstrated by them, we would point to the sequels of this event to find examples of missions-related decision making that are more directly applicable today. The saga of John Mark is a case in point.

The Case of the Deserting Disciple

John Mark, cousin of Barnabas, was being discipled by Barnabas and Saul at the time of their call (Acts 12:25). So they took him along as a helper, although he had not been named by the Holy Spirit (Acts 13:2,5). Mark's service was apparently satisfactory through the first stage of the mission. But before the team began the arduous trek from Perga to Pisidian Antioch, Mark abandoned the project and returned home to Jerusalem (Acts 13:13). The reason is not stated by Luke.

Paul and Barnabas completed a tour of central Asia Minor, returned to Antioch, and reported on "all [the] things that God had done with them and how He had opened a door of faith to the Gentiles" (Acts 14:27). Then they remained in Antioch for "a long time" (Acts 14:28).

The second missionary journey was proposed by Paul to Barnabas after the Jerusalem Council: "'Let us return and visit the brethren in every city in which we proclaimed the word of the Lord, and see how they are'" (Acts 15:36). It is worth noting that the text does not attribute this idea to the Holy Spirit, as was the case with the first journey. It was apparently generated by Paul's desire to fulfill Christ's commission to see believers taught and come to maturity. His suggestion is an example of initiative taken by a spiritually mature man who is intent on accomplishing God's moral will in a wise manner.

There was apparently no discussion as to whether God had called them to make this trip. What was discussed, with great intensity, was whether they should take along John Mark. Barnabas, who wasn't one to give up on people, wanted to take him. Paul, who placed a premium on loyalty, perseverance, and proven competence, wasn't willing to risk another desertion. The issue, once again, was not John Mark's call or lack thereof. The issue was his demonstrated qualifications (Acts 15:37-38).

In the absence of agreement or any direct word from God, they decided to separate and form two new teams (Acts 15:39). Barnabas took Mark and headed for Cyprus which was familiar territory to both of them. "Paul chose Silas" (Acts 15:40), a proven leader with the prophetic gift (Acts 15:32), and with the blessings of the church headed for Asia Minor.

Mark Him Well

Though Barnabas and Mark drop out of sight in Acts, Mark surfaces again in the epistles. Ironically, it is from the pen of Paul that we learn that Barnabas' confidence in Mark bore fruit.

During Paul's first Roman imprisonment, Mark was one of several helpers who stood by him (Philemon 24). In his letter to the Colossians penned at that time, Paul gave this commendation:

> Aristarchus, my fellow prisoner, sends you his greetings; and also Barnabas' cousin Mark (about whom you received instructions: if he comes to you, welcome him); and also Jesus who is called Justus; these are the only fellow workers for the kingdom of God who are from the circumcision; and they have proved to be an encouragement to me (Colossians 4:10-11).

A few years later, during Paul's final imprisonment in Rome, he sent this word to Timothy: "Pick up Mark and bring him with you, for he is useful to me for service" (2 Timothy 4:11).

As far as Paul was concerned, the issue was always personal qualifications. When Mark proved his worth (probably through his ministry with Barnabas in Cyprus), Paul did not hesitate to make him a member of his team and commend him for his conscientiousness.

When at First You Don't Succeed...

Returning now to Paul's second journey in Acts 16, we find a different scenario unfolding. When Paul and Silas left Antioch, they still did not have a helper. Paul's disappointment with John Mark did not, however, cause him to abandon the idea of on-the-job training for young men. When he and Silas came to Lystra, Paul was impressed by a young disciple named Timothy. A convert from Paul's previous mission there, Timothy was chosen to become John Mark's replacement (Acts 16:3). His credentials are briefly established in the text: He was a disciple who "was well spoken of by the brethren" in those parts (Acts 16:1-2). Again, it was demonstrated spiritual qualifications, rather than a call, that proved to be decisive in the choice.

The wisdom of choosing Timothy for this role was to be confirmed over and over again in the years to follow. We know more of this assistant to the apostle than any other of Paul's fellow workers. Timothy was given significant responsibilities for ministry and he consistently fulfilled his assignments (see 1 Thessalonians 3:1-2, 6).

In his commendation of Timothy to the Philippian church, Paul gave his ultimate accolade to his beloved protégé:

> But you know of his proven worth that he served with me in the furtherance of the gospel like a child serving his

father. Therefore I hope to send him immediately.... (Philippians 2:22-23).

As with John Mark and Timothy, Paul explained the sending of all of his fellow workers to various churches on the basis of their proven ability to minister. Such proven character was the case with Epaphroditus (Philippians 2:25-30), sister Phoebe (Romans 16:1-2), Stephanas, Fortunatus, and Achaicus (1 Corinthians 16:17-18), Tychicus (Ephesians 6:21-22), Epaphras (Colossians 1:7-8; 4:12-13), an unnamed brother (2 Corinthians 8:22), and even the converted runaway slave Onesimus (Colossians 4:9; Philemon 10-13).

Our purpose in this review of missionary activity in the New Testament is to establish this fact: Once missionary outreach was set in motion by the Holy Spirit in Acts 13, all subsequent decisions related to missions were made on the basis of applied wisdom. (The one exception to this process was the Macedonian Call in Acts 16:6-10, which we discussed earlier.) In the actual practice of the New Testament church, the decisions concerning timing, destinations, and personnel were all made by the appropriate people with a view to obeying God's moral will in the most effective manner possible. There is a remarkable absence of any reference to the call of God beyond Acts 16.

DECIDING WHO SHOULD GO

As we were preparing the material for this chapter, we thought it would be good to get input on current perspectives from those directly involved in missions. We wrote to a dozen missionary agencies and asked, "What kind of people are you looking for to become missionaries? What qualifications have you established? What advice do you give to people who are considering a career in missions?" Frankly, we were wondering what degree of importance is attached to a sense of calling as compared with other criteria.

If the replies we received are representative of current thinking among mission boards, the present mentality might be summarized as follows: While a sense of call is considered to be important by most, other qualities and qualifications are far more determinative in the actual selection process. Some missionary leaders even admit to being wary about someone's claim to a call from God. Michael

C. Griffiths, former general director of the Overseas Missionary Fellowship, gives this candid explanation:

> Oddly enough, mission societies are wary of commitment too. They often seem to have a healthy skepticism about our guidance. Not everybody who fancies himself climbing the Himalayas or who feels attracted to the glamour of tribal work is necessarily suitable for the work. The high percentage of people who feel called to glamorous fields makes one a little skeptical. Missions are not eager to saddle themselves with impractical romantics who want to join the Mission and see the world. You may be wary about approaching a mission, but you will find them equally cautious about you. They will try to size you up very carefully. If they don't, you should become more wary still![1]

In fact, there is at least one missionary society, Sudan Interior Mission, that is willing to consider candidates who cannot pinpoint a decisive call to the mission field. General Director Emeritus Dr. Raymond J. Davis and General Director Dr. Ian M. Hay were asked:

> How does SIM react to a person who expresses an interest in foreign service, but who can't honestly say he has had a missionary "call"?

Replied Dr. Hay:

> SIM reacts with understanding. We want those people who are first of all committed in their lives to the lordship of Christ, people who understand that their basic responsibility is to do the will of God as outlined in the Scriptures. The person who comes with this attitude is precisely the type of person we're looking for, whether he understands what a "call" is or not. Actually, the use of that word bothers me. There's a lot of misunderstanding regarding a "call." The word has assumed overtones that I think we can do without.

Dr. Davis added:

> The concept of a "call" as a necessary introductory experience for serving God cannot be scripturally substantiated. Some, like Paul, did have such an experience, but

many others didn't. We've built up the idea of a "call" into something which simply was not known in the days of the early church.[2]

There are missions leaders at the other end of the spectrum for whom a sense of divine call is considered indispensable. At the pragmatic level, however, most agencies leave the genuineness of a call to the individual and evaluate the candidate according to very practical standards. In the final analysis, if the missionary agency concludes that the applicant is unsuited to be a missionary, they will have no part in sending him, whether he claims a "call" or not. As Griffiths observes: "Most missions have had plenty of experience with people who have been hard to live with or hard to live down. They are not going to rush taking you on, however highly you may value your own services."[3]

Significantly, there is essential agreement among mission boards as to the basic requirements for missionaries. These may be categorized as qualities and qualifications. A list of *qualities* that we have compiled so far draws the following profile: patient, psychologically mature, emotionally stable, teachable, reliable, dependable, goal oriented, person oriented, assertive, servant-minded, self-reliant, energetic, steadfast, tactful, serious, loyal, immovable, flexible, gentle, tenderhearted, conscientious, disciplined, generous, meek, wholehearted, concerned, humble, practical, humorous, friendly, holy, discerning, progressive, motivated, and able to leap tall buildings in a single bound. (That last item is optional, depending on the assignment.) Michael Griffiths puts such lists in proper perspective when he notes, "It is the fruit of the Spirit we need more than anything else."[4]

Missions educator Dr. George Peters gives an accurate summary of the categories of missionary *qualifications.*

> In general, the preparation and qualifications of a missionary candidate are measured by several standards and labeled as:
> 1. Spiritual qualifications
> 2. Doctrinal qualifications
> 3. Academic qualifications
> 4. Physical qualifications
> 5. Personality qualifications
> 6. Social qualifications.[5]

The specifics in each of the general areas listed above vary from agency to agency and from assignment to assignment. But they have been forged on the anvil of hard experience by the application of spiritual wisdom. In actual experience, whether the traditional view of guidance is maintained or not, it appears that the twentieth century Church is applying the same principles of wisdom in decision making as the first century Church.[6]

The Bottom Line

In bringing this discussion of missions to a conclusion, we would submit this applicational principle: *Rather than waiting for some kind of mystical "call" from God, every believer should respond to the revealed will of God by giving serious consideration to becoming a cross-cultural missionary.*

Having given sufficient coverage to the difficulties of the missionary task, we now need to look at the reasons for considering personal involvement. There are at least three.

1. *The Command.* Christ's Great Commission to "'make disciples of all the nations'" was given to the Church and remains in effect "even to the end of the age" (Matthew 28:19-20). For the believer, personal involvement in the cause of world missions *is not optional.* We don't need a call—we've already been commissioned. Every single Christian is to be making some contribution to the objective of world evangelization and discipleship. (The variety of ways in which people can be directly involved will be noted below.) Since some must carry the gospel to unreached peoples, it follows that every Christian should be available to do so. We are all under orders.

2. *The Need.* The statistics are so mind boggling that they cannot be fully comprehended. But this is the way it is:

> Three billion of earth's people are not Christians. Over two billion of those are completely separated from anyone who can share the gospel with them. The two billion plus will be reached only by cross-cultural missionaries.[7]

3. *The Provision.* The Head of the Church has given to some of His people the personal strength, resources, and gifts to do the job. Obedience to the command to be faithful stewards requires all

believers to evaluate whether they have the God-given capability to best fulfill the Great Commission by personally taking the gospel to people in another culture. Those who do should go. Those who don't should send.

THE ROAD TO THE MISSION FIELD

Here Am I—Now What?

For those who are prepared to respond openly to the challenge of the Great Commission, we would suggest embarking upon a personal project which, if pursued to culmination in a missionary vocation, would entail at least seven steps. (Since any number of things could rule out a career in cross-cultural ministry, such a project could be sovereignly interrupted, and hence completed, short of the foreign field. Nevertheless, if one is to become a missionary, this is the course to follow.)

1. *Commitment.* The first issue, really, is availability. And that issue ought to be settled by grateful submission to the Lordship of Christ (Luke 9:23-26; 14:25-35). One reason there aren't more missionaries is not that God hasn't called more; it's because more people haven't responded to the clear commission already given. There might be many valid reasons for not becoming a missionary; but unwillingness is not one of them (Luke 9:59-62).

2. *Investigation.* An important means for gaining wisdom is the gathering of facts. Ask questions: What do missionaries do? What does it take to become a missionary? What does it cost? What does it require?

The realities are sobering. "It takes six to ten years after college graduation to become an effective cross-cultural missionary."[8] But while gathering facts about the cost, be sure to collect data from God's Word and experienced missionaries concerning the anticipated return on the investment. What, in all the world, could possibly be worth the kind of cost that is required of missionaries?

3. *Involvement.* Every believer who reads this book can personally and actively participate in Christ's worldwide mission right now. The first means is effectively bearing witness to Christ right in one's own "Jerusalem." Coupled with such evangelistic involvement must be the exercise of whatever gifts and abilities God has given for ministry in the context of a local church (Ephesians 4:11-16). Such ongoing ministry represents obedience to God's

moral will and perpetually equips for broader ministry, perhaps cross-culturally, in the future.

Further, the responsibility that every Christian has to contribute to global outreach can be fulfilled in a variety of ways. These include the indispensable support roles of intercessory prayer and financial investment. Additionally, Christians in the sending church could do more to minister to the needs of the missionaries who represent them: writing letters regularly, sharing prayer requests and answers, providing spiritual food through taped Bible messages, sending "fun money"—in short, anticipating needs and taking creative steps to meet them. Such ministry to the Church's "front-liners" would undoubtedly make them more effective in their work; and it would give supporters the sense of satisfaction that comes from being a contributing member of the team.

Other individuals are needed to promote the challenge of world missions in local churches—to light a fire under the people and fan it! Sunday school teachers with a heart for missions and the ability to communicate a vision may be used of God to launch boys and girls on a journey that ends on a foreign field. Christians with the ability to organize could do the legwork necessary to put on truly significant missions conferences for the local church. The possibilities are limited only by laziness and by limiting ourselves to the list of things we've always done.

4. *Evaluation.* Each believer should take a personal inventory of himself, evaluating his potential by the standard of missionary qualities and qualifications. Some factors may immediately rule out a career in missions: health limitations, an unsaved spouse, or lack of opportunity for adequate training, to cite some examples. Personal weaknesses do not necessarily disqualify but may be corrected through education, training, help from others, increasing maturity, or some other manifestation of the grace of God. In some cases, wisdom will indicate that a particular Christian can make more of a contribution to missions through a vocation at home. In other cases, the believer will discover in himself the raw material from which missionaries are made. When that happens, that individual should deliberately set out on a course whereby that raw material can be shaped by the Potter into a finished vessel—suitable for service on a foreign field.

Such an inventory should be taken periodically throughout one's life. Some people who were prevented from becoming missionaries when they were young adults have found doors of opportunity opening at later times. And some who have developed proficiency in a "secular occupation" have discovered that their skills were needed on the mission field in a vital support role. Those kinds of possibilities need to be pursued in the evaluation process.

5. *Consultation.* Personal evaluation should not be carried out in a vacuum. The New Testament carefully records the involvement of local churches in recognizing, choosing, and sending those best suited for international outreach. Since the missionary serves as the representative of the sending church, it stands to reason that the church should have a determinative role in the evaluation and selection process.

First, the local church must stimulate an interest in missions among the people. Second, the church should take some initiative in approaching apparently qualified members with the challenge of personal involvement as potential missionaries. Third, the Christian who is considering a vocation in missions should seek the counsel of mature believers who are in a position to evaluate his or her potential for cross-cultural ministry.

6. *Preparation.* As long as the light remains green, the potential missionary should take the individual steps that will lead to the foreign field. The most important of these steps, whether one becomes a missionary or not, is to enroll in the school of spiritual growth. The motto of that school is: "Discipline yourself for the purpose of godliness" (1 Timothy 4:7).

Second, personal involvement in world missions while still at home provides excellent preparation for serving abroad.

And third, the individual must deliberately proceed to meet the requirements set up by the mission agencies. Although there are exceptions, most missionary societies include the following: adequate education (usually a college degree), a certain amount of formal Bible training, experience in Christian ministry, cross-cultural exposure, development of facility in witnessing, commitment to a mission agency, language acquisition, and training in specialized skills as necessary for a particular assignment. Throughout the process, the would-be missionary would do well to become acquainted with the history of missions and principles of cross-cultural communication.

7. *Prayer*. Pray for wisdom, strength, and open doors of opportunity. And submit, in advance, to the sovereign will of the Lord of the harvest (Luke 10:2). Then proceed, as you pray, to obey His moral will — with the confidence that He is at work in you "both to will and to work for His good pleasure" (Philippians 2:13).

Notes

1. Michael C. Griffiths, *You and God's Work Overseas* (Downers Grove, Ill.: InterVarsity Press, 1967), pp. 23-24.

2. "No Voice From Heaven?," *Africa Now*, November-December 1979, pp. 2-5. This article is also available in reprint form from Sudan Interior Mission, Cedar Grove, NJ 07009.

3. Griffiths, *You and God's Work Overseas*, pp. 24-25.

4. Michael C. Griffiths, *Give Up Your Small Ambitions* (Chicago: Moody Press, 1970), p. 56.

5. George W. Peters, *A Biblical Theology of Missions* (Chicago: Moody Press, 1972), p. 292.

6. I observed this reality first-hand when I represented Multnomah School of the Bible at the 1979 InterVarsity Missions Conference at Urbana, Illinois. By the end of that conference, 1,471 of the 16,500 delegates had signed a statement which read, "I believe it is God's will for me to serve Him abroad, and I will make prayer and inquiry to this end." Yet not one of the 165 mission agencies present apologized for laying out their very exacting requirements for service. Many students came directly from mission-board booths to the one where I was working and said, "The missionary agencies tell me that I need at least one year of good solid Bible training on the college level. What does your school offer along that line?" I was there to inform students that Multnomah has an excellent program that has been set up specifically to meet the requirements of mission boards.

7. Ed Dayton, "How To Get There from Urbana," *World Vision*, January, 1980, p. 16.

8. Ibid., p. 17.

Chapter 21

Vocation, Education, and Wisdom

*I*f men and women of antiquity could somehow be transported through time to our present era and culture, they would probably be dumbfounded by the number and kinds of choices that are granted to individuals in our society. As we have already noted, during Bible times parents exercised a decisive control in the arrangement of marriages. For the most part, a man's choice of vocation was similarly determined. Sons usually took up the occupations of their fathers, working the land or using the tools that were passed along from one generation to another.[1] Daughters became wives. Asking a young Israelite if he had discovered God's will for his life's work would probably elicit a blank stare.

Not so today. For young people of our time and culture, the "Big Three" among the decisions of life are marriage, vocation, and education—though not necessarily in that order. The choices are personal and the options are almost limitless (at least in theory). Given the multitude of possibilities and the importance of the decisions, the urgent search by many Christians for definitive guidance in these areas is certainly understandable. It is at least ironic that our frantic quest for the vocational "dot" was no more of an issue to the saints of A.D. 50 than, say, the eating of meat sacrificed to idols is to us today.

That is not to say that biblical revelation is obsolete or irrelevant. For while the burning issues of yesterday give way to the new concerns of today, the principles of God's Word remain remarkably contemporary. So even though the apostolic world differed in many respects from our own, the vocational guidance provided by the Holy Spirit through Scripture is entirely adequate — even for our individualistic age.

GOD'S WILL FOR YOUR WORK

Some of that guidance has already been discussed in chapters 19 and 20. There we observed that while God has called certain individuals to specific tasks in the past, such divine assignments are the exception to the rule. The idea of each Christian being "called" of God to his life's work fits the model offered by the traditional view very nicely. But it just doesn't correspond to the experience of most of the saints in either testament.[2]

For those who are not called to some vocation by direct revelation, the choice of a career or job falls in the area of freedom — a decision to be made on the basis of wisdom. For when one reads the biblical passages directly related to the subject of work, one finds the same principle which governs choices pertaining to singleness and marriage: The believer's decision about his vocation is *regulated* and affected by the moral will of God, but *not determined* by it.

Worship While You Work

The moral will of God as set forth in the New Testament epistles concerning the Christian's work may be summarized by the following principles:[3]

1. Insofar as he has the opportunity, the Christian man is to find gainful employment (2 Thessalonians 3:10-11). The believer who refuses to work is severely censured.

2. The obligation to provide for one's own family is one of the highest priorities a Christian man has (1 Timothy 5:8).

3. The Christian's vocation must be lawful (Ephesians 4:28).

4. The Christian's work is to be characterized by:
   a) Sincerity of heart (Ephesians 6:5; Colossians 3:22-23)
   b) Enthusiasm and diligence (Ephesians 6:6; Colossians 3:23; 2 Thessalonians 3:8; cf. Ecclesiastes 9:10)
   c) Reverence and devotion to Christ (Ephesians 6:5-6; Colossians 3:22-23)
   d) Good will (Ephesians 6:7)
   e) Discipline (2 Thessalonians 3:11)
   f) Quietness (2 Thessalonians 3:12)
   g) Cooperation (Titus 2:9)
   h) Honesty (Titus 2:10)
   i) Integrity (Ephesians 6:6)
   j) Efficiency (Ephesians 5:16)
   k) Gratitude (Colossians 3:17)
   l) Generosity (Ephesians 4:28)
5. In the exercise of his vocation, the Christian should make it his goal:
   a) To earn his food (2 Thessalonians 3:10)
   b) To provide adequately for those of his own family (1 Timothy 5:8)
   c) To behave properly toward outsiders and not be in any need (1 Thessalonians 4:11-12)
   d) To avoid being a burden to others (2 Thessalonians 3:8)
   e) To earn enough to meet his own needs and have some left over to contribute to the needs of others (Ephesians 4:28)
   f) To set a good example for others (2 Thessalonians 3:9)
   g) To preserve God's reputation (1 Timothy 6:1)
   h) To adorn the doctrine of God in every respect (Titus 2:10)—that is, to manifest a consistency between profession and practice
6. In his relationship with his employer, the Christian worker:
   a) Must be submissive and obedient, as unto the Lord (Ephesians 6:5; Colossians 3:22; Titus 2:9; 1 Peter 2:18)

b) Must be diligent in his work, with the idea that his ultimate superior is the Lord (Ephesians 6:6-8; Colossians 3:23)

c) Must work as hard when no one is watching as he does under direct supervision (Ephesians 6:6)

d) Must regard his employer as worthy of all honor (1 Timothy 6:1) and show respect even to those supervisors who are unreasonable (1 Peter 2:18)

e) Must not take advantage of an employer who is also a believer, but rather serve him all the more out of love (1 Timothy 6:2)

7. In his relationships with his employees, the Christian boss:

a) Must not abuse his workers (Ephesians 6:9)

b) Must treat his employees with justice and fairness (Colossians 4:1)

c) Must apply the golden rule, treating his workers as he would wish to be treated (Ephesians 6:9)

d) Must be fair and prompt in the payment of wages (James 5:4)

e) Must remember that he is accountable to God, the Master of all, for his treatment of his workers (Colossians 4:1)

8. If it does not otherwise violate the moral will of God, the opportunity for vocational change or advancement may be taken (1 Corinthians 7:21).[4]

One's choice of occupation, then, is to be made on the same basis as every other decision within the moral will of God: wisdom and spiritual expediency. The question the believer should ask as he avails himself of God's guidance is: Given my aptitudes, abilities, gifts, desires, and opportunities, which vocation would offer the greatest potential for my service to the Lord and my obedience to His moral will?[5]

Spiritual Gift

The believer's spiritual gift is part of his ability and aptitude and so influences his decision making. The best description of a spiritual gift comes from Paul when he describes it as a "gift", "ministry", "effect," and "manifestation of the Spirit" (1 Corinthians 12:4-7). God gives the *gift* of a spiritual enablement that is seen in a *ministry* which has *effect* for the common good. Believers are gifted differently (1 Corinthians 12:8-11, 29-30) which affects decision making differently.

The moral will of God determines that each believer should use his gift for the common good.

> As each one has received a special gift, employ it in serving one another, as good stewards of the manifold grace of God (1 Peter 4:10; cf. 1 Corinthians 12:7; Romans 12:6-8).

So a believer's life style must include the use of his spiritual gift. Thus, the moral will of God regulates that a gift must be used, but does not dictate when and where it must be used.

The gift of teaching, for example, can be a "full-time" teaching position or a weekly Bible study. The place that the gift is used could be with junior boys or college women, in Sunday school or one-on-one discipleship, in a local church or at a Bible school. These decisions are determined by spiritual expediency. Where can my gift be most wisely used to effectively serve God?

Wisdom also will determine the amount of time and effort used with the exercise of one's gift. The moral will of God prohibits a person from using his gift exclusively while neglecting actions specifically commanded in other passages of Scripture. For instance, fathers are to teach their children (Ephesians 6:4) whether they have the teaching gift or not (Romans 12:7), all believers are to give (1 Corinthians 16:2) though not all have the gift (Romans 12:8), and all believers are to show mercy (Matthew 5:7; Ephesians 4:32), but only some have the gift (Romans 12:8). On the other hand, it is wise to use more time and energy where one has special enablement from God. Certainly Billy Graham must show mercy as a believer, but wisdom guides him to skip some trips to the rest home in favor of a city-wide evangelistic crusade. A greater amount of time and effort is directed by wisdom into those areas where God has gifted and brings the greatest spiritual effect.

We have already demonstrated in chapters 19 and 20 that every believer has an obligation to give valid consideration to "full-time vocational Christian service." Because of all the factors involved, the majority of believers who seriously evaluate that option will probably conclude that they can serve God more effectively through a so-called secular position. A good job offers a natural base from which a man can provide for his family, bear witness to Christ, and contribute to the proclamation of God's Word through his local church and world-wide missions.

A student who was struggling with this kind of decision once shared with me his dilemma. "Some years ago, I had a secular job which I enjoyed. I made a point to share Christ with my fellow workers, and in time I was given the opportunity to lead some Bible studies for people in our company. Those Bible studies were so used of the Lord in the lives of those people that I began to think I should be teaching the Bible full time. I became so gripped with the idea that I told my family and my church that I felt God was calling me into the ministry.

"Now, after several years in the pastorate, I have concluded that I was actually more effective as a servant of Christ in my secular job than I am in church work. I would like to go back to what I was doing, and enjoying, before. The problem is that I cannot just withdraw from full-time ministry and return to my previous vocation."

Though I was pretty sure of the reason, I asked, "Why not?"

"Well," he replied, "since I told everyone that I was called into the pastorate, people would think I was disobeying the Lord if I went back to my old job. Also, it would be very humiliating to admit that I had been mistaken about that call."

What this student needed to understand, first of all, was that no inner feeling had the authority to determine his choices. Once freed from that subjective absolute, he could focus on the right question: "How can I best serve the Lord through my life's work?" To be sure, he had backed himself into a corner with his family and friends by announcing what he had thought was a call from God. That earlier declaration would make it more difficult to reverse his vocational course, even if that is what wisdom indicated. But as far as God was concerned, he was not thereby locked into a less fruitful job for the rest of his life.

More often, in my classes at Multnomah School of the Bible, I meet men and women who are moving in the opposite direction. Though successful in business or some other secular vocation, many of these students came to recognize that the Lord was using them more outside of their job than in it. Now they are studying the Bible to become better equipped to do full-time the ministries which the Lord has been blessing in their "spare" time. Eventually, if they continue on the present course, they will become Bible teachers, pastors, youth workers, and missionaries. Their change in vocational direction was brought about by the same question: "How can I best serve the Lord with my gifts and abilities?"

VOCATIONAL DECISION MAKING: A CASE STUDY

Same Song, Second Verse

It is one thing to grasp abstract principles; it is another to be able to apply them to the concrete situations of life. And so, in seminars that I have conducted on decision making, I have used a personal illustration to help translate the precepts into practice.

The irony of the illustration is that it so closely resembles the decision I described in the introduction to this book. For both decisions required a choice between two schools. In the first instance, I had to decide where to enroll as a student. In the second, I had to choose where to work as a teacher. In the first case, I experienced great frustration because of my efforts to consistently apply the traditional approach to decision making. In the second—well, the contrast was striking.

Fifteen years separated the two decisions. During that interim, I had worked through a theology of decision making and the will of God. I had become convinced from the Scriptures that my responsibility before God was not to look for an elusive ideal will, but rather to seek clear guidance that was both objective and available.

As a result, when two Bible schools invited me to consider a teaching position on their faculties, I genuinely looked forward to the decision-making process. Rather than becoming anxious about missing my vocational "dot," I was thankful that I had *two* excellent opportunities, instead of just one, or none at all. My prayer for guidance was specific and biblical: I asked for wisdom, believing that God would grant it as He promised. Then I began my search for the wisdom that God said was findable.

I must hasten to add that my new understanding did not magically transform this decision into an easy one. The fact of the matter is that the elements favoring each school were so strong, the choice between them was very difficult. The difference was that I had confidence that the process I was following was scriptural and objective. I knew that I was facing a "no lose" situation, so I was able to relax and enjoy the challenge of making a wise decision.

Try this Decision on for Size

In my seminars, I like to give students a chance to practice applying the wisdom approach to decision making. So I have the group work through my own decision-making situation hypothetically. Students raise questions that they think I should have been asking. I respond by telling them whether I actually pursued those particular questions, and report on what I learned when I did. As the data is compiled, further issues are raised and discussed. And the group participates personally in my decision-making process.

That approach is impossible in a book. But what I can do is reconstruct a session I had recently with a college-career group in a local church. Since my recall is not as absolute as the playback from a tape recorder, we will have to be content with a paraphrase of what was actually said. Hopefully, the reader can participate vicariously.

Student: Before you decided where to teach, you had to decide *whether* to teach. Had that issue already been resolved in your mind?

Garry: By that time, I had concluded from past ministry that God had given me the gift of teaching. It is His moral will that I exercise whatever gift He gives me (Romans 12:6-8; 1 Peter 4:10). So teaching at a Bible college would be an excellent place to exercise that gift.

Student: Where were the schools located?

Garry: One was here in Portland. The other was in my home town in Michigan.

Student: So what's to decide?

(It should be pointed out that these Oregonians intuitively recognized the wisdom of locating in the beautiful Pacific Northwest.)

Home, Sweet Home

Garry: Actually, the location favored the Michigan school—for several reasons. That's where my home church is. I know the area well and have a spiritual concern for my home town. And working there would have brought our whole family together again in one place. Accepting a job close to my parents would be a way of honoring them.

Student: What *did* your parents think? Did you seek their counsel?

Garry: I was initially concerned that my folks might feel slighted if I turned down a job at home when I didn't need to. So I determined that if they would be upset by my selection of the alternative offer, I would regard that as a strong reason for accepting the job at home. I hoped that they would not feel offended if I moved away again. But life is full of such realities, so I prepared myself for such an eventuality.

When we actually sat down to discuss my options, my parents demonstrated the same maturity they have always tried to teach me. The first thing they said was, "You know that we love you, and we would love to have you teaching near home. But we want you to know that our greatest desire is for you to make the best possible decision—not just the one that keeps you close to us." My counselors were first-rate, and the price was right.

As we analyzed the numerous advantages of the school away from home, Mom jokingly said, "Wait a minute. We're not trying to get rid of him." We could laugh because we knew that was true, and because we were not afraid to seek where wisdom would lead us in God's guidance.

Student: Exactly what kind of work did each school want you to do?

Garry: That is an important question because, in this situation, the openings were not identical. The school in the Northwest was offering me the lowest position on the totem pole. The school in the Midwest wanted me not only to teach, but to assume the position of chairman of the Department of Bible and Theology. In terms of opportunity and responsibility, the two positions were clearly unequal.

Student: But at that point in your teaching career, did you think that you could handle the additional pressures of being a department chairman?

Garry: That is a perceptive observation! There is a business axiom to the effect that workers tend to rise to the level of their incompetence. If I had accepted that position of department chairman, the chances are excellent that I would have *started out* at that level. I do have a desire to serve in an administrative capacity, but the offer came four or five years too soon. So I had to conclude that the job descriptions favored the school in the Northwest.

The Power of the Purse

Student: What about the pay scale?

Garry: At that time, I didn't really care what they paid me. So today, I honestly cannot remember what the prospective salaries were. I know that both schools offered more than enough for a single person to live on.

As I have reflected on that aspect of the process, I have concluded that I should have paid more attention to the salary offers. There are at least three reasons for that. First, though both salaries were more than adequate for a single person, there was no guarantee that I would continue to be single in the years ahead. Second, the more money I earn through my work, the more money I can give for the Lord's work. In fact, at that very time I was praying that the Lord would enable me to increase my financial support of Ed and Kay Klotz, missionaries in Nigeria, as well as of my seminary alma mater which God had so greatly used in my life. Third, faculty salaries often reflect the relative stability of a private school and the commitment of its supporters.

In the actual decision, however, the prospective pay package was not a factor.

Student: Did you have an opportunity to teach some classes at each school?

Garry: Yes, I did. Both schools made arrangements for me to teach several class sessions. Then, my presentations were evaluated by students and other faculty members.

Student: Did the various responses help you in your decision?

Garry: Yes. The number and type of questions I got from the students, plus the inaudible clues a teacher picks up, indicated that my teaching had been more appropriate and helpful to the students in the Northwest school.

Who's in Charge around Here?

Many other excellent questions were put to me by the group. They raised the issues of doctrinal stance, school reputation, and opportunities for outside ministry—areas in which the two schools were equally strong.

But one question that I was listening for did not come up: "Who would be your direct boss? To whom would you be responsible? To whom would you have to submit?"

That is an important question in the consideration of the job. For submission to authority is a biblical imperative for believers. Experience teaches that submission to authority is easiest when the one in charge is reasonable, competent, patient, loving, and compatible in personality. Wisdom would indicate that whenever one is in a position to choose his own boss, that choice should be made with great care. For once the commitment is made, the moral will of God that requires submission is binding.

For a teacher in Bible school, the person in authority is the academic dean. So while both schools were scrutinizing me, I was studying the two deans. One of the men was quite different from me in temperament. So I spent more time discussing and debating things with him to see how we would work together. It soon became apparent that I would have no difficulty working with and submitting to either dean. In that regard, there was a plus for both schools.

But Do They Play Soccer?

At both schools I asked about a soccer team. All other things being equal, I wanted to know if there would be opportunity to participate in a sports program. This was not a "top ten" issue. But my love for sports and enjoyment of a temple that is in good working order probably pushed it into the top thirty questions.

Though it may not sound like a very spiritual consideration, the question about sports was one aspect of my search for wisdom. For Scripture commands us to do all things with zeal and enthusiasm. Being able to play soccer or basketball would help me to obey that imperative in my teaching. The physical exercise would be good for my bodily health, and the fun of playing would help me maintain my emotional health. One's personal happiness is a valid consideration in the process of making a wise decision (1 Corinthians 7:40).

To that particular question, the reply of both schools was the same: "You may work out with the school team if you wish."

Everything You Wanted to Know, But...

Much wisdom is available to those who know the right questions to ask. From my subsequent experience as a teacher, I have discovered several areas that would have merited careful investigation — areas that I didn't check out because I didn't know to ask the questions. If I had it to do all over again, I would now make the following additional inquiries:

1. How many different classes will I teach?
2. How much secretarial help will I have for grading assignments and other office work?
3. What type of office equipment and space will be supplied?
4. What will be my responsibilities in publicity and recruitment?
5. How many committee assignments will I be expected to accept?
6. What will be the nature of my relationship to the head of the department?
7. What kind of grading system is used in the school?
8. How often are contracts worked out and signed?

The fact that I did not think of those questions until after the decision was made underscores a couple of corollaries to the principles already stated. First, when we ask for wisdom, that's what God gives us; He does not grant omniscience. I didn't learn everything I could have learned before making my choice. But the wisdom God gave me was entirely sufficient for a sound decision.

Second, the knowledge we acquire through the process of making a decision, as well as the insight acquired *as a result of* our choice, help to prepare us for future decisions. Every decision not only requires wisdom, but becomes a means by which God gives further wisdom for the future. That same process also equips us to give wise counsel to others who are facing similar choices.

Go West, Young Man

In the end, I accepted the position offered by Multnomah School of the Bible in Portland, Oregon. The decision was never cut-and-dried, but it has proved to be a good one. God kept His promises and showed Himself to be faithful in this decision. He gave power, wisdom, and motivation enabling me to make a wise choice within His moral will.

My job has been both fulfilling and taxing over the past four years. Though I have encountered many difficulties, I haven't been tempted to engage in second-guessing, quietly worrying, "Could it be that I missed God's perfect will?" No, God expected me to make the decision, directed by His moral will according to spiritual expediency. He also supplied the guidance and ability to do that. That knowledge has freed me to concentrate fully on serving God where I am, today, with all the energy and ability that He supplies.

God's Will for Your Preparation

Three to Get Ready

Upon graduation from high school, many young people enter a transitional phase in their lives that precedes the commencement of their career. Usually that period of time is utilized to prepare for complete independence from parental support and full participation in the adult community. For many people in our society, the direction to be taken during these determinative years is the first major decision in life for which the individual takes full responsibility.

Because of the differences in time and culture, there are not many passages of Scripture that directly address this particular decision. And so the determinations that a Christian makes with respect to education and training are to be made according to wisdom. The basic question will be: How can I best prepare to serve the Lord through my life and my vocation as an adult? That question articulates the basic issues: (1) the ultimate goal is to serve the Lord in the most effective way possible; (2) the intermediate objective is appropriate preparation; and (3) that preparation should develop the Christian as a person as well as train him for a vocation (though the actual process may take place in stages).

The options open to a young person in our society are abundant: university, college, Bible school, military service, vocational training school, apprenticeship, and so on. Or, the individual can immediately go to work and gain valuable exposure and skills through on-the-job experience. The actual possibilities will be limited by a number of factors: academic aptitude, grades and test scores, openings, financial resources, family circumstances, personal inclinations, individual initiative, and world conditions (peace or war). The person who has concrete ideas about what he wants to do with his life will be in a position to map out a specific course of preparation. The individual whose vocational plans remain unformulated would do well to consider educational opportunities that will be foundational to any career—a liberal arts education or perhaps a tour of duty in the armed forces. Additionally, the Christian young person should weigh the advisability of some formal Bible training to help equip him or her to serve the Lord more effectively through any vocation.

Study to Show Thyself Approved

To the above generalizations, I would add a couple of observations. The first is that education or training does not *in itself* qualify a person for spiritual ministry or a specific vocation. It is only part of the equipping process. For instance, graduation from seminary does not necessarily guarantee a man's suitability to function as a pastor. Seminary can train him so that he is "able to teach" (1 Timothy 3:2) and "able both to exhort in sound doctrine and to refute those who contradict" (Titus 1:9). Those are divinely instituted requirements for elders and so they are very important. But a seminary education does not insure that a man is able to manage his family well, or that he has the spiritual character required of a church leader. A "Master of Theology" with an uncontrolled temper is not ready to pastor a church—though the degree looks nice on the wall.

The second observation is that the individual himself is the most determinative factor in the ultimate success of the preparation. The best university in the world cannot impart a significant amount of knowledge to a lazy student. On the other hand, an industrious student, who is more concerned about genuine learning than grades or a diploma, can gain a good education even from a mediocre school. The self-taught individuals of past generations have proved that a disciplined, motivated learner who only has access to a library will be far better educated than a slothful Ivy Leaguer.

EDUCATIONAL DECISION MAKING: A CASE STUDY

Abraham's Journey to an Unknown Land

To see how the principles of wisdom apply to an educational decision, let's look at a true case history.

I first met John David Abraham and his wife, Carol, in August, 1977. I had come to Klamath Falls, Oregon, to conduct a weekend seminar on "Decision Making and the Will of God." Dave and Carol were active in the church that was sponsoring the meetings, and they were enthusiastic, probing participants in every session. Because of the providential circumstances that led to the crossing of our paths and the course of events that followed, I asked Dave if we could include his story in this book. He graciously consented, and the account that follows is based on his own testimony.

The summer of 1977 was a time of crisis for Carol and Dave. With Carol's graduation from the State University in Springfield, Missouri, the long-delayed decision about what they would do next could no longer be postponed. Dave had graduated from college the previous year, and had been accepted for enrollment at Grace Theological Seminary in Winona Lake, Indiana. For fifteen years he had looked forward to going to seminary. But he had a problem: Though he knew what he wanted to do, he didn't know what God wanted him to do.

The decision they were facing was obviously very important. Carol and Dave were conscientiously seeking to know God's will for this decision. They prayed, talked things over with friends, and discussed the situation at length together. Yet, they could sense no clear-cut leading from the Lord.

Finally, Dave decided that he wouldn't go to seminary until he knew God wanted him to go. So instead of going to Indiana, they moved to Klamath Falls, Oregon, where Dave took some courses in automotive engineering at Oregon Institute of Technology.

They didn't move to Klamath Falls because they felt that was God's will for their place of residence. They went there because they had to live somewhere and they didn't have any better ideas. Basically, Dave decided to go into a holding pattern for a year or so — until he could figure out what he was going to do.

Dave recalls lying awake in bed one night, crying tears of frustration because of his confusion about what God wanted him to do. He had always been taught that if a Christian wasn't where God wanted him to be, he would be miserable. The burden of that pressure weighed doubly heavy on Dave because he was now married, and had to make decisions that were right for his wife as well as for himself.

As he reflected on their situation, Dave decided there certainly wasn't anything in Scripture that said they couldn't move to Oregon. He hadn't robbed or killed anybody to get there. They had left Springfield with all their bills paid, owing nobody anything. So Dave finally decided if he couldn't find anything in the Bible that said his decision was wrong, it must be all right. Still, he wasn't sure.

Once they moved to Klamath Falls, they began to look for a church home. After some investigation (including a hike with their fingers through the Yellow Pages), they began attending Klamath Evangelical Free Church. They had only been to a few services when it was announced that Mr. Garry Friesen of Multnomah School of the Bible would be coming to present some messages on decision making and God's will. Dave's reaction to that announcement still stands out in his memory. "Needless to say, I was really excited. I couldn't believe that I had moved 2,000 miles to hear someone talk about God's will!"

His response to the seminar itself is equally memorable. "What I heard of the freedom that we have in Christ to make decisions based upon His Word was very thrilling," says Dave. "As the truth of God's Word was unfolded before me, I felt as though a load was being taken off my back. What I was hearing was almost too good to be true!"

The Road to Grace

With his new understanding of God's will, Dave was eager to tackle the decision about seminary. He had already gathered a lot of information so he began by listing the reasons for going to seminary:

1. It had been a dream of his for nearly fifteen years to attend seminary. He felt he should at least give it a try so he wouldn't look back later in life and regret that he had passed up the opportunity.

2. He had taken a one year break after leaving Bible college and his interest in seminary training remained.

3. He didn't see how going to seminary could dishonor or displease God. If anything, it would enhance his spiritual growth.

4. He had observed many men who had gone to good seminaries and was impressed with their lives and their love for the Lord.

5. He sought the counsel of his pastor and was encouraged to go.

6. His wife was in favor of it.

7. His parents and in-laws were supportive of the decision to go to seminary.

When Dave tried to come up with some reasons *not* to attend seminary, he could think of none. So the next thing to consider was which seminary to attend. Grace Theological Seminary seemed to be a good choice for several reasons:

1. On the basis of previous investigation, Dave had narrowed his options to four schools — one of which was Grace.

2. To gain admission to two of the seminaries he was considering, he would have had to obtain additional college liberal arts credits.

3. Grace is located in a small town, while the other three are in large cities. In evaluating himself honestly, Dave thought he would enjoy the small town environment more.

4. He had already been previously accepted by Grace and would not have to apply again if he entered that fall.

5. He had accumulated the financial resources for one year of school.

6. He had a good friend who was attending Grace. Dave respected his opinion, and he spoke highly of the school. That further stimulated Dave's interest.

7. Dave's wife was in favor of going to Grace.

On the negative side, Dave could think of three factors that seemed to be against Grace Seminary:

1. The small town environment might require greater adjustment for his "city-slicker" wife.
2. Indiana was a long way from either of their families.
3. In the winter, the climate there is cold and wet. They wondered how difficult it would be to acclimate to it.

The "pros" in favor of going to Grace clearly outweighed the "cons"—both in quantity and in quality. And so they decided to begin moving in that direction. They knew if their decision was contrary to God's sovereign will, He could close the door in any number of ways. (When you pack all your belongings in a rental truck and transport them 2,000 miles, almost anything can happen to change your direction.)

As Dave and Carol evaluated the total picture, they felt they had made a wise decision. Dave saw the move as something that could enhance his spiritual life. They were not leaving any unpaid debts in Oregon and would not be going into debt to go to seminary. Dave had the encouragement of those who knew him best—his wife, pastor, parents, in-laws, and close friends. And he had done everything he knew to do in making the decision. Dave and Carol also knew they could trust the unknown to God.

Grace for Grace

God's provision for the Abrahams as they followed through on their decision is worth noting. They left Oregon early in the summer in order to have plenty of time to find a place to live and a job for Carol. ("It seemed like the wise thing to do.") Upon arrival in Winona Lake, they stayed with some friends in a rooming house while they began their search for more permanent accommodations and employment.

Carol's success in job hunting was remarkable. Her first step was to inquire about job prospects at the local employment office. That same afternoon, the employment office called back with a good possibility. The very next day, she had an interview for a secretarial position—which was what she was looking for. The firm asked her to return the next day to work a few hours so they could evaluate her work and so she could decide if she was interested in working for them. Well, Carol was hired as personal secretary for Ken Anderson, president of Ken Anderson Films. It is a company where Christian fellowship among the workers is an everyday reality. Carol has greatly enjoyed the working conditions and she has the added satisfaction of knowing that her work will have a spiritual impact on the lives of hundreds of people.

The fact that Carol was able to get such a fine job so quickly might have been taken as confirmation that they had "found God's will" in this decision. But their search for housing would have produced the opposite conclusion. They couldn't find a thing. And they ended up staying with friends in very tight quarters for over a month.

Finally, just a few days before school was to start, a house became available for rent. It was a two-bedroom, brick home just down the street from where they were staying. And it was perfect! Dave comments, "That little house is the nicest place we've ever lived in – or probably ever will!"

Dave is now completing his second year at Grace. In the time they have been there, they have experienced a mix of trials and blessings. Their first winter there, the temperature went below zero for thirty straight days – a record breaking winter for that area! They have found that some of their acquaintances don't understand what they are doing and think they are wasting their time. And seminary has proved to be even more difficult than Dave had anticipated. "It is the hardest thing I have ever attempted to do in my life," he confesses.

On the other hand, God has been using these situations and experiences to teach Dave to use his time wisely, to discipline himself, and to depend on Him in every area. Dave gets enthusiastic when he speaks of his seminary experience. "The training I am getting is just fantastic. Sometimes I get so excited about what I am learning that I can hardly stand it. Attending Grace Seminary is the most rewarding thing I have ever done."

Dave and Carol have also gained increased maturity in their understanding of decision making and God's will. "Learning to make decisions on the basis of God's Word and wisdom has required some adjustment and experiential learning. Initially, I rejoiced in the freedom God has given us to make responsible decisions – and I still do. But I discovered that before long, the process was becoming one-sided. I was making decisions, but God didn't seem to be involved at all. I have been learning that even though many decisions rest with me, I am still to remain *dependent* upon God—allowing and expecting Him to accomplish His purposes in my life. His provision for Carol and me since we have been here has been a real demonstration of how God continues to move in our lives, working through and beyond our decisions for His glory."

Notes

1. Pat Alexander, ed., *Eerdman's Family Encyclopedia of the Bible* (Grand Rapids: Wm B. Eerdmans Publishing Co., 1978), p. 226; and Charles F. Pfeiffer, Howard F. Vos, and John Rea, eds., *Wycliffe Bible Encyclopedia*, vol. 2: "Occupations" by Robert H. Belton (Chicago: Moody Press, 1975), p. 1222.

2. In the previous chapter, we refrained from generalizing a principle that God's vocational call has been restricted to those directly engaged in the ministry of the Word. Our hesitation stemmed from the fact that, while such a limitation does characterize God's call to special service in the New Testament, there are a handful of exceptions in the Old Testament: Adam (gardener), Noah (boat builder and zoo keeper), Bezalel and Oholiab (artists), Joshua (general), and all the men drafted into the army to fight Israel's holy wars (see Genesis 2:15; 6:14,19-20; Exodus 31:1-6; Numbers 1:2-3; 27:22-23). And yet, because all of these men were directly involved in carrying forward God's program of redemption, their work cannot be labeled as strictly "secular"—any more than a pilot for Missionary Aviation Fellowship could be so categorized. In any event, whether "sacred" or "secular/sacred," every example of a divine vocational call in the Bible was communicated via special revelation from God.

3. The passages from which these principles are derived are 1 Corinthians 7:21; Ephesians 4:28; 5:16; 6:5-9; Colossians 3:17-4:1; 1 Thessalonians 4:11-12; 2 Thessalonians 3:7-12; 1 Timothy 5:8; 6:1-2; Titus 2:9-10; James 5:4; and 1 Peter 2:18-25. A number of these references pertain to relations between slaves and their masters. Most commentators consider that social condition to be analogous to our arrangements between employees and employers. And so the exhortations directed to Christian slaves and masters are considered to be directly applicable within the contemporary labor-management context. See, for example, F.F. Bruce, "Commentary on the Epistle to the Colossians," in *Commentary on the Epistles to the Ephesians and the Colossians,* The New International Commentary on the New Testament (Grand Rapids: Wm. B. Eerdmans Publishing Co., 1957), pp. 294-96.

4. The decision as to whether one should change jobs is slightly more complicated than one's initial choice of a vocation. That is because, in accepting employment, a worker places himself under certain obligations to his employer. For a Christian to change jobs without violating the moral will of God, he must do so in a manner which will permit him to fulfill his commitments to his present employer. For instance, the Christian employee is not free to abruptly accept a better offer from another company if his sudden departure would do damage to his present employer. Christian integrity would require the giving of adequate notice so that the employer could take appropriate steps to secure a replacement.

Neither does Scripture encourage a believer to change his work just because his working conditions are difficult. (In New Testament times, the option of bailing out was not available to slaves!) Rather, Christians are to appropriate God's grace to grow through the pressure. One application of this principle would be: If the decision rests with you, don't quit your job until in God's sovereignty a better one becomes available.

5. The obvious prerequisite to a wise decision concerning one's vocation is a good understanding of one's aptitudes, abilities, gifts, and desires. Such self-knowledge takes time, a variety of life-experiences, and diligence.

Chapter 22

Giving and Wisdom

*I*t was Jesus Himself who said, " 'It is more blessed to give than to receive' " (Acts 20:35). For many Christians, however, the joy of giving to the Lord has been blunted by the pressure to give—pressure generated by the sheer volume of requests for donations. The number of mailing lists on which the average American believer finds himself seems to grow with each passing month. And so he is barraged with appeals for funds from missionaries, mission organizations, Christian schools, parachurch ministries, counseling centers, evangelistic enterprises, and a variety of home missions. Add to this the financial needs of radio and television ministries ("We need to hear from you this week in order to stay on the air..."), and the less spectacular requirements of the local church, and the effect can be numbing. Most of the appeals come from legitimate, Christ-honoring organizations and individuals who genuinely need financial support to continue their works for the Lord. But many believers become worn out by so many asking for so much—when they have so little.

By learning and applying biblical principles of giving, the Christian can make a significant contribution to the Lord's work—and enjoy doing it. By basing his giving on scriptural guidelines rather than a purely emotional response to appeals, the believer can experience pleasure rather than pressure.

Accordingly, the purpose of this chapter is to set forth biblical principles and priorities for decision making in the area of giving. We will begin by evaluating two common approaches to giving: the tithe and the faith promise.

THE TITHE

10%, 19%, or 22%?

More than one Stewardship Sunday sermon has been preached on the text of Malachi 3:8-10:

> "Will a man rob God? Yet you are robbing Me! But you say, 'How have we robbed Thee?' In tithes and offerings. You are cursed with a curse, for you are robbing Me, the whole nation of you! Bring the whole tithe into the storehouse, so that there may be food in My house, and test Me now in this," says the LORD of hosts, "if I will not open for you the windows of heaven, and pour out for you a blessing until it overflows."

Tithing, a system of financial support employed in Israel during the age of the Old Testament, is practiced by many Christians today. It has the advantages of simplicity, consistency, and discipline. The believer contributes 10 percent of his income to the church, and the church makes all the decisions on distribution. Tithing follows a biblical pattern, and generates considerable revenue in those churches where a high percentage of members practice it. It seems probable that most people who tithe feel that they are doing so in obedience to God's command. And many believe that personal financial prosperity is conditioned upon faithfulness in tithing.

There is certainly nothing wrong with giving a tenth of one's income to the Lord! However, a fuller understanding of the place of tithing in God's overall program will put such a practice in its proper perspective. And that, in turn, will expand the individual's appreciation for God's wisdom as it guides our giving.

The much used text from Malachi contains several points that deserve attention and comment. Note the following details: (1) failure to bring the designated tithes constituted theft from God; (2) the command was to bring the *whole* tithe; (3) it was to be brought to the temple; (4) the temple was to serve as a storehouse, not only for funds, but for food; and (5) as disobedience brought a curse, so obedience would bring material blessing.

Malachi should not have had to bring such a message to Israel. Moses had already done so. It was all contained in Israel's Law. The temple-based ministry was to be supported by the tithes of the people.

The word "tithe" literally means "tenth." In the Mosaic Law, however, there is evidence that the Hebrews were required to bring not one, but probably two, or possibly even three tithes![1] The first tithe was 10 percent of all of one's possessions (Leviticus 27:30-33). It was considered to be "the Lord's" and was used for the support of the Levites as well as the temple ministry (Numbers 18:20-21). A second tithe, taken from whatever produce remained after the primary tithe was given, was set apart for a sacred meal in Jerusalem (Deuteronomy 12:17-18). Another tithe was collected every third year for the welfare of the Levites, strangers, orphans, and widows (Deuteronomy 14:28-29). If this third tithe was separate from the second one (which is possible, but not certain), each Jewish family was obligated to surrender approximately 22 percent of its annual income for spiritual and social purposes.

Because they were required, the tithes of Israel were more like taxes than gifts. That is why failure to submit the "whole tithe" could be described as "robbing God." Furthermore, if one of God's people wanted to express his worship through a voluntary offering, it had to be over and above the 22 percent of his income which was owed (Deuteronomy 12:6, 11; 1 Chronicles 29:6-9, 14). An offering cannot be "freewill" if it is commanded.

Planned Obsolescence

What believers today need to understand is that the tithe, which was foundational to the economic system of the theocratic nation of Israel, is *not* part of the economic system of the church. In the church, there are no taxes, dues, membership fees, or any other prescribed assessments. The ministry of the church is supported as each member gives "as he has purposed in his heart; not grudgingly or under compulsion" (2 Corinthians 9:7). And so, Christians are not under obligation to practice tithing.

This is so for several reasons: (1) the local church does not have the same function as the temple did—the church is not a "storehouse;" (2) the material blessing that was promised as a reward for faithfulness in the Old Testament is not promised to the saints of this age; (3) according to the apostles, the Mosaic Law was expressly set aside for Christians; and (4) the command to tithe is not carried over into New Testament revelation. We will look briefly at each of these facts in turn.

Once it was built in Jerusalem, there was one temple in Israel to which tithes and sacrifices were brought. The sacrifices, which were prescribed for specific sins, were offered there. Such offerings were presented in anticipation of the consummating sacrifice of Christ—the ultimate and final guilt offering (Isaiah 53:10). When Christ died on the cross, the entire sacrificial system was fulfilled and rendered obsolete (Matthew 5:17; 27:51). The temple itself was destroyed under the judgment of God in A.D. 70 (Luke 19:41-44), and will not be rebuilt for certain until the period of the Great Tribulation.

In the absence of the temple, there is nothing in the New Testament to suggest a physical counterpart in the economy of the church. The only "temple" with which Christians have to do is a spiritual one (1 Corinthians 3:16-17). It cannot be maintained that contemporary church buildings are "mini-storehouses," for the New Testament knows nothing of our modern edifices. Therefore, without a temple, it is simply impossible for Christians to comply with the imperatives of Malachi 3.

A second difference between the present age and that of the Old Testament era is that the promise of material blessing for obedience (Leviticus 26:3-5) is no longer applicable.

> Spiritual blessing (Eph. 1:3) and the meeting of material needs (Phil 4:19) are what God promises. Being prospered materially is no necessary sign of deep godliness of faithful tithing; and contrariwise, poverty is no indication of being out of God's will (cf. Paul's own case in Phil. 4:12).[2]

And so the threat of a curse for failing to tithe and the promise of prosperity for those who comply are seen to be applicable only to the "sons of Jacob" to whom the words of Malachi were addressed (3:6).

A New Economy for a New Economy

Even if the temple was still standing in Jerusalem, Christians would not be under the obligation to tithe. For the Mosaic Law has been replaced by the "law of Christ" (1 Corinthians 9:20-21). In the terminology of James, believers today are under the "law of liberty" (James 1:25; 2:12), and the "royal law" of love (James 2:8; cf. Romans 13:8-10). Under the New Covenant, the law of grace is written on the hearts of believers rather than on tablets of stone (2 Corinthians 3:3-6). And so, as a code of life, the Mosaic Law is no longer binding on the children of God (Romans 7:1-6; Galatians 3:19-25; Hebrews 7:11-12).

Now those aspects of the Law of Israel that directly reflect the moral character of God and are appropriate to the age of grace (such as the command to love) were repeated in the New Testament (cf. Leviticus 19:18; 1 John 4:8-11). Such imperatives, and those that were added through apostolic revelation, comprise the moral will of God for this age (Ephesians 3:2-11). As far as the subject of giving is concerned, two questions must be asked about the New Testament revelation. First, does this new revelation continue the Old Testament practice of tithing? Second, is the Church given new guidelines to regulate the practice of giving during the age of grace?

As we have indicated, the answer to the first question is no—tithing is not prescribed for the Church. The concept of the tithe is not included in the apostolic teaching except by way of historical illustration (Hebrews 7:1-10). The answer to the second question is yes—new giving guidelines are established in the New Testament. (These will be discussed later.)

If It Was Good Enough for Abraham...

It has been argued by some Bible students that since the concept of tithing precedes the Mosaic Law, it should be viewed as a universal principle to be applied in every dispensation. This position is based on the correct observation that tithing was practiced by Abraham (Genesis 14:20) and Jacob (Genesis 28:22).

The argument and the correct response are well stated by Ryrie:

> Since Abraham and Jacob both tithed, and since their acts antedated the law, does that not relieve tithing of its legal aspects and make it a valid principle to follow to-

day? The answer would be yes if there were no other guides for giving in the New Testament. . . . but since the New Testament gives us clear principles to govern our giving, there is no need to go back to two isolated examples in the Old Testament for guidance. . . . Not even the most ardent tither would say that the Sabbath should be observed today because it was observed before the law (Exodus 16:23-36), yet this is the very reasoning used in promoting tithing today.[3]

In summary, while the practice of tithing has some advantages, that approach to giving is not prescribed for Christians. The Old Testament pattern is no longer operational. Believers today couldn't obey Malachi 3:8-10 if they wanted to. In the New Testament, the principle of tithing was replaced by the principle of grace giving.

The Tithe: An Unequal Yoke

An understanding of these truths is important applicationally. For some Christians need to be set free from the *burden* of tithing, while others need to be released from the *limitations* of giving a "mere tenth." David Hocking illustrates:

Any study of the percentage of giving in the New Testament must face directly this basic principle: Whatever the percentage, what one sows, he shall reap! The standard of the traditional 10% or the "tithe" might be in some cases to "sow sparingly." In other cases, it would be to "sow bountifully." To illustrate this, here are two men, one who makes $1,000 a year, and one who makes $100,000 a year. The first man gives 10% and he has $900 left to live on; the second man gives 10% and he has $90,000 to live on. That's a far cry from $900! Perhaps the economy only demands $900 to live on; or perhaps $9000 would be more like it. The first man would suffer greatly, while the second would not have a care financially.[4]

Consistent application of the New Testament principle of proportional giving would not only eliminate such inequities, but actually increase the total amount given by Christians for the Lord's work.

THE FAITH PROMISE

A second contemporary system of giving is called the "faith promise." While explanations of the approach differ in detail, the following excerpts from a Christian school publication may be taken as representative:

> "Faith Promise" is the popular name for a plan which, as one writer says, "helps Christians receive far greater blessing through periodic gifts." It is "trusting God for an amount of money which He wants to channel through you for His glory."
>
> A Faith Promise is not just a gift, nor just a pledge of future gifts. It is a promise that, as God supplies the money, you will give a certain amount *over and above* your regular giving. It is a promise of money that you do not yet have nor know about; but you believe that God will provide it, to be given to a certain project or ministry.
>
> The next step, after deciding to use the Faith Promise approach, is to decide on the amount. How can a person know how much to promise? By asking God what additional amount He wants to channel through you. Then by means of His Word and a settled peace that comes with prayer, you will come to a conclusion with thanksgiving to Him.
>
> Now you can look for the extra amount to arrive, usually from an unexpected source. The extra money, perhaps unexpected overtime pay or a repaid dead loan, should be recognized as God's to be used for His work and not for other purposes.

However it is explained, the distinctive features of the plan are as follows: (1) God is the Supplier of the money, the believer is blessed by the privilege of being His channel; (2) the money to be given is to be "over and above" all existing giving commitments; (3) the amount to be given is determined by God and revealed subjectively to the heart of the believer in response to faith and prayer; (4) the money is supplied as the Christian continues to trust God for it; (5) the money will come from unexpected sources; and (6) the destination of the gift is already determined—by the organization that explains the approach.

Faith promise giving is a direct application of the traditional view of guidance. The method assumes that God has already determined a certain amount of money that He wants the believer to give. Through prayer and inward impressions of the Holy Spirit, God is expected to reveal that specific amount to the believer. The amount thereby derived is believed to be God's individual will for the Christian in his giving.

Nothing Succeeds Like Success

As a system of giving, the faith promise method is quite popular. For not only does it harmonize well with the traditional view of decision making, it also works. Churches have found that a properly run faith promise program increases the amount of money given to missions. Mission organizations are able to raise remarkable totals from a single banquet where their work is described and the faith promise method of giving is explained. And they are able to do so without siphoning off funds from other essential ministries. One Christian school presented plans for a much needed building project to the student body of 700 students. Following the faith promise format, those students pledged $70,000 — and that was for money over and above their present giving commitments!

As a system, the faith promise approach to giving is not a biblical plan. But it works, in large measure, because it incorporates two principles that are thoroughly biblical.

First, the method greatly encourages *prayer*. Picture the college student who "in faith" concludes that God wants him to give $300 to the missionary project beyond all his regular giving. This is a student who is motivated to pray! He knows that money cannot come from sources of which he is already aware. He's already tapped all of those! So he prays fervently for "extra" money that he can give to missions. The motivation is excellent, and his prayer fulfills the moral will of God. Many who commit themselves to a faith promise begin to pray with earnest intensity for the first time. God responds to such prayer whether it is part of a faith promise program or not.

Second, the method encourages great *generosity* in giving. This, too, is biblical. Picture again that same student with a $300 faith promise. He is now praying regularly for God to supply what to him is an enormous amount of money. The state legislature enacts a tax rebate and he receives a check in the mail for $34.70. Formerly, he might have put $3.47 in the offering plate at church and spent the rest of it on himself. But not now. Now the whole check goes to the missions project. That is the attitude of generosity in action. Such a response may be a new one for this growing believer. Such generosity pleases the heart of God whether it is part of a faith promise program or not.

Choose a Number

One almost hesitates to criticize something that is characterized by such good qualities and promotes such fine results. But the system of faith promise giving has some flaws that are in need of correction. The first, and foremost, of these is that the method lacks a scriptural basis. The Christian school publication quoted earlier is typical in that most presentations are marked by an absence of references to the Bible.[5] The whole system is built upon the traditional model of guidance. The reason the method is so productive of spiritual results is not because the system as a whole is valid, but because people are challenged to pray and give generously. It is obedience to those biblical principles that God honors—just as He blesses all obedience to His Word.

The fact of the matter is that there are parts of the method which are doctrinally fallacious. The first problem concerns the whole process of determining the amount to be pledged. As we explained in considerable detail in chapter 8, "Impressions Are Impressions," God does not reveal His individual will for our decisions through inner impressions upon our hearts. All of the problems of subjectivity explored in that chapter apply to the question of determining an amount to give. It is not surprising that for some people a whole jumble of figures come to mind, while others draw a blank and are not "impressed" by any amount at all.

The verses that do address this issue correspond perfectly to the principles of decision making explained throughout this book.

Let each one do [i.e., give] just as he has purposed in his heart; not grudgingly or under compulsion; for God loves a cheerful giver (2 Corinthians 9:7).

And in the proportion that any of the disciples had means, each of them determined to send a contribution for the relief of the brethren living in Judea (Acts 11:29).

In both the exhortation (2 Corinthians 9:7) and the example (Acts 11:29), it is the individual believer who purposes or determines whether to give in a specific situation and how much to give. Instead of deciding on the basis of some mystical inner impression, the believer is to make such decisions on the basis of specific guidelines in accordance with established priorities. These are set forth in Scripture and will be discussed more fully later.

Promises, Promises

A second misunderstanding of Scripture that is fostered by the faith promise format relates to the nature of faith. In the explanation, Christians are encouraged to trust God for something that He has not said He will do—namely, come up with a specific amount of money for a specific project within a certain period of time. There is no verse in the Bible that indicates that God will reveal an amount that He wants the believer to give. Nor is there a verse that obligates Him to provide a figure that we decide to pledge. If there were such passages, God's faithfulness would be at stake in the fulfillment of the promise. But to hold God to a promise that He hasn't put on the record isn't faith—it is presumption. Genuine faith must be anchored to verifiable promises. That is what characterized Abraham who was "fully assured that what He [God] *had promised,* He was able also to perform" (Romans 4:21). If God doesn't promise, we can't promise. And an inward impression is not a promise.

Because of these biblical deficiencies, participants in a faith promise program come to false conclusions based on the results. Those who are able to meet their pledges give glory to God and conclude that the system is valid. Giving glory to God is entirely appropriate for He is the One who makes all giving possible (2 Corinthians 9:8-10). But the success of the program does not prove its validity. Only Scripture can do that. And if our understanding of God's Word is correct, we have shown that some aspects of the faith promise system are invalid.

On the other hand, many who don't meet their quota, though they are just as prayerful and generous as others, end up wondering if their faith is weak. Not only is that an inappropriate response, but it robs the giver of joy in giving what God did provide and replaces that joy with false guilt.

Those Bible school students mentioned earlier are a case in point. The $70,000 they pledged represented a very ambitious "step of faith." From the outset of the project, enthusiasm ran high. Students wore buttons reminding them to pray for the successful completion of the goal. But as the deadline drew near, it became increasingly apparent that, barring a miracle, the goal was hopelessly beyond reach.

The amount of money actually given for the project was approximately $12,000—a tremendous contribution from financially-strapped students. Many had given sacrificially, beyond their means, as the Lord enabled them. I had participated as a student in similar giving programs at a Christian college and a seminary. I knew what we had given at those two schools, and these students had surpassed both of those totals. But instead of rejoicing over the $12,000 that had been graciously and generously provided, the student body was more uptight over the gap between the gift and the goal. And I'm sure that over three-fourths of those students came out of that experience questioning their faith.

Interestingly enough, there are two other possible explanations for failure to meet one's faith promise: either God didn't come through, or there is something wrong with the system. We have concluded that it is the latter. But most people dismiss both alternatives and assume that the problem lies with them.

$700 Short on Faith

What is needed is modification of the faith promise format to bring it into complete alignment with Scripture. Perhaps a personal illustration would be helpful here.

When I was in college, I participated in a faith promise project. When the appeal was made, the only figure that came to my mind was $1000. That was a lot of money. I didn't have that kind of money. If I sold everything I had (and I did try to sell a few things that I thought I didn't really need), I could not raise $1000. So I prayed and worked.

What I was able to contribute, as the target date approached, was $300. That was fantastic! I had never given like that in my life. But I was more frustrated than joyful because I was $700 short on faith.

So I began asking God to give me a way to raise the remainder of my pledge. What I came up with was an all-school work day. I organized it and many students participated. By the end of that day we had raised $700.

That made me feel better. But as I reflected on it, I realized that I could not claim that money as the fulfillment of my faith promise. I could say that God answered my prayer for the $1000. But money that was earned through the labor of others was *theirs* to contribute, perhaps as part of their own faith promises.

What I needed to learn was that God hadn't promised to give me $1000. That figure was the product of my own mind. What the Lord did expect me to do was to pray fervently, gratefully accept what He chose to provide, and give generously.

When I went to seminary, I endeavored to apply some of the lessons I had been learning about faith, prayer, and giving. I desired to participate in a particular church ministry for which the people could not pay me. In order to do that, I would need $2000 per semester from other sources. I did not have time to work at another (paying) job and do this ministry. So I prayed and asked God to provide the $2000.

There was no verse in the Bible that said God had to give me that $2000. There was no passage that exempted me from gainful employment. Most of my seminary brothers had to work at one or more outside jobs and there would be nothing wrong with me working for pay somewhere. I was willing to do that and would thank the Lord if He chose to provide for my needs in such a manner. I would ask Him to teach me discipline and patience through that employment and would try to faithfully represent Him before my fellow workers.

But the Lord chose to answer my prayer positively. He provided that $2000 per semester through the gifts of other believers and I was thereby enabled to minister in that church without being a burden to those people. God provided the needed money in that way, not because I had a foolproof system, not because I had more faith than anyone else, not because He was obligated to come up with the amount that came to my mind; but because He is gracious and because He answers prayer.

The two situations that I have described are dissimilar in several respects. But they share a common bottom line: Money had to be provided if a ministry was to function. And what I learned from the first incident helped me to better approach the second one. In the latter instance, I avoided the mistake of locking God into a box of my own construction. I asked Him to provide an income in some manner that would free me to minister without pay. Then I left the outcome to Him. The figure I asked for was not extracted from thin air, but based on specific, anticipated needs. Because God is wiser than we are, the way He chooses to provide will be wiser. And by letting Him act with no strings attached, He gets the glory regardless of the outcome.

BIBLICAL PRINCIPLES OF GIVING

Purposeful, Proportionate Giving

Repeatedly in this chapter, we have alluded to "biblical principles of giving." We've said enough about what they aren't. Now we need to see what they are. The most extended treatment of giving in the New Testament is the presentation found in 2 Corinthians 8 and 9. The reader would do well to carefully read those chapters before continuing on with this material.

The decisions that each believer must make with respect to giving are numerous. Among them are the determinations of how much of one's income to give, and how to distribute what is given. Since we have been discussing various ways of determining the amount to be given, we will look first at those passages that specifically address that issue.

In 2 Corinthians 8 and 9, the phrases that relate to the matter of choosing an amount to give are very instructive:

"according to their ability" (8:3)

"of their own accord" (8:3)

"by your ability" (8:11)

"according to what a man has, not according to what he does not have" (8:12).

All of these expressions are consistent with the summary exhortation of 2 Corinthians 9:7: "Let each one do just as he has purposed in his heart; not grudgingly or under compulsion; for God loves a cheerful giver." This verse rules out the "compulsion" of a required tithe. It also speaks against the extracting of contributions by means of organizational pressure, guilt trips, or emotional manipulation of any sort. The matter is placed squarely on the shoulders of the individual believer who is to give "as he has purposed in his heart." There is no hint of any inward impression; there is no instruction to seek for clues to God's will. 2 Corinthians 9:7 *is* God's will for our giving.

The same point is made in different words in 1 Corinthians 16:2: "On the first day of every week let each one of you put aside and save, *as he may prosper,* that no collections be made when I come." Under grace, the tithe has been replaced by the principle of proportionate giving.

It is not difficult to compute 10 percent of one's income; but how much is "as he may prosper"? It is neither a specific amount nor a particular percentage. The rich should be "rich in good works" (1 Timothy 6:17-18). Those who have nothing are not expected to give anything (2 Corinthians 8:12). Those who have less than enough are to receive from others who have more than enough (2 Corinthians 8:13-14). Those who have little give the little that they can (2 Corinthians 8:2-3). Increasing prosperity should result not only in an increase in the amount given, but in the percentage given. Many Americans should think in terms of 15, 20, 40, or 60 percent of their income. Their "abundance" (2 Corinthians 8:14) should make them abundant givers.

This principle is well illustrated in an incident that occurred during the early years of the Church:

> Now at this time some prophets came down from Jerusalem to Antioch. And one of them named Agabus stood up and began to indicate by the Spirit that there would certainly be a great famine all over the world. And this took place in the reign of Claudius. And *in the proportion that any of the disciples had means, each of them determined to send a contribution* for the relief of the brethren living in Judea (Acts 11:27-29).

The Rich Young Giver

When I was pastoring in a church, a young man in the congregation came to talk to me about giving. He said, "I used to think that the reason I did not give much was because I did not have much. But now that I have quite a bit of money, I find that I still am not contributing very much of it to the Lord's work. How should I give?"

I explained to him the principles of grace giving. Then I suggested that he select a percentage of his income that he thought would be consistent with the degree to which the Lord has blessed him financially. In one week, I promised to follow up our conversation by asking him if he had chosen a specific percentage to give to the Lord.

A week later I checked with him. "Yes," he replied, "I think that 40 percent is about right." I gulped. From next to nothing to 40 percent is a big jump. Nevertheless, I encouraged him to follow his plan for one month and then evaluate. If he felt some adjustment was called for after that trial period (and I was sure he would need to become more realistic), he could change the amount if he wished.

At the end of the month, we discussed his giving. He was full of joy and said it had been a great period in his Christian life. He had invested significantly in the work of the Lord and had derived great satisfaction from his ministry of giving. Moreover, he reported, his new commitment to giving was requiring him to more carefully monitor where the rest of his money went. He was amazed at how much money he had formerly wasted on things he did not really need.

When I suggested that he reconsider the percentage of his income that he would give the following month, he readily agreed. "I have concluded that 40 percent is too little in view of the way God has been prospering me," he declared. "This month, I think 60 percent would be more appropriate."

Later, I overheard one of the young people talking about this same brother. "You know, he doesn't go out and spend away his money on Saturday like he used to. I wonder what's gotten into him." I knew the answer. He was learning to give rather than waste. Abundant giving and careful spending were his new response to God's prospering of his life.

Principles of Grace Giving

To this point, we have emphasized the principle of proportionate giving as a needed corrective to other, less biblical approaches to contribution to the Lord's work. But that principle will be inadequately understood and subject to abuse if it is not seen within the context of other New Testament guidelines that govern the Christian's practice of giving.

Given the space limitations of a single chapter, we cannot hope to fully develop all of these principles. But the following outline, developed primarily from 2 Corinthians 8 and 9, should provide a helpful overview of these guidelines as a basis for further study.[6]

1. God Himself is the Model, Motivator, and Equipper of all Christian giving! (2 Corinthians 8:9; 9:8-10,15).

2. Giving one's money to the Lord is an extension of the prior gift of one's own self (2 Corinthians 8:5; Romans 12:1-2). The donation of a portion of one's wealth is made in the recognition that *everything* the believer has belongs to God (1 Corinthians 4:7; 6:19-20; Luke 19:11ff.; 1 Chronicles 29:14).

3. The ability and motivation to give to the Lord is a function of grace (2 Corinthians 8:1, 3, 6, 7; 9:8-10). Grace is that work of God in the believer that gives both the desire and the power to fulfull God's will.

4. In God's eyes, the *attitude* of the giver is more important than the *amount* given (2 Corinthians 9:7). Accordingly, grace giving is to be characterized by:
   a) Joy (2 Corinthians 8:2)
   b) Cheerfulness (2 Corinthians 9:7)
   c) Liberality (2 Corinthians 8:2)
   d) Sacrifice (2 Corinthians 8:2-3)
   e) Eagerness (2 Corinthians 8:4, 7-8)
   f) Willingness (2 Corinthians 8:12; 9:2)
   g) Perseverance (2 Corinthians 8:10-12)
   h) Integrity (2 Corinthians 8:20-21)

5. Giving is a spiritual exercise in which *all* believers may participate—even poor ones (2 Corinthians 8:2; Luke 21:1-4).

6. The value of a gift is not determined by its amount but by its cost (2 Corinthians 8:2; Luke 21:1-4). The question should not be, "How much can I spare?" but rather, "How much can I sacrifice?" Not "How much can I give?" but, "How much can I give up?"

7. The believer is not expected to give more than he is able. Often, however, Christians find that they can

give more than they thought they could afford!
(2 Corinthians 8:3, 12).

8. The extent of spiritual "treasure" or "fruit" is either
limited or expanded by the extent of the gift (2 Corinthians 9:6; Matthew 6:19-21).

9. The ability to give is granted by God, who gives even
more to those who want to give more (2 Corinthians
9:9-11; Luke 6:38).

10. The opportunity to give is to be viewed as a privilege,
not a compulsive obligation (2 Corinthians 8:4; 9:7).

11. The greatest threat to generous giving is not poverty,
but covetousness (2 Corinthians 9:5; Luke 12:13-34;
Acts 5:1-10).

12. If a promise of financial support is made, every effort
must be made to fulfill it (2 Corinthians 8:10-12; 9:5).

13. The Christian's habitual practice of giving is to be
regular, individual, systematic, proportionate (1 Corinthians 16:1-2).

14. The results of grace giving will include:
   a) A harvest of righteousness (2 Corinthians 9:10;
   Philippians 4:17)
   b) Further enrichment of the giver so that he can give
   more (2 Corinthians 9:11)
   c) Thanksgiving to God (2 Corinthians 9:11-12)
   d) The meeting of needs (2 Corinthians 9:12)
   e) The glorifying of God (2 Corinthians 9:13)
   f) Verification of the message of the gospel (2 Corinthians 9:13; John 13:35)
   g) The offering of reciprocal prayers (2 Corinthians
   9:14)
   h) A strengthening of the bonds of fellowship between believers (2 Corinthians 9:14)

BIBLICAL PRIORITIES IN GIVING

Charity Begins at Home

Once one has decided how much of his income he wishes to give to the Lord, it remains for him to determine the distribution of those funds. Guidance for this decision is provided in the New Testament where priorities are set forth for the use of our money.

Heading the list of priorities is one's *own family*. Paul wrote, "But if anyone does not provide for his own, and especially for those of his household, he has denied the faith, and is worse than an unbeliever" (1 Timothy 5:8). Those are strong words—even for Paul! One's immediate family is given the highest priority in matters of financial provision, as is indicated by the word "especially."

The second sphere of responsibility encompasses one's wider family, or *relatives*. In 1 Timothy 5, much of the discussion centers on the proper care of widows. Paul stresses that the primary responsibility for such care falls on the immediate family rather than the church: "but if any widow has children or grandchildren, let them first learn to practice piety in regard to their own family, and to make some return to their parents; for this is acceptable in the sight of God" (1 Timothy 5:4; see 5:16).

Don't Muzzle the Ox—or the Preacher

The believer also has a financial responsibility to provide for those who are ministering the Word to him. "And let the one who is taught the word share all good things with him who teaches" (Galatians 6:6). If those who receive such spiritual ministry fail to provide for the physical sustenance of the teacher, he will have to curtail his teaching and find other means to support himself and his family. This would lead to the spiritual impoverishment of the church. To be sure, no man is to become a pastor for the purpose of gaining wealth (1 Peter 5:2). But the one who preaches the gospel is entitled to make his living thereby (1 Corinthians 9:11,14; 1 Timothy 5:17-18).

There are some situations, however, in which it is simply not possible for a man to receive a living wage directly from those to whom he is ministering. A new and struggling work often cannot fully support a pastor. An evangelist or missionary reaching into a previously unevangelized area cannot expect local unbelievers to take up an offering for his sake. Thus, we have the opportunity and necessity of providing financial support for those who are ministering to other people in other places.

Robbing Macedonia to Feed Corinth

Such monetary assistance was probably included as part of the church's role in sending out the first two missionaries, Barnabas and Saul (Acts 13:2-3). The believers in the infant church at Philippi began giving to help Paul in his church planting ministry shortly after they were saved (Philippians 4:15-16). The immaturity of the Christians in Corinth forced Paul to rely on gifts from other churches to sustain his ministry there. Paul later wrote to these Corinthians,

> I robbed other churches, taking wages from them to serve you; ...for when the brethren came from Macedonia, they fully supplied my need, and in everything I kept myself from being a burden to you, and will continue to do so (2 Corinthians 11:8-9).

By Paul's reckoning, the responsibility for his support belonged to the saints to whom he was ministering—the Corinthians. Because they neglected to provide for him, he "robbed" other churches for his support. On the other hand, he commended the believers from Macedonia for supplying his needs, even though he was not ministering directly to them.

From the very outset of the church's missionary activity, local churches have viewed financial support of missionaries as a means of direct involvement in the fulfillment of the Great Commission. Thus, a church and its members are expected to first support the ministry to themselves, and then to participate financially in the gospel-spreading work of other messengers in other places (see Acts 1:8).

Rescue the Perishing

Giving to meet physical needs is another responsibility which received emphasis in the ministry of Christ and His apostles (Galatians 6:10; 1 John 3:17). In fact, all of Paul's exhortation in 2 Corinthians 8-9, from which the Church derives many of its principles of giving, was directed toward the collection of relief funds for the impoverished saints in Judea.

The priorities that have been established for the relief of the poor are: believers first, unbelievers second. The needy in one's spiritual family take precedence over those in the world. We may not neglect the needs of unbelievers by caring exclusively for our own. It is not a case of either/or, but of both/and. Paul said, "So then, while we have opportunity, let us do good to all men, and especially to those who are of the household of the faith" (Galatians 6:10).

To sum up: As the Christian responds to the grace of God by being a good steward of his money, he determines the distribution of his funds according to biblical priorities. In general, the order of his giving moves outward, with those who are closest to him having the priority of provision: the immediate family, the extended family, the work of the local church, the work of gospel proclamation, and, finally, the relief of needy believers, then unbelievers. Such an order in giving is part of a sound strategy for outreach. For the long term support of missionary activity requires the prior establishment of a solid base of operations at home.

Passing Out God's Money Is Fun

In recent years, I have adopted the following approach to my own practice of giving. I have chosen a percentage of my income that I contribute to the Lord's work. A portion of what I give goes to my local church to sustain the ministry of those who are sharing the Word with me. I have also decided that half of what I give will go to ministries where the gospel is being proclaimed through evangelism, church planting, and other missionary enterprises. Some of this giving can be channeled through the local church, and some can go directly to the persons or agencies in which I have a personal interest.

When it comes to giving money to meet physical needs, I used to get all tensed up. The reason, quite simply, is that there are so many needs—many more than I could ever hope to meet. I felt guilty every time I heard a moving story of someone's plight, or saw a picture of starving people. I found I was being motivated almost entirely by the pull of my emotions, rather than responding to the instructions of Scripture.

So I determined that about 10 percent of the money I give to the Lord will go for the meeting of needs. I have established what I call the "Need Fund." Every payday, the appropriate amount of money is put aside in that fund. That money is devoted for the Lord's use to meet needs. Whenever I learn of a need, if there is money in my "Need Fund," I have the joy of passing it out. And if there is nothing in that fund when I learn of a need, I don't have to feel guilty about not giving.

Of course, I'm not restricted to giving only what's in that fund. If the situation warrants it, I can divert moneys that were earmarked for other purposes to meet an urgent need. Some circumstances call for sacrificial giving. Sometimes, when I hear of a special need and the reserves are depleted, I ask the Lord to provide some additional money that I can give. If He chooses to do so, I have the joy of passing it along. And if He doesn't, I can trust Him to supply that need through other channels.

God has entrusted to His children the privilege and responsibility of wisely utilizing this world's goods to attain spiritual fruit. The freedom that Christians have to make decisions about giving can be exploited by some for their own selfish needs. But not for long. For God is not mocked—a man will reap as he sows (Galatians 6:6-10). And those who freely give as they have freely received (Matthew 10:8), will experience great joy and blessing as recipients of God's abundant grace (2 Corinthians 9:6-12).

"Thanks be to God for His indescribable gift!" (2 Corinthians 9:15).

Notes

1. O.T. Allis, *God Spake By Moses* (Nutley, N.J.: The Presbyterian and Reformed Publishing Company, 1975), p. 143, n. 1; Merrill F. Unger, *Unger's Bible Dictionary,* s.v. "Tithe," (Chicago: Moody Press, 1957); Charles C. Ryrie, *Balancing the Christian Life* (Chicago: Moody Press, 1969), p. 86; Paul Levertoff, "Tithe," *The International Standard Bible Encyclopedia,* James Orr, ed. (Grand Rapids: Wm. B. Eerdmans Publishing Co., 1939), vol. 5, pp. 2987-88.

2. Ryrie, *Christian Life,* p. 88.

3. Ibid.

4. David L. Hocking, "Biblical Pattern of Giving" (First Brethren Church, Long Beach, Ca., n.d.)

5. The only verse that I have ever heard cited in support of the faith promise plan is 2 Corinthians 9:5: "So I thought it necessary to urge the brethren that they would go on ahead to you and arrange beforehand your previously promised bountiful gift, that the same might be ready as a bountiful gift, and not affected by covetousness." The only point of continuity between this verse and the faith promise

method is a "previously promised...gift." Apart from that similarity, none of the distinctive features of faith promise giving are even mentioned. It is not even clear that the "previously promised" gift was to be a specific amount—only that it was to be "bountiful."

6. Other relevant passages that merit study with respect to giving include: Matthew 6:19-24; Luke 6:38; 12:13-34; 16:1-13; 19:11-27; 21:1-4; Romans 12:8; 1 Corinthians 16:1-2; Galatians 6:6-10; Philippians 4:14-19; 1 Timothy 5:8, 17-18; 6:6-19; 2 Timothy 3:1-2; Titus 1:7; Hebrews 13:16; James 1:11; 5:1-6; 1 John 3:17-18.

Chapter 23

Wisdom When Christians Differ

O ne of the major premises of this book is that in those areas where the Bible gives no command or principle (in nonmoral decisions), the believer is free and responsible to choose his own course of action. Any decision made within the moral will of God, we have argued, is acceptable to God.

Ironically, there are some decisions in which it is easier to please God than to please our fellow Christians. Given the nature of humanity and the reality of freedom of choice, it is inevitable that believers are going to come to different conclusions concerning what is permissible and what is not. That fact has caused no small amount of trouble in the history of the Church. For people tend to feel threatened by disagreement. And Christians, being less than perfect, have not always responded to their differences with an overabundance of charity or wisdom.

Our overreactions tend to move toward one of two opposite extremes. On the one hand, there is the Christian who relishes his freedom and appreciates his direct accountability to God. He basically ignores the opinions of others, and lets the chips fall where they may. If others get offended by his enjoyment of Christian liberty, that's their problem.

The other extreme is represented by the sensitive saint who values his position in the Body of Christ. Recognizing his accountability to the other members of the Body, he bends over backwards to keep from violating anyone's convictions. If he bends over far enough for long enough, he eventually discovers that he can't move at all.

Most Christians recognize instinctively that neither of these two extremes is appropriate. We cannot ignore our differences; neither can we be immobilized by them. And yet we must have some basis for making decisions that takes the opinions of others into account. How are we to relate to fellow believers who differ with us regarding decisions in the area of freedom? It is that question that we will attempt to answer in this chapter.

God Didn't Goof

Part of God's design for the Church is that it should successfully manifest unity in diversity. It was His intent that people with divergent personalities, nationalities, gifts, abilities, tastes, and backgrounds should become unified in Christ without sacrificing personal distinctiveness (1 Corinthians 12:12-27; Colossians 3:11).

Accordingly, God does not view differences of opinion in the area of freedom as a bad thing. The inevitability of such variance of thought is not seen as a flaw in an otherwise beautiful plan. It rather represents one more situation in which the supernatural character of the Church, and its observable distinctiveness as a living organism, may be manifested before the world (John 13:35; 17:20-21).

What God desires, then, is not uniformity of opinion but unity of relationship (Romans 15:5-7).[1]

And so, instead of trying to eliminate divergence of opinion, the Holy Spirit has given specific instructions to guide our response to it. Most of that revelation is concentrated in Romans 14 and 15, and 1 Corinthians 8-10.

THE MEAT DEBATE

In this Corner, the Carnivores

This divine direction was occasioned by some specific problems that cropped up in the Church during the first century. Believers were lining up on opposite sides of issues where no definitive revelation had been received. The test case which eventually warranted apostolic comment concerned the propriety of eating meat.

There were actually two variations on this one theme. Dr. F.F. Bruce gives this excellent explanation of the problem in the church at Rome:

> The question of what kinds of food might and might not be taken agitated the early Church in various ways. One of these ways affected Jewish Christians more particularly. The Jewish food-laws, which had been observed by the nation from its earliest days, were one of the principal features distinguishing the Jews from their Gentile neighbours. Not only was the flesh of certain animals absolutely prohibited; the blood of all animals was absolutely prohibited, and "clean" animals slaughtered for food had to be killed in such a way that their blood was completely drained away. Since one could never be sure that meat eaten by non-Jews was free from every suspicion of illegality in one respect or another, it was impossible for an orthodox Jew to share a meal with a Gentile. Indeed, it was difficult enough for a strict Jew to share a meal with a fellow-Jew whom he suspected of laxity in these matters....
>
> Peter, in his vision on the roof of Simon the tanner's house in Joppa, learned not to count as unclean anything or anyone that God had pronounced clean, and thanks to that lesson he consented almost immediately to visit the Gentile Cornelius at Caesarea and accept his hospitality. But it was long before the majority of Jewish Christians could think of following his example.[2]

The problem in Rome, owing possibly to the sensitivities of the Jewish element, concerned whether it was permissible to eat any meat at all. The debate in Corinth differed in one detail. There, the spiritual ramifications of eating meat that had *previously been offered to idols* were hotly disputed.

> The buying of butcher-meat in pagan cities such as Corinth and Rome presented some Christians with a conscientious problem. Much of the flesh exposed for sale in the market came from animals which had originally been sacrificed to a pagan deity. The pagan deity received his

token portion; the rest of the flesh might be sold by the temple authorities to the retail merchants, and many pagan purchasers might be willing to pay a little more for their meat because it had been "consecrated" to some deity. Among the Christians there were some with a robust conscience who knew that the meat was neither better nor worse for its association with the pagan deity, and were quite happy to eat it; others were not so happy about it, and felt that somehow the meat had become "infected" by its idolatrous association.[3]

Other issues arose as well.[4] But Paul specifically addressed the issues of meat eating to establish principles which are to govern the exercise of Christian liberty in the social context of differing opinions.

To give a framework to our presentation in this chapter and the next, we are going to articulate five principles for decision making when Christians differ, based on Paul's treatment in Romans 14 and 15. The textual support for these guidelines will be established from both of our key passages (Romans 14-15; 1 Corinthians 8-10) as each principle is explained in detail.

Decision Making When Christians Differ
Romans 14:1-15:13

1. Learn to distinguish between matters of command and matters of freedom (14:14, 20).
2. On debatable issues, cultivate your own convictions (14:5).
3. Allow your brother the freedom to determine his own convictions—even when they differ from yours (14:1-12).
4. Let your liberty be limited, when necessary, by love (14:13-15:2).
5. Follow Christ as the model and motivator of servanthood (15:3-13).

Figure 33

DEFINING THE AREA OF FREEDOM

Principle 1: Learn to Distinguish Between Matters of Command and Matters of Freedom.

While Paul was discussing the specific subject of eating meat, he placed that issue in a broader category. He was talking about decisions that fall within the area of freedom. The alternatives being considered (to eat or to refrain from eating) were neither right nor wrong in themselves. Scripture does not command meat eating; neither does it forbid meat eating. And so the question must be answered by each believer on other grounds.

Paul's vocabulary makes it clear that he was discussing matters of freedom. In Romans 14:14,20, the rightness or wrongness of eating meat are declared to be a matter of personal opinion. The terms in 1 Corinthians are even more precise: "This *liberty* of yours" (8:9); "a *right*" (9:4-6); "all things are *lawful*" (10:23); *"freedom"* (10:29).

This distinction between what is commanded and what is left to the choice of each believer is a critical one. For the principles that Paul establishes in these chapters govern only those differences that arise in the area of freedom. If a believer departs from a tenet of gospel truth, or violates an explicit command of Scripture, different principles governing the response of the church go into effect.[5] On the fundamentals of the faith there is no room for compromise, no tolerance of diversity of viewpoint.

Unfortunately, experience has revealed that gaining a consensus on where to draw the line between matters of command and matters of freedom is not easy. Hindsight perceives that in any given culture and generation, the absolutes of human tradition invariably move beyond the explicit imperatives of Scripture.

In Paul's day, to eat meat or not to eat meat—that was the question. But what about today? Dr. Richard Seume gives a personal example where the issue was not *what* one ate, but rather *where* and *when* one ate:

> In the early days of one of my pastorates, I found my lot cast among a group of believers with very strong convictions about certain peripheral matters, including eating in a public restaurant on Sunday. Before coming to that assembly, this matter had not been a problem with me; indeed, I had never even considered it a problem.

One Sunday evening, on my way to the service, I stopped off at the hospital to visit several patients and then stopped in at a diner for a quick snack. It happened that the place was filled with a cacophony of music, which hardly prepared me for the message. During the course of my sermon, I mentioned the incident in passing, little realizing that my own congregation as well as the radio audience in that metropolitan area had other thoughts about such a thing.

When I returned home that night after the service, I was scarcely in the house before the telephone rang, and a rough voice at the other end said, "Brother, I vant to ask you something. If you had died in dat diner tonight, where would you haf gone?"

Without hesitation, I replied, "Why, to heaven, my friend."

"Nothing of it, you would have gone straight to hell!"[6]

The twentieth century American church has managed to divide itself over a whole range of issues. The list below contains issues that I have personally encountered. In every case, there are sincere believers who consider the activity in question prohibited by God, while equally sincere brothers maintain that participation is permitted within the Christian's freedom:

attending movies
watching television
working for pay
   on Sunday
mowing the lawn
   on Sunday
fishing on Sunday
drinking wine
   in moderation
cooking with wine
attending the theatre
   for live drama
participating in sports
participating in
   contact sports
eating food in the
   church building

wearing two-piece swim
   suits (women)
mixed swimming
playing pool
playing cards
gambling for recreation
buying insurance
smoking
dancing
wearing pant suits
   to church (women)
using a Bible translation
   other than King James
raising tobacco
playing guitars in church
listening to rock music

wearing makeup
(women)

wearing beards (men)

wearing hair over the
ears (men)

wearing hair cut above
the shoulders (women)

kissing (unmarried
couples)

wearing skirts above
the knee

playing the saxophone
in church

taking sedatives

speaking in tongues

going to a psychiatrist

People who read this list tend to react with laughter and in-credulity. On the one hand, they chuckle at the items that are "ob-viously" in the area of freedom. On the other hand, they can't believe that anyone could feel free before God to do the things that are "obviously" forbidden by principles of Scripture. And yet if we asked ten different believers of various ages and backgrounds from different parts of the country to separate those activities into categories of "permissible" and "not permissible," we would likely end up with *ten different sets* of lists.

A primary reason for this state of affairs is that biblical com-mands tend to be general in character. They require holiness, love, separation from the world, good stewardship of resources, per-sonal consecration, and the like. Such directives will be obeyed in different ways in different settings. Serious conflict arises when personal or cultural *applications* of divine imperatives are added to the list of universal *absolutes*.[7]

Such applications may be valid, and therefore binding for those who recognize them. The danger stems from not distinguishing between the scriptural command in its more general formulation and the specific manner in which it is obeyed in a given setting. Human traditions — the accumulation of particular applica-tions — tend to concretize over a period of time.

In Paul's day, the imperatives of holiness and separation from the world were applied by some believers to the detail of eating meat. And so in that case, the real disagreement was not over the activity itself, but rather the spiritual ramifications of the ac-tivity — i.e., whether the eating of meat would result in spiritual defilement.

Such a distinction between the activity (which in itself is neutral) and the ramifications (which may have moral implications) characterizes all debated questions. However, in the heat of debate, most people lose sight of that distinction. And all too often, the activity itself is perceived in moral terms of "right" and "wrong." When this happens, argumentation becomes highly emotional and the ability to reason objectively is lost. So is any hope of maintaining unity.

Accordingly, part of Paul's objective in Romans and 1 Corinthians was to bring his readers to an awareness of the nature of the disagreement: "But food will not commend us to God; we are neither the worse if we do not eat, nor the better if we do eat" (1 Corinthians 8:8). Eating meat is, in itself, neutral. But if a person is convinced that by eating meat he violates God's standard of holiness, then eating meat becomes sinful to him (Romans 14:14; 1 Corinthians 8:7).

Likewise, believers today need to learn to differentiate between biblical principle and specific application. That must be the first step. Dr. John R.W. Stott says it well:

> First, we must distinguish more clearly between tradition and Scripture. Most of us Christian people have a set of cherished beliefs and practices, probably inherited from our parents or learned in childhood from the church. Too many of us have accepted them uncritically en bloc. And evangelical believers are by no means free of this tendency. For example, our "touch not; taste not; handle not" has often been "smoke not, drink not, dance not." I am not expressing an opinion on whether we should or should not engage in these habits. What I am saying is that Scripture contains no explicit pronouncements on them. These prohibitions belong therefore to 'the traditions of the evangelical elders'; they are not part of the Word of God.[8]

Decision Making When Christians Differ
Romans 14:1-15:13

1. Learn to distinguish between matters of command and matters of freedom (14:14, 20).

DEVELOPING PERSONAL CONVICTIONS

Principle 2: On Debatable Issues, Cultivate Your Own Convictions.

This principle is established in a single statement: "Let each man be fully convinced in his own mind" (Romans 14:5).

Specifically referring to noncommanded issues, Paul underscores the reality of the believer's freedom and responsibility. There is freedom because the matter is not dictated one way or the other by God; and there is responsibility because the individual is expected to come to a personal decision based on solid reasons. In the final analysis, his decision will be his own application of whichever general commands he is able to bring to bear on the question. Thus it will be a decision within the moral will of God.

The Examined Life Is Worth Living

The verses that follow Romans 14:5 contain several reasons why each believer needs to come to his own convictions on the debated issues. The first of these, suggested in verses 6-8, is that the Christian is to lead a purposeful life. And that central purpose is to please and serve the Lord. This fact is emphasized by the repetition of the prepositional phrases (italicized) in verses 6 and 8:

> He who observes the day, observes it *for the Lord,* and he who eats, does so *for the Lord,* for he gives thanks *to God;* and he who eats not, *for the Lord* he does not eat, and gives thanks *to God . . .* for if we live, we live *for the Lord,* or if we die, we die *for the Lord;* therefore whether we live or die, *we are the Lord's* (Romans 14:6,8).

Accordingly, the purposeful disciple doesn't do something simply for his own purposes, but he seeks to do something because it will serve the Lord. Becoming fully convinced is the process whereby the believer determines the positive merits of his conviction.

Second, each man should be fully convinced in his own mind because "each one of us shall give account of himself to God" for the way in which we exercise our freedom and responsibility (Romans 14:12). Since the reasons for our choices shall be evaluated by the Righteous Judge, they better be sound!

A third value of personal convictions stems from the fact that enjoyment of our Christian freedom is one of our spiritual blessings for which we thank God: "The faith which you have, have as your own conviction before God. Happy is he who does not condemn himself in what he approves" (Romans 14:22; cf. verse 6). It follows that one cannot enjoy his freedom if he is not sure of it.

In fact, being unsettled in one's mind could result in actually sinning against the conscience: "But he who doubts is condemned if he eats, because his eating is not from faith; and whatever is not from faith is sin" (Romans 14:23).

Finally, being fully convinced permits one to be responsible for convictions that are truly his own—it keeps him from being held hostage to someone else's views on an issue (1 Corinthians 10:29-30; Colossians 2:16-23).

Convince Thyself

Being convinced that one should be convinced in his own mind about debatable issues, the thoughtful reader of Paul's explanation raises a question: How does one go about developing his own convictions?[9]

Most of the answer to that question has already been outlined elsewhere in this book. (See the discussion on finding wisdom in chapter 11, "Competent to Choose," and the suggestions for following "wisdom signs" in chapter 16, "Making a Good Thing Better.") From Romans and 1 Corinthians, Paul stresses two additional points. First, one must adopt the proper life-focus: "...we live *for the Lord*" (Romans 14:8). Thinking of our various activities as acts of worship will clarify many issues immediately.

Second, it is important to ask the right questions. Several good ones are suggested by Paul's discussion in 1 Corinthians 10:23-11:1:

Is there anything wrong with this activity? Is it lawful? (10:23)

Is it profitable? (10:23)

Is it edifying? (10:23)

Is it self-serving at the expense of someone else's benefit? (10:33; Romans 15:1-2)

Is this something I can thank God for? (10:30; Romans 14:6)

Is this something that will glorify God? (10:31)

Is this worth imitating? (11:1)

Is this following the example of Christ? (11:1; Romans 15:7-8).

Decision Making When Christians Differ
Romans 14:1-15:13

1. Learn to distinguish between matters of command and matters of freedom (14:14, 20).
2. **On debatable issues, cultivate your own convictions (14:5).**

ACCEPTANCE AND ACCOUNTABILITY

Principle 3: Allow Your Brother the Freedom to Determine His Own Convictions—Even When They Differ From Yours.

This principle is implicit in the statement: "Let each man be fully convinced in his own mind" (Romans 14:5). But it is developed in detail through the first twelve verses of Romans 14.

In this segment, Paul actually argues for two related principles which, taken together, provide the basis for the summary statement recorded above.

The first of these is the *principle of acceptance:* Though we differ in our opinions, we are to manifest unity in our relationships. This facet of Paul's argument is found in some of the opening statements of the chapter:

> Now *accept* the one who is weak in faith. . . . (Romans 14:1; cf. 15:7). Let not him who eats *regard with contempt* him who does not eat, and let not him who does not eat *judge* him who eats, for God has accepted him (Romans 14:3; cf. 14:10).

Obviously, the verbs are determinative in understanding these statements, and the key verb is "accept." The word literally denotes "to take to oneself." W.E. Vine observed that in the New Testament this verb is "always in the middle voice, signifying a special interest on the part of the receiver, suggesting a welcome"[10] (cf. Philemon 17). As far as Paul was concerned, different opinions about nonessentials should not be permitted to adversely affect fellowship between believers.

The positive concept of acceptance is further qualified by two negative verbs, "regard with contempt" and "judge." To "regard with contempt" is to despise or "look down upon" (NIV). It is the attitude of spiritual superiority that characterized the self-righteous

Pharisee toward the humble publican in Jesus' parable (Luke 18:9-14).

The corresponding negative, "judge," has the sense of "criticize, find fault with, condemn."[11] Warnings against this propensity to elevate self by putting others down are frequent in the New Testament, beginning with the admonition of Jesus, "Do not judge lest you be judged" (Matthew 7:1-5; cf. Romans 2:1-3; James 4:11-12).

The tendency of the less strict (with greater freedom) is going to be to regard the others with contempt, labeling them as "legalistic." The more strict (with more inhibitions) are going to be more vulnerable to the temptation to be judgmental, regarding the strong as "loose" or "unprincipled." Either reaction is evidence of an attitude of spiritual superiority—i.e., pride. Both negatives are to be discarded for the positive: "Wherefore, accept one another, just as Christ also accepted us to the glory of God" (Romans 15:7).

Let the Judge Judge

To support the concept of acceptance, Paul adds the *principle of accountability:* All believers are ultimately accountable to God; therefore, we should resist the temptation to judge others and concentrate on making sure our own convictions are sound.

Beginning with 14:4, Paul demonstrated the inappropriateness of one believer judging another for his convictions in matters of debate. As a fellow servant, the brother lacks the authority to pass judgment. Further, in his tendency to criticize his brother's actions, he is focusing on the wrong thing. For in matters of debate, motivation is more important than the act itself (14:6).[12]

Instead of worrying about the differing views of a brother, the mature believer accepts him and lets God deal with his opinions. That is God's business. He has assumed responsibility for that brother. He is at work in that brother's life (14:4). And He isn't finished yet.

Significantly, God's evaluation of a man's life comes at the end of the construction project, while fellow Christians tend to critique it at various points along the way.

Since these things are true, says Paul, let the Judge do the judging. Unlike you, He knows what He's doing.

Again, John R.W. Stott concisely summarizes the second and third principles:

No Christian can escape the responsibility of trying to think biblically and to decide conscientiously about such ethical questions as these. He then has liberty to refrain or to practice at his discretion. But he has no liberty either to impose his traditions on others or to stand in judgment on others if they disagree with him. We need to say to ourselves again and again, as Christ taught the Pharisees, that "Scripture is obligatory, but tradition optional."[13]

Of Meat and Movies

In one generation the issue of difference between believers may be eating meat and in another attending movies. But in either case it takes wisdom, maturity, and grace to be convinced and consistent with one's convictions and yet fully loving and accepting of the brother who disagrees. The following narrative helps to illustrate this balance.

"Dad, could I go to the theater tonight to see the Disney movie they're showing there? I hear it's really good."

Dan Jones looked up from the sports page he had been reading. His thirteen-year-old son, Bob, was sitting on the sofa opposite him.

"Don't you already know the answer to that question?" Dan replied, returning to his article.

"Well, I thought maybe you'd change your mind this time."

Dan put the paper down in his lap and looked at Bob. "Why did you think that, son?"

"Because Mr. Saunders is taking Jerry and Karen to see it. I thought maybe you'd let me go if I went with them."

"Bob, your mother and I have given this matter very careful thought and we've decided that our family won't attend movie theaters. We've explained the reasons to you and those reasons haven't changed."

"But it's not fair!" exploded Bob, fighting back the tears.

"You don't feel it's fair that Jerry and Karen get to go to movies when you're not allowed to?"

"That's right," said Bob, wiping one eye with the back of his hand.

Dan placed the newspaper on the floor and leaned forward in his chair. "Son, I can see how it wouldn't seem fair to you, right now. So why don't we talk about it awhile? I think you're old enough to understand why we do what we do."

Bob nodded. "OK. Go ahead."

"The first thing I want you to understand, Bob, is that when we don't permit you to do something, it's not because we don't want you to have fun."

"I know that," admitted Bob.

"What we're trying to do is to be faithful to what God has instructed us in His Word." Dan picked up a Bible from the side table next to his chair and opened it. "Do you remember what Romans 12:2 says?"

Again Bob nodded, then quoted: "And do not be conformed to this world, but be transformed by the renewing of your mind,. . ."

"That's right," said Dan. "We're trying to avoid conformity to the world—its values, its goals, its way of thinking, its means of success, and definitions of happiness—and we want our minds to be transformed so that we learn to see life the way God does. We feel that the movies being made today work against those goals—even the films that are rated 'G.' They may not all show sensuous or excessively violent behavior, but they still portray many of the world's values that Christians must not adopt."

"But just because they show those things, that doesn't mean that I'll go out and do them," reasoned Bob.

"That's true, son," replied Dan. "But the problem is that most of the time we're unaware of the way we've been influenced. Instead of our minds being renewed as we watch movies, they're actually being subtly shaped and molded to conform to the world's perspective. We get brainwashed without even realizing it.

"Now we realize that we can't block out all of the world's influences on our minds, but we can guard against overexposure. We just don't feel that it's right to invest time and money in something that can hurt us like that."

"Then how come Mr. Saunders takes his kids to see some movies?"

"He obviously doesn't see things the same way I do."

"But he reads the same Bible and he teaches Sunday school. He's even on the church board, just like you. How do you know that you're right and he's wrong?" challenged Bob.

"That's not what I said," replied Dan. "I said that he doesn't see some things the same way I do."

Bob looked puzzled. "But doesn't that mean that one of you is right and the other one's wrong?"

"Not necessarily." Dan grinned at his befuddled son. "Bob, very few people fully understand what I'm about to explain to you. If you can grasp it now, as you begin your teenage years, your life will be much more enjoyable and hassle-free in the years ahead."

Bob's attention was absolute.

"First, let me ask you a question," began Dan. "Where in the Bible does it say anything about going to movies?"

"In Romans 12:2," replied Bob. "We just talked about that."

"I know," said Dan, "but did that verse say anything specifically about *movies?*"

"Well, no, not specifically."

"Do you know of any other verses that talk about movies?"

"No, of course not." The light went on in Bob's mind. "Movies hadn't been invented when the Bible was written."

"Right," said Dan. "So we don't have a verse that says 'Thou shalt not go to movies.' Neither do we have one that says, 'Thou shalt go to movies,' or even one that says, 'It's OK to go to G-rated movies, but no others.' Do you see what I'm getting at?"

"I think so," replied Bob. "The Bible doesn't say anything about movies one way or the other."

"Right. You see, while the Bible gives a number of specific commands concerning many areas of life, it doesn't try to give us rules about every single thing a person might think or do. Instead, God has given us more general principles to apply to specific situations."

"Like Romans 12:2."

"That's right. And each believer is responsible before God to determine how those principles ought to be applied to the specific situations of life."

"OK, I understand that," said Bob thoughtfully. "But what happens if two Christians come to different conclusions? Who decides which one's right and which one's wrong?"

"Not 'if,' Bob, 'when.' One of the things I think you're beginning to see is that there are actually many subjects on which Christians disagree. Sometimes those disagreements are due to immaturity on the part of one or more of the people involved. But just as often, equally mature Christians come to differing conclusions."

"Like you and Mr. Saunders?"

Dan laughed, "Well, I don't know how mature we are, but I would say that we're about the same spiritual age.

"Fortunately, the writers of the Bible knew there'd be disagreements among believers in areas where the Bible doesn't specifically command. In those days, the issue wasn't movies—instead, people debated whether it was all right to eat meat."

"What could they see wrong with eating meat?" asked Bob.

"Sometimes it was because the meat had been previously offered in pagan worship to idols. Other times, I think it had to do more with the Old Testament food regulations. But in any case some believers definitely thought it was wrong. In Romans 14, Paul talked about these things. Let me read it aloud and as you listen, imagine that he's talking about movies."

Dan fumbled for a moment, taking out of the pages of his Bible all the Sunday school papers which had been put there after church the day before. Then he began to read:

> Now accept the one who is weak in faith, but not for the purpose of passing judgment on his opinions. One man has faith that he may eat all things, but he who is weak eats vegetables only. Let not him who eats regard with contempt him who does not eat, and let not him who does not eat judge him who eats, for God has accepted him. Who are you to judge the servant of another? To his own master he stands or falls; and stand he will, for the Lord is able to make him stand. One man regards one day above another, another regards every day alike. Let each man be fully convinced in his own mind.
>
> But you, why do you judge your brother? Or you again, why do you regard your brother with contempt? For we shall all stand before the judgment seat of God. For it is written, "As I live, says the LORD, every knee shall bow to Me, and every tongue shall give praise to God." So then each one of us shall give account of himself to God (Romans 14:1-5, 10-12).

Dan looked up at Bob. "Now what did Paul say we should do about these kinds of disagreements?"

"One thing was that we shouldn't criticize or judge that other person," replied Bob.

"And why not?" asked Dan.

"Because that's the Lord's business," answered Bob. "Each of us has to answer for our own decisions before God."

"That's right," said Dan. "In our case, even though Mr. Saunders thinks it's all right to take his children to some movies, and I don't think it's all right for me to do the same, he's not to look down on me for my standards, and I'm not to criticize him for his differing opinion. He isn't accountable to me—he's accountable to the Lord. And I, too, am accountable to the Lord."

Bob was silent for a few moments as he digested what his father was saying. Then he asked, "Is that why you wouldn't say that Mr. Saunders is wrong, even though you're so sure you're right?"

"That's one reason, son. Another reason is that Mr. Saunders might be right in his opinion."

Question marks appeared all over Bob's face. "How could that be?"

"In verse 5 of Romans 14, Paul said, 'Let each man be fully convinced in his own mind.' That means that we're to weigh things very carefully and have good reasons for our opinions. If I concluded that it would be wrong for me to take my family to a movie, but I went ahead and did it anyway, I would be sinning against my conscience. That's why it says in the last verse of Romans 14: 'But he who doubts is condemned if he eats, because his eating is not from faith; and whatever is not from faith is sin.'

"But if Mr. Saunders carefully considered the issue in light of scriptural principles, and decided before God that it was all right for him to attend certain movies, he could do so without offending his conscience. Furthermore, he shouldn't feel guilty because he knows I've come to a different conclusion—not if he's fully convinced in his own mind."

"Do you mean," questioned Bob, "that the very same thing could be wrong for you, but all right for Mr. Saunders?"

"That's exactly what I believe Paul is saying in Romans 14."

"Wow!" exclaimed Bob. "I never knew that."

Dan smiled at his son. "Can you handle one more man-sized idea?"

"I don't know, but I'll try."

"All right," continued Dan. "Here it is: Not only might the same activity be wrong for one person, and all right for another, but the same activity might be wrong for a person at one time in his life, but proper at a later time."

"You'd better give me an example of that one, Dad."

"OK. Do you remember the old black buggy that we ride in when we visit Grandma and Grandpa back on the farm?"

"I sure do," exclaimed Bob. "Last summer, Grandpa let me hold the reins and guide the horse."

"Well, when I was your age we attended a church where the people believed that it was wrong to drive or ride in an automobile."

"Really?"

"That's right. So all the years I was growing up, I felt that cars were sinful. When I was a couple of years older than you are, though, a friend of mine, who was a Christian but didn't belong to my church, bought his very own car. He knew how we believed, but he still talked me into going for a ride with him—he was so proud of that car. It was really fun. But afterwards, I felt very guilty. I had sinned against my conscience. Later, I told my father and he disciplined me for my disobedience. I also confessed my sin to the Lord and the feeling of guilt went away.

"As I grew up and began to study the Bible more for myself, I read Romans 14 and similar passages. I realized that the Bible doesn't say anything about cars one way or the other. I gradually came to see that in many ways, cars are much more suitable as vehicles of transportation than horse-drawn buggies. I also realized that it wasn't sinful to ride in automobiles."

"What about Grandma and Grandpa?" asked Bob. "They have a car now don't they?"

"Yes, they do. It took them longer to accept their freedom in this area because the belief was so deeply ingrained in them. There are still some Christians today who feel very strongly that it's wrong to ride in a car.

"The point I'm making, Bob, is that because of my convictions when I was growing up, at that time it was wrong for me to ride in a car. But later, as I realized that I was free to choose whether or not to ride in cars, I became fully convinced in my own mind that it was all right. From that time on, I could drive a car without sinning."

"I think I understand what you're saying," said Bob. He thought for a moment, then asked, "About this movie business, Dad—have you ever discussed it with Mr. Saunders?"

"Well, we haven't talked about it personally," replied Dan, "But we did discuss it once in Sunday school. Several people in the class shared their point of view. I did, and so did Mr. Saunders. Why do you ask?"

Bob was hesitant, but continued. "I was wondering if you could explain to me why he thinks it's all right to attend some movies."

"Well, I don't recall everything he said," replied Dan thoughtfully. "I know he feels that some of the films he's taken his family to see provided decent family entertainment. It's something he feels his family can enjoy together. If he can't take his kids, he doesn't allow them to go alone."

"But what about what you were saying earlier, you know, about not being conformed to the world?"

"Mr. Saunders doesn't feel that the movies he goes to are all that harmful. I think it's fair to say that in his opinion, the values of movie attendance outweigh the dangers. He's very selective, as I've said, about which movies he attends. He also makes a point to discuss the movies with his children afterwards. That way, if he detects that his children might be picking up something they shouldn't, he can correct it and use the situation as an opportunity for instruction."

"That sounds good to me, Dad," said Bob, hopefully. "What's wrong with Mr. Saunders' ideas? Couldn't you do the same thing with us?"

Dan replied, "I don't think there is anything *wrong* with Mr. Saunders' viewpoint in the sense that it's sinful. I believe that he's fully persuaded in his own mind, and that's good enough for me. But I disagree that the values of *any* movie shown in the theater outweigh the dangers, even if they're discussed afterwards. And I think that our family can learn the same lessons in other ways without deliberately exposing ourselves to that worldly influence."

The disappointment on Bob's face needed no further elaboration.

"Are you beginning to think you were born into the wrong family, Bob?" Dan asked gently.

Bob looked up suddenly in dismay, as though he had been caught with his hand in the cookie jar. "Oh, no," he blurted, "I didn't say that!"

"I know you didn't *say* it, son..." replied his father with a smile.

"Wait a minute." Bob sat up straight, his expression reflecting the return of hope. "Didn't you say that in matters where the Bible is silent, *each person* is responsible to make the decision for himself?"

"I was wondering when we were going to get around to this," mused Dan.

Bob looked puzzled momentarily, but continued. "I've been thinking a lot about this whole thing, and I think that I agree with Mr. Saunders."

"You think?"

"Uh, no—I'm, uh, fully convinced in my own mind."

"Sorry, Bob," said Dan. "It was a nice try, but it won't work."

"Why not?"

"Because of another principle of Scripture that I think you'll remember as soon as I tell you the reference."

"Which is?"

"Ephesians 6:1."

Furrows appeared on Bob's forehead as he mentally sorted out his memory verses. Then his face fell.

"What does that verse say, son?"

Reluctantly, Bob quoted, "'Children, obey your parents in the Lord, for this is right.'"

"That's right," said Dan. "Do you recall the fourth verse of that same chapter?"

Bob thought briefly, then recited, "'And, fathers, do not provoke your children to anger; but bring them up in the discipline and instruction of the Lord.'"

Dan asked, "Do you feel that I am provoking you to anger?"

"Not exactly," answered Bob.

"Good," replied Dan. "That shows you're learning how to accept disappointment in a more mature way."

"Yeah, I guess so," murmured Bob unenthusiastically.

Dan waited a moment before continuing. "Bob, I want you to know that I take that verse very seriously. For that matter, so does Mr. Saunders. We feel that God has given us our children as a kind of trust. God has given us the responsibility to bring you kids up in the discipline and instruction of the Lord. We may go at it a little differently, but that's what we're both trying to do to the best of our ability. When I refuse permission for you to do something, it's because I genuinely feel that that activity will not be good for you. I do that because I really care about you."

"I know that, Dad," said Bob, beginning to recover.

"My job," Dan continued, "is to help you grow to manhood. During the next few years, as you earn new privileges by the way you handle increased responsibilities, your mother and I will turn more and more of these decisions over to you. And when you move out on your own, you'll be fully responsible to make all of your own decisions. That's God's design for parents and children. As long as we care for you and support you, you must submit to our authority. And even though that's hard at times, like right now, it will help you in your adult life when you have to submit to the authority of a foreman, or a sergeant, or a dean, or a company president. Your family life is like a laboratory where you learn how to function in the real world. That's how God designed it."

Bob nodded.

"OK, just one more thing and this sermon is over. It has to do with one more of those principles we've been talking about. In several places in the New Testament, we're told to give thanks in everything. Cultivation of a thankful spirit, even in the face of personal disappointment, is one of the most important goals a man can have. A person can be submissive in his behavior without being submissive in his heart. Do you know what I mean?"

"Sure, Dad. I see it at school all the time."

"God isn't interested in our external behavior alone. He wants us to have submissive attitudes as well. Learning to be thankful in all circumstances and situations will really help to develop the kind of submission that is pleasing to the Lord. It doesn't come easily, but the Lord will help you if you ask Him."

Bob nodded.

"End of sermon."

"Amen!" declared Bob in hallowed tones. "We are dismissed."

Dan laughed as Bob got up and headed toward the kitchen. "I wonder what's for supper."

"Say, Bob," called Dan.

Bob stopped and turned back toward his father.

"I was wondering if you'd be free to go to the high school basketball game with me after supper. They're at home tonight against Central."

Bob frowned in mock seriousness. "Well, I was planning to go see this movie, but things didn't work out."

Dan laughed again while Bob continued pondering. "Still, I don't know. Are you sure it's, you know, all right?"

"Fully convinced in my own mind, son, fully convinced."

Dan illustrates that it is possible to be convinced and consistent with one's convictions and yet fully loving and accepting of the brother who disagrees. Dan was neither hurt nor indignant about his fellow deacon attending movies. But what happens when a believer who sees nothing wrong with movies hurts his brother or causes him to get mad and upset by his attendance at movies? That is the important topic of the next chapter.

Decision Making When Christians Differ
Romans 14:1-15:13

1. Learn to distinguish between matters of command and matters of freedom (14:14, 20).
2. On debatable issues, cultivate your own convictions (14:5).
3. **Allow your brother the freedom to determine his own convictions—even when they differ from yours (14:1-12).**

Notes

1. There must, of course, be unity of thought regarding the fundamentals of the faith. The apostle Paul was vigorous in his opposition to those who taught or practiced doctrine that compromised either truth or holiness, especially where it touched the gospel message of justification by grace through faith (cf. Galatians 1:6-9; 2:1-5, 11-16).

2. F.F. Bruce, *The Epistle of Paul to the Romans: An Introduction and Commentary,* The Tyndale New Testament Commentaries (Grand Rapids: Wm. B. Eerdmans Publishing Co., 1963), p. 247.

3. Ibid., p. 249.

4. Paul makes reference to the observance of certain "holy days" in Romans 14:5 and the drinking of wine in Romans 14:21 as other current issues of debate in the first-century Church.

5. Admonition, reproof, and church discipline are the divinely ordered steps that must be taken in the cases of those who depart from the truth by practice or teaching. These responses to rebellion within the church are further discussed in chapter 24.

6. Richard H. Seume, *Shoes for the Road* (Chicago: Moody Press, 1974), p. 59.

7. "In Christian circles, we see conviction in many areas, such as doctrine, the prohibition of certain activities, and methods of operating a church. In most cases we call these 'biblical' convictions, but are they?...

"We must...remember one key fact — *we are twice removed from the Scriptures* when we make applications to our lives from biblical principles. To discern these principles we must make certain assumptions or generalizations about what the Bible says. This removes us one step. Then we make specific application of the principles, the second step. Frequently at this point we become dogmatic and even insist that this particular application is the right way to function, for everyone. It may be, but we must remember that we have thus moved from direct Bible teaching to principle to application."
Jerry White, *Honesty, Morality and Conscience* (Colorado Springs: NavPress, 1979), pp. 222-24.

8. John R.W. Stott, *Christ the Controversialist* (Downers Grove, Ill.: InterVarsity Press, 1970), p. 86.

9. In addition to the material presented in this book, the reader is referred to chapter 12, "How To Develop Biblical Convictions," in White, *Honesty, Morality and Conscience.*

10. W.E. Vine, *Expository Dictionary of New Testament Words,* vol. 3 (Old Tappan, N.J.: Fleming H. Revell Co., 1940), p. 255.

11. William F. Arndt and F. Wilbur Gingrich, trans. *A Greek-English Lexicon of the New Testament and Other Early Christian Literature,* 2nd ed. (Chicago: The University of Chicago Press, 1952), s.v. "κρίνω."

12. "The important thing is that one should 'be fully convinced in his own mind' as to the rightfulness of his observance. More important still is the certitude of the individual that his motivation is his desire to honor the Lord in what he is doing." *Expositor's Bible Commentary,* vol. 10: "Romans" by Everett F. Harrison (Grand Rapids: Zondervan Publishing House, 1976), p. 146.

13. Stott, *Christ the Controversialist,* p. 86.

Chapter 24

Weaker Brothers, Pharisees, and Servants

*M*artin Luther began his treatise, "On the Freedom of a Christian Man," with two striking statements:

> A Christian man is a most free lord of all, subject to none. A Christian man is a most dutiful servant of all, subject to all.[1]

One could hardly expect to find a more concise summary of the apostle's thought in Romans 14:1-15:13. The first sentence captures the essence of the believer's freedom in Christ, the relational ramifications of which are developed in Romans 14:1-12. In the previous chapter of this book, the contents of those verses (and the parallel passages from 1 Corinthians 8-10) were discussed in terms of three principles.

Decision Making When Christians Differ
Romans 14:1-15:13

1. Learn to distinguish between matters of command and matters of freedom (14:14, 20).
2. On debatable issues, cultivate your own convictions (14:5).
3. Allow your brother the freedom to determine his own convictions—even when they differ from yours (14:1-12).

Luther's second observation, that the "free" Christian is by vocation a "dutiful servant," captures the essence of Romans 14:13-15:13. These verses form the central passage for this chapter.

Ideally, if everyone in the Church followed Paul's directions as expressed in the first three principles of Romans 14, there would be no further problems. (And this book would be slightly shorter.) But the characters in the drama of real life tend to deviate from the script. So further instruction was given to guide our responses to those who are not inclined to leave well enough alone.

CARING FOR WEAKER BROTHERS

Such a person, failing to adopt God's perspective on different opinions in the area of freedom, invariably reacts in one of two ways. Either he tries to persuade others to adopt his viewpoint, or he immediately shifts his position into conformity with those who differ—in violation of his own judgment.

Both erroneous reactions are abundantly illustrated in Scripture. The Pharisees in the gospels provide the classic example of those who pressure others to conform to their traditions. But Paul was apparently more concerned for the welfare of those who are too easily influenced by the opinions of others. He called them "weaker brothers," and his message to the church was "Fragile: Handle With Care."

> Therefore let us not judge one another anymore, but rather determine this—not to put an obstacle or a stumbling block in a brother's way. I know and am convinced in the Lord Jesus that nothing is unclean in itself; but to him who thinks anything to be unclean, to him it is unclean. For if because of food your brother is hurt, you are no longer walking according to love. Do not destroy with your food him for whom Christ died. Therefore do not let what is for you a good thing be spoken of as evil; for the kingdom of God is not eating and drinking, but righteousness and peace and joy in the Holy Spirit. For he who in this way serves Christ is acceptable to God and approved by men. So then let us pursue the things which make for peace and the building up of one another. Do not tear down the work of God for the sake of food. All things indeed are clean, but they are evil for the man who

eats and gives offense. It is good not to eat meat or to drink wine, or to do anything by which your brother stumbles. The faith which you have, have as your own conviction before God. Happy is he who does not condemn himself in what he approves. But he who doubts is condemned if he eats, because his eating is not from faith; and whatever is not from faith is sin.

Now we who are strong ought to bear the weaknesses of those without strength and not just please ourselves. Let each of us please his neighbor for his good, to his edification (Romans 14:13-15:2).

Principle 4: Let Your Liberty Be Limited, When Necessary, By Love.

Previously, in a letter to the church of Galatia, Paul had written:

For you were called to freedom, brethren; only do not turn your freedom into an opportunity for the flesh, but through love serve one another (Galatians 5:13).

Sometimes, words like "love" and "serve" suffer from ambiguity. But Paul's instructions in Romans 14 move us out of the realm of the theoretical in a hurry. For it is one thing to graciously permit a brother to hold a different viewpoint; it is quite another to actually restrict my freedom because of his different viewpoint! On the face of it, such a requirement is unfair. But that is the nature of the love that is to characterize the Christian's walk (Romans 14:1). For *agapē* love is other-centered, and it is costly.

Let us not, however, jump to the rash conclusion that this principle negates Christian freedom for all intents and purposes. It does not. The words "when necessary" are an integral part of the fourth principle. They indicate that the limitation of one's freedom is not always required. But they also imply that something is more valuable than the enjoyment of personal liberty. The key to obeying God's will in this regard lies in understanding what that something is.

And so we must begin with some definitions. You can't follow the action unless you know the players. And you can't tell the players without a program. Specifically, we need to carefully identify the "weaker brother" and the "stronger brother." Then we must determine what constitutes a "stumbling block." Doing that will greatly clarify the commands that apply to these relationships within God's family.

Those Without Strength

The weaker brother is recognized by his weakness in four areas of his life. First, he is weak in *faith* (Romans 14:1,23). Paul is not in this instance speaking of saving faith. He means that "this man's faith is not strong enough to enable him to perceive the full liberty he has in Christ to partake."[2] "'Faith' in this sense is a firm and intelligent conviction before God that one is doing what is right, the antithesis of feeling self-condemned in what one permits oneself to do."[3] The best synonym is "conviction."

One reason he is weak in conviction is that he lacks biblical *knowledge:* "However not all men have this knowledge; but some, being accustomed to the idol until now, eat food as if it were sacrificed to an idol; and their conscience being weak is defiled" (1 Corinthians 8:7). Those of whom Paul wrote in this verse were ignorant in several respects. They did not know that an idol was a nonentity (1 Corinthians 8:4). So they didn't know that food offered to a "nothing" could not be spiritually contaminated. In short, their faith was weak because it was misinformed.

The weaker brother is also weak in *conscience* (1 Corinthians 8:7,10,12). Essentially, that means that his conscience is *overly sensitive,* condemning him for things that Scripture declares are permissible.

Finally, this brother is weak in his *will* because he can be influenced to act contrary to his conscience.

> For if someone sees you, who have knowledge, dining in an idol's temple, will not his conscience, if he is weak, be strengthened to eat things sacrificed to idols? (1 Corinthians 8:10).

Specifically, because he is not fully convinced in his own mind, and because of his respect for the judgment of a more mature Christian, the weaker brother might follow his stronger brother's example and violate his own conscience in the process. He is vulnerable to that kind of sin because his will is weak.

With these facts in view, we can approach our definition of a weaker brother by recognizing, first of all, what he is *not*. He is not just any new or immature believer. He is not any Christian who differs from me on some issue. Neither is he simply a brother who differs from me and gets upset because he feels I am wrong. Such folks may have weaknesses, but they do not fit Paul's qualifications for "weaker brothers." They may have what I consider to be a weak viewpoint, but they are not weaker brothers. They are important to God, but they are not discussed in these particular passages on weaker brothers.

A weaker brother is a Christian who, because of the weakness of his faith, knowledge, conscience, and will, can be influenced to sin against his conscience by the example of a differing stronger brother.

Stronger Brothers Exercise

Not surprisingly, the stronger brother is strong in precisely the same areas where the weaker brother is weak: faith (Romans 14:22), knowledge (1 Corinthians 8:7,10), conscience (Romans 14:22), and will (1 Corinthians 10:29-30).

Additionally, those who are strong are always pictured as influencing the weak — it is never the other way around. As a result, the responsibility for guarding the integrity of the relationship is given to the strong (Romans 15:1). In these passages, it is also assumed that the strong are correct in their opinion (Romans 14:14; 1 Corinthians 8:4-7).

However, the stronger brother is not necessarily strong in love (1 Corinthians 8:1), though he ought to be (Romans 15:1-2).

The stronger brother is a Christian who, because of his understanding of Christian freedom and the strength of his conviction, exercises his liberty with full peace of conscience without being improperly influenced by the differing opinions of others.

Thou Shalt Not Kick Thy Brother's Crutch

The third key term requiring careful definition is "stumbling block." The noun is prominent in Romans 14:13,20, and 1 Corinthians 8:9. The verb form is found in Romans 14:21 and 1 Corinthians 8:13.

Originally, the noun denoted the piece of wood that kept open a trap for animals.[4] Later, it came to stand for the snare itself,[5] and still later, it was used of anything that caused a person to stumble (cf. Leviticus 19:14).

In the New Testament, "stumbling block" is used only as a figurative expression.[6] It refers to the tripping up of a person in some moral sense—i.e., the individual stumbles into sin or unbelief.[7]

One fact that is of considerable significance to our study is that this word is employed in two different senses throughout the New Testament. When the verb is in the *active* voice, it means "to cause to fall or stumble." For example, Jesus had severe words for anyone who caused a little child who believed in Him to stumble or fall into sin (Matthew 18:6).[8] In such instances, the fault is charged to the one who puts the stumbling block in the way of another.

But when the verb is in the *passive* voice, it signifies "to stumble over, to be offended." In such cases, the blame is placed on the one who stumbles. For instance, when Jesus returned to His home town of Nazareth, the people "took offense at Him" (Matthew 13:57). Literally, "they stumbled over Him." He was the stumbling block, but they were at fault. For they did not believe in Him (Matthew 13:58).[9]

Give and Take

Another helpful way of explaining this important distinction between these usages of the verb is to say that the active voice means "to *give* offense," while the passive denotes "to *take* offense."[10]

This distinction holds up when the noun form is used. One of the most familiar instances of a blameworthy stumbling block is found in Matthew's account of an exchange between Simon Peter and Jesus:

> And Peter took Him aside and began to rebuke Him, saying, "God forbid it, Lord! This shall never happen to You." But He turned and said to Peter, "Get behind Me, Satan! You are a *stumbling block* to Me; for you are not setting your mind on God's interests, but man's" (Matthew 16:22-23).[11]

On the other hand, Jesus Christ is repeatedly described as a "rock of offense" over which people stumble in unbelief (Romans 9:33; 1 Peter 2:8).[12]

Having made a big deal over the difference between giving offense and taking offense, it is now appropriate to point out that in Romans 14 and 1 Corinthians 8, Paul was concerned only with those who *give* offense.[13] (The opposite thrust of taking offense *is* relevant to this discussion and will be considered again later.) Specifically, he warned stronger brothers not to cause weaker brothers to stumble. At no point is this more clearly evident than in 1 Corinthians 8:12-13:

> And thus, by sinning against the brethren and wounding their conscience when it is weak, you sin against Christ. Therefore, if food causes my brother to stumble, I will never eat meat again, that I might not cause my brother to stumble.

A stumbling block, then, *is an action taken by a stronger brother which, though it would ordinarily qualify as a permissible act of freedom, influences a weaker brother to sin against his conscience.* The responsibility for the sin is charged to the stronger brother because of his insensitivity to the vulnerability of the weaker brother.

A Misguided Missile

This concept is illustrated by something that happened to me when I was a boy. One evening, I was already late for supper when I started home. To make up for lost time, I planned to take a short cut across an open field. When I arrived, I learned to my dismay that the field was no longer "open." It was occupied by several people with bows shooting arrows at targets.

The route I had anticipated taking cut directly across the trajectory of the arrows. Yet to detour around the archers would cost precious minutes. I made a decision to stick to my original flight plan. When I discerned what I thought was a lull in the missile traffic, I took off.

The "whish" sound that I detected just behind my head and the gasp of the spectators confirmed that my decision had not been a good one. What I did, in my juvenile immaturity, was stupid. But the guy who let that arrow fly almost caused me to stumble.

The act of shooting an arrow is perfectly legitimate when done within legal restrictions. So a man may take target practice at an archery range with complete freedom. He is not compelled to do so; neither is he prohibited from practicing. He may shoot arrows if he wishes.

However, if a small boy in his ignorance wanders onto the archery range, the situation changes. The archer is no longer free to release the arrow, even if he has followed all the rules. It is not his fault that the child has crossed the line of fire. Still, he is required to refrain from shooting until there is no danger to the boy. There is nothing wrong with shooting an arrow in itself. But if such an act resulted in injury or death to a "weaker" child, the archer would be held accountable. Even on an archery range, the man with the bow must look before he shoots. The safety of others is of greater importance than the freedom to shoot an arrow.

Paul's logic follows similar lines of thought. Earlier we said that something is more important than one's enjoyment of his Christian freedom. Now we can see what that something is—the spiritual well-being of a weaker brother.

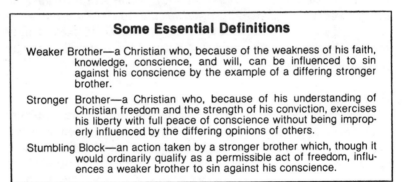

Some Essential Definitions

Weaker Brother—a Christian who, because of the weakness of his faith, knowledge, conscience, and will, can be influenced to sin against his conscience by the example of a differing stronger brother.

Stronger Brother—a Christian who, because of his understanding of Christian freedom and the strength of his conviction, exercises his liberty with full peace of conscience without being improperly influenced by the differing opinions of others.

Stumbling Block—an action taken by a stronger brother which, though it would ordinarily qualify as a permissible act of freedom, influences a weaker brother to sin against his conscience.

Figure 34

A Pound of Prevention

Having defined our key terms, we can now turn our attention to the verbs that really explain the nature of the stronger brother's responsibility—that is, what it means to let one's liberty be limited by love.

An analysis of Romans 14:13-15:2 reveals an even balance between negatives and positives. Since Paul begins this segment with a negative exhortation, we will look first at that side of the relationship.

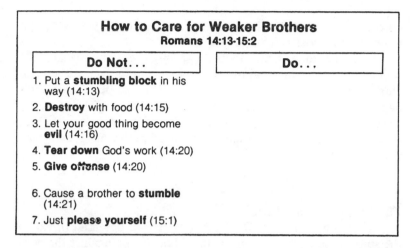

By now, we are accustomed to the meaning of "stumbling block" and "give offense." But the severity of the other terms—"destroy," "evil," "tear down"—may be a little startling. That impression is further reinforced by similar expressions in 1 Corinthians 8: "ruin" a brother for whom Christ died (verse 11); "sin" against the brethren (12); "sin against Christ" (12). One gets the idea that Paul considered this stumbling block business to be pretty serious. The question is, why?

The answer lies in the nature of the weaker brother's vulnerability. In the first place, he is liable to *sin against his conscience* (1 Corinthians 8:10). To some people, that might not sound as serious as the violation of God's law. But God makes no such distinction! (Romans 14:23).

Our Moral Guidance System

The conscience is that part of a man's soul that judges right from wrong. It tells him when he is about to veer off his moral course with some improper thought or action. When he ignores that warning and does what he senses to be wrong, the conscience hauls him into court and condemns him for his transgression. That transaction is experienced as guilt.

At any given point, the standard by which the conscience judges is absolute. It may not be precisely correct in comparison to God's perfect holiness. But the conscience declares guilt or acquittal on the basis of what it construes to be right and wrong at that moment, and does so unequivocally.[14]

Understanding these things can help one appreciate the seriousness of sinning against the conscience. For even if the standard by which the conscience is judging is not as perfect as God's own moral law, the individual reacts *as though it is.* Therefore, to disregard the warnings of the conscience is to choose self over God. And that constitutes rebellion—the sin of going one's own way (Isaiah 53:6).

The Danger of Moral Drift

That is bad enough. But there is a second potential threat to the spiritual life of a weaker brother. For the sin against the conscience can lead just as easily to *sin against God's commands.* Author Jerry White cites an infamous case-in-point:

> Former presidential aide Jeb Stuart Magruder, commenting on the Watergate scandal said, "We had conned ourselves into thinking we weren't doing anything really wrong, and by the time we were doing things that were illegal, we had lost control. We had gone from poor ethical behavior into illegal activities without even realizing it."[15]

This tendency of the flesh to edge us over the line from liberty into license is one of Paul's themes in 1 Corinthians. And so it would be helpful at this point to observe the outline of the apostle's thought through chapters 8, 9, and 10.

He began his response to a question about the propriety of eating meat offered to idols in chapter 8. Though such food was free from any spiritual contamination, Paul declared, there were many believers who were unaware of that fact (8:1-7). So rather than influencing these weaker brothers to sin against their conscience, those with knowledge should refrain from eating this meat (8:8-13).

Chapter 9 consists of a personal testimony by Paul in which he first established his rights as an apostle (9:1-14). He then explained how he had chosen to forego those rights for the spiritual benefit of others (9:15-27).

By way of contrast, he introduced in chapter 10 the contrary example of the children of Israel. Though they had been given tremendous spiritual privileges and resources (10:1-4), they experienced a moral erosion that degenerated from discontent to disobedience to destruction (10:5-10). Their example should serve as a warning to all of God's people that no one is immune to such failure (10:11-13).

The Seduction of Idolatry

The fact of the matter was that the Corinthian believers were in danger of succumbing to the besetting sin of Israel: idolatry (10:14). If they weren't careful, Paul warned, they could slip into idolatry almost without noticing it. For while there was nothing wrong with eating meat that had previously been offered to idols, there was something very wrong with partaking of the temple feasts in which that meat was offered as a sacrifice. In that culture, to participate in a meal that was dedicated to a deity was tantamount to worshipping that god. Furthermore, the Corinthian "gods" were, in fact, demons. So to share in a pagan feast was to have communion with the archfoes of Christ (10:14-22).

That is why, back in 1 Corinthians 8:10, Paul asserted that a stronger brother shouldn't be seen eating in a pagan temple (apparently apart from an official feast). For a weaker brother imitating his example would not only sin against his conscience, he might not possess the spiritual insight to discern any significant difference between obtaining meat at the temple and eating it in the context of a pagan feast.[16]

To sum up: The reason the stronger brother must be careful about harming a weaker brother through his liberty is twofold: (1) the weaker brother might be influenced to sin against his conscience, which is to sin against God; and (2) such an act could be the first step in the downhill slide from liberty into license. It is because of the severity of these potential consequences that Paul admonishes us with such strong terms.

Bricks Are for Building, Not Throwing

To this point, we have emphasized that aspect of Paul's instruction that is essentially preventative. Paul intentionally stressed restraint in the exercise of freedom to keep from hurting a brother. And yet, a mature Christian could conscientiously limit his freedom by love and still fall short of his obligations to his brother. The reason, plainly, is that love is not merely preventive in its expression — it is constructive.

That positive side of the currency of love is readily seen in the rest of the verbs employed by Paul.

How to Care for Weaker Brothers
Romans 14:13-15:2

Do Not . . .	Do . . .
1. Put a **stumbling block** in his way (14:13)	1. Walk according to **love** (14:15)
2. **Destroy** with food (14:15)	2. **Serve** Christ (14:18)
3. Let your good thing become **evil** (14:16)	3. Pursue **peace** (14:19)
4. **Tear down** God's work (14:20)	4. **Build up** one another (14:19)
5. **Give offense** (14:20)	5. **Bear** the weaknesses of the weak (15:1)
6. Cause a brother to **stumble** (14:21)	6. **Please** your neighbor for his good (15:2)
7. Just **please yourself** (15:1)	7. **Edify** him (15:2)

Figure 35

Though not expressly stated, it is implied throughout that the weaker brother's lack of strength is temporary. To use a currently popular metaphor, he is under construction, and "God Isn't Finished With Him Yet" (Romans 14:19-20). The responsibility of the stronger brother, then, is twofold: he is to refrain from tearing down what God is building; and he is to participate constructively in God's work in his brother's life.

> Paul is really not as concerned about "not being a stumbling block" as he is about "becoming a stepping stone." In so many words, then, Paul is saying that to not be a stumbling block is good, but to seek to be a stepping stone is even better. To be a stepping stone means that you are actively seeking ways to help others draw closer to Christ. Being a stepping stone implies that you will be walked on.[17]

The key to a proper attitude, it seems, is perspective. The stronger brother could technically comply with Paul's admonition to limit his freedom, and go around muttering to himself about how much he had "given up for this weakling." But Paul wasn't looking for martyrs—he was recruiting investors to contribute to God's work. The initial investment, the incalculable cost of Christ's life, has already been made (Romans 14:15; 1 Corinthians 8:11). The stronger brother is invited to chip in his two-cents worth to assist in the completion of the project.

That Man in the Hard Hat Is Paul

For Paul, this matter of being a builder, a stepping stone, an investor, was more than just a good preaching point. It was a matter of personal practice:

> For though I am free from all men, I have made myself a slave to all, that I might win the more. And to the Jews I became as a Jew, that I might win Jews; to those who are under the Law, as under the Law, though not being myself under the Law, that I might win those who are under the Law; to those who are without law, as without law, though not being without the law of God but under the law of Christ, that I might win those who are without law. To the weak I became weak, that I might win the weak; I have become all things to all men, that I may by all means save some (1 Corinthians 9:19-22).

> Give no offense either to Jews or to Greeks or to the church of God; just as I also please all men in all things, not seeking my own profit, but the profit of the many, that they may be saved (1 Corinthians 10:32-33).

F.F. Bruce offers this insightful summary:

> Paul enjoyed his Christian liberty to the full. Never was there a Christian more thoroughly emancipated from un-Christian inhibitions and taboos. So completely emancipated was he from spiritual bondage that he was not even in bondage to his emancipation. He conformed to the Jewish way of life when he was in Jewish society as cheerfully as he accommodated himself to Gentile ways when he was living with Gentiles. The interests of the gospel and the highest well-being of men and women were paramount considerations with him, and to these he subordinated everything else.[18]

Accordingly, Paul could write: "Be imitators of me, just as I also am of Christ" (1 Corinthians 11:1).

Careful Enjoyment

To be faithful to Paul's instruction regarding weaker brothers, we need to add a couple of qualifying, and very practical, footnotes. The first is recorded in 1 Corinthians 10:25-27:

> Eat anything that is sold in the meat market, without asking questions for conscience' sake; "for the earth is the Lord's, and all it contains." If one of the unbelievers invites you, and you wish to go, eat anything that is set before you, without asking questions for conscience' sake.

Essentially, Paul's message was, "Enjoy your freedom." The stronger brother is not required to go around taking surveys to determine if a weaker brother is in the vicinity. If the coast appears to be clear, he may proceed to do anything endorsed by his conscience, without worrying about phantom weaker brothers.[19]

Of course, if a weaker brother identifies himself, or if specific clues make the presence of one a distinct possibility, then immediate restraint is in order—as the subsequent verses declare (1 Corinthians 10:28-30).

The second qualification provides the appropriate balance to the first one—without cancelling it out. It consists of two words: "with discretion." Enjoy your freedom with discretion. Put negatively, don't flaunt your freedom.

That piece of wisdom lies behind the rhetorical question of 1 Corinthians 8:10: "For if someone sees you, who have knowledge, dining in an idol's temple, will not his conscience, if he is weak, be strengthened to eat things sacrificed to idols?"

One problem, as Paul saw it, with eating in an idol's temple was that one was more likely to be seen by a weaker brother. To exercise that freedom *with discretion* entailed eating the meat at home or at the private residence of a friend (1 Corinthians 10:25-27). In an environment where it is known that there is widespread disagreement over some matter of conscience, the mature Christian will exercise great care in where and how he enjoys his freedom.

Recognizing Weaker Brothers

As Jews and Gentiles were brought together in the first century Church, one clear evidence of God's grace in their lives was the replacement of hostility and prejudice with a spirit of compassion. The Gentile believers showed sensitivity for their Jewish brethren by avoiding practices that were offensive to them because of their strict upbringing (Acts 15:28-29). And the Jewish saints came to appreciate the revulsion that many Gentile Christians had for certain aspects of their pagan background (1 Corinthians 8:7). In short, they learned where to particularly watch out for weaker brothers.

In our day, there are at least four categories of Christians that merit our loving attention. First, a young adult who is in the process of leaving the parental nest will need some time to sort out his own convictions. Extra sensitivity will be required for those who were reared in a strict, legalistic environment.

The second group is composed of relatively recent converts out of a background of licentiousness. Often, such babes in Christ immediately reject virtually every aspect of their former life style—including some practices that may be perfectly within the believer's sphere of freedom. Such radical purging of the "old" is probably necessary for self-protection until they can gain the spiritual perception to responsibly discern their own perimeters of freedom. It would be a mistake to push these spiritual infants too quickly in the direction of liberty.

A third category would include believers from another country or culture. It is impossible to comprehend the impact our societal milieu has on our convictions—until one spends some time in an alien culture. While we would not wish to be offensive when moving to or traveling in some other part of the country or world, the weaker brother with whom we have contact is more likely to be the foreigner in our midst. His adjustment to *our* standards may take some time. And we will help if we are sensitive to those areas that he finds difficult.

The fourth group is made up of dependent children of convinced, differing brothers. For example, two fathers may hold differing positions regarding attendance at movies, and still accept one another fully. But each man needs to remain alert with respect to his influence on his brother's children. That is especially true when children are seeking external justification for rebelling against parental standards and authority.

These categories of potential weaker brothers are neither ironclad nor exhaustive. But they are worth noting by those who wish to obey God's will and promote His work in the lives of others.

COPING WITH PHARISEES

In all, there are three categories of differing Christians to whom we must properly relate. The believer who is correctly responding to biblical guidelines about decisions in debatable areas is a *convinced differing brother*. I am to accept him and refrain from judging him for his opinions, as he is to do for me. The other classification we have discussed is the *weaker brother*. I am to be alert for him, limiting the exercise of my freedom when my influence might tempt him to sin against his conscience.

There remains a third kind of differing believer that we encounter from time to time. He is one who does not accept me with my differing convictions; who puts pressure on others to conform to his point of view. In terms of stumbling blocks, he *takes offense* when no offense is *given*. The cause of the offense is his own pride or unbelief, rather than improper behavior on the part of the other. He becomes upset, but is not "destroyed." He is not a weaker brother for he is strong in his convictions and will not blindly follow a contrary example. Nor is he a stronger brother, for he is not strong in understanding. He has not fully grasped the nature and reality of Christian freedom and responsibility, especially as it affects relationships with other Christians.

Though not given the same systematic treatment in Romans and 1 Corinthians as the weaker brother, this third character appears frequently on the pages of the New Testament. For purposes of terminology, we will employ the title of the classic example to designate this category of debater — the Pharisee.

By way of definition, the Pharisee is *a professing believer with strong convictions who, because of his own pride, takes offense at those who resist his pressure to conform to his point of view.* By his nature, the Pharisee is most in need of the correctives set forth in Romans 14:1-12. Of the three types of differing brothers, he is also the most difficult to get along with.

Since definitions are often clarified through comparison and contrast, Figure 36 has been prepared to reveal significant differences and similarities.

Categories of Differing Brothers

Weaker Brother	Convinced Brother	Pharisee
He differs from my opinion at times	He differs from my opinion at times	He differs from my opinion at times
He is not fully convinced	He is fully convinced	He is fully convinced
He is sincere	He is convinced and humble	He is convinced and proud
He needs teaching and is open to it	He has been taught, but is open to correction	He has been taught, but is not open to correction
He is surprised at my use of freedom	He accepts me with my differing opinion	He judges or rejects me for my differing conviction
He does not think he can teach me	He is willing to discuss why he differs	He seeks to make me conform to his viewpoint
He is influenced by my example	He is not improperly influenced by my example	He is not influenced by my example
I can cause him to stumble into sin	I cannot cause him to stumble into sin	His pride will cause him to stumble
He is caused to sin by my wrong use of freedom	He is not caused to sin by my use of freedom	He becomes upset by my use of freedom
When I cause him to stumble it is an "offense *given*"	Since he does not stumble, there is no offense at all	When he stumbles over my freedom, it is an "offense *taken*"

Figure 36

Jesus' Thorns in the Flesh

When it comes to responding properly to Pharisees, the disciple would do well to observe the example of the Lord Jesus. For through His interaction with the Pharisees of His day, Christ provided a practical model that determined the outlook of His apostles.[20]

A survey of Jesus' encounters with the Pharisees in the Gospels reveals a progressive pattern of increasing hostility. That is, as Jesus refused to conform to the world view and life style of the Pharisees, their antagonism toward Him intensified. Without wishing to be dogmatic, we believe that that pattern can be traced through seven levels of opposition.

Level 1 — *Observation*: When Jesus emerged on the religious landscape, it wasn't long before the throngs were infiltrated by pharisaic investigators. Almost immediately, tensions began to develop when some Pharisees observed Jesus and/or His disciples doing things (or not doing things) that violated their tradition: dining with "sinners," not fasting on prescribed days, and picking grain on the Sabbath (Mark 2:16, 18, 23-28). In those first encounters, the Pharisees expressed their amazement in the form of a question: "Why?" In each case, Jesus simply gave the reasons for His actions.

Level 2 — *Scrutiny*: The Pharisees began actively watching for infractions of their tradition with the intent of accusing him (Mark 3:2). Jesus' emotional reaction to their hardened hearts was grief and anger (Mark 3:5). He publicly justified an act of healing on the Sabbath, and then He did it in their presence (Matthew 12:11-13).

Level 3 — *Conspiracy*: From that point, the Pharisees "counseled together against Him, as to how they might destroy Him" (Matthew 12:14). Jesus responded by withdrawing from them (Matthew 12:15).

Level 4 — *Slander*: When Jesus expelled a demon from a man who was blind and mute, the Pharisees made their rejection of Him official by attributing His miraculous works to Satan (Matthew 12:22-37). Jesus refuted their faulty logic and rebuked them personally for the first time.

Level 5 — *Accusation*: The conflict escalated as Pharisees accused Jesus' disciples of violating the tradition of the elders (Matthew 15:1-2). Jesus' response was very frontal. This was the first time He called them "hypocrites" to their face (Matthew 15:7). This was the first time He challenged them on the cardinal error — transgressing the commandment of God for the sake of their tradition (Matthew 15:3). And this was the first time He spoke of the Pharisees directly to His disciples:

> Then the disciples came and said to Him, "Do You know that the Pharisees were offended when they heard this statement?" But He answered and said, "Every plant which My heavenly Father did not plant shall be rooted up. Let them alone; they are blind guides of the blind.

And if a blind man guides a blind man, both will fall into
a pit" (Matthew 15:12-14).

Level 6—*Manipulation*: Thereafter, all questioning by the
Pharisees was designed to incriminate Jesus with the authorities or
alienate Him from the people (Matthew 22:15; Mark 10:1-12;
12:13-17). For His part, Jesus skillfully parried all attempts to im-
pale Him on the horns of a dilemma (Luke 20:26, 39-40). He also
began to warn His disciples and the multitudes about the hypocrisy
and false teaching of the Pharisees (Matthew 16:6-12; 21:33-46;
Mark 8:15; Luke 12:1; 18:9-14).

Level 7—*Destruction*: As the Pharisees were plotting with the
rest of the religious establishment to kill Jesus, He delivered a
scathing denunciation of them and their form of "religion" (Matthew 23).

Fencing With Pharisees

While the encounters that we are likely to have with
"Pharisees" will never be as severe as those experienced by Christ,
the fact that He had to deal with His antagonists at every stage is of
benefit to us. With our situation in view, the following observations seem relevant:

1. Jesus did not go out of His way to avoid doing things
    that He knew would offend the Pharisees.
2. The Pharisees always took the initiative in the various
    confrontations.
3. When questioned or accused by the Pharisees during
    the early stages, Jesus simply answered their ques-
    tions and explained the reasons for His actions.
4. At the point where the Pharisees began to effectively
    dissuade people from following Him, Jesus began to
    rebuke them with greater force.
5. He also, at that point, began to warn His followers
    about them, instructing the multitudes in parabolic
    form about their teaching.
6. The specific instructions that Jesus gave His disciples
    were: Beware, and leave them alone.

7. When Jesus challenged the Pharisees personally, the
target of His attack was the content of their *doctrine*
(i.e., when they supplanted the commands of God
with their own tradition), the phoniness of their *practice* (hypocrisy), and the destructive effect of their influence in the lives of others.

Bending Over Backwards

Now, by placing the pertinent apostolic exhortations alongside
the patterns of Christ's example, we can establish some specific
guidelines for relating to the pharisaic brethren among us.

1. *Beware* of becoming a Pharisee (Matthew 16:12;
   Luke 12:1; Romans 14:3). Basically, a Pharisee is one
   who fails to distinguish between divine command and
   personal application. He absolutizes the application—not just for himself, but for everyone else as
   well.
2. When questioned by a Pharisee, graciously *explain*
   the reasons for your convictions (Colossians 4:6;
   2 Timothy 2:24-25; 1 Peter 3:14-16).
3. Don't *capitulate* to his pressure to conform to his absolutes (Colossians 2:8, 16-23), especially on matters
   of gospel principle (Galatians 2:3-5).
4. Pursue *peace* (Romans 12:18; 14:19). Your goal is to
   build him up. If he rejects your efforts to establish
   harmony, leave him alone and commit him to God
   (Matthew 15:12-14).
5. *Admonish* everyone in the church to beware of the
   dangers of Pharisaism (Romans 15:14). Instruct and
   exhort the Pharisee in the context of public ministry
   to the members of the Body.[21]

Pulling the Thorn

The first five guidelines are applicable to relationships with
"passive Pharisees"—that is, those who take offense at the liberty
of others but don't otherwise create division in the church. The
final two steps are reserved for the "aggressive Pharisee."

6. At the point at which the Pharisee begins to cause spiritual damage to others, the church, and/or the reputation of the Lord, *confront* him privately and seek to help him change his course (Matthew 18:15; Galatians 6:1; 1 Thessalonians 5:14; 2 Thessalonians 3:14-15).

7. If private reproof does not restore the brother, then the steps that Christ spelled out for *church discipline* are called for (Matthew 18:15-20). The final step of excommunication is equivalent to Christ's public rebuke of those who so vigorously opposed Him (Matthew 23).

As brothers and sisters in the family of God and fellow members of the Body of Christ, we all have responsibilities to one another. Most of the relational imperatives in the New Testament are constructive in nature. But some are corrective. When correction is called for, the straying brother will more readily respond with repentance when confronted by one who has earned the reputation of a servant through a consistent ministry of edification. As much as anyone in the church, the Pharisee needs the loving up-building of a caring family. To conclude this portion of our study, we return to a comparison of the three categories of differing brothers. This time, our focus is on the manner in which the mature believer is to relate to each of the three.

Relating to Differing Brothers		
Weaker Brother	**Convinced Brother**	**Pharisee**
I need never give him offense	I will not be able to give him offense	I will not be able to prevent his taking offense
I become a willing slave to his conscience	I am free to exercise my freedom	I will not allow him to enslave me to his standards
I must limit my freedom to avoid sinning against him	I need not limit my freedom on his account	I may choose to limit my freedom to keep him from getting upset at me

Figure 37

The Bunker Hill Principle

One final question: What should I do if I cannot determine whether my differing brother is a weaker brother or a Pharisee? Apply the Bunker Hill Principle: Don't fire until you see the whites of his eyes. That is, assume he is a weaker brother and refrain from exercising your freedom until the person in the line of fire is correctly identified or removed from the area of danger. Even if he proves to have pharisaic tendencies, you may find it expedient to sacrifice your freedom for the sake of removing obstacles to his spiritual growth (cf. Acts 15:28-29).

Decision Making When Christians Differ
Romans 14:1-15:13

1. Learn to distinguish between matters of command and matters of freedom (14:14, 20).
2. On debatable issues, cultivate your own convictions (14:5).
3. Allow your brother the freedom to determine his own convictions—even when they differ from yours (14:1-12).
4. **Let your liberty be limited, when necessary, by love (14:13-15:2).**

CONCENTRATING ON CHRIST

Principle 5: Follow Christ as the Model and Motivator of Servanthood.

While virtually everyone recognizes that society would be delightfully transformed if all men would live in accordance with Paul's principles, perhaps the most striking thing about his instructions is how contrary to human nature they are. Men don't naturally extend such consideration as he has been describing to others. In truth, unless men adopt a servant mentality, Paul's exhortation is hopelessly unrealistic. Men want to be sovereigns, not servants.

But therein lies the supernatural character of Christianity. When a human life is infused with the divine Presence, the quest for sovereignty is superceded by a compulsion to serve. In fact, the more the saint becomes like his Savior (which is the whole point of God's construction project), the more servant-minded he becomes. Which is why the apostles so frequently paused in the midst of their expositions to point to the Example. And Romans 15 is no exception.

Let each of us please his neighbor for his good, to his edification. For even Christ did not please Himself; but as it is written, "The reproaches of those who reproached Thee fell upon Me." For whatever was written in earlier times was written for our instruction, that through perseverance and the encouragement of the Scriptures we might have hope. Now may the God who gives perseverance and encouragement grant you to be of the same mind with one another according to Christ Jesus; that with one accord you may with one voice glorify the God and Father of our Lord Jesus Christ.

Wherefore, accept one another, just as Christ also accepted us to the glory of God. For I say that Christ has become a servant to the circumcision on behalf of the truth of God to confirm the promises given to the fathers, and for the Gentiles to glorify God for His mercy. (Romans 15:2-9).

Christ's School for Servants

There are a number of reasons for this apostolic habit of clinching a point by focusing on Christ as the Prime Example. The first concerns perspective and is well described in Everett F. Harrison's comments on verses 5-6:

So Paul prays for a spirit of unity (like-mindedness) that will minimize individual differences as all fix their attention on Christ as the pattern for their own lives (cf. v. 3). This does not mean that believers are intended to see cye-to-eye on everything, but that the more Christ fills the spiritual vision, the greater will be the cohesiveness of the church. The centripetal magnetism of the Lord can effectively counter the centrifugal force of individual judgment and opinion.[22]

The second reason for pointing to Christ is motivational. Those who are the beneficiaries of the Servant's love ought to be compelled thereby to accept and serve others (Romans 15:7).

The primary benefit in throwing the spotlight on the Master Model is instructional. Beyond telling us that we ought to be servants, He shows us how. When Paul says, "Christ has become a servant" (Romans 15:8), we are reminded of both the nature and scope of that self-humiliation as described in Philippians 2:5-11.

And that, in turn, calls to mind Paul's plea to those believers to manifest that very same servant's attitude in their relationship with one another:

> Make my joy complete by being of the same mind, maintaining the same love, united in spirit, intent on one purpose. Do nothing from selfishness or empty conceit, but with humility of mind let each of you regard one another as more important than himself;...Have this attitude in yourselves which was also in Christ Jesus,...(Philippians 2:2-3,5).

> What the apostle is saying to these people is that the next time they find themselves squaring off in a fighter's stance they should switch to a servant's posture. For that is what the mind of Christ is more than anything else—a posture, kneeling and washing one another's feet. It's loving and giving as we have been loved and given to.[23]

Only the Strong Serve

The final point may be the most important: The ability, the enablement to serve others as Christ serves comes from God Himself.

> Now may the God who gives perseverance and encouragement grant you to be of the same mind with one another according to Christ Jesus (Romans 15:5).

That's why the fifth principle points to Jesus not only as the Model but also as the Motivator of our obedience. For all the instructions, even with the complete diagram, would only mock us if His enablement was lacking.

A significant part of the excitement that comes in understanding and then responding to these truths stems from the realization that God's construction projects are not limited to weaker brothers. As we follow Christ as the Model of servanthood, He will give the perseverance and encouragement that we need. Now that's motivation!

Decision Making When Christians Differ
Romans 14:1-15:13

1. Learn to distinguish between matters of command and matters of freedom (14:14, 20).
2. On debatable issues, cultivate your own convictions (14:5).
3. Allow your brother the freedom to determine his own convictions—even when they differ from yours (14:1-12).
4. Let your liberty be limited, when necessary, by love (14:13-15:2).
5. **Follow Christ as the model and motivator of servanthood (15:3-13).**

Notes

1. F.F. Bruce, *The Epistle of Paul to the Romans: An Introduction and Commentary* (Grand Rapids: Wm. B. Eerdmans Publishing Co., 1963), p. 246, quoting "On the Freedom of a Christian Man." (Cf. 1 Corinthians 9:19.)

2. Frank E. Gaebelein, gen. ed., *The Expositor's Bible Commentary*, vol. 10: "Romans" by Everett F. Harrison (Grand Rapids: Zondervan Publishing House, 1976), p. 145.

3. Bruce, *Romans*, p. 253.

4. Colin Brown, ed., *The New International Dictionary of New Testament Theology*, s.v. "Offence, Scandal, Stumbling Block" (Grand Rapids: Zondervan Publishing House, 1976)

5. W.E. Vine, *Expository Dictionary of New Testament Words*, vol. 3 (Old Tappan, N.J.: Fleming H. Revell Co., 1940), p. 129.

6. Ibid.

7. Brown, *Dictionary of New Testament Theology*, s.v. "Offence, Scandal, Stumbling Block."

8. Other verses where *skandalizō* occurs in the active voice with the sense of "to cause to stumble" include Matthew 5:29-30 and the parallel passages in Mark and Luke.

9. Other verses where *skandalizomai* occurs in the passive voice with the sense of "to stumble over" include Matthew 11:6; 15:12; 26:31,33; and other parallel passages in Mark and Luke.

10. Brown, *Dictionary of New Testament Theology*, s.v. "Offence, Scandal, Stumbling Block."

11. Other verses where *skandalon* represents a stumbling block that causes others to stumble include Matthew 18:7; Romans 16:17; Revelation 2:14; and parallel passages.

12. Other verses where *skandalon* represents something at which others take offense include 1 Corinthians 1:23 and Galatians 5:11.

13. In Romans 14:13, the synonym to stumbling block, translated "obstacle," is *proskomma*, which is literally something against which someone may strike his foot. The verb, *proskoptō*, is found in 1 Corinthians 10:32, and is translated "to give offense." Paul used these synonyms in the same way that he employed *skandalon* and *skandalizō*.

14. Jerry White, *Honesty, Morality and Conscience* (Colorado Springs: Navpress, 1979), pp. 28-29, 35-36. White's second and third chapters, "Your Conscience—Friend or Foe" and "How to Use and Respond to Your Conscience" are recommended for his development of the biblical data regarding the conscience.

15. Ibid., p. 83.

16. This paragraph offers one possible view of harmonizing 1 Corinthians 8:10 and 10:19-22. In the former, eating in an idol's temple is considered a sin because it causes the weak to stumble. However, in 10:19-22 the eating of meat sacrificed to idols in the temple context is viewed as idolatry and always wrong. The view suggested in this book takes 8:10 to be eating in the temple apart from a pagan festival and thus not worshiping demons (1 Corinthians 10:20). It is possible to harmonize also by saying that eating in the festival was not pagan worship if the believer had no part in the sacrifice of the food. Even better is the alternative suggested by Hodge that eating in the idol temple in 8:10 is wrong for two reasons (hurting the weak and idolatry), but Paul only mentions its harm of the weak until he gets to the second problem of idolatry in chapter 10. "Here he views the matter simply under the aspect of *an offence,* or in reference to its effect on the weaker brethren, and therefore says nothing of the sinfulness of the act in itself." Charles Hodge, *An Exposition of the First Epistle to the Corinthians* (Grand Rapids: Wm. B. Eerdmans Publishing Co., n.d.), pp. 147-48.

17. Fritz Ridenour, *How to Be a Christian In An Unchristian World* (Glendale: Regal Books, 1967), p. 136.

18. Bruce, *Romans,* p. 243.

19. This is supported by C.K. Barrett's observations on Romans 14:21: "This does not mean that all Christians should take vows of abstinence. The infinitives 'to eat' and 'to drink' are aorists, and the meaning seems to be that if on any particular occasion it seems likely that to eat flesh or to drink wine will cause a brother to stumble, it is right on that occasion to abstain. Eating and drinking are not wrong in themselves, and on other occasions the danger may not arise." C.K. Barrett, *A Commentary on the Epistle to the Romans* (New York: Harper and Row, 1957), p. 266.

20. A systematic treatment of Christ's encounters with the Pharisees is found in John R.W. Stott's excellent volume, *Christ the Controversialist* (Downers Grove, Ill.: InterVarsity Press, 1970).

21. In the New Testament epistles, admonition is a form of exhortation, often with the idea of warning. Most of the time it refers to preventive warning rather than confrontation over a specific problem. In every instance but one (2 Thessalonians 3:15, where "admonish" is used in the sense of "reprove"), the admonition is directed toward a *group* of people. Of primary concern in admonition is the attitude of the one who is doing the exhorting. Key verses on this ministry include Romans 15:14; Acts 20:31; 1 Corinthians 4:14; Colossians 1:28-29 and 3:16. See also the very practical discussion by Gene A. Getz in *Building Up One Another* (Wheaton: Victor Books, 1979), pp. 51-59.

22. Harrison, *Expositor's Bible Commentary,* 10:152-53.

23. Ben Patterson, "A Small Pump at the Edge of the Swamp?," *Leadership: A Practical Journal for Church Leaders* 1 (Spring 1980): 45.

Conclusion

*W*e have covered a lot of terrain through the pages of this
book. It would probably be helpful to quickly review where
we have been.

Part 1 was an honest attempt to present the main beliefs of the
traditional view of God's guidance. It was presented in fictional,
narrative form to create interest and to avoid speaking directly
against any believers who hold this viewpoint. The imaginary
seminar on God's will allowed for a clear presentation of the traditional view in order to promote profitable evaluation and
discussion.

Part 2 was a critique of the strengths and weaknesses of the
traditional view. It was shown that God does not have an ideal individual will as presented by the traditional view. Such an "individual will of God" cannot be established by reason, experience,
biblical example, or biblical teaching (chapters 5 and 6). We saw
that the practice of looking for a "dot" in the center of God's will (a
dot that does not exist) has created needless frustration in decision
making.

We saw further that the traditional view contains several applicational difficulties (chapters 7 and 8). First, the traditional view
must be abandoned in the "minor" decisions of life. Second, it provides no adequate means for dealing with genuinely equal options.
Third, it tends to promote immature approaches to decision mak-

ing. Finally, the traditional view can appeal only to subjective sources of knowledge and thus is denied the possibility of objective certainty in finding God's individual will.

Part 3 proposed an alternative to the traditional view which we have called the "way of wisdom" and is summarized by the following chart.

Principles of Decision Making
The Way of Wisdom

1. In those areas specifically addressed by the Bible, the revealed commands and principles of God (His moral will) are to be obeyed.

2. In those areas where the Bible gives no command or principle (nonmoral decisions), the believer is free and responsible to choose his own course of action. Any decision made within the moral will of God is acceptable to God.

3. In nonmoral decisions, the objective of the Christian is to make wise decisions on the basis of spiritual expediency.

4. In all decisions, the believer should humbly submit, in advance, to the outworking of God's sovereign will as it touches each decision.

The way of wisdom has avoided the weaknesses of the traditional view while it has built upon its strengths. The priority of the moral will of God and the reality of the sovereign will of God have been maintained. The idea that God has an ideal individual will for each believer which must be discovered in order to make right decisions has been abandoned along with all the difficulties it has created. God-given moral freedom in certain areas has been recognized as biblical; and the use of that freedom is regulated by God's moral will and wisdom.

Finally, *Part 4* took us from the quiet study of God's guidance principles to the noisy reality of everyday decision making. The way of wisdom was applied to the specific, concrete, and often difficult decisions of life. These included: marriage choices, mission involvement, vocational choices, giving priorities, and disagreement on debatable issues. Part 4 not only fleshed out the principles of Part 3, but added further scriptural support for the way of wisdom.

A reader of this book may have one of three possible responses to the view presented here. He may agree. He may disagree. Or he may want to think further before he decides.

The one who agrees needs to remember that he is to love and fully accept every believer who holds to the traditional view. He should not condemn, criticize, or look down on the one who disagrees with him (Romans 14:4). Rather, they should discuss the Scriptures together, always remembering that the goal of such discussion is to honor and understand the Scriptures, not to win the argument.

The one who disagrees with the teaching of guidance found in this book should remember that he, too, is to love and accept the brother who wrote it. And he is to love and accept those who agree with it even though he considers them mistaken in their understanding of Scripture.

For the one who is not sure whether he agrees or disagrees, his response is most crucial. First, he should make it his goal to search the Scriptures concerning guidance so that he may become fully convinced before the Lord. Second, he should not begin following this new presentation of guidance until he *is* fully convinced. He should continue to follow his previous conviction so that his actions will be of faith and not of doubt (Romans 14:23). If he is not sure, but goes ahead and attempts to follow the way of wisdom, doubts and self-condemnation are likely to follow (Romans 14:22-23). He should follow the traditional view until he is convinced of another view.

As evangelicals we have good reason to love the Scriptures and that love should be encouraged. However, we also have a tendency to love not only Scripture, but our own interpretation of that Scripture. When our view is questioned we are tempted to be upset, defensive, careless with our words, and more desirous of winning an argument than honoring and discussing the Bible. Discussions then look surprisingly like arguments. Being fully convinced (Romans 14:5) does not require one to be defensive, argumentative, or closed to differing opinions. The searcher for scriptural truth wants to hear the best arguments against his view so that he may strengthen the weaknesses in his position, may properly understand the views of others, and may change his own view when truth so dictates.

My relationship with Jack, a pastor and close spiritual brother, is a constant reminder to me that love and unity among believers who disagree can and should exist. We do not agree completely on the teaching of guidance and God's will, but God has blessed our ministry and unity with each other. I so enjoy ministering with Jack that when he asks me to speak at a church retreat I can never think of the word "no." Some of his church family have commented to us that we should minister together permanently because of our joy and unity.

At a retreat, a lady in Jack's church overheard us talking and good-naturedly chiding each other about our area of disagreement. Genuinely surprised that we held differing views on the subject, she said, "I didn't think you two disagreed on anything since you work together so well." I jokingly responded, "Well, your pastor is wrong on this issue." Then, putting an arm around Jack, I added, "But Romans 14 says we are to love and accept each other." We laughed—but Jack and I meant it. Love and acceptance of differing believers is not optional but vital in maintaining the unity of the Spirit in the bond of peace. The world will not identify true believers by their view of guidance, but by their love for one another (John 13:35).

A student who knew my view of guidance once approached me looking very concerned. With some difficulty he said, "You know you're going to hurt a lot of people if you go ahead and write a book with this wrong view of God's will." I had the presence of mind to answer little and listen much to this brother. But his statement remained on my mind and concerned me. Would I in fact be hurting some people by writing this book? If so, how could I justify my efforts to have it published? I was not able to give him a good answer on the spot, but I have since found answers to those questions.

First, Romans 14 recognizes that we will have differences of opinion that will not result in harm if we love and accept one another and continue to search the Scriptures to be fully convinced in our own minds.

Second, this book does not claim to speak with the authority of Scripture, but only to be the teaching of a concerned believer who is fully convinced that the way of wisdom is what the Bible teaches.

Finally, if the way of wisdom is wrong and the traditional view correct, this book will help the traditional view by raising questions that the traditional view must answer to strengthen its position.

It is for this purpose—the clarification of scriptural truth so that God's people might better fulfill His moral will—that I have written this book. It is my hope that the way of wisdom will become a way of life for many—for the glory of God.

Scripture Index

1 Corinthians

2 Corinthians

Subject Index